DESTINY

DESTINY

Edited by **Patricia G. Steinhoff**

with the translation assistance of
Lina J. Terrell, Ryoko Yamamoto, Kazumi Higashikubo,
Shinji Kojima, Eiko Saeki, Kazutoh Ishida, and Midori Ishida

THE SECRET OPERATIONS OF THE YODOGŌ EXILES

Translation of

SHUKUMEI
YODOGŌ BŌMEISHA NO HIMITSU KŌSAKU

by **Kōji Takazawa**

University of Hawai'i Press
Honolulu

22 21 20 19 18 17   6 5 4 3 2 1

Library of Congress Cataloging-in-Publication Data

Names: Takazawa, Kōji, author. | Steinhoff, Patricia G.,
    editor. | Terrell, Lina, translator. | Yamamoto, Ryoko,
    translator. | Higashikubo, Kazumi, translator. | Kojima,
    Shinji, translator. | Saeki, Eiko, translator. | Ishida,
    Kazutoh, translator. | Ishida, Midori, translator.
Title: Destiny : the secret operations of the Yodogō exiles
    / by Koji Takazawa ; edited by Patricia G. Steinhoff
    with the translation assistance of Lina J. Terrell, Ryoko
    Yamamoto, Kazumi Higashikubo, Shinji Kojima, Eiko
    Saeki, Kazutoh Ishida, and Midori Ishida.
Other titles: Shukumei. English
Description: Honolulu : University of Hawai'i Press,
    [2017] | Includes bibliographical references and index.
Identifiers: LCCN 2016059830| ISBN 9780824872786 (hbk
    ; alk. paper) | ISBN 9780824872793 (pbk ; alk. paper)
Subjects: LCSH: Nihon Sekigun. | Radicals—Japan. | Japa-
    nese—Korea (North)
Classification: LCC HX411.R463 T3513 2017 | DDC
    322.4/20952—dc23
LC record available at https://lccn.loc.gov/2016059830

Designed by Wanda China

CONTENTS

LIST OF FIGURES

ACKNOWLEDGMENTS

My thanks go first to the University of Hawai'i Japan Endowment, which is administered through the Center for Japanese Studies. Small grants from the endowment have supported the Takazawa Collection over many years and have also provided direct support for editing this book and preparing it for publication. When I was unable to travel to North Korea to visit the Yodogō group as originally planned in the early 1990s, funds remaining from a fellowship I received from the Harry Frank Guggenheim Foundation were used to hire the graduate students who did the initial translation. In effect, Takazawa Kōji had already accomplished what I had hoped to learn from the Yodogō group and had gone far beyond what I could have done. The publication of this English translation of his book completes the work.

Special thanks are due to the graduate students who produced the first rough translations from the Japanese: Ryoko Yamamoto translated chapters 2–4 and 17–19; Shinji Kojima did chapters 5, 6, and 27–29; Eiko Saeki did chapters 7–9 and 20–22; Kazumi Higashikubo did chapters 10–12 and 23–26; Kazutoh Ishida did chapters 13, 14, and 32–33; and Midori Ishida did chapters 15, 16, 30, and 31. I did the first rough drafts of the prologue, chapter 1, the epilogue, and Takazawa's afterword for the English translation. Lina Terrell was hired based on the wonders she performed on an initial test of the rough translation of chapter 2, and she performed the same magic on the rest of the translation. Thanks to Christopher Bondy and Kristyn Martin, who provided additional assistance at critical points in this long process.

Asger Rojle Christensen and Robert Boynton, both of whom were doing their own research on North Korea and were interested in the Yodogō group, read an earlier draft of the manuscript and offered helpful comments as did two anonymous reviewers for the University of Hawai'i

Press. Nancy Sack, Pamela Conley, Dave McFarland, Emmy Lou Belcher, and my husband, Bill Steinhoff, also read the translation and provided helpful comments. Masako Ikeda, as the University of Hawai'i Press editor in charge of the book, has read the original several times and has provided another set of eyes to ensure that the translation remains true to the original. Susan Stone improved the text further with her copy editing. All remaining errors are my responsibility.

The original Japanese publication incorporated news photos plus many photographs that Takazawa Kōji took or acquired during his research. Noriko Shiratori and Wanda China prepared the photos for print publication. Thanks also to *Mainichi Shimbun*, Keystone, and the Getty Archives for permission to use historical news photos of key events.

EDITOR'S INTRODUCTION

The author of this book, Takazawa Kōji, is a former student activist who went on to become an author, editor, and independent investigative journalist. He has broad knowledge about the Japanese New Left and close ties to some of its surviving participants and institutions. When I began doing research in Tokyo on the Red Army Faction in the early 1980s, he was one of the first persons introduced to me as an informant. He lent me research materials and introduced me to people to interview, sometimes bringing one or two people to a coffee shop meeting and skillfully eliciting discussion of topics I would never have known to ask about. We became friends and later collaborators on various projects. He facilitated the Japanese publication of my study of the Red Army Faction and the United Red Army (Steinhoff 1991). In 1993 he donated his vast collection of materials on the New Left to the University of Hawai'i, and our collaboration expanded as my students and I worked to catalog the Japanese-language materials.

During the late 1960s and early 1970s, Takazawa was a student member of the New Left organization known as Bund (Kyōsanshugisha Dōmei) and became part of the Red Army Faction when it broke with Bund in the summer of 1969. He helped to produce the Red Army's publications and knew some members of the Red Army group that hijacked a plane to North Korea in 1970, including the group's leader, Tamiya Takamaro, and Yoshida Kintarō. Although at the time the hijackers were simply known as members of the Red Army Faction, the media later labeled them the Yodogō group, using the name of the Japan Airlines plane they had hijacked to Pyongyang. The group announced their conversion to the North Korean *juche* ideology two years after their arrival in Pyongyang, but little was heard from them for many years after that.

Juche is the Korean term for the ideology promulgated by North

Korean leader Kim Il Sung in the 1960s, which became the official belief system of North Korea in 1972 (Suh 2013). Takazawa wrote the term *juche* (or *chuche*) in the phonetic script that Japanese use for foreign words (*katakana*), to distinguish it from the Japanese word that uses the same Chinese characters. These Chinese characters are read in Japanese as *shutai,* and the concept of *shutai* or *shutaisei,* like *juche,* is usually translated as self-reliance or autonomy, but herein lies great confusion. The Japanese version refers to individual self-reliance or independent agency, whereas the North Korean concept of *juche* really refers to the self-reliance and independence of the nation as a whole. In Kim Il Sung's writings that are studied and followed as the national ideology, *juche* represents the basic path for the nation that everyone must believe and follow, encompassing the three pillars of national political independence, economic autonomy, and independent national defense. The Korean version is thus prescribed at the national level and leaves no room for individuals to have their own independent views. In late 1960s Japan, *shutaisei* was a very popular term among New Left students, who understood it as personal agency, or the ability to think for oneself and act on the basis of one's own convictions. The Japanese meaning is thus radically different from the North Korean ideology. To avoid confusion, the Korean word *juche* is left untranslated when it appears in Takazawa's text in *katakana.* Passages in the text written with Japanese characters but clearly referring to the North Korean ideology have been translated using "national self-reliance."

When the youngest of the hijackers, Shibata Yasuhiro, was suddenly arrested in Japan in 1988, communications between the group in North Korea and their associates in Japan began to open up. Shibata's lawyer went to North Korea to consult with the group, and a support group was mobilized for Shibata's trial. Although Takazawa was not directly involved in the trial support activity, he was close to both Shibata's lawyer and the organizer of the support group, Yamanaka Yukio of the Relief Contact Center (Kyūen Renraku Sentā). Takazawa soon visited North Korea and reestablished his ties to Tamiya. In the early 1990s, he helped edit and publish some of the Yodogō group's writings and visited North Korea several more times.

Initially, their associates in Japan thought the Yodogō members were living isolated and constricted lives in North Korea, but their real situation gradually became clearer after the 1992 revelation by Kim Il Sung that they had Japanese wives and children. They lived comfortably in a large private compound on the outskirts of Pyongyang. Takazawa published a book based on interviews with several of the wives in 1995. By then, however, he had become suspicious of the stories they told, which did not coincide with other information he had gathered, and he even warned me not to treat it as factual information for my research. He particularly wondered about the members who were missing when he visited, about which he heard some things in private conversations with Tamiya. After Tamiya's sudden death in 1995, he launched his own investigation, poring over the details of the materials he had and the many documents that the Japanese police had collected but had not understood. Subsequently, he traveled to Europe to follow the group's traces there. The result was this book, which exposed the involvement of the Yodogō group in North Korea in the kidnapping or luring of several young Japanese to North Korea.

I happened to be in Tokyo shortly after the book was published in the summer of 1998. Takazawa met me at a coffee shop to warn me that the book had caused a big storm, and he hoped I would not get caught up in the conflict because of our association. He had stopped going to his usual haunts in Tokyo. In fact, he arrived at our meeting by taxi and avoided using public transportation. In addition to the uproar the book had caused among his friends, there was real concern that he might be the target of North Korean agents in Japan. Yet at another level he was enjoying the conflict, which had the flavor of the internal fights within student movement groups in the 1960s.

I thought the people I had come to know through Takazawa, who also had ties to the group in North Korea, might refuse to talk to me, but that proved not to be the case. Instead, they were eager to tell me how angry they were about what Takazawa had written. When pressed, however, most of them acknowledged that what he wrote was probably true and that it matched some of what they had also heard. They were angry because he had told the truth instead of giving first priority to his friendships with the group in North Korea and also because they feared his exposé might jeopardize the group's precarious situation. The Japanese group in North Korea responded to the book by denying any connection to luring the three young Japanese from Europe to North Korea, despite his documentation. They launched a campaign of character assassination against Takazawa through pamphlets and letters to small movement newspapers in Japan. In one publication they even accused me of being an agent of the Cargill Corporation, which had recently had a dispute with North Korea over a grain shipment. At the time I had never heard of the Cargill Corporation.

The following year the book won the Kodansha Prize for Nonfiction, Japan's most prestigious award for nonfiction writing, and it subsequently came out in a paperback edition. It has since been translated into Korean and published in South Korea. Takazawa's careful research was confirmed when the North Korean government acknowledged publicly in 2002 that it had kidnapped thirteen Japanese citizens during the 1970s and 1980s; the three people that Takazawa had connected to the Yodogō hijackers in North Korea were on the official list.

Although *Destiny* is best known for its investigative journalism on the kidnappings, it won the Kodansha Prize because it is much more than that. Takazawa crafted the book so that it reads like a suspense novel or detective story and keeps the reader enthralled. He also employs some novelistic techniques, such as opening a chapter with a dramatization of an incident told from the perspective of one of the participants. We have highlighted these passages in the translation. Also woven through the book, and deepening its impact, is the parallel story of how Takazawa came to reevaluate his relationship to the group and what they had become. It is definitely not an academic monograph; rather, it is a powerful nonfiction work with the appeal of a novel.

By the time of the kidnapping revelations by the North Korean government, the Japanese graduate students who worked with me in the Takazawa Collection had all read the book, and they suggested that we should do an English translation of it. Takazawa agreed to give us the English-language rights. The University of Hawai'i Press expressed its interest in publishing the translation after receiving a positive recommendation from a noted Japanese scholar who read the Japanese version. He confirmed that it was an important work worthy of translation but was not a scholarly treatise and should not be treated as one. Our translation respects the original nature of the work, but with Takazawa's full cooperation I have added editor's footnotes to fill in essential background, clarify details, and explain special terms he has used, in order to make the story intelligible to an American audience.

The translation has been very much a collective product. Six native Japanese graduate students at the University of Hawai'i—Ryoko Yamamoto, Kazumi Higashikubo, Shinji Kojima, Eiko Saeki, Kazutoh Ishida, and Midori Ishida—divided up the chapters and produced rough English drafts. Initially graduate student Christopher Bondy and I intended to polish the translation, but this proved not to be feasible because of time considerations and our limitations as translators. Instead, with a small grant from the University of Hawai'i Japan Studies Endowment, I was able to hire Lina Terrell, a graduate student and professional translator, to rework the rough chapter translations into a strong English narrative that remains true to the original. She and I went over the manuscript together to correct places where the meaning was ambiguous. I have continued to polish the English and have gone back to the original Japanese and retranslated some passages that had been misconstrued because the students did not know the Japanese context and background to the events or specialized language usage within the Japanese New Left, and thus did not understand what was implied.

In this introduction as well as throughout the translation, I have followed the American publishing convention of giving the names of Japanese persons in the Japanese order of last name first; however, I have given the names of the students who worked on the manuscript in English order because they were living in the United States at the time. Yong Suk Song kindly checked the list of North Korean terms and provided correct spellings. For all other foreign terms I have used the standard English translation whenever possible. For Japanese words I have used Kenkyūsha romanization, retaining the macron over all words except those that have become so familiar in English that they no longer require them. I have preserved the spelling of Yodogō, even though many English sources have dropped the macron over the final ō.

Takazawa volunteered to add a new chapter for the English version elaborating on some things that were not included in the original book, including some comments about its reception in Japan and by the Yodogō group. This chapter has been added as an afterword. In addition, he wanted me to add a final chapter bringing the story up to date. Although the story of what happened to the rest of the group in North Korea is not yet over, I have reported it right up to the time the book went to press, based on my own research and many conversations with Takazawa during my frequent research trips to Japan. As years have passed and the translation has remained unpublished, the saga of the Yodogō hijackers and their families continued in real time. My editor's chapter has been revised many times. This final chapter also incorporates some more recent changes in Takazawa's understanding about what happened, as he has reported it to me based on his subsequent research. These points have been marked clearly where they differ from what he wrote in *Destiny*.

In addition to the new chapters, I have added a selected bibliography of related publications plus a timeline at the suggestion of the manuscript reviewers. Takazawa has donated all of his research materials for this book and his subsequent research on North Korea to the Takazawa Collection; these Japanese-language materials demonstrate the breadth and depth of his research and also will serve as a major resource for other scholars in the future. The bibliography in this translation includes only a fraction of all of the materials he used. The bibliographic references to most of the materials are available on the Takazawa Collection website at http://www.takazawa.hawaii.edu.

Neither the original Japanese publication nor the English translation includes scholarly documentation of all sources throughout the text, but Takazawa did provide simple references in the text to all material he cited or quoted directly, mostly from the group's own publications or mass media sources. Graduate student Kristyn Martin went through the manuscript to identify places that needed citations and noted other small errors. I have standardized these citations in the text and included page numbers whenever possible. These references are included in the bibliography. I have taken the liberty of including a few references to my own related English-language publications in the editor's notes, and these are also included in the bibliography. I also asked several friends to read the English translation and point out things that would not be clear to an American reader with no background on Japan. Their comments have been used to further clarify the text and add more explanatory notes. All first-person references in the main text are to Takazawa; all first-person references in this introduction, the acknowledgments, the editor's afterword, and the notes refer to me.

The original Japanese publication of *Destiny* incorporated sixty-three photographs of historical events, people, and places that document the story Takazawa has told. He gave us full permission to include photographs from the original publication that he took himself or acquired during his research, but he was unable to find the original prints or negatives. Fortunately, after we had re-photographed some substitutes, I found the original photographs while preparing his final donation of materials in Japan, just in time. The University of Hawai'i Press has generously permitted us to include thirty-two photographs in this translation. I have selected the most significant ones, occasionally substituting a similar photograph for one that we could not locate or reproduce.

It has taken much longer than anticipated to get this English translation into print, and I am responsible for much of the delay as well as for any remaining flaws in the English translation. The book itself has withstood the test of time, but, sadly, the situation in North Korea continues to unfold with new twists and turns.

DESTINY

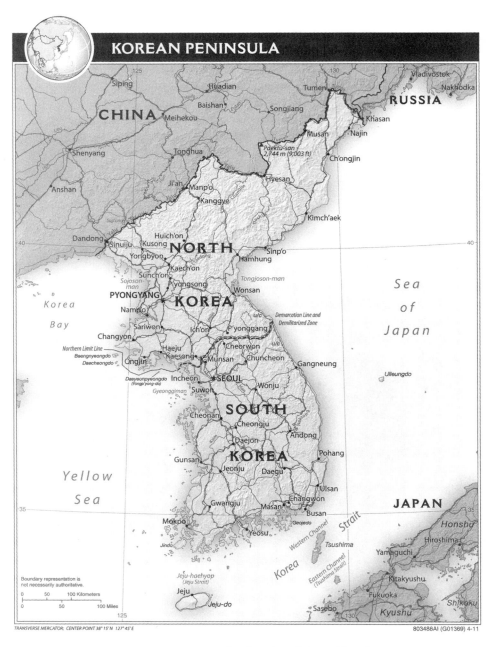

KOREAN PENINSULA

125
Siping
Huadian
Tumen
130
Vladivostok
Nakhodka

RUSSIA

CHINA
Meihekou
Baishan
Songjiang
Khasan

Musan
Najin

Shenyang
Tonghua
Paektu-san
2,744 m (9,003 ft)
Ch'ongjin

Anshan
Ji'an
Manp'o
Hyesan

Kanggye

Kimch'aek

Dandong
Sinuiju
Kusong
NORTH
Sinp'o
40
40
Yongbyon
Huich'on
Hamhung

Kaech'on
Sunch'on
Sojoson-
man
Tongjoson-man

PYONGYANG
Pyongsong
Wonsan

KOREA
Nampo

Korea
Sariwon
Ich'on
P'yonggang
Demarcation Line and
Demilitarized Zone

Bay
Changyon
Haeju
Cheorwon

Northern Limit Line
Baengnyeongdo
Kaesong
Munsan
Chuncheon

Daecheongdo
Ongjin
Incheon
SEOUL
Gangneung
Ulleungdo

Daeyeonpyeongdo
(Yonge'yong-do)
Suwon
Wonju

Gyeonggiman

SOUTH
Cheonan
Cheongju
Andong

Daejon
Pohang

KOREA
Gunsan
Jeonju
Daegu

Sea
of
Japan

Yellow
Gwangju
Masan
Changwon
Ulsan

Sea
Mokpo
Busan
Geojedo
35
35
Yeosu
Western Channel
Strait
JAPAN
Honshu

Jindo
Tsushima
Yamaguchi
Hiroshima

Korea
Eastern Channel
(Tsushima Strait)
Kitakyushu

Boundary representation is
not necessarily authoritative.
Jeju-haehyop
(Jeju Strait)
Fukuoka
Shikoku

0   50   100 Kilometers
0   50   100 Miles
125
Jeju
Jeju-do
Sasebo
130
Kyushu

TRANSVERSE MERCATOR; CENTER POINT 38° 15' N 127° 45' E
803488AI (G01369) 4-11

Map of the Korean Peninsula. Courtesy of University of Texas Libraries.

PROLOGUE

The coffee shop waitress, who had just come on duty, frowned in surprise when a man opened the door and entered quietly. He went directly to a large booth in the rear of the shop and sat down. It looked like it would be another slow day in the coffee shop. Glancing around, the waitress could see two couples occupying separate tables and a young woman who sat at a table across from the lone man's booth. There were no other customers.

As she filled a glass with ice water and set it on a tray, a second man who appeared to be a companion of the first came in. He seemed restless. He hurried over to sit diagonally across from the first man. When she brought the water to the table, the first man abruptly ordered coffee. After turning in the order at the service window, the waitress went to put on a new record. Glancing casually at the door, she saw another new customer come in. He also seemed to be with the men in the large booth. Maybe they were having some kind of meeting. And that was the end of her interest in the matter.

The time passed slowly. The waitress changed the record several times and made several trips to empty the ashtray on the booth table. The two couples had left, and, as she went around refilling water glasses, the waitress saw that the young woman had her eyes closed. It looked as if whoever she was waiting for had not come, and she had fallen asleep.

From time to time, the conversation at the men's table turned angry. There was one man who raised his voice often, ignoring his surroundings. Although on occasion it carried as far as the cash register, the waitress heard nothing of interest in his words. By this time there were more than ten men at the table, but, since some had left earlier, it was hard to say how many there had been altogether.

The waitress glanced at the clock, stifling a yawn. It was nearly closing time. She could hear a train arriving at the station. She began to think of going home and decided to turn off the coffee shop sign a little early. When she returned to the cash register, she saw that the men in the booth had stood up. Though they had been shouting earlier, now they were strangely quiet, standing in a tight group at the register. She thought it was rather odd.

After the men had left, the young woman who had been alone at her table hurried up to the register to pay her bill, as if she was chasing after the men. The waitress later remembered that, along with the scent of her perfume, the woman smelled faintly of disinfectant.

The coffee shop used to be located directly in front of a station on the Yamanote train line that encircles central Tokyo. It had specialized in playing classical music, one of many similar establishments in Tokyo. There remains no record of what music was played in the shop on that day, nor does the waitress have any memory of it. Customers could make requests for music, but none of the men had made any requests to the waitress. They were in the shop on the evening of March 14, 1970, the day the glittering opening ceremony of the Japan World Exposition (Expo '70) had taken place in the Senri hills of Osaka.

There was a reason the waitress was able to unreel that thin thread of memory from an otherwise uneventful evening. About three weeks later, sharp-eyed plainclothes detectives had come to the shop and pressed her for details regarding that day.

The two men who had come to question her carried black notebooks and were overbearing in their manner.

"Tell us everything," pressed the taller of the two.

"Can't you remember anything they discussed?" Their manner had been insistent.

One detective, without bothering to hide his irritation, had pulled out some pictures and spread them on the counter. The faces in the photographs had seemed familiar, but the waitress couldn't be sure. She found it difficult to remember faces she had seen only once.

She suddenly recalled the young woman who had rushed out after the men, but felt no obligation to volunteer this information without being asked.

Almost exactly two weeks after the strange men had held their late-night discussion in the coffee shop across from the station, an event occurred that shook the nation of Japan to its core.

At 7:30 in the morning on March 31, 1970, JAL flight 8315 from Haneda Airport to Fukuoka, nicknamed *Yodogō*, was hijacked by several men who appeared to be extremist student radicals.[1]

---

1. Takazawa refers to the flight both as Flight 351 and as JA8315, apparently because the local flight number was different from the official flight call number

The students held 129 people hostage, including passengers and flight crew, and demanded to go to North Korea. The festival atmosphere enveloping the country at the opening of Expo '70 evaporated instantaneously with the news. This was Japan's first experience with a hijacking, and, for the next several days, live television broadcasts followed the unfolding events closely while the watching nation alternated between hope and despair. The waitress was no exception. She had no idea that she might in some way be connected with the hijackers.

After many stalemates and sudden changes, the hijacked aircraft finally reached Pyongyang's Mirim Airport on the evening of the fourth day. As far as the student radicals were concerned, the hijacking was a success.

When the flight crew finally returned to Japan with the aircraft, people thought the incident was over. It seemed almost miraculous that the terrible situation had concluded without any deaths or injuries. Everyone relaxed, comforted by this quiet resolution.

The waitress soon forgot all about it. In postwar histories of Japan, the *Yodogō* hijacking of a quarter century ago has become a mere footnote of the radical student movement. The hijacking may have come to an end, but in fact there is more to the story of the *Yodogō*.

Some twenty-five years later, in winter, an obituary appeared that carried the name of the leader of the hijackers who had crossed to North Korea. The former waitress of the classical music coffee shop dredged up a vague memory of the man's name. The two police detectives who had come about a week after the hijacking had mentioned the man's name several times. Although she could not recall what she had said to the officers a quarter of a century earlier, she had a clear memory of the man himself.

"That man came up to the register once and bought some cigarettes from me," she recalled. "As I gave him some matches to go with the cigarettes, he turned and said as if to himself, 'I wonder if the cherries are blooming in Ueno yet?' Now, what did I say to him? Maybe something

---

used by air traffic controllers. To avoid confusion, the translation consistently uses the official call number of the flight, JA 8315. Haneda Airport was the main airport for the city of Tokyo until Narita Airport was built in the 1970s. Japan Airlines flights at the time were identified by names in addition to flight numbers. This particular regular flight from Tokyo's Haneda Airport to the city of Fukuoka on the southern island of Kyushu was named "Yodo," and "gō" is the equivalent of "number." The word *yodo* means a pool within a river and is also the name of a river in Osaka, but as the name of this airline flight it is always written in the phonetic alphabet or in the English alphabet and never in its *kanji* character.

like 'If they're blooming early....' I never mentioned this to anyone, not even to the detectives. I even forgot it myself. But I wonder if it meant anything.

"There was something I didn't like about the way the young woman who had been sitting near the men stood up to chase after them. It may have been a young girl's instinctive reaction on my part. I stared after her in a bad temper. I felt a little envious." The former waitress shook her head as if to forget this old, unpleasant memory. She had not thought of it in years.

A quarter of a century may have passed, but the story of the *Yodogō* continues to fly on through the darkness in unmapped fog. The passengers on board this story include not only the nine students and the freed passengers and flight crew, some of whom have passed out of this world, but also many people who became involved through chance encounters.

Actually, the real meaning and the strangest part of the *Yodogō* story really begins at the point where most of us thought it ended.

CHAPTER ONE

The Classical Music Coffee House

One winter exactly twenty years after the Yodogō incident, I settled myself into a seat on board a North Korean People's Airline flight to Pyongyang. It was my first visit, though I would return several times.

The little news available concerning the fates of the student radicals involved in the *Yodogō* hijacking had not been widely disseminated in Japan; most information came from short interviews with representatives of the Japan Socialist Party. I wished to see with my own eyes what had become of them and to confirm that they were still alive and well. About six months before this trip, just after I had returned from covering events in Tian'anmen Square in Beijing, an invitation from the North Korean government had been delivered to me.

At the time, a special single-use passport was required for such a visit to North Korea, obtainable only after observing many formalities and procedures at the Ministry of Foreign Affairs. The temporary passport was necessary because in regular Japanese passports it was printed that Japanese citizens were prohibited from traveling to the Democratic People's Republic of Korea. An invitation from a host institution on the North Korean side was also a necessity.

Not only was travel to North Korea restricted, but there were also obstacles to getting information about it. Even after formalities had been taken care of at the Ministry of Foreign Affairs, it was impossible to confirm the hotel reservations I had made through a travel agency or even to find out which hotel I would be staying at. Consequently, my trip to North Korea remained in doubt until the moment I actually obtained an entry permit from the North Korean Embassy in Beijing.

The journey did not seem real until after the small airplane bound for Pyongyang had taken off from the Beijing airport. I spent the flight watching the changing landscape through the airplane window. Even after gulping down some of the strong Korean beer they were serving on board, I felt too excited to sleep.

The aircraft flew across the Bohai Sea, leaving behind the Chinese mainland, then continued over the Liaodong Peninsula. Eventually, a jumbled, reddish-brown massif came into view: the Korean Peninsula. In places the russet-colored mountains were covered with patches of ice and snow; gradually the world below grew completely white. The fiery colors of the setting sun glowed briefly through the windows, and then suddenly darkness descended. We had arrived in Pyongyang.

Staring down at the world passing below, I thought of the coming meeting with the members of the Yodogō group. I hoped to retrace the true path of events of the *Yodogō* hijacking twenty years before.

This story, thirty years in the making and not over yet, began on the evening of March 14, 1970, in a corner of the Swan, a coffee shop in front of Komagome station in Tokyo featuring classical music. That evening, it was almost certainly Red Army Faction members laying their plans who occupied the large booth at the back of the coffee shop. With Chairman Shiomi Takaya as leader, many important members appeared, including the Military Committee chairman, Tamiya Takamaro, and Konishi Takahiro of the Tokyo University Joint Struggle Committee.[1] Most of the conspirators did not know the ages or even the real names of their associates; they had agreed to use pseudonyms because many of them had warrants out for their arrest. Some of them were meeting for the first time. The group included a sixteen-year-old high school student.

The Red Army Faction had been formed out of the armed conflict faction (Kansai Bund) of the Communist League (Bund) in the summer of 1969,[2] half a year after the defeat of the Tokyo University students in

---

1. The University of Tokyo student conflict featured a new form of organization, an all-campus joint struggle committee (*zenkyōtō*), which elected officers and decided on actions at mass meetings of the student body without regard to their affiliation with a particular student organization. Students at other universities also used this form of organization for their conflicts with campus authorities. *Zenkyōtō* formations are completely different from the All-Japan National Student Organization (Zengakuren). See also Steinhoff 2012.

2. Bund was the nickname of the Communist League, one of the main national student organizations in the Japanese New Left movement. It traced its origins to the late 1950s and had led the student movement during the 1960 anti–

the battle at the Yasuda Auditorium,[3] when the barricades had fallen in one university struggle after another and the movement was gasping for breath under heavy police pressure. At that time, the popular song "Ginza at Twilight" (Tasogare no Ginza) could often be heard playing from static-filled loudspeakers in shopping districts and flowing through the open doors of pachinko parlors.[4] For a while, in imitation of this song, the Bund song "Longing for the Bund" (Akogare no Bunto) was sung to the same tune, but, when Bund failed to achieve its goals in street-fighting, the student activists changed the wording to the more insulting "Bund at Twilight" (Tasogare no Bunto). In the midst of all this, the Red Army Faction was founded by a militant group within Bund to keep alive the hopes of the New Left student movement.

---

security treaty protests. The organization declined considerably after the 1960 protests but was revived in the mid-1960s and expanded later that decade as one of the major student organizations involved in the protest movements of the late 1960s and early 1970s. This revived organization was also known as the "Second Bund." Although Bund proudly traced its continuous history as a national organization from 1958, there were internal factional conflicts. By late 1968, its regional organization based in the Kansai region of western Japan had become more militant and advocated armed conflict to overcome growing police pressure. The central leadership took a more moderate position and in July 1969 expelled the militants, whom they had begun to call the Red Army Faction (Sekigunha). The independent Red Army Faction made its public debut on September 5, 1969, when members battled other groups outside the National Zenkyōtō Alliance Inaugural Congress at Hibiya Amphitheatre.

3. Yasuda Auditorium is a prominent nine-story building with a clock tower on the main Hongō campus of the University of Tokyo, considered the top national university in Japan. It was occupied by students during the Tokyo University conflict in 1968–1969 and was the final site of the two-day conflict between students and several thousand riot police who were sent to clear the building. In 1968 and 1969, a total of 162 college campuses experienced student strikes and building occupations. Riot police were quickly called in to clear buildings of private universities, but public institutions had a strong tradition of not allowing police to enter the campus. National university officials were reluctant to call police onto the campus, so some of these conflicts paralyzed universities for months until the administration finally capitulated and called in the riot police under heavy government pressure.

4. Pachinko is a popular Japanese pinball game played with small steel balls in noisy commercial halls. Players buy a supply of steel balls to start playing, and the pachinko machine periodically disgorges more of them when they hit certain targets. When a player is ready to leave, the stash of steel balls is counted and the player selects from an array of small prizes such as canned goods or trinkets. Gambling for money is illegal in Japan, but these prizes can be exchanged for cash at nearby stores.

On August 28, 1969, the Red Army Faction had held a secret meeting at a government-run guest house in Jogashima, Kanagawa prefecture, to review the progress of the struggle thus far and to decide on plans for the future. They came to the following conclusion: "The methods used until now are inadequate for the 1970 campaign. Passive class struggle theory is useless. We need an active, offensive class struggle. We must organize people's military units immediately and carry out an armed uprising with guns and bombs. We predict that the autumn campaign will be the initial stage of a genuine armed uprising."[5]

The Red Army Faction, dubbed by other radical groups as "Bund's bastards," is well known to have possessed weapons. In the fall of 1969, when police discovered their large-scale training camp at Daibosatsu Peak in Yamanashi prefecture, fifty-three of their members were arrested on charges of possession of illegal firearms and violation of the explosives control law.[6]

After that the Red Army was on the run from the police. Of course, the police were after the people who had escaped from Daibosatsu, but the long arm of the law stretched even to sympathizers who simply attended a public meeting. In those days, there was something called "Red Army crime." No search of Japan's six legal codes would reveal any mention of a statute regarding this crime, but just being associated with the Red Army Faction was grounds for arrest. Faction members were closely watched by the security police; harassment by the authorities was a daily occurrence. If the light changed while a known Red Army Faction member was in the crosswalk, he would be arrested in violation of traffic safety rules. One seen walking along a sidewalk would be delib-

---

5. Takazawa Kōji was told this by someone who was present at the meeting. No record of this secret meeting is noted in Sashō Henshū Iinkai 1975. There is also no record of it in the handwritten internal Sekigunha documents found in the Takazawa Collection, but the content reflects their views at the time.

6. The group had planned a "guerrilla training camp" in the remote mountain area, but police followed them to the location, surprised the whole group while they were sleeping at a mountain inn, and arrested them. The "explosives" were actually small homemade grenades and pipe bombs that the group had developed. The training was needed to ensure that they could throw the devices without blowing themselves up. Japan's explosives control law was originally targeted at bomb-throwing anarchists in the Meiji era and carries potential penalties up to the death penalty, so it is a far more serious charge than gun possession. After the arrests, police discovered that the Red Army Faction had been planning to kidnap Prime Minister Satō, which sharply escalated the security threat the group posed and led to its severe repression.

Figure 1.01. Red Army Faction members after their arrest while sleeping at an inn during their weekend guerrilla training exercise at Mt. Daibosatsu. Lined up for review by a police official, many are barefoot or in slippers. Photo courtesy of The Mainichi Newspapers/AFLO.

erately jostled by police officers, who would then make an arrest on the charge of obstruction of an officer performing his duty.

Even going to a restaurant involved risk of arrest. Plainclothes detectives kept a close watch on Red Army Faction members, waiting until the moment an activist touched his meal with his chopsticks to rush into the restaurant, arrest him, and drag him off to the nearest police station without any explanation of his crime. Any number of charges could be drummed up once the mug shots and fingerprints had been taken. "You hadn't paid for your food yet," the arresting officers would say. "You were trying to cheat the restaurant out of its money."

The security police did not bother to make any distinction between Red Army members and those who only supported them. They devoted much manpower to the surveillance of "suspicious characters" in their "apartment building roller" operations.[7] The Far Left Violence Control

---

7. In an attempt to find and arrest radical students who were hiding out, the police conducted massive searches of all apartment buildings and rooming houses in specific urban neighborhoods where students lived. Police knocked on the door of each unit and asked to look inside. Refusing to let them in was regarded as suspicious behavior and could lead to a full search.

Section of the National Police Agency posted wanted posters with photographs of suspects and advice on how to identify extremists in every
police station and in any location where people were likely to gather,
such as bathhouses, restaurants, neighborhood police boxes,[8] or public
transportation terminals. People who were active late at night, people
with few personal possessions, people who moved frequently, people
who received many visitors to their apartments—all were suspect as
possible left-wing extremists. Citizens were encouraged to form neighborhood watch groups to look out for and report on the activities of
"suspicious characters." Such was the mood of the times.

The hijacking blew through this stifling atmosphere like a fresh
wind. It gave new life to the movement and hope of an escape from the
constant threat of harassment and arrest; it offered another location for
continuing the struggle. Above all, the hijacking was a propaganda hit to
show that the Red Army Faction was alive and well.

The hijackers left behind notes that could be called their last will and
testament. "We will certainly live. Alive, alive—we will survive...even if
only as a tiny slice of human history....To hell with any puny love of a
brush with death! I am absolutely going to survive! Absolutely!"

"I wonder if the weather at Haneda tomorrow will be clear. We may
be embarking on lives of red struggle, aloft on white wings flying in a
straight line between the blue sea and the blue sky...."

"Tomorrow, we will confront Haneda. Whatever the results of this
battle, we have never known anything that raised our courage, confidence, and conviction to such heights....Let us continue to the end. We
are the heroes of the future, Tomorrow's Joe [Ashita no Joe]."[9]

This last was from the notebook of the leader of the hijackers,
Tamiya Takamaro (Sashō Henshū Iinkai 1975, 101).

They had gathered at the Swan to finalize some important details of
their plan. They chose the Japan Airlines flight from Haneda to Fukuoka
and decided on March 27. They confirmed that everyone had already
procured weapons. The only thing remaining that evening was to make

---

8. Japan has a system of neighborhood policing using very small, strate-
gically placed buildings called "police boxes" in which two or three police are
stationed. Some have a room upstairs where arrested persons can be held and
questioned.

9. Ashita no Joe, or "Tomorrow's Joe," was a popular cartoon character
created in 1968. He is an orphan who becomes a juvenile delinquent and then
takes up boxing in jail and overcomes adversity, all of which appealed to the
defiant college students of the day.

the final selection for the hijacking team. Most of the ten or more people attending the meeting announced their determination to join it.

In order to begin a simultaneous world revolution, they urgently needed to establish an international base, and that was the purpose of the hijacking. Their choice of initial destination was the Democratic People's Republic of Korea: North Korea. The previous year, a Kyoto University student known as O had been secretly dispatched to Cuba to explore the possibility of sending a group there. In the end, they decided against Cuba, mainly because it was too far away. The reasoning may have been simple, but to the hijackers it was a momentous decision to exercise their own free will to further the "struggle." They wanted to act. Chairman Shiomi Takaya had developed some theories about the "world transition" and "international bases," but they included little or no concrete strategy or accurate information to accompany the preparations. The activists at the Swan were nervous, but they had a vision.

It was an era that permitted the young to be visionaries. Of course, there were those among the conspirators who also had other dreams. One member, a Red Army activist who nurtured ambitions as a musician and had hair down to his shoulders, decided against going. The urge toward revolutionary activism and the dream of a musical career were not as incompatible as they might seem. Old posters of the wanted members of the Yodogō group show another man with long hair. Though now Wakabayashi Moriaki acts as the spokesman for the Yodogō group in North Korea, he once had many eager fans as the head of the GS band Hadaka Rariizu.[10] And the rock group Zunō Keisatsu (The Brain Police) frequently performed its own song about the Red Army, "Declaration of World Revolution."[11]

---

10. GS, short for "group sound," was a term coined in Japan in the aftermath of the Beatles' first Tokyo concerts in 1966 to describe the legions of new rock and roll bands with strange semi-Western names that emerged in the next few years. These long-haired groups dressed in flamboyant outfits and featured a combination of instruments and vocal harmonizing to produce a distinctive "group sound." The name of this particular GS band combined the Japanese word for naked with the British slang term for hard candy, "lollies" (from lollipops), to produce a catchy but nonsensical name.

11. This band (Zunō Keisatsu) was led by rock musician Panta, who based it on the name of the song "Who Are the Brain Police?" on the first album by guitarist and composer Frank Zappa's rock band The Mothers of Invention, which was popular in Japan at the time. Guitarist Panta was a great fan of Zappa and was also close to the Red Army Faction. Zunō Keisatsu's first albums were suppressed by the police because of the Red Army Faction connections in their songs. They were reissued over thirty years later.

Wakabayashi had questioned the old methods of struggle ever since the battle over Yasuda Auditorium at Tokyo University, and he had instantly declared his intention of joining in the hijacking. However, the other long-haired musician refused to go along. His friends tried to persuade him, but he did not change his mind.

"Come on, let's go together."

"We'll be back by the autumn."

Why wouldn't he go with them? He had a reason: "I do not want to cut my hair."

Their knowledge of North Korea may have been somewhat vague, but all the conspirators knew North Korea to be a workers' nation, with a proletarian dictatorship—probably not a place to tolerate long hair.

As it was, the hijacking plan hit a snag. Red Army Faction chairman Shiomi Takaya, after spending the night at a safe house near Komagome station, was arrested by an officer of the Tokyo metropolitan security police as he got into a taxi with another Red Army member. Shiomi ran off, but the policemen caught him easily and arrested him on an outstanding warrant on suspicion of violating the explosives control law during the International Antiwar Day the previous autumn. This was the beginning of nineteen years in prison for Shiomi.

Upon arresting him, the police confiscated Shiomi's notebook, which contained his notes about the hijacking. They found the two English capital letters "HJ" in several places. Although the authorities closely examined the contents of the confiscated notebook, they could not figure out what "HJ" meant.

At just about the moment when Shiomi was being chased down by the police, elsewhere in the city, Tamiya Takamaro was sitting in the coffee shop Renoir, waiting to meet Shiomi. They had some last-minute arrangements to make for the hijacking. But, though he waited long past the agreed time, Shiomi did not appear.

When he found out about Shiomi's arrest, Tamiya's resolve wavered. Should they continue with the hijacking? Should they call it off? Should they go through with it and at the same time try to break Shiomi out of jail?

There were several in the group who felt they should call off the hijacking, fearing that, once they were in North Korea, they might not be able to return home.

"No way. We'll be back. You'll be eating rice cooked in the same pot by fall. After we get military training, we'll be great revolutionary heroes. There's nothing to worry about," Tamiya reassured them. "More important, we have to figure out a way to get in touch with each other once we get back to Japan."

He tilted his head in thought for a moment. "Okay, let's do it like this," he said. When he finished speaking, there was laughter at his idea.

"Yeah, that's how it'll be!"

So, after some worry, Tamiya came to a decision. They would carry out the hijacking on schedule and not try to break Shiomi out of jail yet.

The day before they left, Tamiya wrote a "departure announcement": "We are going to North Korea determined to do everything necessary to receive military training and remake ourselves into great revolutionary heroes. No matter what hardships we must endure, we will return across the sea to Japan to stand at the head of the armed revolution.... We are determined to go; we are equally determined to return to Japan, no matter how high the walls between the nations may stand" (Sashō Henshū Iinkai 1975, 100).

Tamiya made his final decision at the last minute. It would not be too late for them to try to spring their chairman out of jail when they returned to Japan. They had to be patient and wait until fall, he thought. Once Japan had become a battlefield, they would free Shiomi, who would be eager to meet them again once the revolution had started. For now, they needed to become leaders to guide the way for others to follow. Tamiya envisioned the streets of the capital as the battleground of the revolution to come.

As things turned out, Tamiya's dream never came to pass.

Tamiya and the other hijackers did not meet Shiomi again until a summer twenty years after the hijacking when Shiomi, having served his full sentence, was able to visit Pyongyang for the first time. After Shiomi's release, Tamiya tried to explain the circumstances to him in the following simple message:

> I waited for you for a long time at Renoir. You did not come even after the time we had agreed upon. I looked for you in the pachinko parlors where you liked to go, but I couldn't find you. In the afternoon, I learned you had been arrested.
>
> So I thought about what we had to do. Should we leave you there and do as you had planned? Should we rescue you? On the one hand, it seemed to be our duty if one of us was arrested to make rescue a priority and at the same time continue the struggle. On the other hand, when I considered doing both, I remembered the old saying: "Chase two rabbits at the same time and you won't catch either one." So in the end we came here. You, my

brother, had to spend twenty years in prison. Had you been able
to come with us, would things have been better, I wonder? (letter
from Tamiya to Takazawa, read at welcome party on occasion of
Shiomi Takaya's release from prison in 1990)

Things moved quickly once Tamiya had reached his decision. One
by one he selected those who would accompany him. They procured what
weapons they could. Pipe bombs prepared for the International Antiwar
Day protests of the previous year, Japanese swords stolen from relatives'
houses, toy guns—they took what they could find.

They prepared as thoroughly as possible. Rearranging the desks
and chairs in a classroom at Tokyo University, they practiced hijacking
scenarios. With some of them taking the parts of the hijacked passengers, they worked out what each member's separate role would be. They
had very little time left before the day of reckoning, March 27.

But the hijacking was postponed suddenly on March 27. Tamiya
reluctantly decided to call it off when he was already on board the airplane they were planning to hijack. For a variety of reasons, not all of
their number had been able to make the flight.

Some of the members had never flown before. They did not realize
how much time the boarding procedures would take or that passengers
are all given assigned seats. For that matter, some of them did not even
know where to buy their plane tickets. They had scouted out an airport,
but that had been a small local facility. Yonago Airport in rural Tottori
prefecture in no way compared to Haneda. In addition, a key member,
Konishi Takahiro, was late because he lingered for a last good-bye with
his girlfriend.

Tamiya was flabbergasted when he realized he had less than half
of his team on board the flight to Fukuoka. This was no way to run a
hijacking. Despite all the planning and all their roles being decided, they
were going to have to cancel. He made a sign summoning one of his
nearby associates to his seat. Tamiya could not stand up himself, since
that was the signal to the others to begin the action. He relayed the
message to the others: the hijacking was off.

At the same time, those who had been too late to board the plane
arrived in twos and threes at a coffee shop in the city. They were rigid
with suspense. They worried that the others would go through with the
hijacking despite their reduced numbers. The radio in the coffee shop
was tuned to the news, and they listened anxiously. The flight was due
to arrive at Fukuoka at any minute.

"We've been listening to the news the whole time and haven't heard anything. It must be all right," Konishi said to a member who arrived a little later.

That day, the JAL flight landed without incident at its usual time at Itazuke Airport in Fukuoka. Among the passengers, the would-be hijackers glumly descended the stairs of the airplane. So, what should they do now? They contacted by telephone the others who had missed the flight. Although they needed to meet, none of them had much money since they had all planned on going straight to North Korea. That night they returned from Fukuoka to Tokyo by night train. They were exhausted. It never occurred to them to return to Tokyo by plane.

Tamiya changed the date of the hijacking to the thirty-first. He went over with the others the new plan for boarding the flight from Haneda.

On the morning of March 31, the nine men who gathered at Haneda Airport went through the boarding procedure separately. The aircraft was a Boeing 727 and, like many airplanes in those days, had a nickname, the *Yodogō*. A few members who had promised to join the venture did not appear, but this time Tamiya had no intention of calling things off. In 1970, there were no metal detectors or body security checks, and they were able to carry all of their weapons on board with them. In fact, it was this hijacking that spurred the authorities to institute the security measures that have made metal detectors and X-ray of luggage routine practices at Japanese airports ever since.

At 7:30 a.m., after taking off a little late from Haneda Airport, the *Yodogō* was hijacked by Red Army Faction students as it flew over Mt. Fuji.

"We are the Red Army Faction! We are going to North Korea!"

It took the pilot, Captain Ishida Shinji, a few minutes to realize they were serious.

Several men stood in the shadows of the lobby at Haneda Airport watching as Tamiya and his companions checked in for the flight to Fukuoka. One of them carried a camera. The next day, on April 1, the evening papers carried an astounding headline with a photograph: "These are the criminals!"

The photo showed three men in long coats as disguises, carrying long, narrow bags that could easily accommodate something like a sword. There was no doubt they were indeed the hijackers. But the statement in the article that the photograph had been taken by "a casual observer in the airport lobby" was disingenuous. In fact, the men who "just happened" to be in the lobby were undercover police detectives who had followed the Red Army Faction members to the airport. They had observed as the hijackers boarded the *Yodogō*. Their only action was to forward the names of the students and the flight number to the Far Left Violence Control Section of the Fukuoka police. Clearly, the police still had not deciphered the meaning of the letters "HJ" in the notebook confiscated from Shiomi.

However, in the following days, the letters "HJ" in the notebook were cited as evidence in Shiomi Takaya's indictment as a co-conspirator in the hijacking on charges of assault with a deadly weapon, international kidnapping, theft of an airplane, and taking hostages.[12]

In 1990, my own flight from Beijing took a little over an hour and a half to arrive at the airport in Pyongyang. The little airplane circled above Sun'an Airport several times before descending. There were almost no lights to be seen. The airplane dove down into the darkness to make the approach for a landing.

After a short taxi, the aircraft came to a stop in the center of the tarmac; the passengers began descending the steps to the frozen runway in a fierce wind that blew powdery snow in violent swirls. The searchlights picked out the barely visible portrait of Kim Il Sung mounted on the airport administration building.

The airport was deserted and silent. It had been twenty years since the hijacking, and the fall of 1970, when the hijackers had said they would return, was long past. What had happened to those youths who had crossed over to North Korea? How had their thoughts and feelings changed?

Once I had proceeded through customs and passport control, two members of the original Yodogō team were waiting for me with smiling faces. It was New Year's Day.

---

12. There was no crime of airline hijacking in Japan in 1970, as no hijacking had ever been committed and no threat was perceived. Unable to charge them with hijacking, the police used every available criminal charge they could think of.

CHAPTER TWO

Sky Pirates

A message of "Skyjack!" was received at the Haneda Airport control tower from Japan Airlines flight 8315, known as the *Yodogō*, a little after 7:30 a.m. on March 31, 1970, as the aircraft was flying over the southern face of Mt. Fuji. News of the emergency was instantly transmitted to the relevant authorities. By 7:35 a.m., tension was running high in the JAL operation control department. Emergency operation headquarters were immediately established at Haneda Airport.

That day Flight 8315, bound for Fukuoka, had taken off from Haneda Airport at 7:21 a.m., after a delay of ten minutes past its scheduled departure time. Ten minutes had passed, and the aircraft was just leveling out at its cruising altitude.

The "fasten seatbelts" sign had just been turned off.

This was the signal, and several men in the front section stood up. The flight attendants had just started handing out heated towels to the passengers.

The men ran to the cockpit.

There was shouting.

The sound of people being hit.

The thud of a door slamming.

Passengers stared as the men struggled with the flight crew. Some passengers were on the verge of standing up; others did not yet understand what was happening.

Two of the men stormed the cockpit brandishing a Japanese sword and what looked like dynamite. They yelled at the pilots, "We are the Red Army Faction! You will fly to Pyongyang, North Korea!"

The threatening shouts continued. "If you do not go to North Korea, we have bombs! We will detonate them here!"

Captain Ishida Shinji spoke quickly. "We have only enough fuel to get to Fukuoka."

"So land at Fukuoka and refuel! Then we will continue on to North Korea!" was the immediate reply.

For a moment, Captain Ishida was confused. He wasn't sure where they meant. In his mind, there was no place called "Pyongyang"; he had always known it by its Japanese name of "Heijō."

A few of the men came back into the main cabin. One grabbed a microphone from the hand of a dazed flight attendant.

"We are the Red Army Faction. This plane has been hijacked to North Korea. We have explosives. If you resist us, we will blow up the plane," he announced in one breath.

7:40 a.m.: The aircraft is over Nagoya. Captain Ishida has finally calmed down enough to take the microphone and make an announcement to the passengers in the cabin.

"This is the captain speaking. We have been taken over by a group called the Red Army Faction. For your own safety, please do not resist them. Please remain quiet and stay seated. We are presently flying over the city of Nagoya. Please remain calm and stay seated...."

At that moment, the Komaki Self-Defense Force base receives an order from the Self-Defense Agency to send up a reconnaissance plane. By 7:50 a.m., the reconnaissance plane is following the *Yodogō*. It will stay with the passenger jet all the way to Fukuoka.

On board the aircraft, the hijackers are striding up and down the aisles carrying swords, knives, and pipe bombs. They are intimidating the passengers, consolidating their control. Suddenly, a baby in the back row starts to cry. His frightened mother begs one of the men, "May I just give him some milk?" The man is indecisive for a moment but finally brings a small container of milk from the galley and gives it to the woman. By this time, the cabin is under the hijackers' complete control.

7:52 a.m.: An emergency radio message from the *Yodogō* arrives at the Japan Airlines routing section. The message is logged at the airport in Fukuoka by on-duty personnel: "North Korea, fifteen people, going to North Korea." The estimation that the hijackers number about fifteen makes its first appearance in this note.

Shortly after this, at 7:53 a.m., Osaka Airport receives the following message: "Fukuoka landing decided. Skyjackers have bombs. They say they will detonate the bombs if their attempt fails. Absolutely no one

Figure 2.01. Hijacked Japan Airlines plane parked at Fukuoka's Itazuke Airport, with its name, *Yodo*, clearly visible on the fuselage. Photo courtesy of The Mainichi Newspapers/AFLO.

may approach the aircraft while we refuel at Fukuoka. We will continue on to Heijō after refueling. We request maps and directions."

8:59 a.m.: *Yodogō* lands at Fukuoka's Itazuke Airport.

9:13 a.m.: A message arrives at the Fukuoka airport's routing section from the *Yodogō*, which is standing on the tarmac after landing. "Remove the newspaper reporters. We will probably fly to North Korea using visual flight references.[1] We will cross the 38th parallel on the east coast and fly west from there."

9:42 a.m.: "Give us some kind of map, even a junior high textbook map would do. Please bring something."

North Korea has no diplomatic ties with Japan. It will be the first time anyone in the *Yodogō* crew, including Captain Ishida, has been there. They have nothing to rely on but maps and intuition. This is the moment when Ishida accepts the fact that he must fly to North Korea.

---

1. They could only fly visually because Japanese airlines and airport controllers had no relations with their counterparts in North Korea. They did not even know where the airport for Pyongyang was located.

News of the airplane hijacking spreads immediately around the entire nation. TV and radio broadcast live news flashes, and the newspapers print special editions. Besides the media, anxious family members and curious onlookers gather at Fukuoka airport. The festive mood raised by Expo '70 has quite disappeared. In an attempt to prevent the aircraft from continuing on to North Korea, the National Police Agency orders the Fukuoka Police to block the *Yodogō* from taking off. Japan Airlines, not wishing to lose its airplane to North Korea for an unspecified amount of time, drags out the refueling time for as long as possible. But none of this seems to have any effect. There is no change from the *Yodogō*, standing near the terminal's gate 5.

The paralysis breaks at about 1:40 p.m. Suddenly, twenty-three children and elderly people are released from the aircraft. A resolution appears to be at hand. But the door, once opened, is shut and locked again.

Immediately after, the airplane begins to move slowly.

There is a commotion among the security team; journalists hustle over to ask the team leader what is going on.

"The plane is moving! *Yodogō* has started moving! There are still ninety-nine passengers on board! *Yodogō* has started moving from gate 5 at Fukuoka airport with passengers still aboard!" The news reporter is screaming at his camera.

The aircraft taxies out to the central runway and picks up speed for takeoff. There is no way of preventing it.

It is 1:59 p.m. The *Yodogō* turns toward the Sea of Japan and leaves the vicinity of the Fukuoka airport.

In the cockpit of the hijacked aircraft, Captain Ishida is astounded by the map he has been given. Certainly his request was very sudden, but is this the best they could do? He clamps his teeth in irritation. The Fukuoka airport routing section has delivered nothing less than a copy of a line map from a junior high school textbook! It is possible to make out the shape of the Korean Peninsula but nothing more. How can he fly to North Korea with this map? Ishida is about to throw the map to his copilot, Ezaki Teiichirō, when he notices a handwritten note at the top of the map.

"No aviation map; tune in to 121.5 MC."

In the cabin of the *Yodogō*, the Red Army students are screaming with excitement and jubilation.

"We're going to Pyongyang! Pyongyang!"

"At last, we are going to Pyongyang!"

Much later, a passenger describing this moment said, "They were so young."

At about the time the airplane flies out over the Sea of Japan and levels off its flight path, the leader of the hijackers, Tamiya Takamaro, takes the cabin microphone.

"This plane is flying to North Korea. We will go to Pyongyang and make it a base of operations for the international revolution. Later we plan to fly to Cuba, Vietnam, or Cambodia."

There is some agitation in the cabin at his words. To calm the passengers down, Tamiya adds, "Even though we are all going to Pyongyang, you should all be able to return to Japan in a week or two, or in a month at the most."

About thirty-five minutes after its takeoff from the Fukuoka airport, the *Yodogō* reaches the skies over the island of Ullung. They have perfect visibility. Captain Ishida recognizes the island by its shape and changes heading to north by northwest. The airplane turns gently and continues on in the new direction.

At that moment, a fighter jet becomes visible through the right window of the cockpit. Sunlight reflects blindingly from its silver wings. From the cockpit, the fighter jet's pilot looks very near. The pilot is making a thumbs-down gesture.

He repeats the gesture and seems to be signaling for the *Yodogō* to decrease altitude. Ishida reluctantly begins to descend. The jet fighter continues to hold its position to the right of the cockpit. A second fighter jet is visible.

All Ishida can tell about the pilots is that they have Asian facial features. The fighter jets carry no identifying marks. There is no telling where they have come from. The *Yodogō* has provoked a scramble of jet fighters of unknown nationality over the Sea of Japan. The escorting jets force a more westerly course than the original north by northwest direction.

A landmass colored in reds and greens appears below. This must be the Korean Peninsula, and apparently they are over South Korea. The atmosphere in the cockpit becomes very tense. They have not yet crossed the DMZ. The 38th parallel is ahead of them. It appears they will cross the 38th parallel and enter North Korean air space not far from the Sea of Japan.

Ishida calls one of the Red Army militants into the cockpit. "Have you contacted the North Koreans?" he asks.

The answer is simple: "We have not made contact. We won't know whether they will take us until we get there."

The cockpit crew feels a chill run through them. Ishida begins desperately calling the Pyongyang control tower. "This is JA flight 8315. Please respond!" Then, in English, "Pyongyang approach control, Pyongyang...." There is no response from Pyongyang.

Unless they raise a response, they will have to cross the DMZ without permission. It is common knowledge among pilots that the air space above the DMZ is a no-fly zone. Even with previous authorization, their safety in the no-fly zone is not guaranteed. In fact, there is a formal agreement that an aircraft above the DMZ for any reason can be shot down. There would be no grounds for complaint or redress if they were met with an anti-aircraft barrage at this moment. And they would get no warnings....

With a silent prayer, Ishida turns the plane northward. They enter the DMZ.

Their fighter jet escorts make rapid turns away from them and disappear. Silence falls. The *Yodogō* flies on in the silent world.

At this time, the Japanese embassy in Seoul and the Staff Office of the Self-Defense Agency near Roppongi, Tokyo, receive a message from the South Korean Air Force radar control, informing them that the *Yodogō* has entered the DMZ no-fly zone. As the course of the *Yodogō* is tracked and traced on a map, the worst possible outcome is foremost in the minds of the staff officers. The *Yodogō*, with 106 people on board, could well come under deadly fire the moment it crosses the 38th parallel.

If that happened, it would inevitably precipitate an international incident. There would also be the pressing question of responsibility. Was there nothing that could have been done in Fukuoka? Everyone is sweating in fear.

The moment of crisis is fast approaching. Within the next ten minutes, all questions will be answered.

In the cockpit of the *Yodogō*, Captain Ishida slowly turns his eyes toward his watch.

The aircraft has already entered North Korean air space. There is no anti-aircraft fire. An incredible silence reigns.

At 2:52 p.m. on March 31, seven and one-half hours after taking off from Haneda Airport, the *Yodogō* crosses the DMZ. In the cockpit, the flight crew finally allows relief to appear on their faces. Ishida rubs at his sweating face with the palm of his hand. The Red Army militant on watch in the cockpit remains silent, standing with his arms crossed.

The only sound in the cockpit is the captain's voice as he repeatedly requests a response from the control tower.

"Pyongyang, Pyongyang, please respond. Pyongyang, this is JA 8315. Pyongyang, please respond...." At that moment, there is a faint response on emergency radio frequency 121.5 MC.

"This is Pyongyang. This is..." Though the reception is breaking up, the cockpit crew can hear the words clearly. "This is Pyongyang. Tune your radio to contact frequency 134.1 MC. Repeat, this is Pyongyang. Tune your radio to contact frequency 134.1 MC."

They are repeatedly requested to change radio frequencies. As instructed on the map he received in Fukuoka, Ishida has the radio tuned to 121.5 MC. Now, following instructions again, he switches the dial to 134.1 MC.

Once the radio is set at a new frequency, a clear voice speaking in English can be heard issuing from it. "This is Pyongyang approach control. This is Pyongyang...."

Barely fifteen minutes have passed since they crossed into the DMZ no-fly zone. The *Yodogō* flies on, following the guidance of the disembodied voice. In a very short time, they will arrive at Pyongyang.

Just after 3:10 p.m., panic erupts once again in the security control room of the Japanese embassy in Seoul, which has been monitoring the flight path of the *Yodogō*. Something strange is going on.

"The *Yodogō* is heading south! It's heading south! If it continues on this heading, it will cross back over the DMZ!"

The security officer feels his mind go blank for a moment. Even if he wished to, there is no way he can contact the *Yodogō* from this room. Nightmarish scenes chase through his mind.

The South Korean Air Force radar control also clearly shows that the aircraft has made a U-turn.

In the cockpit of the *Yodogō*, an airport comes into sight. It is Pyongyang. The aircraft gradually descends.

"This is Pyongyang approach control. Please maintain your approach path...."

Captain Ishida suffers a moment of unease but allows the airplane to descend farther and enter the landing approach path. The ground rises up in front of them, and the body of the aircraft shudders with the shock of landing. Ishida steadies the aircraft. The fuselage creaks, and they come to a complete stop in the middle of the tarmac.

The time is 3:19 p.m.

"Finally, we have arrived in North Korea! We have imposed on you, but we will soon be able to release you."

A militant wearing dark sunglasses speaks over the cabin speaker system. There is a murmur, and a cheer rises from the passengers. The Red Army students can also be heard cheering. They have finally arrived in Pyongyang!

"We're in Pyongyang!"

"We have arrived in Pyongyang!"

The men repeat this to each other again and again. Even the passengers can see they are overjoyed.

Some among the passengers have already begun gathering their effects. The hijackers also begin preparing to disembark. Although the curtains on the windows are drawn, a passenger later recalled thinking that the few glimpses of the outside seemed strange, that it didn't seem like a communist country. The aircraft stands on the runway without moving.

Soon the stairs are rolled up to the fuselage.

The men cautiously begin opening the door, when suddenly a cry is heard.

"No!" The shout is from Tamiya Takamaro, the leader of the hijackers. "This isn't Pyongyang! We've been tricked! Those are foreign cars and American military planes!"

At that instant, from where he is standing guard in the cockpit, Konishi Takahiro realizes he can see an aircraft at the edge of the airfield with "NW" painted on its tail: it is a Northwest Airlines jetliner.

The militants grow tense.

Some of their faces are white with fear and anger. They all simultaneously remove from their pockets the pipe bombs that have remained hidden until now. In the cockpit, the men question Captain Ishida. He is not sure what to make of the situation either. The hijacker who stood watch in the cockpit through the flight knows very well that Ishida landed following only instructions that came from the radio voice identifying itself clearly as Pyongyang.

Anxiety spreads quickly among the passengers. A disturbance gathers momentum in the cabin.

Outside the aircraft, an announcement can be heard blasting over loudspeakers.

"This is the Democratic People's Republic of Korea. You are all welcome. Please disembark from the aircraft now. We welcome all of you who are against Japanese imperialism!"

The men look at each other. Pyongyang? When they peer through the windows, they see women dressed in traditional Korean *chima chogori* waiting on the runway holding welcome bouquets. The hijackers are confused.

A bus is parked under the stairs next to the aircraft, waiting to carry the passengers to the terminal.

Tamiya Takamaro shouts through the door to the driver of the bus, "This is Seoul, isn't it?"

The driver, caught off-guard, answers, "Yes!" in English.

By this time the hijackers have largely recovered their self-control, and they regain their presence of mind. A Korean official continues to insist on the radio that this is in fact Pyongyang. Tamiya has an idea.

"In that case, bring us a big picture of Kim Il Sung!"

Of all the things he could have asked for, Tamiya has requested the one thing that cannot be found in South Korea no matter how long one searches.

The *Yodogō,* having been forced through trickery to land at Kimpo Airport in South Korea, now faced a long wait with the situation in deadlock. Passengers and crew remained confined inside the narrow body of the aircraft for four days and three nights. It was the longest hijacking holdout in history.

How was the idea for the deception conceived and carried out? Even now, this question has not been completely answered, but the Japan Airlines Operations office stated afterward that, as soon as the incident began to unfold, they asked the U.S. military for assistance. The security department of the National Police Agency revealed that they had ordered the Fukuoka Prefectural Police to analyze the possibility of forcing the aircraft to land at another airport in Japan or in South Korea.

The U.S. military released the information that a little after 3:00 p.m., soon after the *Yodogō* had entered the DMZ, eight North Korean MIG jets scrambled to meet the aircraft, and there was some anti-aircraft fire.

At the first press conference after his release, Captain Ishida denied that any MIGs had appeared. The hijackers' leader, Tamiya Takamaro, also strongly denied this when I asked him in a much later interview in Pyongyang. It is not true that the *Yodogō* completely altered its course because of an attack by MIGs or anti-aircraft fire. It is generally believed that the South Korean Air Force heard the *Yodogō*'s emergency radio request for a response from the ground and responded. Although the mystery is not completely cleared up, the incident does reveal the degree and structure of cooperation between U.S., Japanese, and Korean military forces, which none of the hijackers could have imagined.

However, this forced landing at Kimpo Airport, unplanned though it was, will have a powerful effect in changing their fates later in the story.

CHAPTER THREE

Airport in Disguise

A little after 5:00 p.m. on the evening of the third day, about fifty hours after the *Yodogō* was tricked into landing at Korea's Kimpo Airport, there were signs that the long stalemate was about to break. Parliamentary Vice-Minister of Transportation Yamamura Shinjirō had contacted the hijackers to propose a hostage exchange.[1]

This was an unexpected development.

Inside the aircraft, Tamiya and the others had a short discussion of the proposal.

Most were of the opinion that they should accept the offer in order to break the stalemate more quickly. If possible, they wished to take the passengers with them to Pyongyang, but their opponents were doing everything they could to prevent this, and the stalemate might continue indefinitely. The hijackers were well; the passengers, however, were growing more restless as conditions in the cabin worsened. In addition, the hijackers felt the vice-minister might act as a hold on their opponents. But with fewer hostages the enemy might be more willing to take drastic steps. How should they decide?

The final decision came down to the leader, Tamiya Takamaro.

"We'll accept."

The faces of the other hijackers brightened for an instant. They

---

1. In Japan's parliamentary system, elected members of the majority party in the parliament (called the Diet) may be appointed as cabinet ministers or as vice-ministers of particular government ministries. Yamamura was a Diet member from the majority Liberal Democratic Party who had been appointed to this political post in the Transportation Ministry.

all felt the risk was necessary, even if the final chances of success were small. Shortly after 6:00 p.m., the response was sent out over the wireless radio: "We accept the offer."

During the early hours of the siege, the hijackers had passed out magazines and books to the passengers, saying, "Please read these if you get bored." They were Marxist-Leninist works, the only reading material they had brought. Now the rear toilets were full to overflowing, and an awful smell pervaded the cabin. Only the front toilets still functioned, and it was very hot. The air-conditioning had long since stopped; the air was stale. On top of all that, hunger was becoming an issue.

"They have reached their limit," thought Tamiya as he observed the passengers' faces. Aloud he said, "We will free you tomorrow." A cheer went up from the passengers.

It was 7:30 p.m. on April 2, sixty hours since the hijacking had begun.

From the second day of the hijacking, Japan had been embroiled in a public discussion of the hostage situation. Experts in various fields had babbled nonstop on television and in newspapers, and the media had accused the government of incompetence and inaction. Psychologists had analyzed the stresses of confinement and pronounced that "the passengers are reaching the end of their tethers. Their captors may suffer from psychological fatigue." Military experts talked of the possibilities of a breakthrough, and sociologists lectured on the background of the hijacking. There were even those who had suggested that sleeping drugs be mixed into the food supply. But these critics and experts had all forgotten one important point: for the hijackers, this was a military operation. They might feel physical exhaustion, but there would be no "psychological fatigue." This is what everyone got wrong.

In fact, as was often noted afterwards, the hijackers remained in high spirits throughout the incident even though they barely slept. Tamiya Takamaro especially exhibited a level of energy and concentration that seemed superhuman even to his colleagues.

So, although there were floods of comments and opinions to be heard from every corner, no one had suggested a useful solution. The unheard-of idea of using Vice-Minister Yamamura in a hostage exchange was a last-resort option for the government. Yamamura revealed his own anxiety and unease when he later confessed, "To tell you the truth, my legs were shaking."

On board the *Yodogō*, on the evening of the third day since their forced landing at Kimpo Airport in Seoul, Tamiya sat and reviewed all that had happened.

When he had understood that the airport he thought was Pyongyang was in fact Kimpo, he had been infuriated. This anger had sustained him ever since. He knew very well the sorts of scheming that must have been going on outside the aircraft. Even though they were making progress toward breaking the stalemate, Tamiya knew there were any number of possible traps and pitfalls into which he might yet fall. They must be cautious, more than cautious; it was not possible to be too cautious. Yet they must also be willing to take risks. This he had learned from his experience as a student radical, when Tamiya's daring had earned him the admiration of his fellows. He had only to trust himself, he told himself. He was sure they would succeed.

Years later, Tamiya commented, "At that time, all I could do was believe in myself. Believing in myself meant believing in my comrades. It was the only thing to do. But it's different now. I don't believe in myself. I believe in my comrades, and I believe in the things we are trying to accomplish together."

Tamiya's total focus on their task had let him realize they had landed not at Pyongyang, but at Seoul. Now Tamiya became thoughtful. Had they stepped out of the aircraft on landing at Seoul, how would things have turned out? A chill ran down his back.

On the first day, after they had decided to sit out the siege inside the airplane, a voice could be heard thundering through a loudspeaker outside.

"Allow the innocent passengers to disembark. We will give you everything else you demand. If not, you will absolutely not be allowed to fly out of Korea."

They learned later the voice was that of the chief of the International Affairs division of the Seoul city police. The announcement was repeated again and again.

Their only response was "We can wait ten, even twenty hours. This is a matter of life or death to us. Let us go north."

Late that first night, they had sensed a large group of people outside the aircraft. Nothing was visible in the complete darkness outside the cockpit window, but they had felt the presence of people. There was some hint of murmuring, of movement. A look at the passengers had shown them to be asleep, exhausted. The hijackers guessed it was a specialist team from the Korean army, and clearly they had surrounded the aircraft. One of the hijackers had shouted out of the cockpit window, "We will blow ourselves up!"

The feeling of an invisible presence had continued for a while, but finally it faded, leaving only the darkness.

After a short while, a transmission had come across the radio. The voice introduced itself as Director Jeong of the Department of National Security and said, "We guarantee you a safe takeoff if you will release the hostages."

Tamiya had made no reply; time had passed sluggishly. As the sky slowly lightened toward dawn, they took turns sleeping.

April 1, second day

With the arrival of morning, passengers could be heard asking for food. The hijackers had taken a microphone and announced to the cabin, "Instead of asking for food, we are demanding to go to North Korea. If we ask for food now, they will think we have given up on our demands to go to North Korea...."

Shortly after 11:00 a.m., Kaneyama Masahide, the Japanese ambassador to Korea, had come to the *Yodogō* and spoken through a loudspeaker so he could be heard inside the cabin. "Do not make light of your lives. You are still young. You should think of the future and not act rashly!"

"We can't trust the words of some lying diplomat."

"And I would like to ask, do the North Koreans know you are coming?"

The hijackers made no immediate response. After a pause, one of them said, "We have not made contact."

However, soon after this conversation, the Japanese government received an informal message from the North Korean side: "We guarantee safe passage through Korean air space. All aboard the aircraft will be treated humanely." That day toward evening, Japanese Minister of Transportation Hashimoto Tomisaburō, Vice-Minister Yamamura, and others arrived at Kimpo Airport aboard a government charter flight. At 7:00 p.m., in Minister Hashimoto's presence, Vice-Minister Yamamura and Minister Baek of the Korean Ministry of Transportation had opened a radio transmission with the hijackers on the *Yodogō*. Captain Ishida and Tamiya Takamaro responded.

"We demand to fly to Pyongyang tomorrow morning at 6:00 a.m.," said Tamiya.

Captain Ishida: "We all thought Seoul was Pyongyang. We cannot eat, nor can we sleep. We have very bad air. Last night, the temperature in the cabin rose to 40 degrees Celsius. We do not have enough oxygen. The Koreans have offered us air, but there is worry that there will be some kind of gas mixed into it. The passengers are exhausted. They are hungry, and if the situation continues, I fear for their safety. We must make the passengers' safety our first priority, even though the demands of the Korean government should also be taken into account...."

Commissioner Baek: "We are putting the safety of the passengers first. But if an aircraft of unknown nationality flies north through our airspace, it is our policy, as of any other government, to force a landing. We forced the landing for the sake of the passengers' safety."

Tamiya: "Then how did you know to trick us into landing by pretending to be Pyongyang?"

Commissioner Baek: "Because we had received information about your intentions beforehand. We acted for the safety of the passengers. And let me ask you, what would you have done in our place?"

Tamiya: "Bring out Ambassador Kaneyama. I want an answer soon. Stop your tricky games and deal straight with us!"

Vice-Minister Yamamura: "You must realize that the Korean government has been more than generous. If we can just be sure of the safety of the passengers, you will be able to fly to your destination."

The transmission had lasted about fifteen minutes.

Figure 3.01. A crowd of reporters and cameramen watch the *Yodogō* from a vantage point at the outer edge of Seoul's Kimpo Airport, held back by South Korean soldiers lined up in a ditch in front of them. Photo courtesy of The Mainichi Newspapers/AFLO.

April 2, third day

At 3:20 a.m., the telex machine at the Japanese government special task-force headquarters clattered out a message. It was an official communication from the North Korean Red Cross, forwarded by the Japanese Red Cross:

Item: The safety of the aircraft is guaranteed.
Item: All aboard will be treated humanely.
Item: The aircraft will be returned.

This was merely confirmation of the unofficial message received the day before but significant all the same: the North Korean government had made an official decision. Tamiya and his cohorts did not know it then, but the Japanese government's decision to allow the Red Army hijackers to continue to North Korea began to crystallize with the receipt of this telex. Until then, the general attitude within the government had been a flat refusal, with everyone including Foreign Minister Kiichi Aichi insisting that the North Koreans would not take the hijackers. The basis for this belief was the unconfirmed report leaked from the U.S. military of anti-aircraft fire. But, with this message, some voices within the government reversed their stance: the *Yodogō* should be allowed to continue to North Korea; and the sooner the better, to ensure the safety of the passengers. The only concern was first to secure the release of as many hostages as possible.

Daybreak, fifty hours since the hijacking started

7:30 a.m.: Food and water for two hundred people is delivered to the aircraft.

9:00 a.m.: After minimal maintenance, the aircraft is towed back to the runway and parked, facing north.

The hijackers, however, had not yet been notified of the Japanese government's decision. At 11:00 a.m., Minister Hashimoto held a press conference at Kimpo Airport and told reporters in an official statement, "We will not allow the aircraft to depart for Pyongyang with the passengers still aboard." Then, the Korean Cabinet released an official statement: "We will guarantee at all costs the safety and release of the passengers at Kimpo Airport. If the hijackers do not respond to this

demand, the JAL aircraft will never be allowed to leave." This announcement had been made at precisely noon. The hijackers ground their teeth
in frustration and fury when they heard this. They could all feel the thick
walls of an impossible situation closing in around them.

"Shit!"

"They are making fools of us!"

The hijackers muttered curses. Even today, many of the hostage
passengers can still clearly recall the frustration and anger of their
captors.

Tamiya had taken the microphone and addressed the cabin in a
quiet voice. "We are going to North Korea as the first leg of our journey
to Cuba and Vietnam. We have said our plan is to study the revolution
as thoroughly as we can, then return to conduct it in Japan. We have
done this because we love Japan...." Tamiya became thoughtful. He had
made this speech not only to explain to the passengers the hijackers'
motivations, but also to strengthen the resolve of his companions. It had
worked better at reinforcing the unity of the hijackers than at giving a
theoretical explanation to the passengers, and it was the best thing that
Tamiya could do as a leader. By the time Tamiya's voice became more
impassioned, the other hijackers had regained their composure.

Just then, there was a small disturbance in the front of the cabin.
One of the hijackers had seen a passenger objecting to the speech and
prodded his back with the handle of a Japanese sword.

The passengers were nearing the limits of their tolerance of the
tight, cramped conditions of the cabin. At this provocation, frustration
burst out.

"Kill me, then! If you are going to kill me, just do it!" the older man
had shouted. He started to stand up, still yelling. A stir went through the
entire cabin. Tamiya approached the man slowly.

"If you tell me to kill you, I will," he said in a tight, deep voice. The
sword was put into his hand. Instantly, the cabin became completely
quiet. The passenger who had angrily shouted out also fell silent and
settled down. A long moment stretched out. No sound could be heard.

That had been earlier in the afternoon. Afterwards, time passed
slowly, almost painfully. Then the wireless radio in the cockpit had
received an emergency message. It was Yamamura's proposal of the
hostage exchange, with himself as collateral. Tamiya continued to review
carefully all the events up to this moment. When he had thought through
everything, he called subleader Konishi Takahiro over and issued several
instructions.

Fourth day

Time passed quickly in the predawn of April 3. Socialist Party Diet member Abe Sukeya,[2] from a district in Niigata prefecture, had come to Seoul at the hijackers' request to act as their spokesman, arriving aboard a special charter at forty-eight minutes past midnight. He met with Vice-Minister Yamamura and Ambassador Kaneyama aboard the airplane he had arrived on, and they worked out the procedure for releasing the hostages and how to handle all the agencies involved.

Military security around Kimpo Airport had been beefed up. The area of restricted access extended beyond the edges of the airfield, with a steel-mesh fence surrounding the area and camouflaged troops bearing automatic weapons keeping guard twenty-four hours a day. The greatest worry of the Korean government was that the hijacking incident might provoke other terrorist attacks. The danger of bombing attacks came not only from South Koreans opposed to allowing the *Yodogō* to continue to its destination in the north, but also from North Korean sympathizers taking advantage of the uproar to commit acts of violence. Increased security measures were in place throughout the entire country as well as in the vicinity of the airport and the city of Seoul. The longer the deadlock lasted, the greater the danger of a terrorist attack. The military alert status extended even to Panmunjon village in the DMZ.

The responses of the television and print media had also been heated. Every Japanese television network was reporting live from Kimpo Airport, and articles concerning the hijacking had been taking up most of the print space in the newspapers.

With the news of the hostage exchange proposal, the atmosphere in the cabin gradually eased. Above all, the passengers were relieved to think they would be freed the next day. The faces of the Red Army students were more relaxed as well. Although they still did not reveal their real names, they began to tell the passengers about themselves, their upbringing, and their worldviews. When some of them started discussing the difficult theories of the Red Army and the "international

---

2. The hijackers did not trust politicians from the conservative Liberal Democratic Party, but they trusted opposition Socialist Party members of parliament, some of whom had ties to North Korea. They requested that this person serve as their representative in the delicate negotiations, and, in the crisis, Japanese authorities flew him to Seoul to assist.

revolutionary base theory" that had provided the theoretical basis for the hijacking, some passengers heckled them to explain in terms easier to understand. Many of the captives felt comfortable enough to ask to speak, and the atmosphere continued to lighten. Some sang "Return to the North" to send the hijackers on their way. These exchanges continued until late in the night.

Also late that night, Konishi Takahiro lowered a seatback tray, opened a notebook, and began writing his "Memorandum." The improvement of relations with the hostages did not mean that all danger had passed. If by some accident they did blow up the aircraft before arriving in Pyongyang, the hijackers had to be sure to leave a record of the events of the last few days. They had not landed at Kimpo to refuel or by mistake but had been tricked into the landing by a military conspiracy on the part of Japan, the United States, and South Korea. This truth had to be told. Konishi's leader, Tamiya, had instructed Konishi to write this essay. "In this aircraft cabin, where we can feel so acutely the thickness and weight of the wall of reality that divides nations and peoples," he wrote, "we wish to make some statements on this struggle, our own struggle, and the larger class struggle of which this is a part" (Sashō Henshū Iinkai 1975, 107).

Thus Konishi started his memorandum in the midst of the hijacking incident. He paused to think and then finished the rest in one sweep. He thought of the friends he had left behind in Japan. Although the essay was full of difficult political jargon, the words flowed easily. The hand holding the pen moved quickly, impatiently.

> The true facts must be made clear. This is an issue that the proletariat of Japan, no, of the whole world, must understand. This airplane we seized landed in Fukuoka to refuel. Why were we deliberately hindered for so long from taking off? Clearly, it was because the Japanese government needed this time to negotiate with the South Korean government. They conspired to trick us into landing at Seoul airport by making us think it was Pyongyang. When our airplane had flown north across the western Japan Sea to the Korean Peninsula (we certainly crossed the 38th parallel), an airport responded to our call for Pyongyang. This "Pyongyang Airport" gave us landing directions that led us to Seoul, not Pyongyang. Thus it was not some mistake or emergency of ours that led us to land at Seoul. We were forced into landing at Seoul by the Japanese and Korean governments. Then

we had no choice but to tighten our control of the passengers aboard the aircraft (though of course this did not involve physically restraining them) and to strengthen our resolve to set off a suicide explosion as a last resort.

Our struggle is still only in its first stage. Whether or not we will be able to get to North Korea and whether or not we may receive military training and then fly to Vietnam or Cuba once we reach North Korea—all is uncertain at this point. It is a completely unknown world. But we have confidence. It is our own personal actions that have opened up the situation and made this possible, and that is what will condense it into the practical conditions that make the rest possible. (Sashō Henshū Iinkai 1975, 108–110)

Konishi raised his head. By the time he finished writing, the cabin had become quiet. Overcome with exhaustion from the events of the day, the passengers had settled into sleep. Konishi took up his pen again to add: "April 3, a soldier of the Communist Alliance Red Army Faction, aboard an airplane at Seoul, South Korea." And, finally, "Konishi Takahiro."

Negotiations for the hostage exchange began at 10:00 a.m. the next morning. Diet member Abe and Vice-Minister Yamamura approached the *Yodogō* where it sat on the runway and began direct discussions through a cockpit window. The negotiations stumbled; they could not agree on procedure. Yamamura did not have the authority to agree to the hijackers' conditions and had to return to the airport facility to consult with Japanese government officials. More than an hour passed. At 11:10 a.m., he came back to the cockpit window to continue talks.

"Allow half of the hostages to disembark. Then I will come on board in exchange." But this was not the only condition. "And send off one of your members with the first group of hostages. When the last one has been released, we will return your man."

When Tamiya accepted these terms, the negotiation stage was complete.

2:20 p.m.: Time to begin the hostage exchange. Tamiya takes the speaker microphone and surveys the cabin.

"Now it is time for us to part ways," he says. "We wish to convey our thanks to you. Thank you, everyone. Let's have a little farewell celebration."

They pass out sandwiches, rice balls, and juice to all the passengers.

"We will fight to the end on behalf of the world's oppressed proletariat. We will persist and do our best until the end. We have caused you unhappiness, but we hope you will understand that we did it because we love Japan, and we want to make Japan a better place for all."

Then Tamiya recited the poem "Kawanakajima."[3] Afterwards, the released hostages spoke often of this episode, and the moment became very famous.

> The hushed whispers of riding crops cross the river
> Dawn reveals a thousand soldiers standing by their battle flag
> Damnation! After polishing this sword for ten years
> The big snake escapes under a shooting star.[4]

Tamiya's resonant but high-pitched voice echoed through the cabin. The hostages applauded.

The atmosphere in the cabin was one of relief at the thought of imminent release as well as a strange sense of intimacy. It had been four days since takeoff from Haneda Airport and seventy-nine hours since the initial surprise of the hijacking.

After Tamiya's "party," the passengers began preparing to disembark from the aircraft in a predetermined order.

The door opened.

2:27 p.m.: The first passenger can be seen behind a stewardess standing in the hatch. A woman in kimono; a man wearing a suit; passengers begin descending the staircase. Unexpected cheers rise from the watching reporters. A dull roar can be heard from the crowd standing at a distance.

The *Yodogō* is completely ringed in by a troop of Korean soldiers standing at a distance of about 100 meters. In addition, fully armed soldiers stand by in trucks all over the airport.

When half of the hostages have descended, Vice-Minister Yama-

---

3. This traditional Chinese-style poem commemorates a series of famous battles in the sixteenth century known as the battles of Kawanakajima. Kawanakajima, or "island in the middle of the river," is actually the name of the plain on which parts of the battles were fought. The series of battles and particularly the fourth battle in 1561 have become enduring themes in Japanese popular culture, in Noh and Kabuki as well as in modern films, television drama series, anime, and computer games. This particular poem is often memorized by students, so Tamiya could recite it, and at least some of the passengers on the plane knew what it was.

4. There are many English translations of this poem because of its wide circulation in contemporary Japanese popular culture. This translation is in a novel: Hal Gold's *Neutral War* (Gold 2003, 203).

mura makes a sign from the bottom of the stairs. It is the signal for the hijackers to send down their exchange "hostage," Tanaka Yoshimi.

Tanaka stands in the aircraft hatch.

Vice-Minister Yamamura sets one foot on the bottom step of the stairs.

The hijackers, the hostages, the Japanese government officials at the bottom of the stairs, the Korean government officials—everyone watches breathlessly.

Tanaka takes one step down the stairs.

Seeing this, Yamamura ascends a step.

Tanaka slowly descends another step.

Step by step, Yamamura approaches the aircraft's cabin. He carries a small cloth-wrapped bundle in his hand.

The two men pass each other in silence at the midway point. It's a moment of tension for both sides. Yamamura's steps are shaky.

As soon as he reached the bottom of the stairs, Tanaka was taken

Figure 3.02. The last hostage leaves the hijacked plane at Seoul's Kimpo Airport, as Tanaka Yoshimi, the Red Army's "substitute hostage," passes him halfway up the stairway. Photo courtesy of The Mainichi Newspapers/AFLO.

into custody by the South Korean side. Inside the cabin, Yamamura took a seat as requested.

Once this "hostage exchange" was complete, the second group of passengers was released. At this moment, Yamamura stood up suddenly and approached the door. He appeared to want to make a peace sign to the onlookers. The hijackers panicked. If he had disembarked then, it could have jeopardized the entire venture. They hurriedly pulled him away from the door and tied his hands with rope. He remained so until all the passengers had descended the stairs and the hijackers' "hostage" member had been returned to them.

While he waited outside the aircraft, Tanaka was addressed by a puzzled member of the South Korean team. Though his Japanese was not very good, his meaning was clear.

"Why are you going to North Korea? If you go there, your life will be hard...."

Tanaka said nothing.

The man tried several times to engage Tanaka in conversation, until finally Tanaka shouted, "Shut up! I don't want to talk to you!"

The man stopped his attempts to speak, but for some reason Tanaka to this day clearly remembers the large man who tried in such halting words to speak with him.

The last passenger appears at the top of the staircase.

Once again, "hostages" must be exchanged. Tanaka is escorted back to the foot of the steps. The passenger at the top puts out one foot. Tanaka ascends one step. When they meet in the middle, they both simultaneously hold out their hands and shake.

"Take care of yourself; keep a sharp eye out always," says the passenger.

"Well, take care. Until we meet again!" Tanaka is smiling. He often recalls this friendly moment in the years to come. He mentions it in his memoirs written twenty years after the hijacking (Tamiya et al. 1990, 141–142).

The "hostage exchange" is complete. Some among the newly released hostages wave handkerchiefs at the aircraft.

On April 3, eighty-three hours after being hijacked, the *Yodogō* departed from Kimpo Airport en route to Pyongyang, North Korea. The flight crew remained aboard the aircraft. The sunset faded from the sky, and night fell.

In the gathering darkness, the *Yodogō* took off with the students of the Red Army Faction.

The time was 6:04 p.m.

CHAPTER FOUR

Exile into Darkness

One question has remained in my mind ever since I began tracking the paths of the Yodogō hijackers: If the *Yodogō* had not been tricked into landing at Kimpo Airport, would the affair have ended differently?

"If" is a taboo word in writing factual history. It is meaningless to ask questions like "If things had been like such and such, how would they have turned out?" If, if, if....Once you start saying that, the truth remains vague and ambiguous, hidden behind speculation. However, I am going to give in to temptation and indulge in some speculation.

During the hijacking, several people asked the hijackers at different times whether they had made any contact with the North Korean side. Their answer, in harsh tones, was always "We have not made any contact. We do not know if they will accept us." In the original hijacking plan, Cuba was the destination. The planners had even made contact with Cuba, going as far as sending one of their members there. But complications with this plan made them decide at the last minute to change their destination to North Korea. Cuba was simply too far away, on the other side of the world. The danger was not so much the distance, but the increased risk of being caught and arrested each time they had to stop to refuel. I have found no evidence showing the Red Army members tried to contact North Korea during their planning period. There certainly is no sign that the nine hijackers professed love for North Korea or that they espoused "Kim Il Sung–ism" or "*juche* ideology."[1] Tamiya had even declared, "I will recruit Kim Il Sung [for the Red Army Faction]!"

---

1. See the explanation of *juche* ideology in the editor's introduction.

Twenty years after the hijacking, they admitted in their published memoirs that they did not know until the moment they landed whether they would be welcomed.

"We didn't know," wrote Abe Kimihiro, "if we would be chased off the moment we landed at Pyongyang or be thrown into prison…or if we would be told to take off again immediately."

However, against all expectations, North Korea accepted them. They not only were allowed to remain but were treated like heroes. As Wakabayashi Moriaki wrote,

> We were put up at a hotel in Pyongyang the first night. We almost expected to be escorted straight to an internment camp, so it was unexpectedly nice treatment.
>
> After a meeting with the authorities, we were shown to the hotel dining room. Vice-Minister Yamamura and Captain Ishida as well as the rest of the crew were seated at a neighboring table. The meal consisted of a full-course Korean banquet. Mr. Yamamura's eyes were quite round as he commented, "This is incredible!" I had never eaten such a banquet before, and I didn't understand what was so incredible about it, but I remember being excited about eating white rice. Before we left Japan, we figured there would be nothing but sorghum in the north, so we went out for one last Japanese meal. But, as it happens, rice from the northern part of the peninsula is really delicious. During the colonial period, rice from the northern province of Hwanghae-do was supplied to the Japanese imperial family. (Tamiya et al. 1990, 155–156)

What was the reason for this unexpectedly warm treatment? Here I wish to enter the forbidden domain of speculation, of "what if…" in a historical account.

For four days, as the crisis unfolded, Kimpo Airport and Korea were the focus of attention from the entire world. The news coverage was broadcast not only in Korea and Japan, but across the planet. The whole world looked on as the deadlock continued. As far as North Korea was concerned, these men were heroes, and the story of their arrival in Pyongyang, despite the combined efforts of the Japanese police, the Japanese National Defense Force, the South Korean National Air Force, and the United States Air Force, provided their greatest propaganda triumph ever. From the moment they were forced to land at Kimpo Airport, the hijackers' act took on unintended additional political significance.

They became game pieces in the conflict between North and South in the Korean Peninsula. When the *Yodogō* took off from Kimpo to land at Pyongyang, the whole affair was transformed for North Korea into a major governmental propaganda coup of international proportions. Simultaneously, it became for North Korea a victory over South Korea.

So, had the *Yodogō* not endured the hours of impasse at Kimpo or had they flown directly from Haneda Airport to land at Pyongyang, there would have been no great Yodogō story. The North Korean government might simply have handed over the offenders in response to an extradition request from Japan. In that case, they probably would have used the return of the hijackers as a trump card in foreign relations games with Japan, wielding it, for example, to leverage compensation money for damages inflicted during the Second World War. Quite possibly, as the hijackers themselves half expected, they could have been thrown into an internment camp as political criminals. The ideology of the Red Army was not compatible with the political realities of Kim Il Sung's North Korea.

However, sometimes history smiles on us with irony. Contrary to the intent of the combined Japanese, American, and Korean governments, the forced landing of the *Yodogō* at Kimpo Airport profoundly complicated events.

Immediately after the incident, the North Korean government responded to the Japanese extradition request with the statement "We will not be the agents of the Japanese police." The "reckless hijacking" by the Red Army students, which could rationally be considered a small, almost accidental event, had suddenly grown into a showcase event displaying "socialist Korea" to a world caught in the Cold War of the 1970s. And it did not end there. The self-exile of a group of students from the "rotten capitalist society of Japan" was perfect material to further demonstrate to the people of North Korea the excellence of Kim Il Sung's leadership.

Let's turn the scene back, once more, to the interior of the aircraft. When the *Yodogō* took off from Kimpo Airport, still on board were Captain Ishida Shinji, Copilot Ezaki Teiichirō, Flight Engineer Aihara Toshio, Vice-Minister of Tranportation Yamamura Shinjirō, and the nine Red Army students, who included

Tamiya Takamaro, leader, 27;
Konishi Takahiro, Tokyo University Joint Struggle Committee subleader, 25;

Okamoto Takeshi, Kyoto University, 24;
Akagi Shirō, 22;
Wakabayashi Moriaki, 23;
Abe Kimihiro, 22;
Tanaka Yoshimi, 21;
Yoshida Kintarō, 20;
Shibata Yasuhiro, 16.

Okamoto Takeshi was the older brother of Okamoto Kozo, who was later imprisoned by the Israeli government for his role in the 1972 attack at Lod International Airport in Tel Aviv. Yoshida Kintarō was a worker active in Bund's Antiwar Youth Committee. Shibata Yasuhiro had not yet graduated from high school (in the newspaper articles of the period, he is referred to as "Boy S"). The rest were also activists in Bund, the Red Army Faction, and the Joint Struggle Committee (Zenkyōtō).[2] Some of the members joined the hijacking group immediately after finishing jail terms following their arrests during the fighting at the University of Tokyo in 1969. Tamiya Takamaro was a Bund activist from Osaka City University and served as an officer and the military leader of the Red Army Faction.

Even as I write this, I am struck once again at how young they were. For that matter, even Minister Yamamura, the substitute hostage, was only thirty-six at the time. Captain Ishida was the oldest at forty-seven.

At the time of takeoff, no one was sure of the identity of all the hijackers. Not until after the *Yodogō* had returned to Japan did the police identify them all, based on fingerprints left in the cabin and passengers' testimony.

Shortly after taking off for Pyongyang, Yamamura Shinjirō and the Red Army students aboard the *Yodogō* engaged in a conversation.

"You have been through a difficult time. Are you doing all right?"

"No, no, I'm fine."

"No need for you to be so nervous. We are not going to hurt you." They laughed. "Please just relax."

"Thank you, thank you, thank you."

"What kind of a reaction has there been out there to this whole affair?"

"Oh, well, there is a huge uproar. After all, it's the first time ever...."

Yamamura is finally getting used to the situation.

---

2. See chapter 1, notes 2 and 3.

"But I'll be OK in the next election, with this."

This statement makes the hijackers roar with amusement. Suddenly, Yamamura's face becomes serious, and he asks the students, "What is going to happen when we get to North Korea?"

"Oh, well, we don't really know. We might all be thrown into an internment camp. But you'll probably be all right, won't you?"

"Mmm, we don't have diplomatic relations with this country, so I really have no idea."

Yamamura opens the cloth-wrapped bundle he has brought aboard with him. "I brought this stuff just in case." There are undershirts and underpants inside.

Soon Yamamura loosens up even more and begins criticizing his colleagues, other Liberal Democratic Party (LDP) members of the Japanese national Diet.

"That guy is always showing off and making too much noise. He avoids the dirty work, only takes on what makes him look good. Nobody really trusts him. These days there aren't that many people in the LDP who have the guts to take on a fight and sacrifice themselves to make things happen. Government would really benefit if more people like you got involved. Well, it's true" (Tamiya et al. 1990, 143–144).

This last is flattery.

The conversation with Diet member Yamamura must have been a memorable experience for the hijackers. In that winter twenty years later, over dinner in Pyongyang, they spoke of their encounter for a few minutes. Their memories were vivid. This was when I asked them for their memoirs. They made a very quick job of it, and, when it came time for me to return home, I had a thick bundle of manuscripts in my luggage.

One of the stories they told about Yamamura concerns what happened after their arrival in Pyongyang, when they were being examined by a North Korean official. Abe Kimihiro described it:

> Each of us declared our name and occupation. Then it was Vice-Minister Yamamura's turn. However reduced in circumstances, he was still a member of the Japanese Diet and a vice-minister in the national government. He must have felt he had to say something.
>
> "Well, er, at this time, North Korea...," he stumbled a little.
>
> The official gave him a withering look and said, "Our country has an official name!"

Yamamura seemed to take note and tried again.

"Korea...." He was unable to say any more.

Finally, after some struggle, trying to incorporate words like "people" and "democratic," he came up with "Korean People's Democratic Republic" (the correct title is the Democratic People's Republic of Korea). His expression seemed to say, "There, that should do it!" I would say this was probably a standard type of performance of Japanese LDP politicians. What came next was funny.

The official asked him his occupation, and Yamamura answered eagerly. His chest puffed with pride, he said, "I am a member of the Diet."

Of course, Yamamura did not expect in North Korea to have people start to bow and scrape at the mention of the words "Diet member," but he did look a little haughty. The official showed no sign whatsoever of being impressed but simply repeated the question, "What is your occupation?"

Yamamura was nonplussed. "I am a member of the Diet," he repeated.

"What I am asking is, what is your occupation?"

With some loss of confidence, Yamamura repeats again, "Well, I, er, I am a member of the Diet...."

The same question and answer were repeated several times. The official finally seemed to give up and moved on to the next person. (Tamiya et al. 1990, 154)

The point the Yodogō members were making here is that, in North Korea, "Diet member" is not an occupation in itself but merely someone who is a representative of the people of the nation. So a Diet member should also have an occupation.

I listened with great interest to their stories. More than anything, they were the only ones who could tell me what had happened after the takeoff from Kimpo Airport. It was a great topic to talk about over drinks.

About an hour after taking off from Seoul, the *Yodogō* reached the skies over Pyongyang. In order to avoid flying over the DMZ, they had flown out past the eastern sea coast to turn north then west at Wonsan. Captain Ishida continually requested communication with the Pyongyang control tower, but there was no response.

The airplane circled above Pyongyang for a long time. As they descended, streets laid out in straight lines and what looked like apartment buildings became visible in the dim lights. There were even a few neon lights.

The students were caught with a sudden anxiety.

"Aren't neon lights usually used for advertisements?"

"Is this really North Korea?"

"Are they trying to trick us again?"

They recalled the long, unpleasant hours of waiting at Kimpo Airport.

There was still no response from the Pyongyang control tower. The *Yodogō* continued to circle up and down in a spiral above the city. Captain Ishida had his eyes fixed on the ground below, but he could see no airport where they might land. Suddenly he saw something resembling a small airstrip. He made a final decision as captain.

"We have no choice. We have to land there."

A dim memory had risen to the surface of the captain's mind. In the final months of World War II, he had been a training officer for the special attack corps, the suicide mission pilots. During that period, he had received some part of his own training in the Korean Peninsula, and, if his memory was correct, this was the training runway they had used then. But surely this airstrip was not now in use? And, even if it were still in use, Ishida knew this runway built by the Japanese imperial governor-general was a relic of the past.

With still no response from the control tower, they had to risk it. He turned to Konishi Takahiro, keeping watch in the cockpit, to confirm his decision.

"I don't know if that airstrip is in service now, but, since we can't find any other airport in the area, we have no choice but to land there. I cannot guarantee our complete safely, but will this be all right?"

Konishi took Ishida's words as a threat, thinking that even now Ishida was trying to interfere with their plans. His face dark, he bit out his words harshly, "It doesn't matter. Land there." Konishi communicated the captain's decision to the other Red Army members and Vice-Minister Yamamura in the cabin.

"It seems to be some kind of old training airstrip, and he said the plane might break up. Watch out."

However, as we know, Captain Ishida's experience and knowledge ensured success.

Once again, the airplane circled down and prepared to land. The landing strip visible from the cockpit window did not show a single light. The darkness seemed solid. The *Yodogō* plunged nose-first into the black depths.

BANG! Then a thundering rumble, another BANG, more shudder-ing shakes, and a deafening roar as the aircraft bounced up and down. Nearly at the end of the runway, the captain slammed on the brakes. The noise of the reverse jets thundered through the cabin. The hijackers clung to seat backs and struggled to keep themselves upright. None of them were belted into their seats. Finally the aircraft came to a complete stop, and Captain Ishida heaved a sigh of relief. Copilot Ezaki's forehead dripped with sweat. They were a step away from the end of the runway.

It was 7:20 p.m. Eighty-four hours had passed since they took off from Haneda Airport (Tamiya et al. 1990, 150–152).

The aircraft was silent. There was not a single sound. Suddenly, out of the complete darkness around the runway, searchlights flared up in all four directions. A vehicle could be heard approaching. Looking out the window, they saw armed men in military uniforms climbing out of it.

The pilots became the intermediaries, since the hijackers refused to disembark first and risk becoming separated. Ishida and Ezaki exited the aircraft.

The power was off inside the cabin; total darkness. Several minutes passed in a strange atmosphere of relief at having landed safely mixed with anxiety at what the future might hold. Yamamura continued to sit quietly. The pilots returned.

"They say to come out," Copilot Ezaki informed the hijackers.

In the dark, they tried to see each other's faces.

"Well, then, let's go!" leader Tamiya's cheerful voice rang out in the darkness.

When they descended the stairs set at the rear door of the aircraft, they saw the *Yodogō* had been surrounded by a crowd of people.

It was cold. They shivered. Twenty years later, they still recalled that, though it was April, the temperature felt like it was below freezing.

On leaving the aircraft, the students were immediately disarmed by the soldiers. A dull Japanese sword, a toy pistol, a mountaineering knife, a pipe bomb that might or might not actually work—these items were laid out on the runway. The soldiers took the items one by one to examine them. When one of them picked up the pistol, Abe Kimihiro said without thinking, "Toy, toy!"

He was embarrassed more than anything. He wanted to point out that it was a toy before they noticed it themselves, but it was not clear whether the translator picked up on the English word.

Once the soldiers had finished, the students were directed to board a bus. Their anxiety increased since they didn't know what their desti-

Figure 4.01. North Korean soldiers disarm the Yodogō hijackers on their arrival in Pyongyang. Photo courtesy of The Mainichi Newspapers/AFLO.

nation was. As the bus pulled away, they all turned to look back at the runway. The *Yodogō* sat in the darkness, alone. There was no going back.

Through the bus windows, Pyongyang lay dark and deserted. The streets and the trees lining them were visible in the headlights. Eventually the bus came to a wide river and stopped in front of a large building. The river was the Daedong, which flows through the center of Pyongyang. Later they recalled that at first they didn't realize it was a river but thought it was a lake called Daedong. The bus had stopped in front of the Pyongyang Hotel, which still stands today. Although now it has been surpassed by newer hotels such as the Koryo, in 1970 the Pyongyang Hotel was the best hotel for foreign visitors to North Korea.

As soon as the nine arrived at the hotel, they were questioned by a government official. The official asked each of them their names, occupations, and ages, and then had one final question:

"Why have you come to our country?"

"We have come to receive military training."

Tamiya Takamaro jumped to his feet and began to speak with passion on the Red Army's theories of "simultaneous world revolution" and "bases for the international revolution." The modern period after the Russian revolution was a transition through a socialist phase to the realization of a communist society, and preparations to renew the revolution had to be undertaken. Countries ruled by the proletariat had to function as the logistical bases for the world revolution. International government borders made it impossible for any one country to achieve its revolution alone. In order for a proletarian nation to become a true communist society, it must take a position amidst a continuous world revolution....Tamiya's speech lasted for nearly thirty minutes.

The North Korean official listened quietly for a time, then nodded as if in understanding. "So do you wish to return immediately to Japan, or do you wish to stay here?"

Tamiya, caught off-guard by his question, answered hastily, "We can't go back immediately. We want to stay here."

At his words, the official was quiet for a long moment.

"Fine, then. However, I think you need some more education first."

So saying, the official stood up. Apparently they were not to be immediately deported. The students felt relieved. Once the interrogation was over, the official informed them that a meal had been prepared for them.

When they arrived at the hotel restaurant, they found the luxurious Korean banquet laid out on the tables with beer and other drinks. That evening, the white rice had an exceptional flavor. It was their first real meal in four days. Later they commented that it was like a party. A somewhat inebriated Captain Ishida came over to Tamiya and they toasted each other. At the next table, Yamamura Shinjirō appeared to be enjoying himself.

One could say that the *Yodogō* began a quarter-century-long flight through darkness with the hijackers' message to their comrades in Japan: "No matter how high the walls between the nations may stand, we will return by fall."

However, the "fall" of their return has yet to come, even after the passage of some thirty years. The hijacking itself had been a success with their arrival in Pyongyang, but their temporary military training course turned out to be a trap. Although their safe landing at the Mirim airstrip was a public triumph, at the same time, it was a personal disaster. After their disappearance, nothing was heard of these men for twenty years. These decades are a dark blank in the story of the Yodogō. On that night of April 3, 1970, the Red Army Faction student hijackers entered into an exile in darkness.

CHAPTER FIVE

Pyongyang

A certain fateful day can mark the moment when all traces of a person whom we have been following closely suddenly disappear. The flow of information concerning our subject dries up abruptly. We hear nothing more of how he is living or where. In this kind of situation we usually say "his whereabouts are unknown" or "he has disappeared." These words perfectly describe the situation after the Red Army Faction students arrived in Pyongyang. Of course, they did not "disappear" but spent the first several years in Pyongyang undergoing intensive daily ideological and lifestyle remolding ("brainwashing"). But, to us, their lives in Pyongyang were a blank during those years. It was as if a wire had been cut, with silence falling suddenly after all the noise. They might as well have hijacked themselves across the river of the dead.

This impression may just be in contrast to the flood of information that preceded the moment of the hijackers' disappearance. The testimony of every passenger aboard the *Yodogō* was public information; there was not a newspaper, magazine, or weekly tabloid that had neglected to cover the subject. Live, unceasing, on-the-spot television coverage had provided countless images of the crisis. There is even a recording of the speech Tamiya made to the passengers aboard the *Yodogō*. On this tape, Tamiya is shouting at the top of his lungs, his distinctive, piercing voice delivering a political speech in language listeners found very difficult to understand. With such a proliferation of information, viewers could easily imagine themselves at the scene.

But the hijackers' daily lives in Pyongyang remained a blank. Not only were there no relations between the two countries, but there was no news of the students and no way to make contact with them. The public knew only that they had indeed gone to North Korea, and many believed, without reason, that they were jailed there. Twenty years passed.

When I visited North Korea for the first time, I received my entry visa from the North Korean embassy in Beijing, but, because I was traveling privately and not as a member of a delegation or a tour group, there were many annoying bureaucratic difficulties. North Korea was in many ways much more remote in those days than it is now. When my departure date neared, several friends and colleagues held a small farewell party. Everyone said the same two things: they wished that I would have luck in discovering what had become of the Yodogō hijackers and that I should return safely to Japan. They seemed to regard this journey as a momentous event: though the two countries are divided only by the narrow Sea of Japan, the atmosphere at the party was one of sending a traveler off to the end of the world.

On my arrival in Pyongyang, I checked into the Koryo Hotel on Changuang Avenue. Tamiya was waiting for me in the hotel lobby. A man of rather small physique, he stood in the shadow of one of the pillars in the lobby, his head tilted slightly to the side. Memory can fade with the passage of time, but this was indeed Tamiya, leader of that student movement of twenty years past. But I was struck by the impression that this man, the leader of that long ago hijacking, did not seem comfortable in the luxurious hotel lobby.

That evening, we enjoyed a fabulous banquet in a private dining room at the hotel, in the company of several high-ranking North Korean Workers' Party members. After the meal, we moved to another room in the hotel and continued our party late into the night. My interest and excitement overcame any travel exhaustion: here I was, in North Korea! It was not a place one ordinarily visited. In addition, here were the Yodogō hijackers themselves who had come to meet me, and, with twenty years of catching up to do, we had plenty to talk about. Later, alone in the dark of my room, I had difficulty falling asleep.

The next morning, I awoke once in the early predawn. The snowy streets of Pyongyang were visible in the half-dark outside the window. I could see an elderly woman, stooped over, walking down the snow-covered street, and, as my eyes adjusted, I discerned several people making their way along the freezing road. This was my first glimpse of Pyongyang. I wondered briefly where the woman could be going so early in the morning, but soon I fell back to sleep. Later, when my watch alarm began beeping some distance from the bed, I arose and pulled aside the curtains to see the snow on the street glittering brilliantly in the sunshine. The dim early morning scene had quite vanished. A bus disgorged its passengers; people descended stairs into the subway. It was in every way a typical morning.

From that day, we were busy touring Pyongyang. We visited, one after the other, Mangyondae, Kim Il Sung's birthplace that has been turned into a shrine; Kim Il Sung Square; the Museum of the Korean Revolution and the giant statue of Kim Il Sung at Mansudae; the statue of Chollima, the flying horse of Korean legend; the Daedong River; the circus; the theater; the Children's Palace; and collective farms. The May Day Stadium, Gaeseonmun; Botongan Park; the Memorial to the Patriots of the Revolution at Mt. Teson; the Juche Tower of Ideology; the People's University—anything we could think of worth seeing in Pyongyang, we visited. One morning before dawn, we boarded a train at Pyongyang Station to visit Mt. Myohyang, where the International Friendship Exhibition Hall contains many of the gifts received from international visitors along with statues of Kim Il Sung and his son, Kim Jong Il. Every day, at the evening meals and for hours late into the night, we continued talking.

We were chatting animatedly in the coffee shop at the hotel, when I was suddenly inspired with an idea.

"I know. Let's call Shiomi-san!"

"Do you know his telephone number?" Tamiya asked.

Just before I left Japan for Pyongyang, Shiomi Takaya, the original leader of the Red Army Faction, had been released from Fuchū Prison after finishing his sentence of nineteen years and nine months. On the afternoon of his release, I attended a small welcome-back party held for him in a pub near the Kokubunji station in Tokyo. I had taken the opportunity at the time to tell him I would be traveling in just a few days to North Korea to meet with the Yodogō hijackers. Just as the last twenty years had passed in exile for Tamiya, so had they for Shiomi. It seemed a strange coincidence that these two figures, so intimately connected with the Yodogō hijacking and so long absent from the scene, should both reemerge into the light of day at the same time. I didn't think there was much I could do for them, but I thought I could at least act as a go-between for their reunion. I noted down Shiomi's phone number from my pocket planner, went to the hotel post office to request an international phone call, and waited while the operator made the connection.

"Please use the booth on the left for your phone call," she told me.

"Yoboseyo! [Hello?]"

I spoke into the receiver. Shiomi's wife answered, surprised by the unexpected call. I explained briefly that I was in Pyongyang with Tamiya and asked if I could speak with her husband.

Before he could come to the phone, I handed the receiver to Tamiya. I wanted to make this first conversation as dramatic as possible. Finally, after a silence lasting twenty years, these two would be speaking to each other again.

"Is that Shiomi?" Tamiya said into the telephone.

I stepped quietly out of the booth.

One evening a few days after my arrival, we had a New Year's party. We celebrated the New Year seated at low tables in a Japanese-style room. We sang songs, accompanied by Abe Kimihiro on the guitar. When the party was at its height, someone said, "Now's probably a good time to do it."

"Yes, that's right."

Everyone turned to Tamiya. He stood up. This was the first time I heard Tamiya recite "Kawanakajima," the poem he had recited on board the *Yodogō* during the hijacking.

The recitation brought vivid images to my mind of those years when universities everywhere in Japan were blocked and barricaded, and helmeted students filled the city streets. But the fires had soon been extinguished, and now the campuses languished under a strange air of emptiness. I wondered about these men, living in this foreign country: what had the seasons of their years been like? The answer to this question was finally going to become clear, after twenty years of mystery.

For several days after their arrival at the Pyongyang Hotel, the Yodogō hijackers were put on a kind of probation. The North Korean government was having trouble deciding what to do with them.

In contrast, the flight crew and Vice-Minister Yamamura were allowed to return to Japan after a day of rest, and they arrived safely at Haneda airport in the *Yodogō*. On April 5, the Metropolitan Police began their investigation of the aircraft in a hangar of the Japan Airlines maintenance facility. The investigators found a dagger in a white sheath in the cockpit, apparently left behind by the hijackers. The next day, on April 6, Minister of Transport Hashimoto Tomisaburō awarded Captain Ishida and the crew commendations for "saving the lives of all the passengers, along with the airplane." The media praised Captain Ishida and his crew for their cool-headedness during the crisis, and they suddenly became the heroes of the day. Yamamura was referred to as "Yamamura Shinjirō, the Man," and a popular singer of the day, Kasuga Hachiro,

Figure 5.01. Vice Transportation Minister Yamamura addresses the welcoming crowd after his safe return to Haneda Airport in Tokyo. Photo courtesy of The Mainichi Newspapers/AFLO.

Figure 5.02. Yamamura's reunion with his family. Photo courtesy of The Mainichi Newspapers/AFLO.

released a song about him. And, as he had expected, Yamamura won his next election by a landslide. The hijacking crisis was over.

On the fourth morning after their arrival at the hotel, the Red Army Faction students received a visit from cadres of the Workers' Party.

"Gather up your luggage, please."

Several black Russian-made Volgas were standing at the hotel lobby entrance. The hijackers were instructed to get into the cars.

"What is going on? What are they going to do with us?" Anxiety filled them.

The cars carried them away from the center of the city. Soon they had traveled beyond the city streets and entered a pine forest. The journey continued over a hill and passed through a stretch of farmland. Occasionally they glimpsed soldiers. The students' biggest worry was that they were being conveyed to an airport to be forced to board an airplane for repatriation to Japan. They also feared the possibility of prison or an internment camp.

Once they had left the farming district, the cars climbed a small rise to a gated entrance guarded by soldiers. Entering, the Volgas stopped in front of an elegant building. It began to appear that prison did not await them.

Two single-story concrete buildings stood together, surrounded by pine woods, with the bright water of the Daedong River visible through the trees. Brilliant yellow forsythia and tiny flowers in a multitude of colors bloomed in the garden. This place was a Workers' Party guest house.

Inside one of the low buildings there were several rooms, each furnished with beds, desks, and other furniture for two occupants. The other building contained public rooms such as the dining hall, meeting rooms, and a movie theater. In the living room hung an elaborate chandelier, and every room had a portrait of Kim Il Sung on the wall. A spring breeze still carrying a bite of winter blew through opened windows. Outside, across the Daedong, collective farms lay surrounded by their fields.

Tamiya chatted with the Workers' Party cadre through the translator with a cheerful, smiling face. They would be staying at this guest house. The students had finally understood that they were not to be imprisoned or repatriated but would be allowed to remain and live here. All nine wore similar smiles and happy looks on their faces.

Tamiya turned to his fellows and said, "From tomorrow, people." Everyone nodded, ready.

They were in a dream. But they believed they could make their dreams reality and that in the near future, one day in the autumn, they would leave this place and return to Japan in triumph. They would be heroes of the revolution.

In the meantime, this guest house was to be their residence. It was still their home when I met them, twenty years later.

The Red Army students decided to begin a strict routine from the next morning. Because they considered themselves soldiers, they made discipline a priority. They set a time to rise and determined to exercise before breakfast. In small groups, they discussed repeatedly what they could do with their time here in North Korea. Some wished to study theory. In Japan, caught up in protest activities, they had never had time to read the classics, so others felt they ought to read the works of Marx and Lenin. Above all, they all wished to receive military training. They had gone to great lengths to come to this place to receive military training, and they must not miss the opportunity while they had it.

Outside their quarters, they raised a flag of the Red Army that they had brought with them. The red flag fluttered in the breeze coming across the river.

The North Korean Workers' Party had promised to dispatch cadres to serve as instructors for the students, and the students prepared to make their self-introductions. For the first time they told each other their true names, since they had continued to use pseudonyms when addressing each other. Before the hijacking, the group had met in full only twice. Since they did not even know each other's names, it is hardly surprising to learn they had no agreed upon plan to follow now, after their arrival in North Korea. Tamiya quickly called a meeting so they could agree on a plan. The discussion grew heated: suddenly they were no longer dealing with an amorphous future. They found themselves in Pyongyang, but they still had no firm ideas of what they wished to do.

The meeting resulted in the entire group agreeing on three resolutions, embodied in three slogans. Much later, Tamiya read the slogans to me one by one and explained their meaning:

Item: We live and die together.

Item: We will defend and nurture the simultaneous world revolutionary transition.

Item: To complete the success of the hijacking, let us prepare for a triumphant return to Japan!

"We risked our lives in the hijacking, and we fought together," explained Tamiya. "We could only rely on each other. Furthermore, we had no idea what the future held, so we felt like we had to take the initiative and decide our path for ourselves. If we stood together, we would have hope. We had to trust and help each other. And we had to unite to ensure the victory of the world revolution. Then also, we were soldiers of the Red Army. The idea of simultaneous world revolution was the Red Army's philosophical starting point. Our purpose in the hijacking was to set off the initial stage of the world revolution, which would hurry up the process. We had to establish a 'World Party' with simultaneous revolution as its central tenet. We had to discuss and come to an agreement with the North Korean people as to the legitimacy of simultaneous world revolution....Third, the hijacking itself was not the point. The idea was to come to North Korea to educate ourselves about politics, ideology, and military science, then to return to Japan to use our new skills to fight effectively. That is why we thought our hijacking would be a complete success only when we finally managed to return to Japan....How we would return to Japan was something we hadn't yet figured out."

In retrospect, these slogans formulated by consensus evoke pity, even pain. When they were formulated, the hijackers did not think they had completed their venture, and this gave them hope. So, what brought about the later change in their ideology, the degeneration of their hopes? Given his political and ideological stance when he told me about them, the explanation Tamiya gave of these slogans seems to be an admission of defeat.

After laying out their three slogans, they debated what to request of the Workers' Party. Several differing opinions were aired. It was impossible to agree on any one thing. According to Tamiya, the talk went something like the following:

"We came to get military training, so I think that is all we need."

"That is so one-sided. This is a good opportunity for us to study philosophy and economics."

"No, simultaneous world revolution is our central tenet, so it would be better if we formed our own study group to read the Marxist-Leninist books and Red Army pamphlets we brought with us."

"I want to study about socialism. What we need is a platform."

"What do you mean, 'platform'? No, I want to study economics. To tell the truth, I don't know anything about economics."

"I want to study philosophy."

"You? Philosophy? With that face?"

"What, philosophy is about looks?"

"No, I think our main goal should be to engage in military training, since in the end we are dedicated to the principle of simultaneous world revolution. Like learning about the North Koreans' experience in fighting against the Japanese occupation and such...."

"The anti-Japanese fighters used guerrilla tactics. Were you thinking we could use guerrilla tactics to fight in the mountains of Japan?"

"No, that's not it. I think we could gain some valuable general insights from their firsthand experience. How much do you really understand about military strategy?"

As one of the passengers aboard the hijacked airplane had remarked, "They were so young." Perhaps so, but they were also perfectly serious. In the end, they agreed to make the following five requests:

Item: Military training
Item: A solution for our return to Japan sometime this year
Item: Lectures on philosophy, economics, and the Korean Anti-Japanese Resistance
Item: Training field trips
Item: Japanese newspapers and magazines; access to a radio

These requests were immediately relayed to the Workers' Party. The response to the request for military training: "We will consider it."

As for returning to Japan: "It was a rash decision on your part to come here, and this will not be a simple matter. We will do what we can. Please consider any future requests carefully."

Lectures began immediately. A curriculum was developed, and a teacher was dispatched to deliver the lectures every day at the appointed time. The professors from the Social Sciences Institute in Pyongyang spoke in soft tones, but there was no room for compromise in interpreting their message. Their text was Kim Il Sung's writings, and the topic of study was his personal leadership ideology, the only ideology acceptable in North Korea. Other lectures covered the revolutionary history of North Korea and the history of the international labor movement.

Their wish to go on field trips was soon granted. To learn about the resistance movement against Japan, they visited museums dedicated to the Revolution, as well as historical sites, and listened to lectures afterwards. They were usually asked to write opinion essays on what they had seen and heard after these trips. They saw their first real guns at the Museum of the Revolution at Mansudae, and afterwards one of the opinion essays stated only, in a mix of English and Japanese, "I Love jū" (I love guns). When their guide read this, he could not stifle a quick laugh.

Once a week they watched ideological movies. Many of the movies were about the Korean resistance against the Japanese; others concerned the accomplishments of Kim Il Sung or were socialist propaganda vehicles. The first two movies were documentaries, titled *North Korea Today* and *Brother and Sister Visit the Motherland*, both excruciatingly long and wordy. Without fail, there was a discussion session afterwards.

Apparently, they were not very diligent students in those early days, mainly because the lectures had nothing to do with the topics they wished to study. Where they had wanted to study economics and Marxist-Leninist texts, they were given lectures on *juche*[1] ideology and the "masterpieces" of Kim Il Sung. The professors said: "*Juche* ideology is the modern Marxism-Leninism, creatively developed from the latter. It follows the Marxist-Leninist model. At times of revolution we respect the model, while preserving our own creativity and independence. Therefore *juche* ideology includes and supersedes Marxist-Leninist theory; nothing more is needed. *Juche* ideology is the only modern guiding philosophy that the world's working classes need."

It was only after their arrival in Pyongyang that the hijackers heard of *juche* (self-reliance). And they could not easily agree with the professors' words. As far as the Red Army Faction was concerned, even if this was ideology well suited to the circumstances in communist North Korea, it was still just a local brand of Marxism-Leninism.

"I can't stand these lectures. They're worthless." Some complained about the classes; others just slept through them. A few pretended to be listening while actually reading Marxist-Leninist texts, piling up other books on their desks so the lecturers could not see. There were frequent run-ins with the instructors.

"Revolution in just one country will bring change."

"Revolution in just one country is impossible."

"Even Marx spoke of 'the simultaneous world revolution.'"

Things went as far as shouting in anger at the head professor of

---

1. *Juche* ideology is the official ideology of North Korea, based on the writings of Kim Il Sung. The characters for *juche* are the same as the characters for self-reliance or subjecthood in Japanese. The Japanese philosophical concept of *shutaisei*, or independent subjecthood, was a much debated and admired quality among New Left students in the late 1960s but was understood in quite a different way from the North Korean *juche* concept. Where the name of the official ideology is used, we have kept it as *juche*, but, when the concept is repeated in the context of a long quotation, we sometimes render it as "self-reliance."

juche ideology at the Social Sciences Institute, "Do you people really know anything about Marxism?!"

Akagi Shirō reminisced about earning the nickname "Anti-Dühring" from his fellows because of his tendency to challenge their professors by quoting Engels' *Anti-Dühring* and Marx' *Critique of the Gotha Program.*[2]

Consequently, their daily routine had two parts: the days were spent studying *juche* ideology and the evenings, Shiomi's theory of the transition into simultaneous world revolution. Once classes were finished for the day, they conducted their own study sessions and discussions to meet the requirements of item 2 on their list of slogans: "We will ensure the success of simultaneous world revolution."

They not only studied and debated issues. Their physical training sessions were an important part of their schedule as well.

"Military training! Military training! Always military training!" wrote Abe Kimihiro. "If we didn't get military training, then we had no reason for coming. Of course, we also needed to study philosophy and economy, and the history of revolution and the like, but only in order to engage more effectively in the military struggle. I had no intention of studying obediently like some college student!"

"Because one of our motives for coming to North Korea was to receive military training, our daily routine also included running in the mornings. It felt very good to run in the fresh, early morning air, far from the city. We agreed that we shouldn't just run but that we should "run in the spirit of activism." So we shattered the still of the early Korean mornings by shouting out our Red Army slogan of "Achieve the Uprising, Victory in War!"

However, they were immediately obliged to stop this demonstration. They received a message from the Workers' Party: "You can be

---

2. Friedrich Engels wrote and published *Herr Eugen Dühring's Revolution in Science* in 1878 and in 1880 arranged three chapters of it as a pamphlet titled *Socialism: Utopian and Scientific,* which is often known as *Anti-Dühring.* This version became widely known as a popular introduction to Marxism and would have been part of the basic reading in Marxism for Japanese New Left students. Karl Marx's *Critique of the Gotha Program* was published in 1891 as the basis for a new party platform for the German Social Democratic Party, but Marx had written it some fourteen years earlier as a set of notes critiquing the platform that was proposed for the Gotha Congress in 1875. It was attractive to youthful students of Marx both because of its exposition of some key philosophical issues in Marxism and because of its argumentative style.

heard on all the nearby farms. Wouldn't it be best if you stopped shouting your slogan?"

"What's wrong with being heard?"

A counselor from the Party advised them, "You might have some trouble if it got out in the neighborhood that some Japanese people are doing something here" (Tamiya et al. 1990, 170).

The hijackers had no response to this, the perfect squelch.

"Oh, well, then. We agree that it might be best not to let such a rumor get out...." Although not completely satisfied with this explanation, they decided to give in.

Since their arrival in Pyongyang, the Red Army students' world had been completely circumscribed by the North Korean Workers' Party. Even if they tried, they would not have been able to escape its control. When they became restive, the manipulation simply became more intensive. Escape was impossible. A little later in their studies of *juche,* they came across the term "the art of guidance." Handled skillfully, a person can be made to believe a decision has been made completely freely, without either restrictions or coercion on the part of a handler. But no one wants to believe he can be controlled in such a way, so he thinks his decision has been made of his own will. The "art of guidance" is a highly developed form of mind control, and, when the students agreed to give up the show of activist spirit on their early morning runs, they took their first voluntary step into the embrace of the Workers' Party. They chose to interpret their instructor's advice in a positive way: "Isn't this a sign that our request for military training is going to be accepted?"

Instead of shouting slogans, they cleared out a three-kilometer-long running course in the pine woods around their residence, adding in an exercise area with horizontal and parallel bars. Sweating allowed them a small sense of fulfillment. With the help of some Korean workers, they enlarged the open ground even more and made a field large enough to play soccer. Every day in their small square of land, they spent themselves to build up their physical strength. Naturally, they were not allowed to wander around freely outside.

"The only thing we worked really hard at was the physical exercise," wrote Abe Kimihiro. "Anyway, I went all out. It was an urgent matter, since we thought the plan was to return in the autumn and lead the revolt."

The men felt swim training was an important element in building up physical fitness, and they had a qualified coach in Okamoto Takeshi, who had been a star on his Kumamoto High School swim team. They added a round-trip swim across the nearby Daedong River into their training regimen, a distance of some 300 meters. On occasion they completed the swim fully dressed, always keeping in mind that all their training was aimed at military preparedness, not just building up their physical strength.

The season had shifted to summer, and soon it would be autumn, the time for their departure. Still no military training curriculum had been offered, and there was no firm date set for their return to Japan.

I had been in Pyongyang for about a week.

One afternoon, I was walking around in the city with Tamiya Takamaro and a few of the others. We were strolling along the avenue from the downtown department store toward the fountain park near Mangyondae, when we met several pairs of newlywed couples, the new brides dressed in bright *chima chogori.* It was the custom of the middle class in North Korea to take their wedding pictures in front of the fountain in this park. The park, the fountain, and the large bronze statue of Kim Il Sung are featured in these photos. I suddenly wondered how it had gone for these men.

"Have none of you married?"

One of them answered, "We haven't yet given up on the revolution."

"Just because you get married doesn't mean you have to quit the revolution, does it?"

"Do you know anyone suitable?"

"But aren't there lots of beautiful women in North Korea?"

The faces of the women I had met since coming to Pyongyang came to mind. Though I had met them only in passing, some of them had been charming and lovely. It seemed most natural that at some time in twenty years they would have met and married someone suitable.

"If you know anyone, please introduce me!"

"Sure."

"Korean women are difficult. North Korean women think only of North Korea. They think only of the revolution in their own country."

"Is that so?"

"We think of the revolution in Japan, and at some point we must return to Japan. We wouldn't be able to take North Korean women with us then...."

During this conversation, I thought of a rumor I had heard in Japan just before I left to the effect that Okamoto Takeshi had married a Korean woman, and they had a child.

"But what about Okamoto? He married a woman here, didn't he?"

There was a moment of silence.

"Okamoto has decided not to return to Japan and to have his bones buried here. North Korean citizenship and family relations are complicated, and he sometimes has a tough time."

The conversation ended there, and I had the strong impression I was being warned not to ask any more questions. Looking back now, I know they were all already long-married by then.

I did not, in the end, meet either Okamoto Takeshi or Tanaka Yoshimi on that trip. Konishi Takahiro had departed a few days before on a business trip, and the others told me that, if I waited a few days, he would be back. I should have liked to meet the whole group, but I didn't feel there was any point in insisting. I was satisfied just to know that they were alive and well somewhere in Pyongyang.

"Since we came here, a lot has happened, hasn't it? Even in Japan," Tamiya Takamaro said suddenly.

Indeed, a lot had happened. Too much to remember everything, I thought to myself.

While the *Yodogō* was sitting in deadlock on the runway at Kimpo Airport in 1970, the national Red Army Faction had decided to hold a political rally at Hibiya Auditorium on the evening of the first of April. However, this became the first indoor rally in Japan to be banned by the authorities since the end of World War II, all owing to the hijacking. Lines of riot police surrounded the auditorium as if martial law had been declared. The protest movement in 1970 had been vigorous and active; but it was about to enter a long period of retreat. Many activists had been arrested and imprisoned, and those not imprisoned could not resist the changing times. The Red Army Faction's party newspaper, *Sekigun* (Red Army), attracted attention when it published a special edition devoted to the hijacking, with the text of Tamiya's departure proclamation and Konishi's "Declaration of War from Seoul." Tamiya's claim of "We are tomorrow's Joes" was much repeated. An activist who had been arrested at the same time as Shiomi Takaya but later released was rearrested at the time of the hijacking. In addition, several people were arrested as accomplices to the hijacking. Throughout the country, dozens of university campuses suspected of harboring Red Army Faction bases were subjected to forced searches, including Kyoto, Dōshisha, and Ritsumeikan universities, as well as Shibaura Institute of Technology and the Tokyo Medical and Dental University.

In Osaka, the 1970 Japan World Expo drew increasing crowds every day to its site in the Senri hills, and its theme song by Minami Haruo was heard in every corner of the country. The heat of summer came. Every day, as the fiery glow of the setting sun burned the tatami mats in my tiny room and dyed the evening sky the color of blood, I would set off for my part-time night job. These are my memories of the summer of 1970.

With the arrival of the breezes of autumn, a rumor began circulating, its origin a mystery.

When I met the hijackers twenty years later, I asked: "I heard a rumor that you were back in Japan, that you had been seen in Niigata. The rumor spread with amazing speed....What was the true story with that?" Twenty years after the fact, I was finally able to put this question directly to Tamiya. He shook his head slowly.

"A lot has happened. For both of us...."

"Yes. A lot...."

Tamiya Takamaro accompanied me to the airport on the morning of my departure from Pyongyang.

"Let me ask just one more time. Is your life here truly satisfying? Is there anything you can tell me?"

He replied that all was well, "...but I feel a little uncomfortable...."

It was time to board. I passed through passport control and entered the boarding lounge, then walked across the airport tarmac to board the airplane waiting on the runway. It was the same little twin-engine aircraft in which I had come to North Korea. Through the round window, I could see my companions waving continually. At that moment, I had no idea how many repeat visits I would make to North Korea in the future.

The aircraft began taxiing down the runway and took off. People, cars, buildings, all became tiny, distant dots. Soon Pyongyang had disappeared from view.

CHAPTER SIX

Ideological Remolding

I n those days, as now, there were no direct flights between North Korea and Japan. Traveling between them always means a stopover, often in Moscow or Beijing. North Korean Airlines has only one or two weekly flights to Moscow, Beijing, Khabarovsk, and Sofia. From Japan, the usual transit point is Beijing.

It was a relief to return to Beijing. There, the city hummed with people and cars. Waves of bicycles filled the streets; the crowds were full of energy. Used to the hubbub of metropolitan Tokyo, I had felt uncomfortable in the silence and stillness of Pyongyang. In contrast, Beijing felt like a place where people lived and worked. It was with a strange sense of nostalgia that I wandered among the crowds on Dongdan Street and Chang'an Avenue, near the Qianmen gate and Wangfujing. In Pyongyang, there had been no sense of people living their daily lives, but in Beijing activity swirled around me in all directions.

The martial law imposed in Beijing after the Tian'anmen Square incident in June 1989 had only recently been rescinded, and armed soldiers were still stationed on street corners. Circumstances were hardly normal even in Beijing, but to my eyes, compared to North Korea, people here seemed free to lead their own lives.

A long queue of visitors wishing to pay their respects to the embalmed body of Mao Zedong snaked around his mausoleum in Tian'anmen Square. I watched the scene idly. Bullet scars remained on the Monument to the Heroes of the Revolution, and tread marks left by the Red Army tanks were still clearly visible in the asphalt of the streets.

"I won't mention the name of the country, but it seems to me it wasn't a type of socialism with faith in its people. Revolution is always necessary. Ceaseless revolution. Revolution within the Party is a necessity."

This was Tamiya's response during a conversation in a room at the hotel in Pyongyang, when we were on the subject of the events in Tian'anmen Square and the later turbulence in Eastern Europe. I strongly wished to interrupt him with the question "And what about in North Korea?" Instead, I held my tongue and continued to listen to his words.

When he finished, I merely commented: "Perhaps socialism needs to be reconsidered. It may be quite important for the socialist countries to rethink the issues of socialism. Since you have been an eyewitness of the construction of North Korean socialism, it may be a very valuable experience for you to take another look at the issues as a whole."

Tamiya touched on this theme in his second book, *On Socialism in a Socialist Country* (Hihyōsha, 1990). The manuscript arrived in Japan shortly after my return there, but there was no mention of anything but the brilliance of North Korean socialism.

The year 1990 was a year of world-shaking events.

Soon after the Tian'anmen incident, the Berlin Wall had fallen, followed by Eastern Europe's descent into turbulence. The socialist regime of Romania was destroyed, and its president, Nicolae Ceaușescu, whom Kim Il Sung considered a friend, was executed by a mob. The wave of change continued with the outbreak of the civil war in Yugoslavia, then the disintegration of the Soviet Union in late 1991. At the time, I had no way of knowing that, as a direct result of the collapse of socialism in Eastern Europe, the members of the Yodogō group were being recalled to Pyongyang from their long-term activities there and in Western Europe.

At my hotel in Beijing, I began reading the memoir manuscripts the Yodogō group had given me.

Some of the manuscripts were handwritten, and some had been typed on a word processor; yet others had apparently already been published in magazines or newsletters. Each writer described in detail his life beginning with his experiences as a student activist and the process of joining the Red Army Faction. The essays described the period immediately before and after the hijacking, the atmosphere and events on the airplane, the hijackers' shift of attitude after arriving in Pyongyang, and the current ideological standpoint of each writer. Disappointingly, the stories only continued through the first year of their stay in North Korea. The next twenty years remained a blank. However, their voices, which

I had previously encountered only in political newsletters and articles, came through clearly in the short manuscripts.

Wakabayashi Moriaki had this to say about the days spent in lectures and study: "Our debates took many different tacks. The instructors never directly contradicted us or agreed with us; they just circumvented our arguments. It was as if they were saying, 'Do as you like, we don't care.' We tried to engage them in [Shiomi's theories of] simultaneous world revolution and international bases for revolution, but it was no use. We got absolutely nowhere with it. We soon grew frustrated" (Tamiya et al. 1990, 174).

Abe Kimihiro, on the sought-after military training: "There was no indication we would be granted the military training we had requested to accompany our academic studies. Whenever we asked about the military training, the response was always 'Let us think about it' or 'We are looking into it.' As we gradually figured out, 'Let us think about it' is North Korean for 'This is not possible, but we can think about it.' Or, more clearly, 'No'" (Tamiya et al. 1990, 176).

In short, they were not taken seriously. Their impatience came through clearly in the manuscripts. None of their requests were fulfilled except for the lectures on *juche* ideology and the field trips.

I had one simple question: So why did they remain in North Korea? After all the effort of hijacking an airplane and flying there with the primary goal of receiving military training, why did they remain in North Korea when it became obvious that the military training would not be forthcoming? Why didn't they follow their initial plan of only stopping over in North Korea and continuing on to Cuba or the Middle East? Why couldn't they do that? The more times I read the words "We were not able to get military training," the more I began to feel I was not getting the whole story.

What were the circumstances of their failure to leave North Korea? What prevented them from leaving? Did some powerful force coerce them or even imprison them? The memoirs of their first year's experiences expanded only on the theme of their sense of their own "ideological immaturity" and their growing conviction in the validity of the new ideology.

What I wished most to learn, as I shuffled through the thick sheaf of manuscripts, was the how and why of their conversion to *juche* thought. Although no one could doubt the immaturity of their Red Army ideology, their total submission to *juche* was too extreme to be believable. To put it directly, was their conversion a voluntary matter of free choice, or were they forced into it?

Perhaps North Korea's much-rumored techniques of "brainwashing" really did exist.

The manuscripts contained the statement "We entered into the struggle of systematically reevaluating the errors of our earlier ideology after the middle of 1971." I began to read more carefully from this point. Both Konishi and Wakabayashi wrote about this. Wakabayashi wrote:

> While defending the idea of simultaneous world revolution within our ranks, a serious ideological dilemma was developing.
>
> In contrast to the success of the revolution and reconstruction of North Korea, the failure of our own efforts was obvious. This failure meant our ideology and theory, our party line, our strategy and tactics were all bankrupt....
>
> Tamiya came into my room to talk. I looked up from my book and listened to him. He summarized what our struggle had achieved. I think I answered a number of questions and had several opinions to add. The conversation went on for a while, then Tamiya asked slowly, "So, on whose behalf were you fighting, anyway?"
>
> I was stumped by this sudden question. I turned the question over in my mind, "On whose behalf....On whose behalf....?" The only response that came to mind was "For the people...right?" But I said nothing, feeling at a loss.
>
> Why couldn't I just say, "For the people"? Although I knew what I should say, why could I not say it out loud? Why was I at such a loss for words?
>
> It was from this time that my ideological conversion began. I entered a period of self-examination.
>
> "For what? For whom? Have I ever thought about this? Have I really been working for a grand cause?" Looking back to when I was in Japan, I knew the words "for the people" had seldom crossed my lips. There seemed to be something fishy about them even on those few official occasions when I did say them out loud. It seemed almost hypocritical. I thought it might be because I did not really believe in some of the actions taken in the name of "the people." If someone had asked me if I was fighting "for the people," I would not have been able to answer with confidence. I

must have started out believing it. . . . So why? . . . I began to rethink my childish ideology in order to be able to say, without hesitation and with full responsibility, "for the people." This was the start of my new endeavor. (Tamiya et al. 1990, 183–185)

Konishi wrote:

> We had to face reality. Why, instead of expanding or effectively organizing, were our own organizations collapsing? It must have been because of some fundamental error on our part. While we defended our idea of simultaneous world revolution in debates with our teachers, I became more aware of this issue.
>
> I will not go into the details of the reevaluation that the group undertook but only mention a little of what my own intuition told me.
>
> I had begun to doubt the collective people's power, the power of my comrades, and especially my own power. This doubt grew stronger as the contrast between these and the history and the current reality of the revolution in North Korea became clear. . . .
>
> We had frequently repeated the word "world" when we spoke of the "simultaneous world revolution," the "world revolution," or the "armed and organized world proletariat," but this was mainly because the will of the Japanese people to take the initiative and carry out the revolution in Japan was very weak. (Tamiya et al. 1990, 187)

Ah, so that's how it was. "We had to face reality." That was true. I wondered at the statement that the theory of "simultaneous world revolution" was an expression of the weak will of the Japanese people to take the initiative in achieving their own revolution. But my real question concerned "reality." What kind of reality were the Yodogō hijackers facing after their arrival in North Korea? What kind of reevaluation were they being forced to make? What was the process of their conversion? What was the process of reevaluation? What were the facts? These questions remained in my mind as I continued to read through the memoirs.

I was not so interested in knowing the results of this process: it was fairly obvious from their present ideology and their discussions of their reevaluations what they currently believed. I began to feel irritated. I had more sympathy for the Wakabayashi who, newly arrived in Pyong–

yang, was still sensitive enough to find phrases like "for the people" untrustworthy than I felt for the Wakabayashi who now used the words without hesitation. Suppressing my disgruntlement, I continued to read. The following are from Tanaka Yoshimi and Abe Kimihiro. Tanaka wrote:

> The days since our arrival in Choson passed one by one.[1] The much-awaited "preliminary revolt" did not happen, and, faced with the reality of North Korea, I began to taste how green my own ideological stance was.
>
> On whose behalf had I myself fought in the struggle? To what end? Had I really meant to share in the lives of workers and learn from them? This self-examination led me to the conclusion that I had not been a genuine revolutionary. I determined to eradicate the petit-bourgeois worldview I had held until now and to rebuild from the foundation a revolutionary, popular worldview. (Tamiya et al. 1990, 181)

Abe Kimihiro's memoir reported:

> Each of us underwent a separate ideological conversion. In my case, my moment came during a trip to the east coast in the summer of 1971.
>
> Of course, I had been greatly troubled until then. During our discussions of simultaneous world revolution, I found myself becoming more and more sympathetic to the story of the North Korean revolution. There was the reality of modern North Korea, but I found the story of the anti-Japanese resistance, as we saw it in films, particularly affecting. When I watched the movies, great tears would drip down my face. They were tears of sympathy, for, even though I was very young, I too stood for armed struggle. They were tears of homage and admiration.
>
> However, that was a separate issue from the question of simultaneous world revolution. I may have felt sympathetic to the struggles of the North Korean revolution, but I clung strongly

---

1. Choson is the short-form Korean name for the Democratic People's Republic of Korea (DPRK), or North Korea. It appears frequently in the writings of the Yodogō group when they are quoted in *Destiny*, written in *katakana* to indicate that it is a foreign word. In most cases we have kept it as Choson rather than North Korea.

to my belief that, "under the siege of imperialism, it is impossible to achieve socialism or communism in a single country. Sooner or later, it would collapse. The North Korean revolution is no exception to this." Put simply, I thought any socialist country surrounded by imperialism must be negatively affected by it or even forced to submit to it.

   With the situation thus, we went on a trip to the east coast in July. It was our first such trip and our first outing in a while. Yay! I felt refreshed by the change. The train reached the coast, and we could see the ocean, our first sight of it since our arrival in North Korea. I saw a sentry box from the window of our train as it followed the coastline. It had neat stone walls, and a soldier armed with a bayonet stood within. The area was very clean and looked as if it had been carefully swept. "Ah, yes, North Korea is fighting the fight," I thought to myself. Suddenly, I was overcome by a vision of the glory of North Korea's struggle against U.S. imperialism.

   My whole body began to shake in unbelievable shock. . . . That was the start of my active participation in the work of reevaluating simultaneous world revolution. (Tamiya et al. 1990, 189–190)

It is all well and good to be moved by the sight of a soldier armed with a bayonet standing in a sentry box against the background of a beautiful view of the sea, but it isn't logical. It does not lead to the conviction of the excellence of North Korea. Such an expression is indeed typical of Abe, who later demonstrated talent as a composer and artist, but this passage is not convincing in its reasoning. More significant here is the statement that this was their first trip since coming to Pyongyang, their first outing "in a while," implying that they lived under conditions of near imprisonment.

Tamiya wrote about his own process of conversion:

The principle of simultaneous world revolution had come to seem increasingly hollow. None of us could explain clearly why we had tried so hard to achieve it. But, if we gave up this slogan, we felt our entire reason for existence would disappear, and we would have no idea what we should be struggling for.

   During this period, we were all thinking over various issues. How could we undergo our ideological conversion together? This was the main question in my mind at this time.

Some of my comrades felt deep commitment to the Red Army Faction and the idea of simultaneous world revolution; others had decided that the philosophy of *juche* was correct.

There may have been only nine of us, but there were differences among us all the same. Each had his own opinion. It would not be easy to reach a consensus, though we continued to agree on one thing: "We live and die together." Anyway, we had only each other to rely on. How could there be any life in separating from these comrades and going off on one's own? Therefore none of us had any intention of striking out alone.

For this reason, those of us who thought *juche* ideology was correct in its claims did not go so far as to say that the idea of simultaneous world revolution was nonsense. But someone had to say it. And it came down to me. But even I was reluctant to voice it, since there were still those who clung to the idea, and I could not ignore them.

Despite our slogan of "We live and die together" and despite our shared purpose, the group relations became more awkward as our thoughts and ideology began to differ. In addition, I had come to think that, as long as we held on to our ideas of "simultaneous world revolution," we would not be able to make any progress. We could not move on to the new until we had shed ourselves of the old.

So I proposed to the others that we deal with far more fundamental matters than wasting time in pointless discussions on simultaneous world revolution. Why had we thrown ourselves in with the revolution? Were we really fighting for the workers? Was our own ideology not flawed? By asking these and other questions, we began to revise our own ideological foundations. (Tamiya et al. 1990, 190–191)

Because they could not make any logical progress or discoveries as things stood, Tamiya said they should start over from scratch. As the group's leader, Tamiya's problem was to find a way out of their current deadlock. How could he move the group forward while still preserving their unity? He was not proposing a new theory or a new ideology, which is clear when he refers to their discussions of simultaneous world revolution as "wasting time." He was proposing a whole new life view. Only in this way could they overcome their differences of ideology and theory. "Let's start over," he said. Tamiya's writing here shows frankly how the unity of politics and ideology among the Yodogō group members had at this time disintegrated. There was no orderly or logical process of conversion.

Here I have to touch once again on the circumstances of their decision to stay in North Korea. The haphazardly planned hijacking had not ended in the North Korean Workers' Party forcibly repatriating them or sending them to prison; indeed, the Party had installed them in a first-class hotel. They had nothing in the way of personal items with them and were completely dependent on the Workers' Party for everything from bedding and day clothes to underwear, towels, and toothbrushes. Meals were luxurious, and a chef and an attendant were assigned to them exclusively. They were treated as honored guests.

Despite this, wrote Abe Kimihiro, "we were not very grateful for this treatment. In part, at the time, we took such things for granted; but in part we thought they were trying to placate us, and we resisted the feelings of gratitude. But then we were really impressed when all of us received tailor-made suits. As we were being measured, we had a hard time suppressing our laughter."

> "Huh, a suit. It's my first one."
> "Yeah, me too. Who knew we would have to come to North Korea to get tailor-made suits?"
> Then we all felt the proper gratitude in our hearts. (Tamiya et al. 1990, 163–164)

Here we can clearly see how they underwent a softening-up process. Though they tried to resist it, such good treatment resulted in their "proper" gratitude. And this led gradually to feelings of *giri* (obligation)[2] toward the Workers' Party, which in turn bound them more tightly to it. Their belief in their theories had already been bankrupted; in place of theory, they fell back on ingrained values. Their sense of obligation became their only spiritual prop. At the time, they coined a phrase, "revolutionary *giri*." To whom did they owe this obligation? To the Workers' Party and to Kim Il Sung, who had extended such "heartwarming

---

2. The term *giri* refers to a strong moral obligation in Japanese culture to repay one's benefactors. As radical left students, these men would have been dismissive of such a traditional cultural value, even though they would have felt its pull in their everyday lives. Calling it "revolutionary *giri*" allowed them to experience it positively.

treatment" to them. This phrase "revolutionary *giri*" remains a favorite among them even today.

Thus they were treated hospitably and provided with everything they needed, except freedom. They were forbidden to go out, and they were kept segregated from the "people." Abe Kimihiro wrote about how they tried to cope:

> To release our frustration, we would sneak out and wander around different places. We would slip out after dark and climb a nearby hilltop to watch the surrounding villages. In winter we skated across the Daedong River to the other bank and visited the villages, then came back over a mountain. It was a thrill when we came across military training grounds or sentry boxes. Of course all this was a secret, but I think the statute of limitations has run out, so I'm telling about it. (Tamiya et al. 1990, 177)

He meant the area around the guest house compound where they lived. Describing such ordinary walks as a "thrill" reveals the lack of personal freedom they had in their daily lives. They did not know the location of the compound, nor did anyone tell them how to get around. On those occasions when they went on a field trip or a tour, the Party always provided cars with drivers. So they knew nothing of their surroundings except that they were in North Korea, somewhere in the outskirts of Pyongyang.

Every day their routine included ideological education. However, the instructors and professors sent to them by the Party paid no attention whatsoever to their discussions of theory. The only item on the curriculum was *juche* ideology.

They would rise at 6:00 a.m., eat breakfast, then spend the rest of the morning in study. After lunch there was a short break, followed by classes again. This was the routine, day after day, without change or breaks. After a day of "What is *juche*?" and "What must you do to master it?" there was always time allotted for discussion groups.

There was only one answer to each of the instructors' questions; to anyone answering otherwise, the same lecture would be repeated again and again. But the instructors never pressed for the "correct" answers. By the constant repetition of the same lecture, the group came to understand for themselves that there was only one correct answer.

Eventually, as the lectures continued, they finally got the point. And with that, the first stage of their "education" was complete: there was no escape except by giving the answer the instructors wanted to hear. They saw the light. Though they were insincere, they sought to give the answers the instructors expected. As far as the instructors were concerned, it didn't matter that their answers were insincere. What mattered was the process involved in eliciting the answers.

Though they didn't really believe in what they were saying, they answered according to the ideology of *juche* and suppressed their discontent. But this process they were being subjected to gradually results in a spiritual disconnect, a dismantling of the self. Everything begins to seem hollow, meaningless, pointless. At this point, a strange and new ideology can easily take root: only by accepting a new ideology and absorbing a new set of values and standards can one overcome the terrible sense of emptiness. The Yodogō hijackers eventually saw the light on this path. The instructors waited patiently for their students to reach this stage, and once no one any longer raised any objections, their teachings soaked in like water poured on sand.

It was an extremely effective way to brainwash the students: First probe into the psychology of the subject, then lead him into an independent acceptance of the correct ideology. This was the method of teaching *juche* ideology.

The "self-reliant" choice to accept the teaching means the student does not feel he is being coerced in any way. Instead, once an independent answer is made, more answers that do not contradict the first build up to a logical structure. Thus any doubts entertained along the way mean doubting one's own thinking and require a "self-reliant" reexamination for illogic in one's own argument. It is the beginning of an endless process, an endless recycling around again and again. The only escape from this trap without going mad was to accept *juche* as the only truth.

Slowly but inexorably, the brainwashing continued and finally bore fruit.

In his memoirs, Tamiya Takamaro suddenly launched into the statement "Self-criticism and mutual criticism are the most effective methods for forging a strong ideology and also allow for a decisive summary of one's ideology." Then he continued, "I successfully rebuilt my own set of beliefs in this way, and so did my companions."

At this point, Tamiya's topic changed from his own process of ideological conversion to the process of his companions' achievement of political and organizational unity. I read on with some surprise at this change of direction in his text.

It seemed that Tamiya himself had by this time stepped into the next phase.

I understood this single fact and continued to read with increasingly mixed feelings rising in me. But let us continue to explore some more of Tamiya's text. He wrote:

The best method for forging and strengthening one's ideology is through self-criticism and mutual criticism. First I prepared my own self-criticism, and then I received the criticism of my comrades. In my self-criticism, I acknowledged that, although I subjectively thought I was working on behalf of the people, in fact I was only interested in the narrow goals of the Red Army Faction, and my actions were all motivated by the interests of a small sectarian group. I criticized my tendency toward radical petit-bourgeois thought. Finally, I strongly criticized myself for not holding a properly *juche* attitude.

In a sense, we spoke of self-reliance more than anything else. Especially when we were thinking over our "line" and trying to live according to it, we had only ourselves to rely on. But the true meaning of "establishing a self-reliant attitude" means holding to a masterly attitude and taking responsibility for one's own fate. But how deeply had I thought of Japan's fate or spoken or acted responsibly? Perhaps my words and actions had been little thought out, based only on my own narrow and shallow experiences....

That time my comrades' criticism of me was quite harsh, but I was grateful for it. Frank though their criticism was, it included a strong message of comradely loyalty, insisting that, having come to North Korea with me as the leader, all of us must continue to advance along the correct road.

My comrades gave examples and criticized some actions of mine that I had not noticed before. One said I did not look on them as "comrades" but as "subordinates." Another commented on how, when I spoke of the people fighting in Japan, I tended to speak critically without considering their hardships. One strict criticism questioned whether I was living each day thinking of Japan and thinking of the people. I also began to understand how my least word could wound my comrades, resulting in an obstacle for our solidarity as a group.

Until then, I had thought that, of all of us, I was the one who thought most and acted most on behalf of Japan and its people, so this criticism made me realize for the first time how arrogant I was. I made the devastating discovery that, even when one thinks he is giving all he has for the people, actually achieving this is impossible. In this way, going through this criticism session was a great chance for me to reconsider myself.

In addition, *I began to understand that the method of criticism is a very powerful tool for changing people.* When I was in Japan, I was convinced that people did not change easily and that it was enough for those to change who wished to do so. However, when I underwent this criticism experience, *I realized that, by using this method, any human being could achieve a revolutionary existence.* Following me, all the others began a complete analysis of their ideological beliefs through self-criticism and mutual criticism. (Tamiya et al. 1990, 192–194; emphasis added by Takazawa)

On reaching this point in Tamiya's memoir, I felt a stirring of uneasiness, of anxiety. I had come across something similar before. Dredging the bottom of my mind, I pulled up an old but clear memory from the distant past. This method of which he spoke was the same method that had been used in the snowy Japan Alps in 1972 in the *sōkatsu* and purge during the United Red Army Incident. Then, the processes of self-criticism and mutual criticism had ended in a purge and a massacre by the United Red Army of some of its own members.[3] I already knew the

---

3. In ordinary Japanese a *sōkatsu* is simply an analysis of a recent activity, but here it was a demand for a personal reevaluation of one's behavior and thoughts in an effort to produce ideological change. The United Red Army was a group formed of remnants of the Red Army Faction and a Maoist group called the Revolutionary Left Faction of the Japan Communist Party Kanagawa Committee, whose parent organization had broken with the Japan Communist Party to favor a Maoist line some years earlier. The merged group contained many members who were wanted by the police, and they retreated into the mountains to develop the group's ideology and prepare for future activity. A Maoist-inspired process of self-criticism and mutual criticism introduced by the Revolutionary Left Faction went out of control as the leaders began ordering physical attacks and punishments in the hope of getting members to change their ideas more quickly. The group was isolated in the mountains, and the process of group criticism fed on itself, resulting in the death of a dozen members of the United Red Army group during the winter of 1971–1972. The group's leaders, Mori Tsuneo and Nagata Hiroko, called the demand for such an ideological self-criticism a *sōkatsu*, and this new meaning was popularized in accounts of the purge. For a detailed account of what happened, see Steinhoff 1992. This is a shortened version of the analysis in Steinhoff 1991.

historical fallout from this event. A feeling of disquiet engulfed me as I continued to read.

This method of ideological analysis and personality remolding that Tamiya mentions is common in North Korea, in weekly or monthly criticism meetings, either at the workplace or at district party meetings. At this point it was unclear whether Tamiya's discovery came out of his intensive exposure to Kim Il Sung's take on Stalinism or whether he had picked up on it from his experience in the New Left movement in Japan, which was influenced by traces of Stalinism.

This method is structured so that only by criticizing others can one become more revolutionary. Making criticism is part of one's disciplinary duties, and the criticism can be for anything from general lifestyle to daily acts and words because everyday behavior is taken to indicate one's ideology. The criticism escalates in a spiral that cannot be stopped, since he who gives the most devastating criticisms gains the upper hand. There may be the rare example of success with the method in situations where there is total trust between the members of the group. But in his memoir Tamiya had clearly stated that "relations became more awkward as our thoughts and ideology began to differ."

The disintegration of the unity of the Yodogō group came through clearly in the memoirs. If giving harsh criticism showed great revolutionary disposition, then the end result was obvious. The endless rounds of self-criticism and mutual criticism gradually wore away the distinction between friend and enemy, ending with the loss of all friendship. Soon enough the comrades who once swore to "live and die together" were targeting trivialities and fiercely denouncing each other. They mistakenly came to see finding an enemy within the organization as a meaningful political activity. In this, their standard of judgment was their newly acquired *juche* ideology. From this time on, this ideology became their supreme guiding beacon.

The day came when they took down the three slogans they had posted on the walls of the guest house. Not only "We will defend and nurture simultaneous world revolution," but also their first resolution of "We live and die together" was torn down and thrown away.

The group of Red Army Faction members who had flown to North Korea were germinating the bud of disaster at the same time that, just across the Sea of Japan at a winter camp in the Japan Alps, the harried United Red Army was about to commit its own terrible mistake.

There seemed to be a deep and fateful connection here in that both cases were clashes with outside ideologies that resulted in calamity. In the United Red Army, there was friction over the Maoist principles of the Cultural Revolution. For the Yodogō hijackers, there was the unavoidable encounter with Kim Il Sung's principle of *juche*, or self-reliance. Just this similarity is enough to give one shivers. But it is deeply puzzling that the dissolution of both groups in such a short time was not due to problems of theory or tactics but to problems with the social values of duty, morale, and ethics.

Having read thus far, I finally put away the manuscript. I was tired from my travels. And I felt a growing anxiety regarding what remained to be read.

Outside my hotel window, the sprawling city of Beijing was completely obscured by the night's darkness. Suddenly I sensed an evil presence flying in the pitch black, screaming grotesquely. It was the same evil darkness I had seen in the spring of 1972 in Karuizawa, looking at the Myōgi mountain range where the United Red Army purges had taken place.

I edited and published the Yodogō group's memoirs several months later in Japan under the title *Twenty Years after Takeoff: To North Korea on the "Yodogō"* (Tamiya et al. 1990). Yoshida Kintarō's name is not included in the list of authors. In addition, just when the first proofs were ready for proofreading, I received an urgent message from the Yodogō group requesting the deletion of Okamoto Takeshi's segment of the manuscript. The reason they gave was "Okamoto no longer wishes to return to Japan. Because the publication of this manuscript is a step in our move to return, his name cannot be listed with ours."

CHAPTER SEVEN

Kim's Golden Eggs

Kim Il Sung was in a good mood.

He held a letter in his hand. From the window of his office, he could see the streets of Pyongyang spreading out below, construction starting on a huge building. Kim Il Sung let out a small chuckle as he looked out on the scene.

"So they were 'golden eggs' after all."[1]

Two years earlier, when the Red Army Faction students had hijacked the JAL airliner, Kim Il Sung had been traveling. Upon receiving an emergency communication from Pyongyang, the premier (as he was called at the time; the title "chairman" was adopted later) had casually quipped to the people around him, "They will be my 'golden eggs.'" When he heard that the Japanese government had requested the return of the hijackers to Japan, he gave the order, "Stand firm, refuse. They were unable to arrest the students while they were on Japanese soil, and they couldn't do anything in Seoul either. Asking for them after they get to Pyongyang is presumptuous....We are not the tools of the Japanese National Police!"

The letter the premier now held in his hand was from the nine Red Army Faction students.

It had been reverently delivered to him that morning by Comrade Ho Dam of the Department of Foreign Affairs. Since the time of the Yodogō's arrival in Pyongyang from Kimpo Airport, Ho Dam had been appointed by the Central Committee of the Workers' Party as the hijackers' handler. After making a New

---

1. The character for Kim Il Sung's family name is the same as the character for "gold" in Japanese; hence the title of this chapter has the double meaning of "Kim's eggs" and "golden eggs," as in "the goose that laid the golden egg."

Year's greeting, the letter announced that the Yodogō group members had rid themselves of the impure ideology they had held in Japan and that they wished to declare their loyalty and pledge allegiance to Kim Il Sung.

Kim Il Sung returned to his desk and called Ho Dam in.

"So how are they doing?"

Standing at attention, Ho Dam answered, "It took a long time to straighten out their ideas, as they had been poisoned by bad ideology, but progress has been good. Recently, on their own initiative, they took on the premier's works, and they are now enjoying these studies. Soon their character remolding will be complete, and they will be very loyal juche *warriors of our Comrade the Premier, our Great Leader. The instructors at first thought it was a hopeless case, but they have done their best."*

Kim Il Sung nodded.

The letter, which still lay open on the office desk, had been written by the Yodogō students themselves.

To the Premier, our revered Comrade Kim Il Sung:

The nine of us who came to the Democratic People's Republic of Korea the year before last aboard the *Yodogō* send our respectful best wishes for the New Year. We apologize for our failure to send even one letter in these two years.

In this first letter, we wish to express above all our deep gratitude for the unheard-of degree of warm consideration that has been shown to us.

We have studied and thought about many things in these wonderful surroundings. From the example of the revolution and the establishment of the Democratic People's Republic of Korea, from our study of the Premier's ideas and theories that give firm guidelines in all matters, and based on our organizational life under your revolutionary guidance, we have been able to profoundly review our petit-bourgeois views on revolution.

The Premier's unlimited love for Korea and the people of Korea, and his belief in the power of the masses taught us that we were lacking in something very important. We were not prepared to dedicate ourselves completely to the cause of the Japanese people and the Japanese revolution, nor did we have a firm faith in the historical duties of the Japanese working class or the construction of socialism. We did not fully understand the hardships and demands laid upon the Japanese people or how we could fight these problems together with them; we did not even understand what it meant to establish socialism under a proletarian dictatorship. This is why it seemed impossible to us for a single country alone to establish a proletarian dictatorship in the face of the worldwide imperialist counterrevolution.

Under the generous and revolutionary guidance of our Comrade the Premier, we have finally come to understand the connection between Leader, Party, the classes, and the masses, and the source of authority for the proletarian dictatorship, and why together these become the power that reaches for socialism and communism. We understand that it is possible to develop a socialist economy through the people's own efforts to reform; when under the correct guidance of the Leader and the Party, workers take back the means of production and become the central figures of the nation, struggling for unceasing revolution through organized collective life and education in political thought.

We did not come to comprehend these matters only through study or through the example of the reality of the Korean revolution, but also through the study of our own organizational life. With revolutionary guidance, we came to understand the deep truth that the emancipation of the people of each nation must depend on the strength of the people's own self-reliant (*juche*) thought. The Premier's teachings show us that true Marxism-Leninism must be maintained in the revolutionary struggle in any country; and also that socialism and communism will prevail, even when facing the power-hungry ambitions and counteroffensives of other countries, if the people and the Party are properly united in establishing the fundamental self-reliant attitude and in independently advancing the construction and revolution of their country according to its situation to realize socialism and communism, avoiding dogmatism, flunkeyism, and imperialist ambitions.

Now, having reevaluated our extreme-left opportunism and anarchism, we are finally at the stage of starting the struggle for the victory of the Japanese revolution, based on *juche* ideology. Above all, our starting point must be to completely revolutionize ourselves and then, with the examples of our Comrade the Premier and the Korean Workers' Party as our highest models, to become revolutionaries prepared to give our lives on behalf of the revolution of Japan and the Japanese people. Even if this does not become a struggle with the authorities, we do not think it will in any way be easy. However, we absolutely believe that victory is assured as long as the nine of us continue to feel this passion for the revolution and as long as we have the unmatched support and revolutionary guidance of our Comrade the Premier. We take this opportunity to thank the Premier for the warmth of the proletarian internationalism he has shown us these last two years. We hereby pledge that whatever difficulties we might meet, we will overcome them to see this struggle through to the end.

Finally, we wish to congratulate the Premier on reaching his sixtieth year. May he achieve ever more success in his unification of Korea, his construction of socialism and communism, and his mission in the international communist movement. We rest our pen with a prayer for his long life.

From the Japanese revolutionaries receiving training for the revolution of Japan in the Democratic People's Republic of Korea.

December 31, 1971

This is the text of the first letter that the Yodogō group sent to Premier Kim Il Sung. The results of their ideological remolding are clear, just six months after their conversions. After the unavoidable dismantling of their theory and belief systems—and their identity crises—they no doubt quickly mastered the once strange-seeming *juche* ideology and Kim Il Sung's teachings. They probably absorbed this ideology like a sea sponge absorbs water.

Abe Kimihiro wrote:

We all became motivated in our studies. Our lights-out time was 11:00 p.m., but several of us asked the manager to delay and stayed up studying until 1:00 or 2:00 a.m. As we had been focusing on protecting our theory of simultaneous world revolution, we had not been paying much attention to the lectures, so we started by reviewing them. If you change your point of view, everything can seem 180 degrees different. I wished many times I had started sooner.

The important thing about our studies is the emphasis we laid on reading original texts. Rather than lectures, we based our

studies directly on the works of Chairman Kim Il Sung. First we
read the entire five volumes of his *Collected Works*. After reading
through each work, we outlined its contents. We wrote down the
important points, summarized the main ideas and lessons, and
then discussed them together. (Tamiya et al. 1990, 196)

At some point in the history of North Korea, writing a letter bearing
New Year's greetings to the "Great Leader" Kim Il Sung had become a
national custom. Two years after their arrival in Pyongyang, the Yodogō
group was allowed to write such a letter under the guidance of their
instructors. This meant that the instructors had decided the group had
largely completed their thought-remolding process. The letter was carried from the instructors to Kim Il Sung by Comrade Ho Dam via the
Party's Central Committee.

Unexpectedly, the letter pleased Kim Il Sung. Later, the Yodogō
group sent a second letter congratulating the premier on reaching his
sixtieth birthday on April 15, and this pleased him as well. He even mentioned the matter to a group of Japanese journalists visiting North Korea.

The year 1972 was a strange year. Looking back, it was a water-
shed in the postwar history of Japan, with the occurrence of many
value-transforming events. Richard Nixon and Mao Zedong held their
widely reported conversation, and initial contacts were reestablished
between the United States and China. The sleeping socialist giant had
made a historic handshake with the capitalist giant. In addition, the following year the so-called oil shock threw Japan into a black-market turmoil reminiscent of the burned and rubble-strewn early postwar years.
People rushed to stock up on toilet paper, and the prices of gasoline and
paper rose sharply. The government called for energy-saving measures,
with late-night television broadcasts being canceled and neon signs in
the city streets turned off. The period of high economic growth ended,
and the term "Showa Renaissance" fell out of use. The sense of being in
the postwar era faded, along with the common use of terms like antiwar,
the Japan-U.S. Security Treaty, and democracy. And in February there
was the incident at the Asama mountain villa in Karuizawa.

Five members of the United Red Army, chased into the mountain-
ous region of the southern Japanese Alps, barricaded themselves into a
mountain villa belonging to the Kawai Musical Instrument Manufactur-
ing Company, taking as hostage the wife of the building manager. The
siege lasted for ten days, including gun battles with the riot police. In
July the year before, the United Red Army had been formed when the Red

Army entered a military alliance with the Maoist Japan Communist Party Revolutionary Left Faction (Kakusa). The siege ended only when the riot police demolished the front of the villa with a huge ball and crane. The story, however, does not end there: afterwards, the bodies of several of their student comrades were discovered buried near their base in Haruna and the caves of Mt. Myogi, and the reality of the unprecedented purge and murder of their own members came to light. Altogether, fourteen bodies were found.[2] This was the "United Red Army Incident," after which the New Left movement in Japan declined and the Red Army Faction inside Japan was in shambles.

This incident had a serious impact on the Yodogō group in Pyongyang. By the spring of 1972, their ideological remolding was nearly completed. The events in Japan brought about the final step of their conversions, since it extinguished their last hope of fighting the revolution together with their comrades there.

Tanaka Yoshimi wrote about this in his section of the memoirs. He was excited about this new *juche* ideology and had been looking forward to telling the comrades he had left behind in Japan all about it: "The most important thing, even though we can't return legally to Japan and even if we have to swim there, is to teach them the *truth* [i.e., *juche* ideology] and for the entire Red Army to change its line.... I believed this. We seriously discussed this issue among our group as well" (Tamiya et al. 1990, 182; emphasis and note in brackets added by Takazawa).

The United Red Army incident and ensuing destruction of the Red Army Faction in Japan meant there was no one to whom they should transmit their newly discovered ideology. The annihilation of their organization in Japan made them worry about more pragmatic matters as well. Konishi Yasuhiro wrote: "The newspaper reported a series of arrests of Red Army Faction members. What was going on? This was crushing our organization in Japan. What would become of us? We had still not received the training, military or otherwise, that we had requested. If on top of this we lost our home power base, then no one on the North Korean side would listen to our demands. I could not help feeling stunned" (Tamiya et al. 1990, 186–187).

It is not surprising that the Yodogō Red Army Faction members were confused and panicked by the shocking news of the purge of their

---

2. This count includes twelve from the United Red Army purge plus two that members of the Revolutionary Left Faction had murdered as suspected spies the previous summer at a different location.

comrades and the disintegration of the party. Their parent organization, to which they wished to return after their daring feat of hijacking an airplane and flying to North Korea, was destroyed. It is not difficult to imagine that they must have felt as if they had climbed up to the roof and then suddenly had their ladders stolen from under them.

"Why is this happening?!"

Tamiya Takamaro ground his teeth in chagrin. The top leader of the United Red Army arrested by the police, Mori Tsuneo, had been a student junior to Tamiya at Osaka City University. He remembered Mori as a timid and weak university student. On New Year's Day of the following year, Mori would hang himself in his solitary jail cell in Tokyo.

Tanaka Yoshimi thought of other comrades.

One of the bodies of the purged United Red Army members had been that of Yamada Takashi. A student at Kyoto University, he had been an activist in the Kyoto prefectural level student federation and had become a member of the Red Army's Politburo. Having nothing appropriate to wear for the hijacking, Tanaka had borrowed a suit from Yamada. He had had no way of returning the suit after his arrival in Pyongyang, and now it became a memorial.

All of them were caught up in memories of their former comrades, and they spent long hours in discussion.

There were those who said, "The idea of armed insurrection itself is wrong."

"And that isn't all. Their ideology and their policy line were wrong, too."

"I wonder if it wasn't an inevitable consequence of their not thinking in terms of *juche?*"

"Yes, it certainly wasn't from a lack of personal qualifications. I guess it has to be seen as a problem with their theory and strategy."

This was their conclusion. The mistakes of the United Red Army were due to ideology and strategies they themselves had once adhered to. The Yodogō Red Army members were all in mutual agreement on this.

"When a struggle that isn't based on trust of the people becomes too radical and aggressive, it isn't revolutionary. The important things are to trust the people and to have a revolutionary worldview based on the ideology of *juche*" (Tamiya et al. 1990, 186).

After these events, they leaned more and more heavily on *juche* ideology and the teachings of Kim Il Sung. From this time onward, they began to develop their own organization and principles.

Kim Il Sung was showing a cheerful face to the group of Japanese journalists. That year, on April 27, he gave an interview to them while dining
at the Cabinet office building. The three organizations representing the
Japanese press corps were NHK, the *Asahi Shimbun*, and Kyōdō News
Service.[3] The interview continued for an unprecedented four and a half
hours, and during the meal the subject of the Yodogō students came up.

"They are under the instruction of the education branch of the
Central Committee of the Workers' Party. When they arrived, they were
anarchists. They were continually spouting fantastical things like 'We
will engage in the world revolution' and 'the world revolution will soon
be upon us.' But they have now improved somewhat.

"I have recently received two letters from them, one with New
Year's greetings, the other to congratulate me on my sixtieth birthday.
Their ideological stance looks like it's improving, too.

"They were quite troublesome at first but now not at all.

"I am letting them study in educational surroundings three or four
times better than that of most university students in this country.

"They may go sightseeing in Pyongyang; they see movies on Saturdays. We even take them around in cars."

One reporter wrote with surprise, "Kim Il Sung kept on talking in
very good humor."

He even spoke of the hijackers' return to Japan.

"There is no need for them to stay here very long, but we aren't
going to help the Japanese police. If the police weren't going to arrest
them, I would let them go back now. They're still young, and they'll
want to get married...."

Kim Il Sung laughed loudly.

No one there at that time, not even Kim Il Sung himself, realized
how prophetic these casual words would turn out to be.

One of the reporters, emboldened by drink, said he would like to
meet the students.

Perhaps, in the back of his mind, Kim Il Sung was surprised by this
level of interest in the Yodogō hijackers. But he laughed again loudly and
said, "They have not been interested in meeting Japanese journalists up

---

3. NHK is the Japanese national broadcasting company, the Japanese equivalent of the BBC. *Asahi Shimbun* is one of Japan's leading national daily newspapers, widely regarded as the Japanese equivalent of the *New York Times* in its
reputation, and Kyōdō News Service is the major Japanese news service. Having
all three present means that this was a major news event for Japan.

until now. I think they feel a little embarrassed. But I'll talk it over with the Party and let them know of your interest. If they agree, then we will organize a meeting for you."

For some reason, Kim Il Sung was in a very good mood.

The meeting took place three days later in the middle of the night. It was 12:30 a.m., the first of May. The press conference was held in a reception room at the Pyongyang Hotel. The reporters, scheduled to return to Japan later that day, had suddenly been notified late in the evening that the Yodogō hijackers had agreed to be interviewed. Earlier in the day, the Yodogō Red Army Faction leader, Tamiya, had been told by their Party instructor to meet with the Japanese press corps, and the instructor had them go through a simple rehearsal. They traveled in luxury cars provided by the Party to the hotel where the bright lights of NHK television awaited them.

Tamiya, wearing a neat suit and glasses with heavy black rims, led the way into the meeting room. Konishi and the others followed, all wearing suits in the same shade of gray and identical badges on their chests with Kim Il Sung's portrait in gold against a red flag. The presentation went without a flaw. Only Shibata Yasuhiro, still a minor at that time, was absent with a cold.

"It's been a while since I last met with Japanese people," said Tamiya in greeting.

Throughout the press conference, he and the others frequently repeated their admiration of Kim Il Sung and *juche* ideology, and expressed their praise of North Korean socialism.

Akagi Shirō: "I was obsessed with visions of the revolution, saying I would die in armed struggle or that I would fight in the world revolution, in the Japanese revolution. But it was all mere sentiment."

Tanaka Yoshimi: "I joined the student movement only because I was angry. Looking back, I think my actions were based only on my own subjective viewpoint."

Yoshida Kintarō: "There were few students focused on the revolution, and few youths were antiwar. So I was always confused, and I couldn't devote myself to the revolution."

Speaking on the hijacking, Tamiya said, "I have no regrets about the hijacking. But it was an ordeal for the passengers, and I would like to thank them for their cooperation despite everything. Given our immaturity at the time, it was the only way we knew to manage things."

Konishi Takahiro explained, "Communists must take responsibility for the revolution. We must serve the people. When I was studying the Korean partisans in the anti-Japanese resistance, I saw that Kim Il Sung did not impose on the people even during the worst of the fighting. That means if we look at our hijacking from a historical perspective, it was a mistake. However, it was the hijacking that led us to the thought of Kim Il Sung," he added.

They all had views to share about the United Red Army incident, and their criticisms were all based in their *juche* ideology.

"They were isolated from the masses, and they had no tradition of revolution. As a result, they were afraid and chased into a corner, and they forgot that the basic principle of revolution is always to stand together. And it led to the most tragic result, of comrades killing each other out of suspicion."

"Whatever their subjective aims may have been, the result was to help the counterrevolutionary forces and the reactionary forces."

The interview ended with them sending messages to their families: "Please tell our families we are growing into excellent revolutionaries. We have fulfilling lives, doing what we believe in, and we hope they will understand our feelings" (*Asahi Shimbun*, May 1, 1972, Tokyo and Osaka morning editions, p. 1).

With that, the interview was over.

It was, however, big news that they should appear before the Japanese press corps, since it had been two years since the hijacking, and their fates had previously been unknown.

The press conference with the Japanese press was also an excellent opportunity for the Workers' Party leadership to show that their work of "brainwashing" (or thought remolding) was largely completed.

The Workers' Party newspaper, *Labor News*, ran the following article about the group's interview with the Japanese reporters:

> The atmosphere of the meeting was friendly, with ideas being exchanged with laughter from beginning to end.... The Japanese youths said they had learned many things since coming to Korea and also that the mountains and rivers of Japan are beautiful and its people hard-working. They said if they could just rouse the people up, they believed they would be able to build a magnificent society. They said that the wonderful reality of modern Korea, where the people are "One for all and all for one," could be the future reality of Japan as well.... The Japanese youths said that, in the past, the immaturity of their own ideology prevented them from correct views on revolution, with the result that they could

not see clearly the Japanese reality, and so they pursued their struggle divorced from reality. They said they had not been able to comprehend the fundamental truth that they must trust in the power of the Japanese people and fight together with them for a single purpose. Finally, they said they have found the true path by studying the great thought of Premier Kim Il Sung. (*Labor News*, May 3, 1972)

Of course, news of the interview quickly spread in Japan, provoking many responses. The remaining members of the Red Army Faction could not deny that the Yodogō members had completely changed their ideology and strategic principles. There remained in them no trace of the ideas of the Red Army Faction. With their organization still in extreme disorder after the United Red Army incident, the remaining Red Army activists learned that, even in North Korea, far away across the sea, their ideas and strategies had been completely destroyed. Articles mocking the turnaround of the Red Army Faction's fortunes appeared in the weekly magazines. The content of the press conference seemed to be taken as a personal denial of the heroism of the hijacking and the abandonment of their duty to build up revolutionary bases. There was a rumor that Tamiya and the rest of the Yodogō group had been expelled from the Red Army Faction.

In response to this rumor, the Red Army Faction issued a statement criticizing the article about Tamiya's expulsion. Giving a brief summary of the contents of the interview, the statement said that the details of their conversion could not be clearly understood just from the interview and, somewhat defensively, that it was not difficult "to understand that they had matured greatly and outgrown the childish and self-satisfied attitudes of the former Red Army Faction." The statement objected only to the Yodogō members' critical comments on the United Red Army's taking of a hostage in the Asama mountain villa incident, saying in their defense that it "was not to make a deal or for protection." This must have been written by still-faithful volunteers, since the Red Army Faction at the time was hardly organized enough to release such a statement, but it shows the powerful influence of the Yodogō group's press conference.

A few days after the midnight press conference, Tamiya was summoned by their Workers' Party supervisor and informed that they would be presented to the Premier. It was very sudden. That day, the group was told to line up in front of the guest house and wait.

Wearing the tailored gray suits given to them by the Workers' Party and with the "Great Leader" Kim Il Sung badges bright on their chests, all of them stood in line with an air of profound reverence.

They stood there without breaking the line for a long time.

Finally, several pitch-black Mercedes-Benz cars rolled through the guest house gates and slowly climbed the slope to come to a gentle stop in front of them. A few men stepped out of the first Mercedes, and lined up to stand at attention as well. The nine Yodogō members held themselves stiffly erect, eyeing them. Soon, a figure they knew well emerged from the back of a Mercedes farther down the line of cars. It was the face from the portraits; it was Kim Il Sung himself.

The nine of them stood even more rigidly, some with legs starting to shake from tension. They felt overwhelmed by the presence of the "Revered Leader," whom they were meeting for the first time.

In a voice that shook slightly, Tamiya spoke words of praise to the "Great Revered Leader" and expressed thanks on behalf of the group for all the kindness that had been shown to them. Kim Il Sung appeared to be in a good mood that day, too. He listened to Tamiya's tribute with a smile.

After the greetings, Kim Il Sung put his hand on Tamiya's shoulder. He looked the nine of them over and said, "You are my golden eggs!"

That day, two years after their arrival in Pyongyang, the Yodogō students met Kim Il Sung for the first time. It was a reward to them for doing so well in the press conference a few days before. From that day on, Kim Il Sung placed his confidence in Tamiya as the leader of the group. Furthermore, Kim Il Sung and the North Korean Workers' Party expected the Yodogō group to achieve the "revolution of Japan." In other words, they were entrusted with the central role of converting Japan to *juche* ideology under the guiding hand of Kim Il Sung. As proof of his esteem, the "Revered Premier" gave Tamiya an honorary gift: an Omega gold watch.

After giving them some advice on how to conduct the revolution in Japan, Kim Il Sung hosted a big party at the guest house. Several members from the Central Committee of the Workers' Party attended the party as well as officials from the Unification Bureau and the Southern Resistance Committee of the Workers' Party.[4]

---

4. The Unification Bureau deals with the reunification of North and South Korea, whereas the Southern Resistance Committee is the segment of the North Korean Workers' Party tasked with bringing about a *juche* revolution in South Korea.

In reply to the confidence Kim Il Sung expressed in them, the Yodogō members pledged their obedience and loyalty to him there under the gorgeous chandeliers.

> After the bloody battle on the slopes of Mt. Chanpaik
> After the bloody battle in the flow of the Amur River
> Today free Korea thrives
> Ah, that name, beloved, our General
> Ah, that name, brilliant, General Kim Il Sung
> Singing together "The Song of General Kim Il Sung," many voices
>   continued to praise the "Great Revered Leader."

The Yodogō group kept this audience with Kim Il Sung a tight secret, never announcing it in public. In answer to a question at an interview with Japanese media after Kim's death, they even said, "We would have liked to have met him at least once. We are disappointed we never got to meet him." Their purpose in keeping this secret was to appear independent and politically unconnected, camouflaging the fact that they were merely the puppets of the Workers' Party. In addition, the Workers' Party wished to keep its manipulation of the Yodogō group secret for international and diplomatic reasons.

However, May 6, the day Kim Il Sung visited the guest house, became an important anniversary for them. They affected the technique used by Tawara Machi in her best-selling book of poems, *Sarada Kinenbi* (Salad Anniversary), and wrote poems with the line "May 6 is the ** anniversary," filling in the asterisks with words such as "revolution," "audience," or "Party foundation." Ironically, years later, in 1988, the youngest Yodogō member, Shibata Yasuhiro, was arrested on this date after having slipped secretly into Japan. The group immediately printed pamphlets proclaiming "May 6 is the homecoming anniversary."

On May 6, the day they had their audience with the "Revered Leader," Kim's golden eggs hatched beautifully, becoming faithful *juche* warriors for the North Korean Workers' Party. After this initial meeting, Kim Il Sung granted several more audiences to the Yodogō group.

CHAPTER EIGHT

The Secret Invitation

A t the end of May 1972, a violent event in the Middle East shook the world, far away from both Japan and the Korean Peninsula, where the Red Army Faction group in Pyongyang had thrown themselves with renewed vigor into their studies of *juche* ideology after their first audience with Kim Il Sung.

Immediately after Air France flight 132 from Paris bound for Tel Aviv arrived at its final destination, three Japanese gunmen who had boarded the aircraft in Rome opened fire with automatic rifles in the baggage claim area. More than one hundred people were killed or wounded. Two of the attackers were killed in the ensuing gunfight with airport security personnel, and the third was taken prisoner by the Israeli Army. This was the attack on the Tel Aviv airport by the Arab Red Army (later known as the Japanese Red Army).

Let us briefly shift our attention away from North Korea toward the Middle East. At first glance, this attack has no connection to this story, but, in fact, the Yodogō Red Army Faction group in Pyongyang was subtly linked to this event.

The first news of the event was released in the *Mainichi Shimbun*:

Late on the evening of May 30, three Japanese gunmen opened fire with automatic rifles and threw at least five hand grenades in the arrivals lobby of Lod International airport in Tel Aviv, Israel, injuring seventy-two and killing twenty-five. Arab guerrillas immediately announced they had sponsored the attack, and the one surviving arrested gunman confessed to acting on ideology promoted by the "Japanese Red Star Army." Other foreign news outlets report that the gunman confessed to be a part of the Red Army. There is no group called the "Red Star Army" in Japan, but it is thought to have a strong connection with the Red Army Faction. The Japanese Embassy in Tel Aviv is conducting an intensive investigation of the facts. Many details remain unclear, including contradictory reports that one of the gunmen may have been a woman. The strife in the Middle East has a long history, but this is the first case of direct Japanese involvement. The repercussions of this attack will inevitably cause a shock wave in both Israel and the international community. (*Mainichi Shimbun*, May 31, 1972, evening edition, p. 1)

The incident was reported on televised news all over the world that evening and in newspapers the following morning. The British Broadcasting Company (BBC) devoted several days of coverage to the event and the reactions of other Middle Eastern countries. The Jap-

Figure 8.01. Bloody baggage area at Tel Aviv airport after the attack in 1972. Photo courtesy of Keystone and Getty Photo Archives.

anese newspapers, just recovering from the onslaught of news over the United Red Army incident, were again inundated with articles on the Red Army. Not only the newspapers but all mass media, including television and magazines, were filled once again with reports on the Red Army.

The immediate announcement by the PFLP (Popular Front for the Liberation of Palestine) made it clear that the surprise attack was part of the Palestinian liberation movement and that its code name had been "Deir Yassin." The long years of bloody ethnic conflict in the Middle East lay behind the attack. The code name "Deir Yassin" referred to a Palestinian village burned to the ground by a Jewish terrorist group on April 9, 1948, under the British Mandate. It had been a small village south of Jerusalem, and all 250 inhabitants had been massacred. There were reports that the surprise attack on Tel Aviv airport was in revenge for this genocidal act.

News media in the Arab world were full of praise for the success of the attack. The government-run news services of Libya, Egypt, Syria, Iraq, and others ran ceaseless broadcasts supporting it, all to the accompaniment of the "Internationale."

The Egyptian newspaper *Al Akhbar* wrote, "People who think this incident was brutal must realize this was the natural reaction to the unprecedented brutality shown when Israel, upon becoming a nation, forced people off of their ancestral lands."

Lebanon's *Daily Star:* "The Palestinian people, forced from their fatherland, have no other recourse than to drag the rest of the world into the abyss with them."

Al Anwar, also out of Lebanon: "The passion of the Palestinian people made the Japanese heroes willing to die for them. Justice for Palestine is still alive in the hearts of the world's free people."

Of course, the news reached the Yodogō group in Pyongyang. At the time, listening to the NHK news broadcast was part of their daily routine, and they soon knew the main facts of the attack. Later, the Workers' Party also passed on newspaper articles and summaries of general opinion about it. The Workers' Party published a booklet titled *Correspondence Notes* to inform senior Party cadres of overseas news and events, and the Yodogō members also received a copy of it.

When they learned the details of the attack at the airport in Tel Aviv, the nine Yodogō members experienced a deep shock.

Just like the Yodogō group, the Arab Red Army that took the leading role in the attack was a group that had gone to the Middle East for the

Red Army Faction's purpose of constructing international bases for the world revolution.

The names of the three Japanese commandos became clear, too. The two who died in the gunfight were Okudaira Tsuyoshi ("Bashim" Okudaira) and Yasuda Yasuyuki ("Salaha" Yasuda), and the arrested gunman was Okamoto Kōzō ("Ahmad" Okamoto).

Tamiya was caught up in remembering the face of Shigenobu Fusako when she had been an activist with him in Japan. Shigenobu was the leader of the Arab Red Army.[1] She was not someone whom Tamiya got along with easily, nor could he compete with her. Tamiya later wrote about her, telling of their first meeting when he came from Osaka to join in the labor movement:

> [I had also] come to Tokyo. I was supposed to join in the district party activities.... I heard of this sharp girl who worked in a jewelry shop in the Ginza, and I met with her because we were to conduct activities together. But I was disappointed by her. The girl standing in front of me just seemed to be a bourgeois girl dressed in flashy clothes. As soon as I saw her, I lost interest in whatever activities she might have planned. This woman turned out to be Shigenobu Fusako, who is now so well known. Later, when we started working together, I realized my first impression of her had been completely wrong. When I said this to her, it turned out she didn't like me either when we met, thinking, "Why is this hayseed from Kansai so full of himself?" (Tamiya et al. 1990, 47)

When he heard the news about Tel Aviv, Tamiya felt that once again he was trailing behind. He had led the spectacular hijacking, and

---

1. Shigenobu Fusako was the only actual member of the Red Army Faction who went to the Middlle East initially to pursue the international revolutionary bases plan. Okudaira Tsuyoshi, who went with her, belonged to a Kyoto Partisans group that had loose ties to the Red Army. The next few members who joined them came from Okudaira's associates, except for Okamoto Kōzō, who was also not a member of the Red Army Faction but was invited to go with the promise that he would be able to see his brother in North Korea. However, Shigenobu's communications to Japan, including a film by Wakamatsu Kōji and Adachi Masao titled *Red Army–PFLP World Revolutionary Declaration* that was shown on college campuses in 1971, presented the group in the Middle East as an extension of the Red Army Faction. Shigenobu called the group in the Middle East the Arab Red Army to distinguish it from the Red Army Faction and the United Red Army in Japan.

they had recklessly flown to North Korea, only to find themselves now near-captives spending their days in study. Shigenobu and her group had left Japan nearly a year later than the Yodogō group, yet already they were achieving results in the Arab world. This annoyed Tamiya.

Okamoto Takeshi got the worst shock of all from the news of the attack. The lone survivor of the three commandos, Okamoto Kōzō, was his younger brother.

The Tel Aviv airport attack was the first armed action of the Arab Red Army. It was planned in cooperation with the PFLP, as part of the latter's retaliations against Israel, but there was a deeper motive on the part of the Arab Red Army: it was a criticism of the Red Army Faction's role in the purge and massacre during the United Red Army incident. Immediately after the United Red Army incident became known, Shigenobu had sent a message to a mass political rally held by the Red Army in Japan:

> Comrades of the United Red Army, farewell! As a Red Army soldier, filled with dreams and courage, I announce my parting from you. I part from you to prepare for the true revolution. I part from you to confirm my unwavering determination....
>
> Without going through any direct confrontations with the enemy, trying to achieve the illusion of "communization" by disciplining your comrades internally only promotes evil despotism....You comrades of the United Red Army who killed your own members, do you understand my feelings when I still call you comrades? None of us has the right to kill our own group members. (Shigenobu 1972, 83)

The faces of her close comrades in Japan were burned deeply into Shigenobu's heart. She worried about the Red Army Faction, which had both raised her and been raised by her. She agonized forever over the true meaning of their struggle, the true meaning of internationalism. Then she decided to join with the Popular Front for the Liberation of Palestine for the surprise attack at Tel Aviv airport.[2] To Shigenobu, it

---

2. At the time Takazawa wrote this book, it was widely believed that Shigenobu herself had planned and agreed to the Tel Aviv airport attack. However, trial testimony and her writings after her return to Japan in 2000 make clear that she was mainly involved in public relations activities in the Middle East. The attack was planned by PFLP and carried out by the three men, who were

was a protest against and an antithesis to the defeat of the United Red Army in Japan. In this way, the tragedy of the United Red Army incident unavoidably and deeply affected the Arab Red Army as well.

On rereading, Shigenobu's declaration seems to shed light not only on the United Red Army, but also on the Yodogō Red Army Faction members. "Trying to achieve the illusion of 'communization' by disciplining your comrades internally only promotes evil despotism," she wrote. These words describe the contemporary circumstances of North Korea as well as those of the Yodogō group. In an ironic twist of history, her message was delivered to the Red Army rally on March 31, 1972, the second anniversary of the Yodogō hijacking.

The Tel Aviv airport attack had repercussions all over the world. The Western world began to fear terrorism, and zealots in the Arab world shouted in raucous celebration.

However, the countries of the West and the Middle East were not alone in their concern over the attack. In the extreme north of the Far East, in the capital of the northern half of the Korean Peninsula, a group of people were full of praise for the surprise attack. They were the Korean Workers' Party.

Soon after the attack, Tamiya was summoned by his Party counselor to receive an important message. He went, nervous, and what he heard was not encouraging: he knew the plan he was told to undertake would not work. In short, he was instructed to "bring in the Arab Red Army!" The Southern Resistance Committee of the North Korean Workers' Party was fulsome in its praise of the Arab Red Army and of Shigenobu Fusako and her group, who would later become famous as the Japanese Red Army. Tamiya was assigned the task of making contact with the Red Army Faction in the Middle East. The cadres of the Southern Resistance Committee wished to adopt the tactics of the Tel Aviv airport attack in their own efforts against South Korea.

From the point of view of the Workers' Party, the various Japanese groups—the United Red Army in Japan, the Arab Red Army in the Middle East, and the Yodogō Red Army in North Korea, fresh from pledging its loyalty to Kim Il Sung—were all one entity. They were all one Japanese radical group, with no distinctions between them.

---

individual volunteers with PFLP operating under its military authority, and PFLP took responsibility for it. She had misgivings about it based on her limited knowledge of the plan, but, after the participants were identified as Japanese, she was pressed by PFLP to announce that the "Arab Red Army," as she called it, had carried it out. See Shigenobu 2009, 114–125.

The Southern Resistance Committee was in charge of conducting special activities in South Korea. It conducted operations such as the Cheongwadae incident of 1968, in which the residence of the South Korean president was the target of a planned attack by North Korean military infiltrators. Thirty-one operatives, dressed in South Korean military gear, managed to slip into Seoul and were in the vicinity of the presidential residence when they were discovered by the South Korean side. Thirty of the men were killed in the ensuing firefight, with one arrested. In 1970, they planted a time bomb in an attempt to assassinate President Park Chunghee when he visited the National Cemetery. Without exception, every attempt at infiltration and assassination thus far had ended in failure.

It was not such a radical step for the leaders of the Southern Resistance Committee to envision an attack on Seoul's Kimpo Airport much like the attack at Tel Aviv airport. Moreover, those who ran the operation would all be Japanese. If the Arab Red Army could be brought in to join forces with the Yodogō Red Army, they could engage in all sorts of terrorist activities. This might be an excellent way to use Kim's golden eggs! Perhaps, for the Yodogō hijackers, Kimpo Airport represented a bitter memory of deception and stalemate. The Workers' Party, however, was entranced by the vision of daring Japanese extremists shouting "Long live Kim Il Sung!" as they sprayed machine gun bullets around Kimpo Airport, setting all of Seoul ablaze in a sea of fire as a part of the campaign against the South. Newspapers all over the world would devote pages and pages to this news. The Cold War was still at its height, and the media of the East would praise and report on it, just as the media of the Arab world had reported on the Tel Aviv attack day after day. Korea's "Great Leader" Kim Il Sung would be exalted and embraced by the world as the "Leader of the World Revolution." Apparently, Red Army comrades could commit this sort of act without hesitation. What with the United Red Army incident and the attack on the airport at Tel Aviv, they didn't seem to care about killing or being killed themselves. The only drawback was that none of them really understood the Great Leader's socialist ideology, which was the one true guide for the workers of the world.

But on one matter the Workers' Party was careful: although, as Kim Il Sung had said, the Yodogō hijackers had much improved since their arrival in Pyongyang, their thought remolding had not yet progressed to the point where they could be dispatched abroad to engage in revolutionary activities.

There was really only one possible plan: their former Red Army Faction companions must come to Pyongyang to study there and be remolded together with the Yodogō group.

Tamiya, obeying the Party's instructions for this plan, wrote several letters. Some of the letters were addressed to the Arab Red Army. They were invitations to come to Pyongyang.

Of course, the final result of this imaginative plan was failure, mainly due to the differences in political ideologies and theories of the groups involved. That is all that needs to be said here. The failure of the plan ensured the failure of the vision. History does not have to report Seoul airport awash in blood. The Yodogō group did not have to die trying to make this happen.

In their book, *Twenty Years after Takeoff* (Tamiya et al. 1990), the Yodogō members make many criticisms of the United Red Army incident of the spring of 1972. They are silent, however, on the Tel Aviv airport attack of two months later. According to their usual argument, any action taken without being firmly based on *juche* ideology is meaningless and must be criticized. This was just too large an incident to simply ignore. It seems strange, even unnatural, that they would do so. The reason for their silence was not that the Arab Red Army members were their former comrades but the existence behind the scenes of this complicated plan.

This fantasy of a few cadres on the North Korean Workers' Party's action committee may have been bankrupt, but a single drop of water can be the beginning of a roaring waterfall, and a tiny crack in an embankment can herald a terrible flood. The only part of the plan that achieved any sort of success was that of bringing other Red Army Faction members to study in Pyongyang. In one case, the Workers' Party's special office in charge of handling matters related to the Yodogō members received an application from a Japanese woman to enter North Korea. This is how it became possible for Konishi Takahiro's girlfriend to join him.

As the metaphor of the water droplet suggests, the entry of this one Japanese woman into North Korea caused an unexpected ripple among the Yodogō hijackers. And, like a rolling stone, the story began to move in an unexpected direction.

CHAPTER NINE

Secret Crossing

I think I met Konishi for the first time in 1969. I was working as a nurse at Tokyo University Hospital.[1] It was around the time when the fighting at Tokyo University was at its worst. Konishi was the chairman of the medical school's joint struggle committee, and it was sometime in the spring of 1969 that we talked for the first time. It was a sudden thing, and we didn't have much time to meet one-on-one, but I felt I could follow him anywhere. I felt complete trust in him. When the hijacking was unfolding, I was convinced it would be successful, just because Konishi was on the airplane. (Takazawa 1995, condensed from pp. 15–32)

Fukui Takako departed from Japan on October 19, 1975. She was already Konishi's girlfriend before he joined the hijacking team as a subleader, having met him while she was working as a nurse at Tokyo University Hospital. After the hijacking, she decided to go to North Korea herself, though it took her five years to get there.

After Konishi had disappeared into North Korea, she yearned to hear from him, but he never contacted her. She agonized over whether her relationship with Konishi had simply ended or whether she had actually been dumped. On top of that, she fretted about her own increasing age, and she was beset by indecision. She would soon be thirty years old,

---

1. The official name of the university in English is the University of Tokyo, but in Japanese it is simply Tokyo University.

and perhaps after thirty she would not be able to go even if she wanted to. Now was the time to go. Though she felt frightened, she thought seriously about the matter.

She hesitated for some time but finally made her decision: she would go and join Konishi in North Korea. There were no formal relations between Japan and North Korea, and no procedures for traveling between them. She desperately sought a way to go. To others, the method she finally resorted to only seemed foolhardy.

Fukui left Japan one morning in October 1975, blessed with a simple message from her mother: "I believe in you."

It was a full seventeen years later, in April 1992, before it became clear that the whole Yodogō group in Pyongyang had wives and children. Kim Il Sung let it drop casually in an answer to a question from a group of reporters from the *Asahi Shimbun*.

He spoke in a press conference on various things, such as that he had seen the Japanese movie *A Fishing Fanatic's Journal.* He thought everyone should have two days off a week. He had seen all forty-three movies of the *It's Hard to Be a Man* series. He thought Tora-san was a good actor. He had learned a lot about Japanese lifestyles, customs, manners, and cityscapes....Then, suddenly, Kim Il Sung said, "The Japanese Red Army members [i.e., the Yodogō group] say they wish to return to Japan, but, if they do, they would have to stand trial. In Korea we have a saying, 'After ten years, even rivers and mountains change.' I think their feelings have changed, too, in many ways. They are married, with children. It has been a long time, so please consider dropping all the charges against them."

No one among the reporters realized the import of these words. Even when this conversation was reported in the newspapers, few people understood what he had said. No one thought that the Yodogō hijackers in Pyongyang would have wives and children.

Despite Kim Il Sung's words, when the Yodogō members officially announced their marriages after this interview, many people were still surprised. Not only did these Yodogō hijackers, whom everyone had thought were incarcerated in North Korea, have wives and children, but their wives were all Japanese women. Because Kim Il Sung's words carried absolute authority, the Yodogō members could not deny what he had said. Among the wives were women whose families had registered them as missing persons. The Japanese media went into a frenzy, with front pages screaming headlines like "MISSING WOMEN ARE YODOGŌ WIVES!"

Soon afterwards, I made another of my numerous trips to Pyongyang. At the Yodogō group's compound in the suburbs of Pyongyang, I met Fukui Takako for the first time and heard from their own mouths the details of the Yodogō wives' secret crossings to North Korea.

In the reception room of the guest house compound, Fukui Takako began to speak slowly. She spoke of matters that until then had remained unclear. The conversation continued from the early evening until late at night. At one point, tired, I put down my notebook and stopped the tape recorder to go out to the terrace to greet the early Pyongyang winter. There, in the outskirts of Pyongyang, the only sound to be heard in the midnight dark was the lonely keening of the cold wind. Fukui Takako's reminiscences started with how she first met Konishi.

"Several other nurses and I had gotten a room near Tokyo University, where we would get together for student meetings and so on, but several medical students on the joint struggle committee would come by as well. Sometime in the spring of 1968, I had gone to the room for some reason or other, and he was there, working hard on a piece of writing. Since I had gone to some of their rallies, I knew his name but little else. This was the first I had seen more than just a glimpse of him....It was just about lunchtime. I was heading back to the hospital by way of a shopping street, when it suddenly occurred to me that he must be hungry. So I bought some food for him and returned to the room. 'Here, this is for you,' I said.[2] That's what happened.

"The next time we talked was in the summer. Every week in my group we were posting flyers to criticize the hospital. That week it happened to be my turn to write the flyer, so that Friday I went to our meeting room to write it. I was deep in the writing when he walked in....So then I finished writing. But we were making the copies on one of those old-fashioned mimeographs, and I only had about three-quarters of the page filled. I was at a loss about what to write to fill the remaining space. 'Now what can I write?' I spoke to myself out loud, but he suddenly said, 'Here, shall I write it for you?' I hesitated a moment, but then I thought that as long as our opinions were the same it wouldn't

---

2. The word she used for giving him the food was *sashiire*, a term for giving provisions to someone carrying out a task but also for sending something in to a person in jail. It was in common use because so many activists were being arrested in those days.

matter who wrote the thing, so I said, 'Well, yes, please, if you don't mind.'

"When he finished writing, he asked me abruptly, 'Do you have a boyfriend?'

" 'No,' I said. Then, 'Where are you from?'

" 'Kanagawa,' I answered. Next, 'How old are you?' When I answered, 'Twenty-three,' he then asked, 'Would you marry me?'

"I was pretty surprised and wondered what was going on. I had just received a marriage proposal!

"Konishi was so busy with his activist work that we didn't get a chance to meet very often. In the beginning, we met maybe once every ten days, and for a while there it was only once a month. He had traveled to the Kansai area to organize students and on New Year's Day sent word for me to come to Osaka. I went, and we spent the three days of the holiday together.

"So, though we hadn't met very many times, I went to Osaka at New Year's. I returned to Tokyo, and I guess it was just about at the end of January during one of our brief meetings when he abruptly announced, 'I am going to Cuba, so it'll be two or three months before we can meet again.' Since I didn't think three months was such a big deal, I was able to say, 'Sure, that's fine.'

"After that, I think it was about March 14, 1970, we were supposed to meet again. I think it was in Komagome, after I finished my shift at the hospital. I waited and waited in a coffee shop near the train station. He was late as always, once again making me wait for him. That day I waited for about two hours.

"When I waited for him, I would always worry that he had been arrested. I worried and waited, but he would usually appear after about two hours. That day, when he was later than usual, I grew tired of the waiting and started dozing a bit. Then I suddenly heard someone say in a very loud voice 'Now, the Korean Peninsula....' This made me wake up with a start of surprise. On the other side of the coffee shop, the only customers besides me were a group of seven or eight men, clustered around Konishi. As for the speaker with the loud voice, I thought to myself, 'That must be Shiomi.' [She laughs.] Looking back now, I think that meeting must have been where they made their plans for the hijacking.

"He must not have said anything about me to his comrades. But thinking we would not be able to meet again, he had asked me to come to the same coffee shop where they were meeting. I could tell which one of them was Shiomi. I became very worried. 'If he keeps on like that, he's going to get arrested....'

"It was just like he was shouting out for all to hear, 'Here I am!' I thought, 'That one is asking for trouble.'

"At the time, I didn't know any of the people at the meeting. I don't think any of them even realized that I was there, since I was sitting alone right on the other side of the shop. There were no other customers, and it was late. They continued their talk about the Korean Peninsula, and I just waited for them to finish. After a pretty long time, they seemed to have finished their discussion, and they left as a group. I hastily followed them out. At first they all stayed together, but then after a few moments he turned back toward me.

"That night the two of us went together to a different place than the others. The next morning, Shiomi was arrested.

"Shortly afterwards, Konishi said to me, 'We won't be able to meet for about a year. But you should pay attention to the news tomorrow.' I just said something like 'OK.' But, when I watched the news the next day, there was nothing special on. It was because he had been late for the first hijacking, and they postponed it. Not knowing this, I wondered what was going on. That afternoon around three o'clock I got a phone call from him, and he said, 'Hey, let's meet again.' So we met. A few days later, 'Well, anyway, once again, tomorrow we're going to try again,' he said. So we met for the last time on the thirtieth of the month. 'Once more, we'll do it tomorrow,' he said! [Laugh.]

"On the thirty-first, there was a big rally in front of the Yasuda auditorium at Tokyo University. I was there, and, because I had to listen to the news, I stood in the back with a radio to my ear. So, when the sudden announcement came that several students had hijacked the JAL flight over Mt. Fuji, I realized that it was this that Konishi had been talking about." (Takazawa 1995, 15–29)

Fukui Takako's story did not stop there. Eighteen years had gone by since she slipped out of Japan and came to Pyongyang. Perhaps because it was the first time she was telling this story to anyone, her words flowed like water bursting through a dam. At times her eyelashes shone with tears. I simply continued to listen to her words, changing the tape when needed.

"I didn't hear anything about him until 1972. They gave a press conference that was broadcast in Japan. In 1973, I turned twenty-seven. Nothing happened, even though a fortuneteller had told me that something wonderful would happen to me when I was twenty-seven. I had been holding fast, waiting for him, thinking that it meant we would meet again. But, of course, we didn't meet. I began to think I would have to do something about it. At about that time, a friend said to me, 'Chinese is pretty interesting,' so I decided to start studying Chinese. If I had too much free time I felt sad and lonely, so I tried to keep busy.

"So, in February and March of 1974, I organized a tour group, and we visited China, since it was still difficult to travel independently in China at the time. And we were able to go only because we were so interested in learning more about China. We wrote down in detail what we wanted to learn in preparation for our departure.

"I had another reason for going to China as well, of course. I wished to visit the North Korean embassy in Beijing, to try to call Konishi directly from there. Of course, that was my real reason.

"But it was no good. I couldn't call him. I went to the embassy. Because I was on a group tour, every day was fully planned. The only free time came on the last day, set aside for shopping. I only had about half a day. The rest of the group went shopping, but I took a taxi to the North Korean embassy. First a man in his forties came out and tried to speak to me in English. But since my English was bad, and perhaps because he felt that he couldn't make a decision on the matter, he ended up calling the ambassador to come and speak to me directly. The ambassador said, 'I understand Japanese, so go ahead and explain in Japanese.' So then we talked in Japanese. I told him my husband was in Pyongyang. I can't remember if I mentioned he was there because he hijacked an airplane though [laughter].

"Anyway, the ambassador said, 'I see. I will contact my country. In the meantime, return to your hotel, and I will let you know what they say.'

" 'I can't return to the hotel to wait, since I have to return to Japan.'

"Staying longer in China meant I would have to separate from my travel group. The ambassador understood this and said, 'Since you came with the group, it's best you stay with them. So this time, go on home with them. I will certainly be in touch with you. Why don't you write a letter now, and I will definitely pass the letter on.'

"So I wrote a letter, and the next day I had no choice but to return to Japan.

"So then I was waiting and wondering when a reply would come. But I thought I might wait forever without a reply ever coming. It began to seem impossible that I could solve such a personal matter in this way, nor did it do any good to just sit there and wait either. On the other hand, I began to think also that maybe I should forget about it and just settle down and devote myself to my work.

"But I was nearing thirty. I thought that, once I had turned thirty, there would be nothing I could do, so now was the time to act, to try and meet him again before I turned thirty.[3] I was thinking all these things, and I remembered what he had written in a letter: 'We are each the masters of our own destinies. We each have within ourselves the power to pioneer our own destinies.' So there I was, thinking I wouldn't be able to do anything about it after I turned thirty, and now was the time to act. So I decided to try and visit the North Korean embassy one more time.

"I really wanted to go to Beijing again, but it was hard to go as a private individual in those days. There was a lot of preparation involved, and it took a long time. My other option was to go to Eastern Europe, and I thought it might be safer in Europe. I decided to go to the embassies in Eastern Europe.

"So, in October of 1975, I left Japan. All I had was a travel bag and one thousand U.S. dollars in traveler's checks.

"First I went to Greece, because I really wanted to visit Athens. From Athens I went to Rome, then I took a train to Florence, and from there I traveled by train through several of the Eastern European countries, visiting the [North] Korean embassies in some of them. They were all rather nice to me. The first time, once again, the person who came out to talk to me decided he couldn't handle this on his own, and he said he would ask the ambassador to talk to me. The ambassador was in a meeting, so

---

3. The conventional expectation at that time in Japan was that a woman who did not marry by the time she reached the age of thirty was destined to remain a spinster all her life.

I had to wait a while. So I waited there, and after a while the ambassador came out and listened to my story.

" 'I understand. Let me get in touch with my country,' he said.

"That time I waited at my hotel. I waited for three days, but no message came at all, so I went to the embassy again to ask. But they said, 'We passed on the message, but we don't know when a reply will come. But don't worry, an answer will definitely come. They will definitely be in touch.'

"So I waited another three days.... Then, finally after three days, the ambassador called the hotel. An embassy staff member would be returning to his home country in one week's time, so perhaps I would like to accompany him to Pyongyang?

"When I arrived in Pyongyang, I thought he would be at the airport to meet me. I even sent him a letter asking him to come and meet me there. But it didn't happen like that at all. He didn't come; instead a North Korean who spoke really good Japanese came out to meet me when I arrived. He immediately said, 'Let's go straight out to where they are all living.' These days the road is pretty good, and we can travel along it quickly, but in those days it was still a bit of a winding mountain road, and it took a good hour to get there from the airport.

"When we drove through the gateway of the compound, the driver sounded the horn, so everyone had come out to await us. I looked all around, but I couldn't see him at first [laugh]. He was there; he was standing in the line with everyone else, and so I couldn't find him at first. Plus, he had gained weight. [Laughter.]

"So anyway, I was standing there looking around with a blank look on my face, wondering a little desperately where he might be. Even now, I get teased for that. 'The look on your face was so funny. You looked stunned,' they say. [Laugh.] Finally, after a moment, I spotted him. That's how it was. It wasn't a very dramatic reunion at all. But that evening they gave me a welcoming party. We had a big feast, and they sang the 'Internationale.'

"I am basically an optimistic person, so I haven't really had any problems since I came to North Korea. The only thing I had trouble getting used to was not drinking any tea. Here people drink coffee after their meals. In those days there weren't any Japanese products available, only Vietnamese coffee. The Vietnamese coffee was pretty good, sure, but of course I wanted to

drink Japanese tea after dinner. But there was only coffee. The
men didn't seem to care; they just drank coffee. For about a year,
I was always thinking, 'Oh, how I want to drink some tea!' But,
once I got used to it, I didn't really think about it anymore."
(Takazawa 1995, 29–46)

When she paused in her story, to tell the truth, I felt a little confused. Her testimony included several facts that provided insights
beyond my commonsense understanding of the hijacking.

While I was listening to her story, I thought of that long-gone classical music coffee shop near Komagome station in Tokyo. After exiting
the train station, you could smell the aroma of coffee out in the street
near the shop.

Those suspicious-looking men had held their conspiracy meeting
in a booth in the back of that coffee shop on the evening of March 14,
1970, about two weeks before the *Yodogō* hijacking.

Fukui said she was in the coffee shop that evening as well. After she
had finished her shift at the hospital, Konishi called her, and she came
to the coffee shop in order to meet him. Tokyo University Hospital is not
far from Komagome station. She said she remembered the evening well.

The scenes she described took me back in an instant to the Tokyo
of twenty years earlier. In the midst of the Pyongyang winter, with the
sound of the bitter wind beating against the window panes in my ears,
memories of the dark and cold of the Tokyo streets and of the atmosphere of that coffee shop rose clearly in my mind.

Her story brought to light one more incredible fact. Before the
hijacking to North Korea, Konishi had told Fukui Takako, "We will
meet again in a year. In a year I will send for you, and you will come to
Pyongyang."

During this interview, Fukui and I had the following exchange.

Takazawa: That is to say, he thought he would be back in Japan in a
              year's time?

Fukui: No, he wasn't going to come back. He said he would send
              for me after one year. He said he would, for sure.

Takazawa: ...er, but their hijack "declaration" ended with the words
              "We will return to Japan."

Fukui: I don't know anything about that, but he said he'd send
              for me. So it doesn't seem like he was going to come back

after one year, does it? He said he'd send for me after a year.

Takazawa: I think you have just told me something very important. Until now, it has been commonly understood that this hijacking was part of the Red Army Faction's effort to establish overseas bases for the revolution. But, according to what you are saying, Konishi was treating the hijacking as an escape into political asylum, right from the beginning.

Fukui: Yes, I think so.

I was puzzled by this information. They had written many times that their decision to come to North Korea was made on the spur of the moment. In light of this, how should we interpret Konishi's words?

When I decided to go back to the beginning to tease out the truth behind the hijacking, I spoke with many people in Japan who were connected with the incident. It gradually became clear to me that the primary purpose of the hijacking was not to run to North Korea. Instead, I became convinced that their real goal was to make their mark by hijacking an airplane, something no one in Japan had ever thought of doing before. This is also a more satisfying explanation of why they were able to change their destination at the last minute from Cuba to North Korea. And it is no surprise that they hadn't approached North Korea ahead of time. More than anything, the hijacking was important to the Red Army Faction for its propaganda value and as a strategic maneuver. Going to North Korea was only a secondary issue. In other words, the destination was not of importance. What was important was to get to a country where they could receive military training and from which they could go to other countries. If they were forced to repatriate, the result would be total failure. A socialist country with no diplomatic ties with Japan fit these requirements very well, so North Korea was nothing more than the easiest choice for them. Certainly none of the hijackers had much information or any real understanding about North Korea.

When my interviews with people who were connected with the incident had made this point quite clear, I began to see from a new perspective this unexpected side to the hijacking that marked the end of the intense antistate struggle of the late 1960s. At least, as far as the hijacking is concerned, I believe this was the truth of the matter and that the general understanding that the whole point of the Yodogō incident was to fly to North Korea is, in fact, incorrect.

So Konishi's words, as related by Fukui Takako in her story, showed that he differed from his fellow hijackers in his ideas and in his understanding of their undertaking, even contradicting them in some matters.

"Naïve" may be the best word to describe Tamiya, who wrote the "departure declaration," and most of the rest of the members involved in the hijacking. But one of them was quite rationally planning on sending for his girlfriend to come to North Korea. Konishi Takahiro was clearly thinking that, once they had crossed over to North Korea, there would be no returning to Japan. Where Tamiya and the others thought they would be gone for "about six months," this practical realist believed it would take "more than a year" to see his girlfriend again. And, furthermore, when they met, it would not be in Japan, because he would have "sent for her" to come to North Korea. This clear thinking on the part of Konishi is in marked contrast with the naïveté of Tamiya and the others.

If the whole point of the hijacking was simply for them to find "political asylum," as Konishi's words as relayed by Fukui Takako imply it was, then it is no surprise that they would have been planning on bringing their girlfriends to North Korea and having families there. And that would be the end of my interest in the story, since it would mean the story of the Yodogō is simply the story of a few men who willingly exiled themselves to North Korea.

After hearing Fukui's account, I felt the outline of this story, now twenty years old, begin to change. Tamiya had written, "We are…determined to return to Japan, no matter how high the walls between the nations may stand…." The starting point of my entire investigation into their story was to find out the truth about why, after making such a strong statement, they had never returned to Japan in all that time. But, in my trips back and forth to Pyongyang, the truth seemed only to become more elusive, more shadowed, more complicated.

However, in the middle of all this mystery, suddenly the stories of their marriages came to light. Konishi's cool rationality, in contrast to the naïveté of Tamiya and the others in the group, was the inspiration behind the unbelievable "Operation Marriage" started by the Yodogō members and the Korean Workers' Party. But before we go on to the truth behind their marriages, let us listen some more to the words of the wives.

CHAPTER TEN

Japanese Wives in North Korea

U nlike Fukui Takako's story, many of the details of how the other wives arrived in North Korea and of how they first met their respective husbands were still obscure. When, where, how they met the men, why they ended up going to North Korea—none among them would go into detail on these matters. They only uttered phrases like "It was destiny" or "We were connected by a red thread of fate." The women said they met these men by chance during their European travels and fell in love without knowing they were the Yodogō hijackers, but common political and philosophical grounds made it easy for the women to choose to go to North Korea.

After Fukui's long testimonial, I had a chance to speak with the other wives. Because the opportunity came up suddenly, I had nothing prepared for the interview. I knew nothing about the other women. However, I had plenty of questions to ask. The interviews I transmit here took place in 1993, their first in the fifteen years since the wives had come to North Korea. At that time, these women were wanted by the Tokyo Metropolitan Security Police for violations of Japanese passport laws, and the Japanese Ministry of Foreign Affairs had ordered them to return their passports as "persons threatening the national interest and public safety of Japan."

The most important questions that immediately sprang to my mind, the questions that I absolutely wished to ask all of them, were, first, by what means had they come to North Korea and, second, how they had met the Yodogō men. The women were very happy to talk about their children and their daily lives in North Korea, but I felt that, if I

Figure 10.01. Four of the Yodogō wives meeting with Takazawa Kōji in Pyongyang. From right, Mizutani Kyōko, Kaneko Emiko, Fukui Takako, Takazawa Kōji, and Kuroda Sakiko. Photo from personal collection of Takazawa Kōji.

didn't know the basic facts of how they came to be there, then I would not be able to understand their present circumstances.

I asked all of them the same list of questions. What were you doing when the *Yodogō* was hijacked? How old were you then? Can you still remember the incident? What did you think of the hijacking at the time? Why did you think about leaving Japan? How and where did you meet your husband for the first time? Who spoke to whom first? When did you first discover that he was one of the Yodogō hijackers? How did you feel when you discovered this? How long after you met did you marry? Did you have a wedding? Are you happy now? What did you think of the student movement? When did you come to North Korea? Before that, what did you think of North Korea? What impressed you about North Korea? How did you first learn about *juche?* Until then, what had you thought of socialism? What impressed you most about North Korea when you first arrived here? Did North Korea meet your expectations? How does it compare to other socialist countries? What is your most vivid memory, your strongest memory of your time here? What has been your saddest experience since coming here? The most shocking? What do you think of Japan? Why do you want your children to go to Japan?

Kaneko Emiko was born in 1955, discovered *juche* when she was a student at a technical college, and as a member of a *juche* study group was active in promoting its ideas. She is married to Akagi Shirō.

Takazawa: First, how long is it since you came here?

Kaneko: I have to pass on that. Let's skip that part.

Takazawa: How did you meet?

Kaneko: We met overseas, in Europe.

Takazawa: Who spoke to whom first? Though my question may be a little intrusive…?

Kaneko: It was him. Akagi-san spoke to me first. You may know this story already, but at the time the men were looking for marriage partners, and they were going to Europe for that purpose. For various reasons…

Takazawa: I have heard that from the others. They say they met by chance, or it just seemed like fate….So, before that, your interest in the Peoples' Republic and your involvement in the *juche* study group—these things had nothing to do with your meeting? You say you just met him by chance?

Kaneko: That's right.

Takazawa: While you were studying in Europe?

Kaneko: Well, you could call it studying, but I was really there to spend some time on my own, to try to be independent, have some experiences. I wasn't studying so much as I was just trying to broaden my outlook. I felt pretty strongly about doing that.

Takazawa: So, there you were, and by chance, somehow, you met him, you say. In your case, you met Akagi Shirō, right?

Kaneko: That's right.

Takazawa: So you didn't have any problem with coming to North Korea?

Kaneko: By chance, I had read an article describing the Peoples' Republic written by someone who had visited. I was pretty impressed by what I read, and I thought I really wanted to go there myself.

Takazawa: And what was your first impression when you got here? Were you impressed?

Kaneko: Of course I was. What impressed me was the equality and
             respect in human relations and the way they all worked
             together as comrades with the same goals. It was a very
             refreshing feeling. Everyone devoted their lives to achiev-
             ing what they dreamed of, doing what they wanted to do,
             and they felt positive about being able to achieve it. I felt
             like it was a place where anything was possible. I felt it
             was not at all different from the lives of simple Japanese
             people.

Takazawa: Was this your first experience of a socialist country?

Kaneko: It was, though later I became familiar with Yugoslavia,
             Eastern Europe, Hungary.

Takazawa: What did you think of North Korea compared to East-
             ern Europe? North Korea is also a socialist country, of
             course....

Kaneko: Well, I think the people in this country believe this to be
             their own system. They created it themselves, and they
             feel strongly that protecting it will ensure their freedom
             as a people. So, for example, when I went to Hungary and
             stayed in an inn there, people would always criticize the
             Soviet Union or their own Socialist party. I really wondered
             to myself how things would turn out for them. Obviously
             it was the difference between the kind of socialism that is
             imposed and the kind that the people choose and build for
             themselves....

Takazawa: The image of this country that you held when you were
             still in Japan, the image that attracted you, wasn't it
             something of an illusion on your part?

Kaneko: Oh, no. Or mostly not, no. But, I have been living here
             continually since 1988, and I have noticed that the road to
             socialism is not always easy or smooth. As in all transi-
             tions, some people get left behind, and others do very well,
             I have noticed.

Takazawa: Do you remember the Yodogō hijacking?

Kaneko: Yes, I do. It was in 1970.

Takazawa: The end of March 1970.

Kaneko: I was very frightened by it. When I heard the news, I was
             very worried there might be a war between Japan and

North Korea. I said to a friend who was visiting our house at the time, "Doesn't this mean there will be a war?" But when he answered, "No, it will be all right," I remember how relieved I felt. I certainly never thought in my wildest dreams that I would become connected like this with one of the Yodogō men!" [Laughter.]

Takazawa: I would like to ask one more thing. Did you soon find out that he was one of the Yodogō men?

Kaneko: I knew nothing about it.

Takazawa: You mean Akagi-san said nothing at all about it?

Kaneko: He didn't say anything.

Takazawa: When did you find out?

Kaneko: After I came here! [Laughter.]

Takazawa: How did you feel when you found out? You must have been shocked. Didn't you feel stunned?

Kaneko: I was pretty surprised. But I had been surprised by a lot of the things he told me when we talked. I wondered, "Oh, what have I gotten into?" But that was just for a little while. I had always wanted to spend my life with someone who had the same goals and ideals as I did, anyway. We had, after all, both gone overseas in accordance with our own inclinations. In this way, I think many of the women here are quite independent in their outlooks. (Takazawa 1995, 114–134)

Kuroda Sakiko was born in 1954, discovered *juche* philosophy while she was a student at a technical college, and was active as a member of a *juche* study group. Later, she crossed over to North Korea, and she is now married to Wakabayashi Moriaki. She is the only one among the women not wanted for violating Japanese passport laws. She has published articles in party newspapers and elsewhere under the name of Wakabayashi Yasuko.

Takazawa: Well, these are pretty routine questions, but I'd like to hear what your motives for coming to North Korea were and how you managed to come, and also how you first met Wakabayashi-san.

Kuroda: How we met....Well, where should I start?

Takazawa: Did you engage in the study of *juche* even when you were
still in Japan?

Kuroda: Well, yes. I studied *juche* in the study group. I thought even
then that *juche* was quite a profound philosophy, really.

Takazawa: About when did you start to feel more deeply impressed by
juche?

Kuroda: I first learned about it when I was a freshman at the
technical college, when I was eighteen. I did some volunteer work when I was a high school student, and that
was probably one of the reasons I ended up going to the
technical college. Then, there was a lot going on, people
asking, do I want to study *juche* ideology, do I want to go
see a movie?...So I didn't really understand the importance of it at first. It wasn't until I was a freshman, almost
nineteen, that I started to gain an understanding of it.
In *juche* ideology, the issue is to take a world view, not
a humanistic view of things, but, in my case, I began to
gain an insight into *juche* from a more humanistic standpoint. Since humans have the power to decide anything, I
thought humans must be the most valuable. I was struck
by this, "Oh, human beings are the most valuable." So that
was what I found I could identify with, after all.

Takazawa: So you decided to go overseas. This is a bit of a change of
subject, but did you go to deepen your understanding of
juche philosophy, or were you just traveling as a tourist?

Kuroda: Both, I guess! [Laughter.] But, of course, I am also interested in Europe. And I met Wakabayashi in Europe....

Takazawa: But—this may be a silly question—perhaps you really did
go to Europe to try and learn more about *juche?*

Kuroda: Well, let me see. I guess in my case, no, rather than going
to learn more about *juche,* I wanted to go and take a look
at Japan from the outside. And, naturally, I also wanted to
see what kind of place Europe was, I wanted to know about
the people who lived there. That was about it. I am a pretty
straightforward person [laughter]; I can tell big lies, but
little ones are hard for me....

          So we met in Europe, see. You know student cafeterias?
          Places where students can take their meals. Maybe Waka-

bayashi didn't have much money either, but anyway the student cafeterias there are pretty good. When I was in Japan, there wasn't a cafeteria at the technical college. It was just a small school. So I don't know how things are at bigger universities in Japan, but there they had everything, including desserts, things like yoghurt, and fruit.

Takazawa: So that was where you met?

Kuroda: That's right. He asked me if I was Japanese. I don't know, but that's how it usually goes, when you're a Japanese overseas. Complete strangers would come up to me just because we were Japanese. But, looking back, I guess it's clear he had an agenda.

Takazawa: Yes, it seems like he must have planned it.

Kuroda: Yes. So I had no idea at first that he was the Wakabayashi involved in the Yodogō thing. But, of course, he was Japanese.

Takazawa: When did you find out? Once your relationship was well under way?

Kuroda: What was it, about a month later? When we talked, what? He tried to prepare me. He would say there was a lot going on, like this.... Well, it was a little different from what most people who were there traveling as tourists would have to say. He talked about problems in Japan. When he understood that I was kind of interested in North Korea myself, since that was his goal, he tried to steer the talk in that direction. Things went like that.

Takazawa: But it really is too much to think all this was by chance, isn't it? That this Wakabayashi, one of the Yodogō men, who was looking for a marriage partner, should just happen to run into you, interested in studying *juche,* in Europe?

Kuroda: Yes, just what was going on, anyway? [Laughter.] I'll leave it you to speculate. So what was going on? Maybe we were joined by some shared ideas about Japan's destiny.... So, how should I say, though I was interested in different social problems in Japan, I still didn't know much about the leftist movement. So I was deeply interested in learning more. I watched the Yodogō incident as it was happening, on television....

Takazawa: Do you still remember it?

Kuroda: Yes, I remember. When there were student demonstrations, I didn't really understand what kind of demands they were making, but I wasn't by any means against them. It just seemed to me that the students were trying very hard to achieve something that they really believed in very strongly.

Takazawa: So what did you think when you found out this man you were with was one of the Yodogō members?

Kuroda: Well, he may have adjusted the conversations a bit for my sake, but we talked quite a lot about North Korea. They themselves—was it in 1975?—had been reevaluating the actions of the Red Army Faction until then, such as how they hadn't been able to initiate a people-centered movement. But, as for saying whether I really understood the importance of his words, I have to admit that I don't think I did, really. Only that they had been struggling in the style of the Red Army Faction, and that, once they came to North Korea, they were evaluating things in such and such a way, and I didn't really have any problem with all this; in fact, I felt attracted by it.

Takazawa: So he proposed to you after the first month?

Kuroda: No, he didn't. In my case, he asked me to go to North Korea. Of course, had I not had some feelings for Wakabayashi, no matter how much I wanted to go to North Korea myself, I would not have considered marriage with him. But, well, this is the result of trying to explore my own destiny. (Takazawa 1995, 135–155)

Mori Yoriko was born in 1953 to a Japanese mother and a North Korean father, who had been brought to Japan to do forced labor. She had grown up surrounded by prejudice and discrimination. She married Tamiya Takamaro in Pyongyang. When she came to North Korea, she carried her father's ashes, to return them to North Korean soil.

Mori: I met Tamiya because, when I came to North Korea, I said I wanted to meet him.

Takazawa: You said so yourself?

Mori: Yes, that's right. It's annoying that everyone keeps saying I was kidnapped. I just wanted to meet him, after all.

Takazawa: After you came to Pyongyang?

Mori: Right, right, after I came to North Korea. But, of course, I knew about him when I was in Japan, too. I knew of him even during his Red Army Faction days.

Takazawa: When you say you knew him, do you mean you knew him personally?

Mori: No, I mean I knew he had come on the *Yodogō* with the Red Army Faction....I think of this as my country as well, so I came here to study for a while, but I thought, since he was another Japanese like me, that I wanted to meet him. He came to visit me. I came to North Korea to return my father's ashes, and I wasn't involved at all in the student movement. And, anyway, Tamiya isn't such a radical. He rather leans to the right. He's the original Japanese person [laughter]. I get a very strong feeling from him of his Japanese ethnicity. But he seemed to be a man ready to take action, and maybe that's why we hit it off. After all, I was able to bring home my father's ashes, a daughter fulfilling her father's wishes. At that time I thought I wanted to take this man back to Japan....

Takazawa: After you first met, did you get many opportunities to speak to him again?

Mori: Yes, yes, but I didn't know anything, and I had nothing like ideology or theory. But it's kind of strange when I think about it, because, by some coincidence or whatever you want to call it, these days I want to find a way to send him back to Japan. My father would always go a little crazy whenever he thought about his homeland. He drank an awful lot. We were a family of five living in a six-tatami-mat room....

Takazawa: Where was that?

Mori: Kawasaki. In a tenement. When he drank, he would cry, and shout, and send the dinner table flying. That happened a lot. Everybody wants their parents to be respectable, but I could hardly call my father a respectable man. Somehow I wanted him to be a good man, though.

Takazawa: How many years has it been since you came here?

Mori: I came in 1977.

Takazawa: According to what you said before, you had been aware
               of the name Tamiya Takamaro ever since the *Yodogō*
               hijacking?

Mori: Yes, I was. Strange, isn't it?

Takazawa: Yes, it's strange.

Mori: Maybe that's why I married him. I watched it all on TV. It
               happened right during the spring break, right? For some
               reason, I was caught up in it, and I kept thinking, "Oh, be
               safe! I want them to be safe!"

Takazawa: You must have felt quite strongly about their attempt to go
               to North Korea?

Mori: Yes, I did.

Takazawa: Did it make you want to go to North Korea with them?

Mori: I didn't want to join them, but I was very happy they made
               it. "Oh, they're safe!" I thought, "That's wonderful!"
               Though I did think I wanted to go North Korea.

Takazawa: When did you start thinking you really wanted to go to
               North Korea?

Mori: In the third grade of elementary school, when I saw the
               movie *Chollima,* and I thought to myself, "I really want to
               go some day!" After that, it grew in me....

Takazawa: Have you been here the whole time since you came in
               1977? You must have gone back and forth a few times?

Mori: To Japan? Of course.

Takazawa: You married Tamiya about six months after you met him,
               and you have been living with the Yodogō group ever
               since?

Mori: Yes, that's right. Was there anywhere else to go? It was
               tough when I was young. I don't much like to talk about
               it, but there was a lot of discrimination. I haven't talked
               about those days even with Tamiya, and I don't really need
               to tell him, either. This is how we are, and he understands
               it; after all, we've been married now for more than ten
               years....Tamiya is not a talkative man. When he is out

with someone, he can talk almost more than necessary. And he has an optimistic personality. But once he comes home, he doesn't talk at all. Mostly he reads books, or he sleeps, one or the other. There isn't really any married couple conversation between us...[laugh]. (Takazawa 1995, 47–84)

Mizutani Kyōko was born in 1956. She became interested in North Korea and began to dream of going there when she was a student at Aichi University. She is married to Tanaka Yoshimi. She was the youngest of the Yodogō wives to come to North Korea. Speaking with her was more like listening to a lecture on *juche* ideology than conducting an interview.

Takazawa: You were still a university student when you first came here, weren't you?

Mizutani: Yes, that's right. I was a student.

Takazawa: Did you study *juche* in college or anything like that?

Mizutani: Well, yes, but not *juche*. I was in the Korean culture club. I had become interested in North Korea, and it was my intention to come here someday. But it's difficult to come here, you know? So I thought I might get a chance to come here if I went and studied abroad.

Takazawa: You mean that, when you went overseas, your plan was that clear right from the beginning?

Mizutani: So, though I definitely thought I wanted to come here, still it was difficult to make that happen. So I decided to go abroad to see if I could get the chance to come here.

Takazawa: And did you, in fact?

Mizutani: What do you mean?

Takazawa: That, overseas....

Mizutani: Oh, yes, yes.

Takazawa: Where did you go?

Mizutani: That I am not going to tell you! [Laughter.]

Takazawa: Europe?

Mizutani: Yes, Europe.

Takazawa: So were you able to finagle an opportunity?

Mizutani: Well, yes. I figured it out myself. Maybe it was kind of like Fukui-san's case? I regarded the Democratic People's Republic of North Korea as...

Takazawa: Was North Korea something like a "lover"?

Mizutani: I was about in my second year of junior high school when that hijacking happened. So there is a bit of a generation gap between us, but even then I was aware that I was against the examination system, or you could even say this awareness was strong enough that I resisted the exam system by escaping into my own private world. With all that, I still ended up going to university, but I decided I wanted to study about the socialist countries of Eastern Europe.

Takazawa: So then you went to Europe, having been interested in North Korea from the beginning. So what year is it that you came here?

Mizutani: 1978.

Takazawa: And you didn't know Tanaka [Yoshimi] at all at that point?

Mizutani: I knew him by then.

Takazawa: So you had already met him in Europe, not after you came here?

Mizutani: Yes, that's right.

Takazawa: How did you meet him?

Mizutani: Oh, I'd rather not go into that. But about that—I was aware of a problem there too, and it's one of the reasons I was thinking of going to North Korea. And at the time, for the men here it was almost like their duty to be looking for marriage partners. So of course they were able to ferret me out. That's so, isn't it? I guess that was like a common ground for us. That's what I think, anyway.

Takazawa: Where did you meet?

Mizutani: Oh, no, no, not that. Let's just say it was by chance..., and, of course, it's likely that he was the one who spoke to me first...[laughter].

Takazawa: So then he proposed to you?

Mizutani: Yes, that's what happened.

Takazawa: What was your impression of this country when you first came here? Was it what you expected? Was it the place you had been looking for, Mizutani-san?

Mizutani: As far as what I was looking for, a purpose in life in Japan or ideals, these were all dead for me. But here in North Korea, things are alive for me. That's what it is. This is the revolution for these people here, after all. And in the end, we have to open ourselves up to that, too. So that's what I think the philosophy of self-reliance is.

[At this point, she engages in a flood of praise for *juche* ideology and "the Great Leader," Kim Il Sung.]

Takazawa: Since that is a very difficult topic indeed, I am going to lower the tone of the conversation a little. There have been rumors that Tanaka-san has been secretly coming into Japan. What is the truth of the matter?

Mizutani: In fact, he has not been going to Japan.

Takazawa: So he isn't in Japan right now?

Mizutani: No, he isn't, and he hasn't been to Japan, either.

Takazawa: I see. But for that matter, he still hasn't come back, has he?

Mizutani: Well, no, that's true....

Takazawa: You must be a little lonely?

Mizutani: [Laughs.]...Well, yes. Even though people say a lot of things about me, like, for instance, "He must not want to come back because his wife is so scary." [Laugh.]

Takazawa: Scary?

Mizutani: It's just that, for men, there isn't anything scarier than women, is there? (Takazawa 1995, 156–189)

Uomoto Tamiko was born in 1952 and joined the student movement while she was still a high school student. Afterwards, she joined the Proletarian Youth League (the former Proletarian Student League, the student organization of the Communist Workers' Party).[1] She went to North Korea on the instructions of the Workers' Party and married Abe Kimihiro after

---

1. The Communist Workers' Party (Kyōrōtō) is a Japanese New Left organization led by Iida Momo. Like many such groups, it had an affiliated student organization. It has no formal relationship with the North Korean Workers' Party.

falling in love with him in Pyongyang. Of the Yodogō wives, she is the only one who was active in the student movement as a university student, and the circumstances of her arrival in North Korea are also different.

Takazawa: How long were you active with the Youth League?

Uomoto: Until I left Japan.

Takazawa: And you hadn't yet encountered *juche* ideology at that stage, had you?

Uomoto: No, I had encountered it. The nature of the Communist Workers' Party was intellectual, so there were a lot of ideas and ideologies coming in all the time. It was like a study group.

Takazawa: How did you meet and come to know Abe-san?

Uomoto: Well, I managed to scrape together a tiny amount of money working as a busgirl. I wanted to see the world. So I used that to escape from Japan. I went to Europe first, by way of Moscow. I was so happy when I arrived in Moscow. I thought, "Wow, so this is a socialist country!" There were red flags flying in the city. And I saw statues of Lenin. But it was hard, because nobody spoke English, or of course Japanese either. France was hard too. Language is not one of my strong points.

Takazawa: Did you see much of Europe?

Uomoto: Yes, most of it. I didn't make it to Spain or Portugal, though, which is too bad. I didn't have any money, either. I worked really hard, washing dishes, waitressing, babysitting, whatever. I met Abe quite by accident, at a place where Japanese people get together. This was some country in Europe, but Japanese would get together to talk, you know? I thought, "Oh, this guy used to be an activist," because he used words like "the structure." I was pretty happy. I was happy just to meet a Japanese ex-activist in a foreign country. My life was pretty hard. . . .

Takazawa: Did you realize he was one of the Yodogō hijackers?

Uomoto: No, I didn't. But there were a few times when I wondered about that. So I tried to catch him, trick him into saying something. Things like, "Perhaps you've been to North Korea before?" Or, "Haven't you been to North Korea yourself?" [Laugh.] But he wasn't fooled. Finally I figured

I was just thinking too much, I had to be wrong, since surely they wouldn't be allowed to leave North Korea, would they? In those days, everyone figured the Yodogō guys were stuck in Pyongyang all the time.

Takazawa: But that wasn't the case, was it? [Laugh.]

Uomoto: Even after I met Abe, I thought my vagabond life would continue forever. Then Abe asked me to help him with his work.

Takazawa: Was that a marriage proposal?

Uomoto: Mmm, I don't know. But I continued for a little while, anyway. I really wanted to see more of Asia, but instead I ended up in Central America. I was able to go and study painting at a university in Mexico.

Takazawa: By Central America, do you mean only Mexico?

Uomoto: No, I went to all sorts of places, though I never did go to Cuba.

Takazawa: What brought you to North Korea? When did you come to Pyongyang?

Uomoto: In fact, I was pregnant when I was in Mexico. So I came to Pyongyang for the delivery. It seemed like a good idea because there is a reliable social welfare system here in North Korea. I guess it was about the winter of 1978 when I came here. (Takazawa 1995, 85–113)

This brings me to the end of my initial profiles of the Yodogō wives Fukui Takako, Kaneko Emiko, Kuroda Sachiko, Mori Yoriko, Mizutani Kyōko, and Uomoto Tamiko. Circumstances were different for each of them, but, unfortunately, with the sole exception of Fukui Takako and her secret crossing to be with her lover, Konishi, these stories of the women's meetings with the Yodogō men and their subsequent entries into North Korea are completely false. Even the stories of their initial encounters in Europe are just imaginative and well-made fictions. So well-made, in fact, that at first I believed everything I heard. But, behind the veil of the tales they were forced to tell me, stories full of the ideology of Kim Il Sung and their exposure to the "art of guidance," there was something, some dimly visible element in their words, that seemed to be telling the truth of what lay deepest in their hearts.

Behind these tales the women told me lay a secret they had to keep. In North Korea, the true story is always hidden behind the fictional one.

CHAPTER ELEVEN

Operation Marriage

I t's easy to imagine the women putting their heads together in desperation, spinning out of air these fanciful wedding stories about their meetings with destiny in Europe, editing and reediting, checking to make sure there were no discrepancies between them. Their task of inventing these stories for themselves represented a heavy political responsibility for the women. Each would spin out a story on her own, then they would all meet to read and criticize each other's work. They strictly pointed out inconsistencies, and each had to be able to answer questions perfectly. This work was their expression of gratitude and loyalty toward their Revered Great Leader Kim Il Sung and their Dear Leader Comrade Kim Jong Il, who had organized their glorious marriages. Were they to inadvertently let the real story come out, it would mean the Revered Great Leader and the Dear Leader Comrade would experience unexpected distress.

Through this process of criticism and reediting, the fictitious fairy tales gradually took on more concrete and realistic shapes. They were stories of romantic love set in Europe. The women's enthusiasm for the task grew as they continued their assignment. They shared their romantic fantasies openly with the whole group, drawing the men into the process of editing their own wedding stories. Eventually they had a set of stories that the whole community agreed on. By this time, many of the women had come to believe that the stories represented their real experiences. Each was an actress on the stage of her own fictitious story.

In the ideology of Kim Il Sung, far more important than the "real" truth of any matter is the "correct" truth: the way that things should be rather than the way things, in fact, are. Probably the women felt no pangs of guilt over the fairy tales they were concocting, since the actual facts of their experiences were, simply put, incorrect. They could not give such "incorrect" stories out as fact. "Truth," by their reading, consisted of the correct facts, that is, the facts as they should have been. Dear Leader Comrade Kim Jong Il should not have been born in the suburbs of Khabarovsk but at the "Sainted Mountain of the Revolution," Mt. Paekto. So, in this ideology, the "correct" fact is that Kim Jong Il was born in a military camp on Mt. Paekto. As far as these women were concerned, their inventions about their meetings "of destiny" with the Yodogō men in Europe and the marriages that came of "the red string of fate" connecting them were believable as the "correct" truth in a way the "real" truth was not. At the very least, they believed their own stories. This construction required by the ideology of *juche,* with complete fictions being told as if they were the real truth, would trip me up many times in my research on this story.

However, I needed and wanted the "real" truth far more than the required "correct" truth of these fairy tales. We have to twist many facts before our eyes in order to accept "correct" facts as truth. I am no adherent of *juche,* nor do I follow the ideology of Kim Il Sung. Here, I have to depart for a while from the wedding stories of these women and relate the circumstances and background of the marriages, based on the facts sitting out in plain view.

About a year after the fact that the Yodogō hijackers had Japanese wives and children came to light, Tamiya and I were lounging on sofas in the guest house in their compound, just the two of us, talking. Once I started flying between Japan and Pyongyang regularly, this happened often.

Tamiya began by saying, "Revolutionaries are human beings too, so we shouldn't have to deny ourselves, we should have wives and children as well....Every one of us should have a family. So I petitioned the Party (the North Korean Workers' Party) to let us start 'Operation Marriage' in order for us to get our own 'revolutionary comrades.'" He went on to tell me several anecdotes about their progress, then ended with an eager look, saying, "I think I was pretty clever with it."

To this day, I remember clearly the innocence in his expression. His demeanor was a mix of shy and bashful, boastful and playful.

Two years later, in the early summer of 1995, about six months before his sudden death, I had my last interview with Tamiya. He spoke about the marriages.

Figure 11.01. Tamiya Takamaro (left) and Takazawa Kōji (right) talking together in Pyongyang. Photo from personal collection of Takazawa Kōji.

"There are probably people who are angry that we are married, but I think that men ought to marry. Men, and women too, should marry. If you're engaged with something that gets in the way of your getting married, I think you'll eventually lose interest in it.... Of course finding a woman means you'll be gaining a wife. But even more important than having a wife, I think it's important to have that closest comrade in your life. So we held a meeting and decided that, before the year was out, we would all have found wives for ourselves.... It became our revolutionary task to find these women, and, within a year or a year and a half, we had all carried out our missions in good faith. That was around 1977, and it was also the beginning of a new era for the Yodogō group." (Tamiya and Takazawa 1996, 206–207)

The story he told, that this "mission," nicknamed "Operation Marriage," was the original idea of the Yodogō men, that they had agreed unanimously to go to Europe and meet Japanese women with whom they would have "revolutionary" romances and that each couple returned together to North Korea for their married lives, is largely the same story the women had related. For Tamiya, this story was the "correct" truth that he had set into action.

I listened to all this without speaking, and Tamiya continued in the same vein for the whole interview.

But perhaps Tamiya's words did not reveal his real thoughts. More than anything, his slight air of shyness gave away his story as false. The stories themselves were clearly worthless, since, after all, the records of the women's travels abroad from Japan could be checked and their travel routes in Europe retraced.

Looking back now, it's possible to see that their stories held contradictions beginning from the very first interviews. There were many places where the different stories didn't match. However, even after I knew the real story, I hesitated in writing about this because, every time I remembered Tamiya's expression when he said, "I was pretty clever with it," I wanted his story to be the true one. I wanted it to be that these men, who had fled to North Korea by hijacking an airplane, like a shot of cannon fire at the climax of the movement at the end of the 1960s, at the very least were able to make their own choices in marriage, acting by their own free will. I was also certain that Tamiya would suffer a loss of face if the true story were to become public.

The facts of "Operation Marriage" are not at all as told by Tamiya and the women. Neither their words nor the contents of their stories were their own. "Operation Marriage" was run by the Workers' Party so that the Yodogō members could marry and have children. More on that below.

Fukui Takako made her journey to North Korea via Athens, Eastern Europe, Belgrade, and Moscow around November of 1975. Konishi Takahiro had already received the letter she had written and sent from the embassy in Beijing in March of 1974. There was no way he could reply to her, but it had been properly delivered to "Yodogō member" Konishi. None of the others to whom he showed her letter thought she would be able to come alone to Pyongyang to visit Konishi. "There is no way a modern Japanese woman would come all the way to North Korea just to see you!"

Tamiya and the others just laughed at him, but Konishi was unperturbed: "No, she will come, for sure."

And sure enough, despite what the rest of his group expected, she really did come to Pyongyang.

"I was astounded. Imagine there being a Japanese woman these days who would come here!" Tamiya said later.

Fukui's arrival on the scene cast a subtle shadow over the whole group. With the intrusion of a woman into their previously all-male group, jealousy stirred among them.

The other men's feelings were complicated. The others began keeping a distance from Konishi, and they were cooler and more formal in their manner toward him. The group's solidarity began to collapse, and the dynamics of their interactions were disrupted. The effect of Konishi's marriage was to bring an element of ordinary life into an arena that was not at all ordinary. Late at night, the sounds of cheerful talk could be heard from their room, and, in the mornings, the laundry of two people would be hanging out to dry on the veranda. According to Fukui Takako, Konishi came close to being bullied by the others because of all this.

The situation worried Tamiya. As group leader, his first thought was that "our group bonding is not strong enough to weather this naturally." After much consideration, he came to a conclusion: "Men preparing for revolution should have wives and children." He felt sure of this. As the oldest member of the group and feeling his responsibility as its leader, Tamiya's next thoughts were that they were all still young, and, if possible, he wished for everyone in the group to have families.

About six months after Fukui had set up household with Konishi in Pyongyang, Tamiya called a group meeting to discuss the marriage issue. It was now six years since they had left Japan, and most of the members of their group had reached a "marriageable" age. For Tamiya, who always tried to strengthen the solidarity of their group, this was a problem that could not be ignored. He concluded, "We all must find women. It is our revolutionary mission to do so."

He had an idea for a plan of action, too. In his role as group leader, he raised the matter with the Workers' Party. It appears that one of Tamiya's motivations for taking this action was his increasing awareness, finally, that their sojourn in North Korea was going to be of long duration.

Tamiya's suggestion to the Party was given high priority. A similar realization of the necessity for a quick solution had arisen within the Party as well. Ever since Konishi's marriage, several unpleasant sexual incidents had come to light concerning the Yodogō men and the women working at the guest compound where they lived. This was the trigger for the Party to become actively involved in running Operation Marriage.

Tamiya had taken his plan to the special section of the Workers' Party that was in charge of the Yodogō group. The Party had created this special section to take direct charge of their affairs in May of 1972, after the Yodogō men had gained the confidence of Kim Il Sung. Its assignment was to direct "anti-Japanese, anti-South" missions, and the top cadre of the section was Kim Jong Il. From the day of their entry into the confidence of Kim Il Sung, the Yodogō group had been directly tied to the central authority of North Korea, under the supervision of a system outside the control of either the government or the Workers' Party.

Tamiya brought his plan to the special section, but he had made one major miscalculation. He had not completely thought through the consequences, to the members of his group and to the as yet unknown women who would become their wives, of suggesting his own plan of action. Operation Marriage began to develop in a direction none of them could have imagined.

When he formed his plan, undoubtedly Tamiya was filled with the romantic idea that they would really be able to go to Europe to find the women there who would be their "comrades." The Workers' Party, however, would not allow this. They could not be allowed to leave North Korea to wander about freely for any purpose. Looking back now, it seems obvious that, in one vital area, the state of their loyalty, the Party handlers could not have regarded their ideological and personal remolding as complete. They had yet to become people who could wander the world without forgetting their total loyalty to the "Great Leader."

The Party's special Yodogō section came up with a plan that was much simpler and would take much less time to complete than Tamiya's Operation Marriage: *arrange for the men to meet the women in Pyongyang and have them get married there* (emphasis in original). The women would be brought from Japan for this purpose. The special section in charge was given the authority to put this plan into action.

Here events diverged greatly from the original plan of the Yodogō group, and Operation Marriage came completely under the control of the Workers' Party. The women who would become the Yodogō brides were selected in Japan by agents of the special section under the command of Kim Jong Il. Many of these women were followers of Kim Il Sung's ideas in Japan or involved to some extent in *juche* workshops. However, choosing candidates was not made easier by that, and it later became clear to me that the agents did not limit themselves only to such women. However, in the interest of keeping the story clear, I will go into more detail on this complication later: the story of the shadow of misery thrown over the group by the confusion and coercion of this period belongs a little later in this recounting.

The women so hurriedly selected as bridal candidates all obtained passports by the beginning of 1977, and they all left the country at about the same time.

Kaneko Emiko, who was a leader in her *juche* study group, received her passport on January 11, 1977, and departed the country from Haneda Airport two weeks later, on January 25. She later married Akagi Shirō.

Mizutani Kyōko, so powerfully attracted to North Korea from her studies in the Korean culture club, received her passport on March 18, 1977. She submitted a request for a leave of absence from her university and, ten days later on March 29, departed from Haneda bound for Hong Kong. She told her family she was going to "study abroad in Bulgaria." This was the basis of her wedding story of having met Tanaka Yoshimi while studying in Eastern Europe. She later married him.

Mori Yoriko, daughter of a Korean national in Japan, got her passport on March 17, 1977, abruptly submitted her resignation at work on March 25, and five days later, on March 30, departed from Haneda for Hong Kong. She later married Tamiya Takamaro.

Kuroda Sakiko and Uomoto Tamiko had arrived a little earlier.

Kuroda, also a leader in her *juche* study group, had left Japan on June 13, 1976, and later married Wakabayashi Moriaki. The story of meeting him in a student cafeteria in Europe was based on her experiences during her later activities there.

Next, Uomoto Tamiko had departed from Haneda on October 7, 1976, bound for Mexico. She probably chose such a distant destination because of her past association with a New Left group. She had to plan with caution, considering the possibility that her name may have been flagged by the security police. Setting out for Mexico on a trip that took her almost completely around the world, she arrived in Pyongyang via northern Europe and Moscow. She married Abe Kimihiro. Her wedding story was based on this journey and on her later activities in Europe.

Just the fact that all the women suddenly left Japan in about the same time period made their stories of the "meetings of destiny" with their future husbands while traveling in Europe sound extremely unlikely.

One of the women had in fact told a close friend before leaving the country, "I can't tell you my destination because it must be kept a strict secret. I won't be able to write any letters. It is work I can do because I am Japanese. I've already received 150,000 yen in advance for expenses."

In a clever arrangement of alibis, most of the women's families received completely innocuous handwritten letters or postcards from them, mailed within Japan and postmarked after the dates of their departures from Japan.

The women were not told when they left the country that they would be marrying the Yodogō men. They did not realize until they were already in North Korea that their journey was not for study or travel purposes, as they had thought, but for the purpose of their very carefully planned marriages. It was too late to turn back. There was nothing they could do but become the Yodogō wives.

Why was it necessary for the Yodogō men to marry quickly?

There were two reasons.

First, the date that had been set for their wedding day was approaching. This is clear from the rush for the women to leave Japan, as noted earlier. Tamiya Takamaro revealed in his last interview that the plan was to complete the "Operation Marriage" mission in about one year's time. Once the Yodogō handlers in the special section had set the plan into action, the dates of the women's departures from Japan all took place within a twelve-month period. We see the extremely hurried departure of the last few women in the winter and early spring of 1977. And, unlike in Uomoto's case, they did not choose distant destinations, but nearby ones like Hong Kong. This means that the date for the marriages was fast approaching. There was no need to spend a long period "brainwashing" the women, as had been necessary for the Red Army Faction hijackers, since they had already been indoctrinated in the tenets of Kim Il Sung's ideology and *juche* in Japan. A few days for a check of ideology and other basics, and then the date of the wedding was upon them. And the date set for their wedding was most likely none other than the anniversary of the day the Yodogō men were presented to the Great Leader, Kim Il Sung, and pledged their loyalty to him. The men of the Yodogō group and their handlers in the special section were united in their conviction that they must show their happiness and gratitude to the Great Leader.

After all the women had arrived in North Korea, the men assembled, and, standing in a line of pairs with their respective brides, they were all married at the same time. It was early May, barely a month since the last of the women had left Japan. Years later, at a press conference in September 1997 on the issue of the return to Japan of the Yodogō children, the youngest member of the Yodogō hijackers, Shibata Yasuhiro, made such comments as "We all had our wedding pictures taken after the ceremony." It must have been a sight reminiscent of a mass wedding at Reverend Moon's Unification Church. The women were *juche* brides, "brides of the Great Leader," dressed in pure white *chima chogori* dresses.

There is an interesting passage in a recent book, *The Statue of Kim Jong Il's Secretary,* by Ho Dam, who worked for years in the foreign affairs bureau of the Korean Workers' Party and later became party secretary of the central Party. In this passage, Kim Jong Il's secretary says that the best way to lighten the Great Leader's stress and workload was to anticipate what he would think and act on it immediately. And, he told Ho Dam, he was happiest when such efforts brought success. We've already seen that Ho Dam, as a Party secretary, was in charge of the affairs of the Yodogō group. When I read these words, I remembered the words of Kim Il Sung in the interview with the Japanese press that had resulted in the Yodogō group's first press conference. Speaking about the Yodogō members, Kim Il Sung had said, "They're still young, and they'll want to get married."

Of course, I don't know what connection there is between the passage in Ho Dam's book and the marriages of the Yodogō group members. But the go-between in the high-speed "Operation Marriage" was Kim Jong Il, appointed to the position of secretary-general of the Workers' Party in October 1997. Herein lies the source of the Yodogō group's loyalty to both Kim Il Sung and Kim Jong Il right up to the present,[1] which reveals the hidden content of their "revolutionary *giri*."

Now on to the second reason.

The Workers' Party had a very special reason for speeding up the marriages of the Yodogō men to take place by a certain date.

First, it completed their ideological conversions with a vow of absolute loyalty to Kim Il Sung. Second, by bearing children they would embody the precept of the ideology of Kim Il Sung that demands the revolution continue in each generation. In addition, children would increase the number of people in their organization. Also, their wives and children would serve as hostages to assure complicity when the Yodogō men were sent on assignments overseas. In fact, they did not start going on overseas assignments until the late 1970s, after their first children had been born.

Is it really possible to assume that, just because the couples matched in their ideological makeup, their marriages would be successful? This is the last unanswered question concerning "Operation Marriage."

During one of our interviews, Mizutani Kyōko, wife of Tanaka Yoshimi, once said something like "I left Japan determined not to marry" (*Marco Polo* [Tokyo], January 1994, p. 142). However, she and the other women still active as Yodogō wives appear to have adjusted well to their fates. A key to this acceptance lies in the fact that, more than becoming the wives of the Yodogō men, they considered themselves married to

---

1. The book was written while Kim Jong Il was still alive.

juche ideology. In this way they were able to accept their destinies. They were first "brides of the Great Leader" and "brides of the Dear Leader Comrade" and only after that were they "Yodogō brides." They were able to accept their marriages as a way of showing their complete loyalty and obedience to the "Great Leader."

The women would sometimes sing a song they had written in praise of the Great Leader or, as in the song, their "Great General."

> To the feet of the Great General, we are daughters who came
>> from afar
> The same happiness we have been given today, we wish forever
>> upon our Great General
> The boundless love of the Great General taught us to be woman
>> revolutionaries
> Such love! Such kindness! We hold it in our hearts, we offer
>> everything to our Great General
> With the guidance of the Great General, the future of Japan will
>> flower
> We are soldiers of the Premier, we advance along the road of
>> loyalty
> O, our fatherly Great General, may you live ten thousand years!
>> (Yao 2002, 109)

There is another song that both the men and the women would sing together:

> You raised us, nameless as we were, and entrusted us with the
>> Japanese revolution
> In the love of our father, our Leader, we faced the glorious battle
>
> The hearts of the people of Japan are united, opened with the
>> power of *juche*
> Holding tight our Great Leader's teachings, we stride forward on
>> the great road of victory
> O, our fatherly Great General, our loyal hearts pray you will live
>> ten thousand years.

Just writing these lines makes my skin crawl, but they capture well the sentiments of the women. Whenever I happened to hear these songs while I was visiting Pyongyang, I felt they had already gone far away. I came to hate the passage of time and the ideology that had twisted them so. Furthermore, I was chilled to my core by the expressions of ecstasy on the women's faces as they sang of their "father," their "Leader." The lyrics are simple enough; they don't need any explanation. The songs thoroughly show that their "independence" and "transformation" were a precious gift bestowed by the "guidance" of Kim Il Sung and Kim Jong Il.

This was the success of the Workers' Party's Operation Marriage. The women were the Yodogō men's "closest comrades" (the expression for "husband and wife" in North Korea). And most of the women accomplished their first duty soon after their marriages: they successfully delivered children of the Yodogō hijackers.

CHAPTER TWELVE

Japanese Village of the Revolution

Many winters had come and gone at the guest house compound in the outskirts of Pyongyang. If the evening snowfall continued overnight, by morning the whole world would be white. Another long winter was about to descend on the village: the snow went away only with the spring thaw. The fog had been heavy that morning, rising out of the Daedong with the change between day and night air temperatures. The village, on a hill skirted by the river as it wandered around a bend in its upper reaches, had lain obscured in milky whiteness. The Daedong was the largest river flowing through Pyongyang, and soon it would be frozen in the grip of full winter. Once it froze, snow would pile up on the ice, and the boundary between the river and the land would disappear. How many winters had it been, anyway? After their arrival on board the Yodogō *in April of 1970, the hijackers had all shivered in the surprisingly cold spring wind that blew as they descended from the airplane. That was the moment Tamiya had understood that they had come to a cold country. Perhaps this country didn't even have a word for "cold," he had thought to himself. Either it was hot here or cold, one or the other. Tamiya looked up at the snow pouring out of the darkness and said to his comrades, "We'll have to shovel snow tomorrow."*

Every winter since their arrival in this country, this task had been a daily chore.

At some point, people had started referring to the Yodogō guest house compound as the "village." It encompassed a large area of land, and they had struggled with the management of the property when it was first given over to them. Early on they had cut down some of the trees to make space for a small sports field. At the very least, they had reasoned, if they could not get the military training they had requested, they could continue to build up their physical strength. They had even laid out a running course in the woods around the compound. But they hadn't really known how to manage such a place.

Things had changed considerably in the village since those early days. The facilities had improved greatly with the addition of several new buildings, and the number of support staff had increased significantly. The Yodogō men cultivated a manner of being masters of the house.

The snow was a special problem; the several full-time employees simply couldn't handle the volume of snow by themselves. Snowfall was much heavier in this area of low mountains than in the low-lying central city, and neglecting it could paralyze the functioning of the compound. These days, clearing the snow was the only matter in which the Yodogō men had to take the initiative, the only remaining responsibility they still had in the day-to-day running of their village. Everything else had been relegated to the staff. The work was also important for the opportunities it gave them to interact with the staff, another circumstance that had greatly changed.

The village was its own isolated little world. It formed a special area totally separate from the surrounding farm villages: the buildings, the landscape—everything in the limited area was different. Screened by a wide perimeter of forest and woodlands, the interior was impossible to see from the outside, and any outsider who wandered lost into the village would have thought the scene very strange. A fence surrounded the village, cordoning it off from the outside world. The area was so extensive that other people in the region were unaware that the fence existed. Sentries stood guard at the entrance gate. Anyone without the proper permit was not permitted to set foot inside. Armed security soldiers patrolled the area outside the fence, and, on the few occasions when some local farmer did lose his way and come too close, he was challenged at gunpoint and his name taken down. The only place the perimeter was not fenced was where it bordered the Daedong River.

However, the village was not only isolated from its neighbors in a geographical sense. Inside the fence, everything else was different, too: language, lifestyle, food, and clothing. The village was a Little Japan.

Within the village, new buildings had sprung up. When the Yodogō hijackers had first arrived, there had been no more than two buildings. Now there was a special foreign goods store for their own use, individual housing with plenty of space for comfortable family living, and a new

Figure 12.01. Only known photo of Yodogō members' residence in the Revolution-ary Village before its recent renovation for tourism, taken from a frame of a video. From personal collection of Takazawa Kōji.

management building. Meeting rooms and classrooms had been added. In two buildings specially built for them, each family occupied a whole floor. The floor plans included bedrooms, a living room, a dining area, a good-quality study area with shelves and a basic book collection, a fully equipped kitchen with a large refrigerator, and a veranda. All the floors were heated, and every room had air-conditioning. The families shared large, luxurious bath facilities, including a sauna.

The population of the village had increased, too. The Party-appointed instructors and teachers permanently stationed in the village lived in their own special accommodations. Their numbers had more than doubled, counting their wives and children, from the number originally assigned to the nine hijackers. In addition, there was a large staff of attendants and workers who saw to the daily running of the village. All the accommodations had hot water at all times, requiring full-time boiler-room staff. There had to be clerks on duty in the shop. The backup generator that ensured electricity at all times had its own maintenance technician. After the children were born, a clinic and childcare section for their exclusive use was set up. Its staff included a nurse, a doctor, and nursery school teachers. Their transportation was a fleet of Mercedes-Benz sedans provided by the Party Central Committee. The cars were available for their use at all times, and, of course, each one came with a full-time driver.

Several young women served as attendants in the dining hall in addition to the kitchen staff. They served their masters gorgeous meals, then stood aside to wait quietly for further orders for refills of beer or wine, or additional dishes of food. The attendants' work was not limited to the dining hall. They also saw to the laundry, the cleaning, and the bed making. In all, the place had the feeling of a royal palace with a flock of courtiers hovering around a royal family.

Besides the instructors, many of the staff and chauffeurs lived there permanently with their families, bringing the population close to one hundred inhabitants. The Yodogō families reigned over all of them.

Other additions included a display platform for the North Korean national flag, a movie theater, a library, and special housing for guests. In North Korea, it is customary to add the word "palace" (*kunjon*) to the names of certain buildings. For example, Pyongyang has a "Student Youth Palace" and a "People's Cultural Palace." The Student Youth Palace is simply a space for extracurricular activities for youths, with a gymnasium and special education programs for gifted children, but it still earns the grandiose name of "palace." In this sense, it was quite fitting to refer to the village as a "palace" as well.

The system inside this palace-village was unique and luxurious. The Yodogō group could use foreign currency in their special store, but they could also shop without any money at all. All they needed to do was inform the shop clerk, and a few days later the items they requested would be delivered. Rice, vegetables, beef, pork, chicken, eggs, salt, sugar—they didn't even have to request these, as a fixed ration of each was delivered each week. The rice was the same superb type presented to the Japanese imperial family during the prewar colonial period; Kim Il Sung ate it every day. The pork and beef were delivered in large uncut 10 kg (22 lb) portions, and the chickens were ordinarily delivered whole, with only their feathers and heads removed. The men have told me in recent years that because of this they became skilled in butchering meat. They surprised me with the story of how even the children could grill their own meat and steaks. But cooking was not a daily chore. The only time the women cooked was on weekends or during holidays, when they entertained themselves by making their own ice cream or baking cakes, bread, and cookies. Otherwise all their meals were prepared by the professional chefs in the dining hall kitchen.

Besides their weekly rations of meat and eggs, the village was provided with daily necessities, groceries and cooking spices as well as extras such as coffee, cigarettes, and convenience goods. Once the store was built, there was easy access to all sorts of Japanese goods as well, such as instant food, Japanese cooking spices, confectioneries, and luxury items. The only goods they have ever mentioned as hard to get were things like Japanese sweet bean paste, dried sour plums, feminine hygiene products, and condoms. Even so, they were always careful to put on a face of nostalgia for former days when their old friends visiting from Japan brought them souvenirs and food gifts—in order to conceal from me the real standard of living they enjoyed back at the "palace."

They received salaries and generous fringe benefits from the national government, though not in return for work they performed. It wouldn't be going too far to say they were being paid to continue their own theoretical studies and political activities. As they wrote in their memoirs, "We received a daily stipend before we started working, and it was higher than the average salary in North Korea. We put away a lot of money every month in savings." They paid no medical expenses, no rent, no educational fees, and no grocery bills. The only thing for which they needed their own money was luxury goods, so they had little need for cash. Naturally, they put most of their salaries into savings.

In public, until recently, the Yodogō group has always maintained that they earned their living working as Japanese teachers and translators. In fact, however, they did very little such work. They did occasionally have a political charge to give some special instruction in native Japanese pronunciation or to give instruction in basic Korean and ideology to people who came from Japan for various purposes. Their most frequent work of this type, however, was translation. They translated from Korean into Japanese, or they edited documents already written in Japanese; they also translated or summarized in Korean an assortment of Japanese articles and other documents. Their services were mainly used by the Party's Information bureau.

The village economy operated under a strange version of the principle of supply and demand. In short, they had only to demand, and the Party supplied. They could get anything they wanted with no effort on their part. They lived in a world of "your wish is our command." This system of supply and demand was not limited to material goods and food items, either: it included their housing and work spaces, entertainment costs, work expenses, even the women obtained under "Operation Marriage." They praised this distortion as a "communist society." The Party's generosity was the true practice of "communism," and their village was a model for the "communist ideology" of "North Korean socialism." For them, their palace-village was in truth the "paradise on earth" that North Korean propaganda so often claimed for its social-ist society. They did not realize that they alone were benefiting from this version of supply and demand, and, even if they had noticed, they would have shrugged it off as a natural situation, because they had been chosen and everything they did was "for the people." A perverted ideal controlled them. Strangely, however, they never made any public statements about their palace as a real model of communist ideology in socialism or as "heaven on earth." For some reason, they wished to keep their living arrangements strictly secret.

Why should it be necessary to keep "heaven on earth" a secret? And why were they granted such a high status, with special protected privileges and a luxurious lifestyle? The answer lies squarely with their winning of the trust and instruction of the "Great Leader," Kim Il Sung.

Above all else, Kim believed they would be the ones to achieve the revolution in Japan. The Yodogō men had his direct confidence as "the only persons who could convert Japan to the ideology of Kim Il Sung." Because they were the men who would raise the revolution in Japan under the flag of the North Korean Labor Party, the "Great Leader" had also advised that they should not live in the style of other North Koreans, but surrounded by a Japanese environment and lifestyle. In order for them to effectively slip unnoticed into Japan and engage in subversive activities, they had to be trained and disciplined in an environment with the same living standards as Japan. Once this advice had been given, the village was no longer just the residence of the Yodogō group, but also the headquarters of the Japan campaign, and its expansion and manage-ment was kept under total secrecy. After this purpose had been clearly defined, the secret could not be allowed to leak.

Agents involved in the activist project referred to the little Japa-nese village in the outskirts of Pyongyang as the "Japanese Village of the Revolution." Of course, there is no indication of the existence of this palace-village on any map sold anywhere in North Korea.

A typical day in the village originally started out early with a wake-up call, "Get up!" Everyone leapt out of bed when the person with whistle duty that day blew loudly. Morning exercise, then a quick wash, raising the red flag, a song in praise of Kim Il Sung, breakfast, and study.

After the wives arrived, the early morning shout of "Get up!" was discontinued, but otherwise the daily routine was largely unchanged: rise at six, go running, breakfast, meeting, study, short nap after lunch, more exercise such as a game of soccer, study, evening meal in the dining hall, after dinner some entertainment such as games or television, possibly more study time for those who wished it, then bed. Even now, their morning routine of exercise, flag raising, and a chorus of songs in praise of Kim Il Sung continues unchanged.

They were often at a loss for things to do for entertainment. Early on, they played cards, charades, and word association games, anything they could think of. They learned a Korean version of bridge and played it often. And hide-and-seek—sometimes when they were in the middle of a game of hide-and-seek in the guest house, the sound of a sudden female scream would ring out across the village, embarrassing all of them. The women attendants would scream with surprise at finding a fully grown man hiding under a desk or in a closet where no one was supposed to be.

They touch on their daily lives in the village in their memoirs. Of course, they are careful not to reveal any details about the village itself.

Among the attendants was a young woman named Chunsim. Wakabayashi Moriaki wrote:

> Chunsim—in Chinese characters, her name meant "heart of spring." She really did have a feeling of spring about her, unself-conscious about her beauty and cheerful good health. She is a vivid figure in our memories of the early period, a youthful North Korean woman working for a short while as an attendant in the dining hall (a waitress, cook's helper, and hostess, all-in-one). She was a model of hard-working North Korean women. One time, the paths around the guest house were being paved, and we were helping the groundskeepers mix the cement. We were totally unaccustomed to this kind of work and were making a clumsy job of it. We didn't have the knack for it yet, and we were panting and sweaty. Korean workers can mix cement and gravel at a high speed. And the mix gets heavier as you add more water. We didn't do too badly to start with, but we started falling further behind as our backs grew tired, our arms started shaking, and we ran out of breath. Seeing this from behind, Chunsim grew annoyed, grabbed a shovel, and wedged herself in among us. "What is this girl doing?" I wondered, and then she started

moving her shovel at an unbelievable speed. "I can't beat that!" I thought and stood and watched in amazement....Chunsim was such a dedicated girl. She was an attendant for these youngsters from Japan. It must have been dull work for a girl of marriageable age. But she never showed the slightest discontent and worked hard on our behalf, seldom going home even on Saturdays and Sundays. She was happy if we were happy; she worried when we lost our appetites; she smiled even when we were grumpy. She may have had one day off in a month, though there were times when she worked two or three months straight without any time off at all. (Tamiya et al. 1990, 224–226)

Another story about one of the women working as an attendant in the "village" came from Abe Kimihiro:

When we first came to North Korea, there was a woman named Ri Taewon on the staff of building managers. She lived in a house about 200 meters away from our building, down toward the Daedong River, and she took care of all sorts of things, like the electricity, yardwork, and building maintenance. She had a little girl named Song-Ok, who was about eight....Quite a long time went by, and I had just about forgotten about them, when, in the summer of 1984, I had gone to Pyongyang for some work, and I was eating noodles in a restaurant. There was a group of girls who looked like college students chattering happily at a nearby table. "Girls are the same everywhere," I thought, and kept eating. Then one of the girls came to my table and greeted me: "Hi!" She was very pretty. She had rather large eyes, much like many Japanese, and she had a certain style to her. She wore a blue blouse and a tight skirt, a blue scarf tied around her throat. She stood smiling at me....I suddenly realized she was that little girl, Song-ok....She said she was a third-year student at Kim Il Sung General University. Her friends, still at the other table, were sending significant looks our way. They were giggling....We went for a walk along the banks of the Daedong River, talking as we went. Then we rode in a boat. There were couples in a few of the other boats, but mostly the boaters were pairs of men or women. When some of the fellows said loudly enough to be heard, "Chou-kuman!" (Well done!), I shot back, "You're just envious!" That was such a wonderful afternoon. (Tamiya et al. 1990, 231–233)

These two excerpts sketch out two simple episodes, but in the backdrop we can make out the privileged lifestyle in which they were set. Dwelling on this fact will not advance this story, however. What is clear is that the group was able to enjoy their lives in North Korea, even while they were receiving a thorough education in Kim Il Sung's ideology.

Life in the village was luxurious, but still the ideology checks were performed continuously. Every week, on Saturdays, they met for a session in which they criticized themselves and each other;[1] in addition to the Saturday session, monthly criticism meetings fell on a set date once a month. The weekly meetings always started with a review and self-critique of what each had accomplished that week, followed by every member delivering severe criticisms. Such criticism would continue until the subject accepted what the others were saying. He could defend himself and try to turn away any censure, but then his defense would be subject to attack as well. The degree of the criticism each delivered determined the degree required for his own self-criticism, and giving insufficient or too-lenient criticism was itself subject to criticism. These sessions were certainly never easy. There were times when their instructors observed the sessions.

At one meeting, the subject was *jishusei*, or "independence."[2]

"So what do you think independence is?"
   "It means I think for myself, and I am responsible...."
   "And to whom do you owe responsibility?"
   "To myself...."
   "No. Wrong."
   "???"

"Being responsible means committing yourself to the des-

---

1. The term used for these sessions and for the individual's self-criticism is *sōkatsu*, which in ordinary Japanese generally means a wrap-up meeting at which a group evaluates the success of an activity. However, within the United Red Army, Mori Tsuneo had used the word to demand that each individual present a self-criticism that would meet his vague and unspecified standards, which led the group into violence against members who could not "achieve a *sōkatsu*." Takazawa uses the term in that sense, to mean the group's demand that the individual produce an ideologically correct self-criticism. See chapter 6, note 3.

2. The term *jishu* means "independent" or "autonomous." It is often used interchangeably with *shutai* or *juche*, with the same radical difference in meaning between the Japanese and North Korean usage. It does not mean the autonomy or independence of the individual, but rather the autonomy and independence of the nation.

tiny of Japan and the world, and to the struggle of the working masses."

"..."

"It never means being responsible only for yourself, apart from all else. That's why you are so cool and calm in your liberalism, because you don't understand this point." (Tamiya et al. 1990, 215–216)

This recollection comes from Abe Kimihiro. The boring and abstract discussions of such basic tenets of *juche* ideology could drag on endlessly.

Akagi Shirō also has a story to tell:

So this is what happened one day. We were playing soccer again. I was playing defense, and I was about to lose the ball, so I tried to kick it out of bounds instead. But I misjudged, and I kicked the other guy's leg, not the ball. He fell and got hurt.

At the meeting that week, I was criticized for this.

"In a situation like that, you injured your comrade because your attitude toward him was incorrect," I was told.

"I intended to kick the ball, but instead things turned out like this. I think I didn't have the right attitude toward him," I said, criticizing myself.

However, those listening did not accept this.

"Why do you say you didn't intend to do it? If you say 'intend,' then there isn't a problem with your thinking, right?"

I felt annoyed. If I intended to do it, then why shouldn't I say "intend to"?

They continued.

"At the very least, it's a fact that you kicked without thinking about your comrade. That's a problem, and couldn't you at least correct your perspective toward him by raising the matter and criticizing yourself for it?" (Tamiya et al. 1990, 216–217)

The writer's bewilderment comes through in this passage, but, in fact, in these self-criticism sessions the correct answer always seemed to be that one's sense of comradeship had not been sufficiently ideologized. In this way, these sessions were also part of their ideological education. However, Akagi's conclusion to this story is clear: "After that, I never used the phrase 'intend to' again in a self-criticism meeting" (Tamiya et al. 1990, 217).

And that may be the real "correct answer." At least, if they avoided using the phrase "intend to," they couldn't be criticized by their colleagues at the meeting or have to be reeducated by one of the Party instructors.

Starting at around the time of the above story, the men also organized a lifestyle committee at the direction of the Workers' Party. The task of the committee was to inspect the group's discipline, public morals, personal cleanliness, and sanitation. Needless to say, even here criticism and self-criticism were required, and each was required to search out the ways in which his associates were lacking.

Such was the daily life of the village, and the days and months flowed on steadily. The luxurious palace life of the village contrasted starkly with the unceasing human remolding that paralleled it. Living in their palace, the Yodogō hijackers were to be reborn as subjects exclusively loyal to Kim Il Sung and Kim Jong Il. Of course, they persisted in their conviction that they had freely and independently chosen their conversions. And, according to their own words, though it was far from being so in fact, they were also loyal and devoted to "serving the people." They never realized that, from a more objective viewpoint, they were nothing more than mercenary puppets tied directly to the central power structure of North Korea.

Once they had become loyal marionettes acting at the will of their instructors and the Party, their daily lives and the content of their curriculum changed unexpectedly. Their much-wished for and often repeated request was finally granted: they were to receive military training.

One day, without notice, construction was started in a corner of the village. A section of the hillside along the Daedong River was sliced out and leveled. Sandbags were piled up and targets lined up against the remaining rough-hewn cliff: a firing range.

Their military training began with learning to handle firearms. They were taught how to disassemble and reassemble Kalashnikov AK-47 automatic rifles and hand pistols. After a lecture, they learned how to clean, repair, assemble, and load the guns, and then went on to practice shooting with live ammunition. They faced the targets set up against the sandbags at the base of the cliff, took aim, and fired. One of them would fire several rounds, and then it was the next one's turn. They were excited finally to be holding guns in their own hands. But was this the military training they had been dreaming of for so long? At the very least, their ideology and goals had changed since the days when they were so eager for their training. It had taken years before military training was granted them, though, looking back, it is logical that the Party took so long before allowing it: it would have been far too dangerous to grant military training to men who might revolt at any moment because their ideological and human remolding was still incomplete.

Once the military training started, the curriculum took off. Besides target shooting, they learned techniques for assembling and shooting their guns rapidly and how to use a machine gun. They were divided into small groups, and the groups competed for the highest scores. Tanaka Yoshimi consistently had the best scores of all, and his shooting skills and quick footwork were envied by all of them. Many of them mentioned it later.

Their instructors were from the People's Army, and the training was conducted with full military discipline. Besides gun handling and shooting, they received a complete education in a range of military skills. Gunpowder, timing devices, signal shots, martial arts including taekwondo and karate, knife fighting, rope skills, digging trenches, camping, crawling on the ground, driving skills, machine and tool use—in short, all aspects of guerrilla warfare and sabotage.

There were times when they were bussed late at night to some wilderness far from the Village of the Revolution. In completely unknown territory, they were ordered off the bus, given rough maps with a few landmarks indicated, and told to spread out. The mission was to pass a checkpoint and arrive at their destination by dawn, in an orienteering exercise made to resemble a real combat situation. They had a kit bag, a helmet, a little food and water. The kit bag was full and heavy. They had no lamps but had to rely on the light of the moon and the stars. Sometimes they would have to pass farmyards on the way, moving very quietly. If they tripped or made any noise, they would be heard, and they might get into great trouble if they were reported to the national security police. Even for military training, this was an unusual exercise, since the surrounding households were not informed of their presence. In this sense, it was very much like real combat: they had to be careful of chickens and dogs. If a dog barked, they were lost. There were times when they even had to fight with dogs without raising their own voices above a whisper. To avoid the night dew, they might take a short nap. They couldn't smoke, since the glow would make them visible targets. As daybreak neared, they lingered at a short distance from their destination. The point of the combat orienteering exercise was not a competition in speed. The main requirement was to follow the planned time schedule.

Once one of the men told me how he had reached the destination in good time. It was cold. Even in summer, it could be chilly before dawn. He could make out some shadowy mounds that seemed to resemble sandbags, just the right size for a hiding place. The best way to keep warm was to keep moving, so he pulled his portable shovel out of his pack and dug down a little way near the edge of a mound. The earth was softer than he expected. Before too long he had made a hole large enough to lie in. He lay down with his back to the rest of the mound, pulling a sheet over himself. From a distance, no one would be able to see he was there; digging such holes was part of their basic military training and was used primarily to escape pursuers or to sleep in enemy territory. When he finally lay down in his hole, he felt himself sink down into the soft soil. His hand brushed against something. Cloth. When he strained to see in the pale moonlight...

"What do you think it was?" he asked me. "It was a grave. A new one, too...."

Even now, earth burials are the most common type in North Korea. A persistent Confucian belief holds that the soul remains in the world after death and that cremating the body would destroy the soul. They bury the body, then pile up earth into a mound above it. It was just such a mound he had chosen to burrow into. Cold tremors ran up and down his spine, and his shivering didn't stop for a long time. It wasn't because of the cold.

Once they were accustomed to handling guns and small firearms, the curriculum moved on: code techniques, decoding, Morse code, coding with random number tables, radio communications technology, wire-tapping technology and methods, tailing techniques, language study, and more. They focused particularly on mind–control techniques that would allow them to control a subject without his being aware of it, on how to distinguish between friends and enemies, and on psychological methods of personality analysis. In short, they were training to work as undercover operatives. Of course, they were required to perfectly conceal their commitment to Kim Il Sung's philosophy and their ideological background, and to learn to appear as perfectly ordinary persons on the surface. This was emphasized and studied in parallel with everything else they were learning.

Years later, when the subject of North Korean spies' use of random number tables came up between us, Tamiya said coolly, "The Japanese mass media and security police persist in thinking that there is such a thing as a random number table. They are out of date, stuck in the past." He continued, "Nobody has such a thing or even needs one."

In fact, random number tables, once almost a synonym for North Korean spies, are rarely used anymore because of the danger in carrying such obvious evidence and also because they are unnecessary since the table can be reconstructed when needed. At any rate, no one in the Yodogō group ever carried a random number table in a pocket or briefcase when working: instead, they had the necessary material perfectly memorized. Otherwise the system worked in exactly the same way.

The only tools necessary to reconstruct a random number table from memory are a piece of paper and a pencil, and a simple memorized slogan or phrase. A set rule applies a corresponding number to each of the letters in the phrase, and a second rule reorders the numbers. Another rule adds a further layer of change with addition or subtraction, creating a simple random number table. A more complex table can be made with further operations using a slide rule or more additions and subtractions. The simple table prevailed, since the contents of their minds could not be seen, and any physical evidence could be destroyed immediately. In addition, they didn't all use the same table, either. It didn't matter if the enemy broke the code for a given message: the ciphering methods in other messages would be different, and even the underlying phrases or slogans could differ based on the season or whether the message was sent in an even or odd month. Whatever the process had involved, the re-created table made it possible to decipher coded short-wave radio messages sent from Pyongyang.

This more modern technique was included in the special education the Yodogō men and women received in their village. The wives relied heavily on this technique in later years when they went to Japan to carry out undercover missions. All of the women's orders were sent in short-wave radio bursts of code (called A1, A2, and A3, depending on whether the code was a modified Morse code, standard Morse code or spoken numbers, or embedded inside a regular broadcast item, respectively), and the women never carried any actual decoding tables with them. Just as Tamiya commented, it is easy to see that the Japanese media and security forces were out of date, stuck in the past.

The curriculum of the classes conducted at the Village of the Revolution consisted entirely of undercover operative techniques. Just as the existence of the "village" had to be kept secret, nothing they were learning could be revealed. They couldn't even reveal that they had been studying these techniques. And by faithfully making it their first priority to keep this training secret, they made progress toward taking on duties as perfect agents.

Snow is falling, piling up. They have finally finished scraping the snow off the road, neatly mounding it on both sides so cars and other vehicles have no problems passing. The village sits on top of a hill. The road slopes gently, but, once the snow freezes into ice, tires slip and the road is very dangerous.

When they have caught their breath after the day's completion of their regular winter duty, an instructor brings a message. Tamiya greets him politely and is told there will be a presentation ceremony in the afternoon. Gifts have arrived from Great Leader Kim Il Sung and Dear Leader Comrade Kim Jong Il. Like the snow shoveling, this is an annual winter activity. Every year since they entered into the direct confidence of Kim Il Sung, they have received generous and auspicious presents during the end of the year gift-giving season.

They also invariably receive gifts on February 16, Kim Jong Il's birthday, and on April 15, Kim Il Sung's: luxurious, rare items and delicacies from around the world. Kim Jong Il likes to hunt, and occasionally a trophy (a stag's head) or a brace of ducks is included.

It was their custom to return this generosity with songs and poems celebrating the Kims and their birthdays, paintings, and ornamental items. But these were not the true gifts they were required to present: the real gifts they had to offer Kim Il Sung and Kim Jong Il were "peace and happiness." Their complete loyalty gave "peace"; the outcomes of their undercover operations created "happiness." The first time I visited North Korea, in the winter of 1990, Tamiya seemed a little despondent, saying he felt inadequate. He must have been expressing his shame at being unable to deliver the outcomes that were expected of him.

Gifts from Kim Il Sung and Kim Jong Il—in addition to being gifts from the men known as "Great Leader" and "Leader Comrade," they were also gifts from the supreme powers of the North Korean nation, and even the message reporting such a delivery required a formal bow. When gifts arrived, a formal presentation ceremony was held in the palace reception room. Each of the Yodogō members would be called forward to stand in a row, starting with Tamiya. After the instructor delivered a few conventional words in praise of Kim Il Sung and Kim Jong Il, he always told them these were tokens of the special regard in which the "Great Leader and Father" and the Party held them. He made a very deep bow to the pictures of father and son Kim hanging on the wall in front of them and addressed a speech to the portraits describing the honor he felt in conducting this presentation ceremony on behalf of the "Great Leader and Father." Then he turned to face Tamiya and the others with great dignity, raised the list of gifts to eye level, and slowly read out the contents. Besides an abundance of prime-quality rice and glutinous rice, the list included

    1 whole beef carcass
    20 chickens
    1 whole mutton carcass
    Mochi rice cakes
    10 boxes Japanese mandarin oranges
    Sea bream, salted salmon, sea kelp, and other seafood
    Herring roe
    Cheese, butter, yoghurt, and other dairy products
    Russian caviar
    Japanese confections
    Canned goods
    Japanese rice wine, cognac, ginseng wine, beer, and so on
    Several kinds of French wine
    Clothing
    Other

Every Japanese product traditional for the celebration of the New Year was included. Naturally, since these items were given especially for the season, they were separate from the daily-use goods. Compared to an average Japanese household's New Year season, it was luxurious. This they owed to Kim Il Sung's decree that they live a Japanese lifestyle.

These Japanese products, groceries, and prepared food items were all procured by organizations such as Chōsen Sōren, the official North Korean organization in Japan, and transported to Wonsan from Niigata port on Japan's northwest coast. Once the goods had arrived in Pyongyang, they were allocated by Party cadres in the special section that oversaw the Yodogō group. Years later, an infuriated cadre of the central committee of Chōsen Sōren once complained bitterly to me: "We didn't ask them to come; why do they get to live so extravagantly? They came to someone else's country of their own choice, but they live in luxury. Isn't the Japanese nation ashamed of them? Can the Japanese people forgive them for their behavior? And why are the Japanese media so interested in this bunch anyway? Everybody knows how hard the economy is in this country. Maybe they're actually enemies of the people!"

Not all the goods transported from Japan were intended for the Yodogō group. Many expensive groceries and luxury goods were brought in for Kim Il Sung and other high-ranking cadres in the Central Committee of the Workers' Party. Certainly much of it must have seemed like needless luxuries to those whose duty it was to procure the goods, giving them a good reason to be angry. And, from a material point of view, the Yodogō group lived very well. They were granted a distorted level of luxury well above what the average Japanese experiences.

Japanese mandarin oranges are highly prized in North Korea. The cold climate prohibits their cultivation, and, besides their food value, mandarins are treasured for the medicinal value of their skins, dried and taken as herbal medicine.

The group once saw the wife of one of the village workers pick a mandarin peel out of the trash and quietly wrap it in paper. When someone asked why she had done so, she answered in a fearful and faint voice, "We have a sick child in the family; I wish to use it to make medicine. Please forgive me; I won't do it again."

This incident made the Yodogō men and their wives decide they would not throw away the peelings of the mandarins they ate, but instead give them to the "North Korean people." Since each of their households received a copious amount of mandarin oranges, they soon collected a big pile of skins. They believed they were giving charity to the "people."

I don't want to say anything more about this episode except that they believed they were acting on behalf of the "people."

The seasons continued to pass over the Japanese village, and several winters and summers went by. They had obtained wives; children had soon added to the village population. The ideological conversions were all but complete. There were no traces left of the former Red Army Faction. The Yodogō hijackers had been remade into a foreign legion of mercenary puppets, completely obedient to Kim Il Sung and the Workers' Party. In the village, they criticized the beliefs they had held during the student movement and while they were active in the Red Army Faction: "We did not believe in the people, and our actions were not based on the people." They formed a new party, the Independent Revolution Party (Jishu Kakumeitō),[3] on the instructions of Kim Il Sung and the Party. Tamiya was its leader, and, although Kim Il Sung's ideology lay at the core of their belief and it was a mere puppet of the Workers' Party, its membership was limited to Japanese people. And, with the establishment of this new party, the Yodogō group was given a new mission.

---

3. The name of their new party uses *jishu* rather than *juche*, in keeping with the basic principle of disguising their relationship to the North Korean state and presenting themselves as an independent Japanese group.

They had to recruit and train Japanese nationals who would become the backbone of the new party and who would in turn recruit and train more new members. There were no longer any obstacles to their going abroad to engage in these activities. A plan was drawn up secretly by the Yodogō members and their Party handlers.

From the late winter of 1979 until the following spring, groups of two or three men and women at a time went to the special waiting room at Sun'an Airport for undercover operatives. They were always with several instructors, and each man and woman flew to Moscow accompanied by an instructor. From Moscow they continued to Vienna. Then, as now, Vienna was the base for many of North Korea's missions; in the 1980s, the Austrian police authorities complained to North Korean officials about the flagrantly illegal activities of its operatives. From Vienna, they spread out into different areas in Europe to conduct their operations, starting with Madrid, Spain.

From this point on, they were directly in charge of "Operation Madrid," that is, the plan for recruiting more Japanese to their cause.

CHAPTER THIRTEEN

Disappearances in Madrid

Madrid. From the airplane window, the city appeared as suddenly as a mirage in the middle of the desolate red-brown plateau of the central Iberian Peninsula. The stark contrast between the sunlight so brilliantly reflected by the rocky landscape and the shadows cast by the olive groves extending to the horizon emphasized the cruel contrast between life and death. After Tamiya Takamaro died suddenly in the Pyongyang winter twenty-five years after the Yodogō hijacking, something made me go on a journey to retrace the Yodogō members' paths in Europe. Madrid was the scene of their first overseas operation.

Many of the young Japanese who wander around Europe end their travels in Madrid. Carrying everything they own stuffed in a rucksack, these backpackers make their way to northern Europe with cheap tickets on the Trans-Siberian Railway,[1] then travel through Paris, Vienna, and

---

1. For many years the Japan-Soviet Friendship Society provided regular travel service from Japan to Europe for just a few hundred dollars. After paying for the trip at the society's Tokyo office, travelers took a small ship from Yokohama to Nakhodka, a port in the Soviet Far East on the Sea of Japan, and then transferred to a train that took them north to Khabarovsk and then to the main Trans-Siberian Railway line for the three-day train trip to Moscow. From there they could travel to European countries by train. The small port of Nakhodka had become the entry port from Japan to the Soviet Union after Vladivostok became the headquarters for the Soviet Far Eastern Fleet in the 1950s and was closed to foreigners. I took that trip myself in 1964 but had to fly from Khabarovsk to Moscow because the conflict between the Soviet Union and the People's Republic of China had disrupted train traffic over part of the route. In later years, travelers were able to fly from Japan to Khabarovsk to connect to the Trans-Siberian Railway or a flight to Moscow, rather than taking the small ship.

elsewhere before resting from their travels in this sultry land. To the east lies the Mediterranean; in the south, the Straits of Gibraltar; farther on, Morocco and Algeria. It is the perfect place to end a mini-adventure.

The Yodogō operatives arrived in the late winter of 1979 and the early spring of the following year to carry out the plan they called "Operation Madrid." Their targets were these young backpackers and exchange students from Japan. Much of the work fell to the "brides of the Great Leader," that is, to the Yodogō wives. The wives were deemed more suited for the work of acquiring Japanese targets because they seemed harmless and softer than the men, whose names and faces were also better known. Spain was the first arena of the wives' overseas activities since leaving Japan for North Korea. Though they stayed for different lengths of time in Madrid, the women left traces of their stays there. When Fukui Takako, Konishi Takahiro's wife, visited the Japanese consulate in Geneva to renew her passport, she told the employee who handled her case that she was going to Spain to visit a friend there.

They may have been in Madrid on "business," but the women enjoyed themselves very much. Winter in Madrid was easier and more pleasant by far than in Pyongyang. Two of the women were pregnant with their second children during this time.

The wives' assignment was to approach and become friendly with potential targets. In the terminology of the cult of Kim Il Sung, the work of gathering a target's personal data is called "identity investigation." Using invitations to sightseeing, meals, and dates as their cover, the women would conduct casual-seeming conversations that elicited information such as a target's name, home address, hobbies, extended family, opinions, interest in social issues, educational background, work history, details about siblings and parents, and whether they or any of their relatives were involved in police or security work. All this information would be put together and shared with the waiting men; together they would make a judgment on whether to continue tracking a particular target. These were the initial steps for feeling out new subjects; if they decided at this point to continue their pursuit, the next step was to collect more detailed information to confirm the target's suitability, followed by an introduction to the Yodogō men pretending to be the women's friends or "fiancés." Probably, once a friendship had been established and they had gained the target's trust, one of the women would extend an invitation for them all to go on a "trip" together. And a Japanese traveler would disappear from the city of Madrid, Spain.

In this period, several Japanese people disappeared without a trace from Madrid, Barcelona, and elsewhere in Spain. Their whereabouts could not be determined, despite the families' many reports of missing persons. The Madrid police made investigations as well, but they could find no clues either. The rumors flew—they may have gone over to Algeria or Morocco, been taken somewhere by boat from the port of Cádiz, somehow gotten involved with the Mafia, or become the victims of an organization engaged in the buying and selling of human organs. As time went by and nothing more was heard, the disappearances faded from the public memory.

However, about eight years after they had been so mysteriously spirited away and never heard from again, a shocking fact came to light concerning these missing persons. A letter from Ishioka Tōru, a college student from Sapporo who had gone missing in Spain, suddenly arrived at his family home in Hokkaido. His family was surprised to read what he had written: "For reasons I cannot reveal, I am now living in North Korea." Even an inventive imagination would have difficulty making a direct connection between Spain and North Korea. However, the suspicion that the students who had disappeared in Spain had actually been abducted to North Korea revived interest in their cases. Most surprisingly, Ishioka's letter included the names of other Japanese people also staying in North Korea, all of them people who had disappeared in Europe.

When this letter arrived in Japan, not a single person had yet begun to suspect the involvement of the Yodogō group in this acquisition of Japanese people, or what they called "Operation Madrid." Ishioka's letter arrived in September 1988. Not only was it unknown then in Japan that the Yodogō hijackers were operating overseas, outside of North Korea, but it was also unimaginable. Not even the security authorities grasped the real situation.

On arriving in Madrid, the first task faced by the Yodogō wives, just like all travelers, was to find a place to stay. First they settled on cheap accommodations in the downtown area, such as hostels and *pensións* where poor travelers were likely to gather. Their method for finding places was simple: they chose them out of a guidebook for young travelers from Japan. They were certain to meet young Japanese with little money in such places. They began work on their mission the day they arrived in Madrid.

Next, the wives enrolled in classes at a Spanish-language school for foreigners. They had two motivations for this: first, to become proficient in Spanish; second, to meet Japanese students. The length of the women's stays differed depending on the exact nature of their work. If the mission would be a lengthy one, as it was when they were scouting and abducting targets, they moved into a *pensión* or an apartment to have a base for their maneuvers. They polished the details of their careful plans.

Even today, the trail the Yodogō wives left in Madrid is still clear in some places and in the memories of several people who live there.

Many of these traces are in the area of Madrid called the Centro, near the square of Puerta del Sol (Gate of the Sun). Around this square, between the Convento de las Descalzas Reales and the Telefónica, the central telephone company building, there is an old part of the city, its streets still paved in cobblestones. This is downtown Madrid.

The *pensión* where Ishioka was staying when he disappeared is in this area; the wives stayed there on their first night in Madrid.

I wanted to see for myself the places in which these disappearances took place. I thought I might be able to discover something new by actually being there.

I took the first steps of my Madrid quest in the center of the city, in the Plaza de España. I gave a bow to the statue of the great Cervantes looking down upon Don Quixote and Sancho Panza, and, crossing the street, I slowly walked up the Gran Vía toward the Telefónica building.

Ishioka, the student from Sapporo, arrived in Madrid at the end of April 1980. He stayed at the Hostal de San Pedro, a simple hotel well known among Japanese backpackers. Backpackers find convenient and cheap accommodations using their noses and an informal information network. Without a doubt, Ishioka heard about this *pensión* somewhere on the road.

Traveling with a friend he had met at his part-time job, Ishioka had left Japan in March aboard an Aeroflot jet flying out of Niigata airport to Khabarovsk, then continued to Europe on the Trans-Siberian Railway. This route, both cheap and satisfying to young travelers' thirst for adventure, had been very popular ever since Itsuki Hiroyuki published his best-selling novel *Young Man Heading for the Wilderness* (*Seinen wa kōya o mezasu*; Bungei Shunjū, 1967).

From Moscow, they turned south, passing through Paris and Lyon to the Mediterranean. They arrived in Barcelona from Marseilles on April 13. Ishioka had recently graduated from the department of Animal and Agricultural Sciences at Nihon University with a degree in food economics. Apparently he wanted to learn more about Spain's dairy industry and was particularly interested in techniques for producing cheese and bread.

After arriving in Madrid alone, Ishioka checked into the Hostal de San Pedro, where he happened to meet another young Japanese man, also newly arrived, who was planning on staying in Spain to study Spanish. The two of them, both strangers in an unknown country, instantly became friends. Their meeting was pure coincidence, but it has special meaning because of the mysterious fate that befell both of them: Matsuki Kaoru, the second young man, also disappeared from Madrid in the spring of 1980, at the same time as Ishioka.

The Gran Vía sloped up in a gentle rise. At the top, I turned right, my eyes taking in the entrance to the metro. Now the street sloped gradually down toward the Puerta del Sol. Along the way, I turned left into a narrow street populated by prostitutes even in the daytime. I was looking for the *pensión* where Ishioka stayed while he was in Madrid. And there it was, about halfway down the street: the old Hostal de San Pedro. It was no longer a *pensión* but apartments; the travel habits of young Japanese seemed to have changed. The Hostal de San Pedro used to be very attractive to the hippie crowd, but, over the years, the number of guests had dwindled, and now young people apparently preferred to stay at more stylish and convenient hotels. The first floor of the building was still occupied by a pharmacy that seemed to be struggling to survive, but the building owner, Pedro Ventisca, had long ago closed the *pensión*.

To get in, someone inside had to buzz open the door for me. I didn't know anyone living there, but I tried ringing the bell anyway, and the resident who finally answered agreed to my request for information. Entering the building, I found a stairwell rising around its open center. As I climbed the spiraling stairs, running my hand on the railing along the wall, I was suddenly certain that this was the right place, the one I had been looking for. I had, in fact, visited other *pensión*s and apartment buildings before this one, but none of them matched the descriptions I had of the San Pedro. Here, the tenant with whom I spoke told me this used to be a *pensión* and gave me the owner's telephone number. I called the eponymous Señor Pedro.

Pedro did not remember much at all. It had, after all, been more than ten years since the disappearances. He told me over the phone that he had thrown away all the records from those days, but he did remember clearly the Japanese foreign student who left all his belongings in his room and never turned up again to collect them. Although it was not unusual for guests to leave their luggage behind, for some reason the fact that this was a student from Japan seemed to strike Pedro as odd. Since no one ever claimed the luggage, he threw it all away. The student who disappeared from this *pensión* was Matsuki Kaoru, the new friend Ishioka had made in Madrid. We know Ishioka stayed there because of

Figure 13.01. Staircase at Hostal San Pedro in Madrid. Photo by Takazawa Kōji.

a postcard he sent to Japan soon after his arrival: the *pensión* links the two victims.

Matsuki was in Madrid to study Spanish. After graduating from high school in Kumamoto, he had entered Nagasaki Junior College of Foreign Languages and then transferred to the faculty of foreign languages at Kyoto Business University, where he majored in Spanish. When he finished there, he had continued on to graduate school at Kyoto University of Foreign Studies. While he was in Kyoto, he was sometimes asked to do some translating in Spanish. Because of this experience, he thought a visit to Spain would be the perfect chance to polish his language skills. He remained determined in the face of his family's objections, and, finally, after he promised to return in one year, they agreed that he could go. So, at the beginning of April 1980, he arrived at Barajas Airport in Madrid, his heart filled with anticipation. At the time of his departure, his father, until then the most adamant in his opposition to the trip, gave Matsuki some money to help him in his studies.

He had come as a language student, so his lifestyle in this foreign country was not a luxurious one. To begin, he looked for a cheap place to stay using a guidebook for backpackers; he ended up at the Hostal San Pedro, which catered to long-term guests. The *pensión* was in a very good location in the center of Madrid, just off the Gran Vía, near the Puerta del Sol and the Plaza Mayor; not too far away lay the Museo del Prado. Most visitors to Madrid spend at least one afternoon wandering around this area. Matsuki may well have had plans to find work in the area by translating for and guiding Japanese visitors.

After leaving the Hostal de San Pedro, I went to see the clock tower and the fountain in Puerta del Sol. Then I returned the way I had come earlier, in order to visit one more *pensión*, the Amadeo. This was once a very popular *pensión* among young Japanese travelers to Madrid, located just behind the central telephone company across the Gran Vía. The sign was still up, but this *pensión* had also closed. Fortunately, the owner, Señora Maria, still lived there. She remembered well the events of that spring. The door opened automatically when I rang the bell; I rode up to her floor on the old-fashioned elevator. Maria was waiting in her apartment with the guest register from 1980. At that time, the place had always been full of young Japanese travelers. Maria was a big fan of Japan, and even now she lived surrounded by the many souvenirs of Japan sent to her by her guests after they returned home. She looked happy as she talked about the young people from those days. One thing seemed to remind her of the next as she continued to talk.

I slowly turned the pages of the guest register spread open on the table and came across some familiar names. Among the people who had checked into the Amadeo on April 20, 1980, I found a Mori Yoriko and a Kuroda Sakiko. Since hotel registers had to be reported to the city

Nombre	Apellidos	Número del parte	Fecha de entrada	Fecha de salida	Lugar a donde se dirige	Observaciones
▬	▬	691946	11-4-80	14-4-80	Barcelona	ME 3532549
▬	▬	691947	11-4-80	16-4-80	Barcelona	ME 8098689
▬	▬	691922	11-4-80	19-4-80	Malaga	ME 5982915
▬	▬	691925	11-4-80	20-5-80	Madrid	ME 7458957
▬	▬	691956	19-4-80	23-4-80	San Sebastian	ME 8946804
▬	▬	691957	19-4-80	23-4-80	Bilbao	ME 8345656
▬	▬	691950	20-4-80	22-4-80	Barcelona	ME 0012297
▬	▬	691951	20-4-80	22-4-80	Barcelona	ME 0012658
▬	▬	691952	20-4-80	23-4-80	Granada	ME 8968983
▬	▬	691953	20-4-80	23-4-80	Granada	ME 7334891
SAKIKO	KURODA	691954	20-4-80	23-4-80	Granada	ME 3480422
YORIKO	MORI	691455	20-4-80	23-4-80	Granada	ME 4317997
▬	NINIRA	691958	23-4-80	24-4-80	Granada	ME 0093021

Figure 13.02. Registry from Hostal Amadeo in Madrid with the names of Kuroda Sakiko and Mori Yoriko. Photo by Takazawa Kōji.

Figure 13.03. Sign at Hostal Amadeo in Madrid. Photo by Takazawa Kōji.

authorities, Maria had kept hers in a very neat and orderly hand. Here and there, city inspection stamps appeared. Besides guests' names, the register showed the dates of arrival and departure, passport numbers, and next destination. According to this register, Mori Yoriko and Kuroda Sakiko (the wives of Tamiya Takamaro and Wakabayashi Moriaki, respectively) had arrived on the same day, stayed three nights, and then left for the city of Granada on the twenty-third. This was in the period when the Yodogō wives were staying in Madrid and near the time when Ishioka and Matsuki disappeared.

For a short moment in April 1980, the paths of Ishioka, recently arrived in Europe via the Trans-Siberian Railway, and Matsuki, just beginning his Spanish studies in Madrid, crossed the path of these Yodogō wives that trailed back from Spain to Pyongyang via Moscow and Vienna. And what exactly happened in that moment? A chance meeting is not always a moment of serendipity. For Ishioka and Matsuki, meeting the Yodogō wives meant the beginning of a terrible misfortune.

Ishioka's footsteps in Madrid do not tell the whole story of his disappearance. After the arrival of his letter from North Korea, by coincidence it became apparent that Ishioka and his travel companion had encountered two of the Yodogō wives in Barcelona, before they even got to Madrid.

If the Amadeo's guest register had included a column showing where guests had traveled from before arriving in Madrid, it would surely have shown that Mori Yoriko and Kuroda Sakiko had come to Madrid from Barcelona.

The incident actually began on April 13, when Ishioka and his friend arrived in Barcelona from Marseilles.

A photograph provided the first lead toward unraveling this story. The photo, taken by chance, gives us an insight into Ishioka's disappearance. In it, he is sitting on a park bench with two women. Found in the mid-1990s, the picture had been taken by Ishioka's travel companion. He had until then completely forgotten about the women in the picture or even that he had taken the picture at all. He was reminded only when the police in Japan finally started reinvestigating the disappearances years later.

Unexpected facts came to light when the photo became public. First, the women sitting on the bench with Ishioka were two of the Yodogō wives, Mori Yoriko and Kuroda Sakiko. The picture had been taken in mid-April of 1980. Thanks to vigorous research conducted by members of the media, we even know that the bench they sat on was at Barcelona's zoo. What else does this photo tell us about Ishioka's disappearance? It and the circumstances around it tell us that the story is not as simple as his arriving in Madrid, meeting the Yodogō wives for the first time, unwittingly becoming a political target of the wives who worked diligently to deepen the friendship, and then being carried off to North Korea. That story, widely disseminated in the media, is not as complex as the story of Ishioka's disappearance suggested by the photograph. In the end, the snapshot provided further details of the abduction of a Japanese person from Spain.

Ishioka and his friend spent two nights in Barcelona, passing the days seeing the sights.

Near Barcelona's França Station lies the Ciutadella Park. In one corner of the park is Barcelona Zoo, famous in particular for its white gorilla. Ishioka and his friend went to the zoo on their last day in the city to see the gorilla. Could it have been by sheer coincidence that they met two mysterious Japanese women also visiting the zoo? The women said they were studying in Barcelona. The four of them walked around the zoo together for a while, chatting a little, but the women did not say much. They soon parted company; the men did not have any time left.

若林佐喜子　　　森順子　　　石岡亨さん

Figure 13.04. From left to right, Kuroda Sakiko, Mori Yoriko, and Ishioka Tōru at Barcelona Zoo. From personal collection of Takazawa Kōji.

They had now been traveling together constantly since they left Japan, and this was the day they had decided they would go their own separate ways for a while. After a month on the road, they had become used to traveling. Each of them had places he wanted to visit and felt confident enough to continue on his own. Ishioka planned to board a train and depart from Spain that day. Before they said good-bye to the women, the men decided they should take a picture as a memento of the afternoon. The women were at first reluctant to sit for a photo but relented when Ishioka said it was for a keepsake. They took turns taking pictures of each other sitting on the bench. Ishioka is smiling directly toward the camera in the picture his friend took; the camera belonged to the friend as well. This is the lucky circumstance that brought the picture to light more than ten years later and began to reveal the true facts of the story.

Ishioka and his friend had agreed to meet one month later in Lyon, France. Ishioka's friend saw him off at the train station, and they parted. But, for some reason, instead of following his plan, Ishioka went to Madrid. Perhaps he suddenly changed his mind. Perhaps his change of plans, his change of mind, was just a spur-of-the-moment coincidence.

But, considering how the Yodogō group operated, considering the type of thinking that is shaped by Kim Il Sung and *juche* ideology, considering the way such North Korean action groups operate, I do not believe Ishioka's change of plans were the result of any coincidence. There can be no doubt the Yodogō wives had interfered.

Now, how can we get at the truth of the circumstances of this incident?

Part of the strategy of the Yodogō group's Operation Madrid included creating opportunities to meet as many Japanese travelers as possible. Therefore, several of them stayed at various cheap *pensiones*, and several attended language schools for the same reason. In addition, they were under orders to "go sightseeing." Visiting tourist spots was an efficient way to meet many Japanese quickly. In addition, not only could they quickly pick out and start conversations with potential targets, if they were going to claim to be living in Spain, they had to show they knew something about such places. This is why, even today, many of the Yodogō wives know more about Spain's tourist spots than most ordinary travelers do.

One of the wives, Uomoto Tamiko, claimed years later in her interview with me that she had never been to Spain or Portugal (see chapter 10). But, on a short visit to Japan in 1980, she apparently described to a neighbor in detail the Spanish landscape and Spanish bullfights.

The women really did visit many sightseeing spots. But, of course, their purpose in repeatedly visiting places with many Japanese visitors was not to see the sights. Had an observer remained to watch a given site for a few days in a row, he might have glimpsed the wives several times. So it is not so strange that the two women were wandering around Barcelona Zoo alone, even if a zoo seems like an odd place to go sightseeing.

According to Ishioka's friend, that morning Ishioka had checked the train schedule for his train time again and again. It's possible that he had already been invited by the women even then, since it is not necessarily the case that their meeting at the zoo was their first. According to the friend, Ishioka had left for the station but had come back again, saying he had gotten the time wrong after all. They used the extra time together to go to the zoo. It is very possible their encounter with the women in the zoo was no coincidence.

It seems likely the women had already given Ishioka the address of the Hostal Amadeo at this point. He wasn't able to stay at the Amadeo because that day it was already booked completely full by the Japanese travelers with whom it was so popular. But perhaps the wives did not feel it was necessary for him to stay there.

Anyway, why were the women in Barcelona that day? It is probably more accurate to say they were in Barcelona on a day trip from their base in Madrid than that they were traveling through on their way to Madrid. At that time, Mori and Kuroda were not the only Yodogō wives staying in Madrid charged with sightseeing missions in various places. Perhaps they had come to Barcelona because the target acquisition was not going very well in Madrid. More likely, they had another reason for visiting Barcelona Zoo: it was a contact location to meet the Yodogō men or a Workers' Party cadre running the operation, to pass on information or receive new instructions. In fact, a zoo is an ideal location for a secret meeting.

If such was the case, it is understandable why the two women made a strange impression on Ishioka's friend when they met. It was in fact Ishioka and his friend who initiated the contact with the women. Ishioka did not know the women well enough to introduce them to his friend, which may be one reason for the feelings of awkwardness that resulted. For the wives, the unexpected encounter with Ishioka and his friend probably came at a time when their actions should have been a secret and unobserved by anyone. If Ishioka was already a target at that point, the wives had every reason to be cautious about this friend who had been with him all the way from Japan. That the situation had flustered the women is clear: the men had addressed them, when it was they who should initiate all contacts; they were very quiet, not talking much at all; and, finally, they actually allowed their picture to be taken, something strictly forbidden when they were on mission. The women must have wished for nothing more than to end the awkward situation and part from the men as soon as possible.

Ishioka met the women again after he arrived in Madrid. Or perhaps, the women accompanied him from Barcelona. From this time, the women entered the next stage of operation with Ishioka: that is, collecting detailed personal information about him. According to the register at the Amadeo, the women were planning on going to Granada next. However, their names do not appear in any of the hotel or *pensión* registers in Granada. Perhaps they were engaged in another mission as well as actively gathering information about Ishioka.

The other mission the Yodogō wives were carrying out was finding a place to live for their planned extended stay in Madrid. They were lucky enough to find a place very soon. In the beginning of May, about a week after they checked out of the Amadeo, the Yodogō group signed a contract for a small but neat apartment in the city. The monthly rent was about 60,000 yen (roughly $240 at the 1980 exchange rate) for a one-bedroom apartment with a separate dining room and kitchen. This apartment became the women's residence and functioned as their base of operations. Many of the Japanese people visiting Madrid in this time period were invited there.

According to the testimony of visitors to the apartment, the women invited young Japanese travelers and served food and drinks they had prepared themselves. They chatted or played cards or other games. Guests would come every evening, leaving around 10:00 p.m. to return to their various hotels. Among them were Ishioka and Matsuki.

One visitor tells a story of being invited by Mori around the middle of May to go on a trip for a few days. Mori had said her fiancé was coming to Vienna on a business trip. Four of them were going to meet him there and then take a tour around Eastern Europe.

The four already slated for the trip included herself, Kuroda, Ishioka, and Matsuki. Of course, the women were "brides of the Premier," so the story of the fiancé was a falsehood. She might not even have been referring to Tamiya, her husband. She could have been talking about any one of the Yodogō men or a Workers' Party cadre running the operation.

The four of them set out from Madrid in mid-May. It was the beginning of a journey through Vienna to North Korea for the two men and two women. Ishioka and Matsuki have not been seen since.

Around the time the four were headed to Vienna and Eastern Europe from Madrid, Ishioka's friend spent a day waiting for him in a hotel in Lyon, but Ishioka never showed up, nor did he send any messages. He should have been able to find the hotel, since it was the same one they had stayed in and liked so much on their first stay in Lyon, barely a month earlier. Although he continued to hope for Ishioka's arrival, eventually the friend gave up. Worried, he returned to Japan alone. After his return, he waited in vain to hear from Ishioka again.

Soon after, an airmail letter was delivered to Ishioka's family home in Hokkaido. It was postmarked June 3, from Vienna. The note was in Ishioka's handwriting, but, strangely, it said, "I am going to Spain next." His family felt reassured when they received the letter that he was continuing to enjoy his travels. However, I have my doubts about both the message and the postmarked date.

Matsuki's family in Kumamoto was becoming increasingly alarmed as time went by and they did not hear from him. They had received nothing but a few simple postcards, giving his address and telephone number in Madrid. Worried, his father contacted the Japanese embassy in Madrid and asked them to check on Matsuki. Eventually, even the Madrid police became involved, but nothing could be found out about Matsuki's whereabouts.

Neither of the fathers ever saw their sons again; both fathers have since died without knowing what had become of them.

My time in Spain was also running out, but there were still many things I wanted to do before I left. One was to look up the Spanish-language school the wives had attended during their stays in Madrid to see if there was anyone who had been around then who could tell me anything. In this, I was luckier than I expected: I found a teacher who had taught the wives at a language school on the Gran Vía until the mid-1980s. He remembered Mori quite well, he said, since her Spanish had been fluent enough for her to skip the beginner's class and go straight to the midlevel group.

The surprising fact here is that the women continued to visit Madrid until at least the mid-1980s. Madrid remained an important base for the Yodogō group's activities even after Operation Madrid was over. There is other information that supports this, namely, the fact that Shibata Yasuhiro, another of the Yodogō men, is known to have stayed in Spain frequently. We know that Shibata had been in Spain several times right up until he was arrested in Japan in May 1988, on charges of smuggling and carrying a forged passport. He had given out business cards printed with the name of the company he claimed to be working for, "Columbus' Egg."

Shibata's visits to Spain had started around 1979 and continued for about a decade. What do these facts mean?

After meeting with the language instructor, I spent my remaining time in Madrid going through the guest registers at several *pensións*. There were additional missing persons whose cases had been on my mind since I had begun my investigations there. Ishioka and Matsuki were not the only people whom the Yodogō operatives had kidnapped to North Korea from Spain. This I had found out by chance through my exchanges with the group; I was searching for clues about the third and fourth missing persons.

But my time had run out. It took thirty minutes to get to the airport even in a fast taxi. That day, I was going to London to continue looking into the events around the disappearance of yet another Japanese exchange student, who had vanished in London: Arimoto Keiko. I had to leave off my investigations in Spain, though a description of my search in Madrid would not be complete without at least mentioning that I did not find everything I was looking for there.

The Iberian Airlines aircraft took off from Barajas Airport and flew straight into the clouds, without allowing another glimpse of the bright *meseta.*

CHAPTER FOURTEEN

Proof of Life

The letter from Ishioka telling his family he was in North Korea arrived in September 1988. More than eight years had passed since he had left Japan.

Dear All:

I hope this finds you well. I apologize for the anxiety I have caused all this time. Matsuki (a graduate student at Kyoto Foreign Studies University) and I are both well. Along with Arimoto Keiko (from Kobe), whom we met along the way, the three of us are helping each other out and living in Pyongyang. I can't be more explicit, but during our travels in Europe we ended up here in North Korea a long time ago. We basically support ourselves here, but we do receive some support and a small daily stipend for living expenses from the North Korean government. However, the economy is bad, and I have to say it is a hardship to be living here for so long. It's especially difficult to get clothes and educational books, and the three of us are having a hard time. Anyway, I wanted to at least let you know that we are all right, and I am going to entrust this letter to a foreign visitor. At any rate, you can set your hearts at ease because the three of us are doing fine. Please contact Matsuki's family (in Kumamoto) and Arimoto's family [address deleted]. In addition, please thank the person who took care of sending this letter for us.

From your son, Tōru

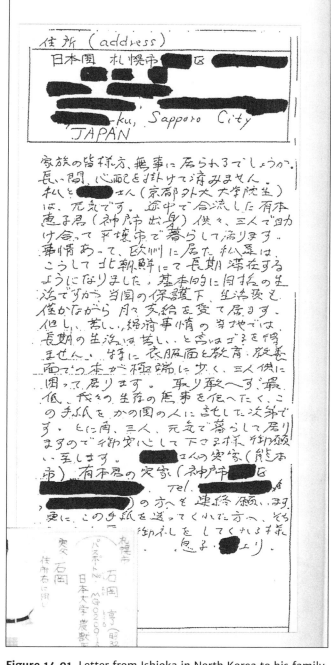

住所 (address)

日本国 札幌市 ▉▉区 ▉▉▉▉▉▉
▉▉▉▉▉▉▉▉▉▉ ▉▉▉▉▉▉▉▉
▉▉▉▉▉▉ -ku, Sapporo City
JAPAN

家族の皆様方、無事に居られるでしょうか。
長い間、心配と御掛けで済みません。
私と▉▉▉エ人（京都外大大学院生）
は、元気です。途中で合流した有本
恵子君（神戸市出身）供々、三人で助
け合って平壌市で暮らして居ります。
事情あって、欧州に居た私達は、
こうして北朝鮮にて長期滞在する
ようになりました。基本的に同様の生
活ですが当国の保護下、生活費も
僅かながら月々支給を受て居ます。
但し、苦しい経済事情の当地では
長期の生活は苦しい、と言はざるを得
ません。特に衣服面と教育・放送
面での本が極端に少く、三人供に
困って居ります。取り敢へず、最
低、我々の生存の無事を伝へたく、こ
の手紙をかの国の人に託した次第で
す。ヒに再、三人、元気で暮らして居り
ますので御安心して下さる様御願
い至します。▉▉エ人の実家（熊本
市）有本君の実家（神戸市▉▉区
▉▉▉▉▉▉▉▉▉▉ Tel.▉▉▉▉▉▉
）の方へ連絡願います。
更に、この手紙を送ってくれた方へ、その
▉▉御礼をしてくれる様、息子▉▉より。

Figure 14.01. Letter from Ishioka in North Korea to his family. Photo by Takazawa Kōji.

Ishioka's family was astounded to receive this letter. That Tōru, of whose whereabouts nothing had been discovered since his disappearance in Spain, should be alive and well in North Korea! No matter how many times they looked the letter over, they couldn't deny that it was in Ishioka's handwriting; even the idiosyncratic use of words and Chinese characters was his own style. The other two names in the letter were unfamiliar, but Ishioka's family used the address he had given to get in touch with Arimoto's family.

Her family in Kobe was bewildered by this sudden phone call from complete strangers in Sapporo. As Ishioka's family explained the circumstances around the call, however, they soon understood that it was in earnest. Arimoto's family had heard nothing from her since 1983, when she had disappeared while studying in London. When Ishioka's family sent them a copy of the letter, they confirmed the photo was of her, and it was her handwriting on the envelope. For Matsuki, the only information the letter gave for his address was Kumamoto City. With some help, they were able to search the local telephone books for Matsuki's home address and telephone number, and they finally contacted his family. They found that Matsuki's family had not heard any news from him either since he disappeared while studying in Spain.

On suddenly finding out that their missing relatives were still alive,

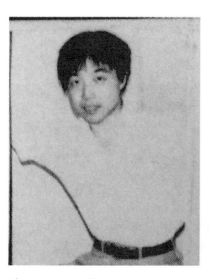 

Figure 14.02. Photos enclosed in letter from North Korea. Ishioka (left), Arimoto Keiko (right). From personal collection of Takazawa Kōji.

after so many years of knowing nothing of their fates, the families felt a moment of relief. But then began a new kind of torment: now they began to suspect that their family members may have been kidnapped by North Korea while studying in Europe. They grew increasingly worried, as they feared that North Korea would never allow people it had abducted to return to Japan. There were no diplomatic relations between Japan and North Korea: neither the families nor the Japanese government had any means by which to confirm or negotiate for the safety of the kidnap victims. The families remained in close contact with each other and took turns in repeatedly petitioning the Ministry of Foreign Affairs and other politicians, begging for help to have their relatives safely returned to Japan. But they received no encouraging responses. Ten painful years went by in this way for the families.

General awareness of the possibility that North Korea had kidnapped Japanese citizens was not aroused until Yokota Megumi's case became public in 1997. It was reported that she had been abducted from the coast of Niigata in northwestern Japan twenty years earlier by North Korean agents, when she was on her way home after badminton practice at her junior high school. She was only thirteen at the time. A North Korean operative who defected to South Korea gave the first testimony about her case, mentioning how his associates had talked about abducting a young Japanese girl while on a mission in Niigata. The circumstances he described fit perfectly with those surrounding the disappearance of Yokota. The news was greeted by the public first with astonishment, then with fury. And, with this news, finally, light began to be shed on the misfortune of the students who had disappeared from Europe and on the abductions of couples from the coasts of Kyushu and along the Sea of Japan. The Association of Families of North Korean Kidnap Victims, organized around this time, began to appeal directly to the public for help and support. The Japanese government was finally forced to begin taking action.

Before setting out on my journey to Europe to retrace the Yodogō group's footsteps there, I visited Ishioka's family in Sapporo. Despite the arrival of early spring, snow still lay in piles on the city's streets, crunching under my shoes.

There, for the first time, I saw with my own eyes the letter Ishioka had written. It was on a sheet of paper torn in half lengthwise, making it long and narrow. At the top, the Ishioka family's address in the Toyohira ward in Sapporo, written in both English and Japanese, was framed in red ink. The letter was addressed to Ishioka himself, not to his parents or his siblings. Above the red box, the word *jūsho* (address) was written in black. Possibly the top part of the letter was written in this way so that, if necessary, the person he asked to mail the letter could just cut out the box and paste it to an envelope.

I could make out faint fold lines in the letter paper. By counting the number of lines and refolding the paper, it was possible to see it had once been folded into the size of a postage stamp. On the back of the paper, written in a square of the same size, was a message: "Please send this letter to Japan (our address is in this letter)."

Ishioka must have prepared this letter to carry in a pocket or wallet in the hope that he would meet someone to whom he could entrust it. He was not in a position to send the letter himself.

In North Korea, any letter with an international address might be opened for inspection; in fact, it is probably most accurate to say that all such mail is opened. Even the letters the Yodogō members sent to me were inspected several times. It was not very pleasant to receive letters that had obviously been opened and read through, but it was better than not receiving them at all. Several letters never reached me in the period when I was still corresponding heavily with people in Pyong-yang. Because my correspondents were members of the Yodogō group, when I met them later, I was able to confirm that the contents of the letters that did not reach me often contained information inconvenient for North Korea. Of course, the letters said nothing directly critical but merely drew a picture of daily life in North Korea or mentioned that some deadline could not be met because of procedural delays of one sort or another. Not only did I not receive all the letters originally sent to me, but it was common that my letters to Pyongyang never arrived either.

The circumstances around Ishioka's letter were different. Ishioka had probably been confined in North Korea ever since his disappear-ance in Spain. Probably he had been subjected to ideological training and character remolding during this time, and, if so, it is unlikely that he was able to go out and walk freely around the city. In fact, his existence in North Korea was a secret, so, even if he had a way to avoid the inspec-tion process, he could not have had the freedom to send letters. He must have prepared the letter to carry with him whenever he had the chance to go out, and, when he happened to meet a foreigner, he passed on the letter to be mailed from that person's home country.

So we can imagine that he carried the tightly folded letter around with him wherever he went. One line in the letter reads, "Anyway, I wanted to at least let you know we are all right." For Ishioka and the other two mentioned, this letter was proof of their existence. It was an affirmation of life.

Not many opportunities to go out present themselves to someone living in Ishioka's circumstances. Several people might be put together in an isolated residence, such as a guest house, and made to live cooperatively. The rare outings would come only for a study trip to further their ideological education or in order to shop in a foreign currency store, always under the strict supervision of a Party handler. But, in such stores, the chances were good that they would run into foreign visitors, and, even under the strictest guard, there must be moments of inattention on the part of the person watching them. There might be a moment to secretly hand over a small folded letter. In case he didn't have time to explain, Ishioka had written on the back, "Please send this letter to Japan." He knew that if he did find someone, chances were he would have no time to talk; thus the note on the back about the address being inside the letter.

The moment would have come unexpectedly; it was risky, but Ishioka took his chance. As it happens, he must have had a little extra time, because he was able to include pictures and some other documents. The person to whom he gave the letter faithfully mailed it upon returning home. The letter was sent from Poland: when it arrived in Japan, the postmark and the stamp were both Polish.

Besides the letter, the envelope contained three photographs glued to Arimoto's travel insurance card. Ishioka must have included them after thinking carefully how to prove that they were alive in North Korea. The photos of Arimoto and Ishioka had most likely been taken in North Korea, and their families' addresses and telephone numbers were written next to the pictures in their own handwriting. The insurance document also showed signs of having been folded very small at some point. The front of the airmail envelope had been addressed to Ishioka's father, in Ishioka's hand; on the back was only his name and "in Pyongyang."

Arimoto Keiko was a student when she was abducted from London in 1983 by Yodogō group members and North Korean operatives, about three years after Ishioka and Matsuki disappeared in Spain. When Ishioka wrote in his letter that they had "met along the way," he probably meant that she had been brought to live in the same guest house where he and Matsuki were undergoing their indoctrination.

Arimoto disappeared only days before she was due back in Japan in

August of 1983. About two months earlier, she had sent to her family a postcard dated June 6, in which she gave the date and time of her return to Japan. "I've bought the ticket," she had written. "So I can tell you the date I'll be back. I leave London on August 2 for Singapore, where I'll stay for about a week. On the ninth I'll fly from there to Osaka. So I'll arrive in Osaka on Singapore Airlines on Tuesday, August 9, at 5:15 p.m. I'll stay here [at the home of her British host family, the Polls] until the end of June, then travel a bit in Europe in July, then return home."

But on that date she was not among the passengers disembarking from the Singapore Airlines flight. The evening before, her family had received an international telegram containing only a few words: FOUND WORK RETURN DELAYED. KEIKO.

The telegram had been sent from Athens at 6:45 p.m. on August 7.

About two months later, in mid-October, the family received an airmail letter from her. Strangely, however, though she wrote that she was working for a trading company, there was no return address on the letter and no indication of when it had been written. The handwriting is certainly hers. Because this letter is important for later events, here it is in full:

> Hello, everyone,
>
> It has been a while now. Are you all well? I'm in Copenhagen now on business. The cool of autumn has come to Europe; it's getting chilly. My job is fun, and I am doing well.
>
> I am traveling all over Europe, so I don't have a mailing address right now, but how are you all doing? I guess [name deleted] has had her baby by now. You must all be very happy. Are they doing well? I want to meet the baby as soon as I can, but I still have some work to do here, so my return to Japan will be delayed for a bit longer.
>
> Copenhagen, where I am now, has one of the highest standards of living in the world, and prices are high, too. When I was here this summer, there were many tourists here, but now there seem to be fewer people around.
>
> Copenhagen is famous for fur, ceramics, glass, and precious metals, among other things, and especially the furs are a lot cheaper here than in Japan. My work is trade-related, so I have learned all about these kinds of things.
>
> When I have time, I will write again. Japan is just entering

into a beautiful season now. I hope you will all take good care of yourselves, and do your best in all your efforts.

from Keiko, in Copenhagen

This letter was the last communication from Arimoto Keiko after she disappeared. Ishioka's letter arrived five years later.

For the last several years, I have had a certain connection with these European disappearances.

Soon after Ishioka's letter arrived, his family petitioned the Ministry of Foreign Affairs and also planned to attend a press conference. However, the press conference was suddenly canceled on the day it was to be held, apparently at the insistence of certain politicians, though the details are unclear. Later someone advised the families to write letters to these missing students presumed to be in Pyongyang. Of course, without knowing the missing students' address, they had to come up with another way to deliver their letters. At the time I was making frequent trips to North Korea with Yamanaka Yukio, who is now head of the "Yodogō Homecoming Humanitarian Association." We were entrusted with these letters by a friend of the families, and we did, in fact, deliver them to Pyongyang. I think we were given this messenger duty only because of our frequent trips back and forth to North Korea.

We did not really understand the details of the situation or the families' motivations. We delivered the letters because we were asked to, nothing more. We thought we could just give the letters to the Yodogō group in Pyongyang, and that would take care of it. We didn't know what was in the letters, only that they were "letters for people in North Korea." After some delay, we handed the letters over to the Yodogō group leader, Tamiya Takamaro, in 1992 or 1993.

I seem to remember saying something like, "These are some letters for some Japanese people in North Korea. If you get a chance, would you please deliver them for me?"

That should have been the end of our duties as messengers. At the time, I was not in the least aware of the Yodogō group's involvement in the abductions of Japanese from Europe. I merely thought that the Yodogō group, having been in North Korea for so long, would know of these people, having heard of them or perhaps even met them somewhere in Pyongyang, which after all is not a very large city. The letters I handed over on that occasion were in fact those that Ishioka's and Arimoto's families, and others, had written to their missing relatives. Knowing as I do now just how deeply involved the Yodogō group was in the abductions of these people, I think I can say with confidence that those letters were by chance successfully delivered to exactly the right people.

I can only imagine how surprised Tamiya was to receive them. He must have been stunned. Struck by my unintentional bull's-eye shot, he could only feign innocence. I think it was lucky I gave him the letters. He understood immediately that we were merely passing on some letters we had been given in Japan. Had I given the letters to a Workers' Party cadre involved in the abductions in the same way, we would have immediately come under suspicion and possibly even been prevented from returning to Japan.

Though I didn't know the whole story behind the letters I had delivered, they continued to bother me for some reason. The following year, when I met Tamiya again, I asked him about the letters. We were in the Japan-Korea Friendship House at the Yodogō compound.

"Let's have a talk. Can you come to my place?"

He did not give a direct answer to my query about the letters. Instead, he told me something else.

He said in a whisper, "There are quite a lot of Japanese here. We don't have contact with them, and we don't really know who is where."

"Really? So many?"

He was silent for a moment.

"We can't contact them." He spoke in a strained voice.

He thought they were living in other guest compounds like this one. There was no need to worry about their lifestyle. That was assured by North Korean socialism. "There are many different people here. We have asked some of them to work together with us, but many refused to join us, saying they didn't want to work with awful Red Army Faction types like us, and left to find other work. Some even returned to Japan."

"Well, I think that if they wish to return to Japan, they should be allowed to. You have to let them return."

"Some did return. They went back to Japan. I guess they are keeping as quiet as possible because they don't want to get into any trouble. We certainly didn't abduct anybody against their will."

Tamiya's profile showed exhaustion. I decided not to ask any further. The look on his face said quite clearly that he did not want to say any more.

Looking back, it seems clear that my unintentional involvement in the story of the abductions of Japanese citizens started if not with this conversation, then with my earlier delivery of those letters.

"Why don't we go and have some coffee?" I suggested.

It had been a short conversation, but I felt completely worn out.

I later spoke with Tamiya in a long interview, published in a book titled *Talking about the Homeland and the People* (*Sokoku to minzoku o kataru*; Tamiya and Takazawa 1996). Besides Tamiya, Abe Kimihiro and Ogawa Jun (not his real name), a later addition to the Yodogō group from Europe, also took part in the interview. Tamiya had the following to say about bringing Japanese people to North Korea:

> Tamiya: We had to start going on overseas missions starting in about 1975. We were in Europe and other places, here and there. After 1970, there were lots of Japanese going to Europe, that is, activists, but they started returning to Japan around 1975.
>
> Abe: That was exactly the case. In the 1980s, there was almost no one left.
>
> Tamiya: What was that novel that Itsuki Hiroyuki wrote?
>
> Takazawa: Do you mean *Young Man Heading into the Wilderness?*
>
> Tamiya: There were a lot of young people who read that and then went traveling in Europe. They took a ship, then continued on the Trans-Siberian Railway.[1]
>
> Takazawa: They were like hitchhikers, weren't they?
>
> Tamiya: Ogawa here was in Europe quite a lot later. Weren't you?
>
> Ogawa: Yes, about ten years later than that.
>
> Tamiya: You are a good example of someone who was there later and got caught.[2] But, even at that time, I thought that the place where we would find the most Japanese people was in Japan. (Tamiya and Takazawa 1996, 204–205)

They spoke this openly in an interview they knew was going to be published because many similar conversations between us had already been made public.

---

1. See chapter 13, note 1.

2. Tamiya uses the term *hikkakatta*, which means to be caught, mixed up in something, or even to be deceived. He is referring to meeting Ogawa in Europe and returning to North Korea with him. See Takazawa's later thoughts about Ogawa in the editor's afterword.

In the spring of 1995, the year Tamiya died so suddenly, he asked me to meet with the families of the vanished students, on his behalf.

"I have a favor to ask of you. And I want to give them a message. Would you meet with them for me? Tell them everyone is well. Ask them just to be patient a little longer."

I didn't know what to say.

Besides reassuring the families that their missing relatives were well, Tamiya had more to add.

"Right now, the more fuss they make, the more complicated the situation becomes. The timing is bad."

This message could be taken as a form of intimidation if the families continued to press the issue. I could not deliver a message like this.

Tamiya realized almost immediately that his words sounded intimidating and tried to rephrase.

"Well, that wasn't any good," he muttered. "It sounds like a threat that way, doesn't it? How should I put it?" I told him I would think about it. Then I would go and see the families.

It wasn't until recently that I finally visited some of the families to tell them about my findings in Pyongyang. The situation had been changing quickly. In addition, Tamiya, who had agreed to help people return to Japan, had died. Most important, it was clear that many of those who had disappeared, even the cases in which the Yodogō group had been involved, were beyond their reach. There was nothing to prevent me from telling the families the truth.

In the beginning, the Yodogō group needed Japanese recruits to expand their own organization. However, their ideological training did not always go well. The failed recruits would be removed from the group and isolated in a Party facility, where they would undergo brainwashing by Party cadres specializing in such work. Once they were removed, these recruits had no contact whatsoever with the Yodogō group. They were completely out of the Yodogō group's reach.

The Yodogō group has not to this day admitted their involvement in the disappearances of Japanese students from Europe. They also continue to insist that "we never brought anyone to North Korea against their will." To be sure, the European abductions are quite different from the violent cases on the Sea of Japan coast where people were carried off in big bags. But, after investigating several cases, it is clear to me that the European cases were not a matter of political persuasion and conversion. Deceit and kidnapping are the only appropriate words for what happened there.

The abductions varied in style. In some, the tool was violence; in others, honeyed words. Whatever the case, the important fact is that these people were not allowed to return to Japan as they wished, and they were forcibly confined to serve some later purpose. In this way, even an abduction that did not involve physical violence was still an abduction. The deceived victims certainly were not at fault. I will go into more detail about the circumstances surrounding the abductions below, but, to put it simply, skilled use of advanced psychological techniques can result in the greatest deception of those most convinced that they will not be deceived. Any contact using seduction and deception that results in confinement has to be called "abduction." We can only begin to see how serious these abductions of students from Europe were by keeping this in mind as we try to shine a light into the darkness surrounding them.

From the moment the Workers' Party had the Yodogō hijackers reconstitute themselves as the Independent Revolution Party, their pressing mission was to expand their organization. The most urgent assignment was to train cadres who would serve as the backbone of the new organization. They had to increase the number of Japanese members. They made the acquisition of Japanese people part of their party agenda. They repeatedly discussed how to achieve the aims of their missions. Besides coming up with concrete ideas, they also raised fundamental issues.

"Is it really acceptable to do this? Do we want to go that far? Is there no other way for us to do this?"

From time to time, one among the men would raise such questions. I would like to record this as proof that the Yodogō men still possessed consciences as human beings.

However, group decisions nearly always suppress minority opinions. More radical plans overwhelm more moderate ones. Such was the case here as well. Doubts were silenced, and anyone who persisted was regarded as unreliable or wavering. Skeptics had no choice but to shut up and go along with the rest of the crowd.

It is an unwritten law in the ideology of Kim Il Sung that adherents may not recruit new members by explicitly declaring their political ideas and opinions. This is because doing so could expose them to unknown dangers by allowing a potential recruit to realize they were followers of Kim Il Sung and believers in *juche*. Therefore, they had to conceal their allegiance until the time was right for disclosure. Instead, they had to use psychological guidance techniques, or the so-called art of guidance, to draw in their unwitting target skillfully. In this way, there was never any attempt to recruit members using political arguments and discussions.

The Yodogō hijackers were able to carry out their operation to "acquire" Japanese people because they accepted an extremely subjective and perverted logic that said, "All we need to do is to bring them to North Korea. As long as we bring them, human beings are flexible, and they will change." They summed it up in their own words: "Having hijacked an airplane to come to this country, we found the truth here, and we were able to reanalyze our own pasts critically. Since even we were able to change, surely there is no human being who can resist being changed by the idea of *juche*." Looking back on all that had happened since the *Yodogō* hijacking, this was indeed a sad conclusion for the *Yodogō*'s hijackers.

So, from the outset, the operation to "acquire" Japanese people was to be based on deception. They had no other means. This seemed like a strange way to go about recruiting people for those Yodogō members who remembered openly expressing their opinions and engaging in political discussion back in the days of their political activism in Japan. It was they who voiced skepticism in their planning meetings and asked whether this was an acceptable way to go about things. Naturally, they were criticized for thinking such things: "Anyone who asks such questions has obviously not truly internalized the ideology of Kim Il Sung."

Because of the deceptions involved in acquiring these people, conflicts arose between the new arrivals and their captors. Ishioka and Matsuki quarreled violently with the Yodogō group soon after their arrival in Pyongyang.

Immediately upon their arrival in Pyongyang, the two young men were isolated in a Party facility to undergo brainwashing. Ishioka and Matsuki, who at first probably regarded their trip to North Korea as another travel adventure, must have become increasingly suspicious about the strange atmosphere and unnatural situation in which they were living. The women who had accompanied them to Pyongyang had disappeared after their arrival. Of course, they were not permitted to go out freely.

At the beginning, instructors from the Workers' Party, as well as several of the Yodogō members including some of the wives, were in charge of their ideological training. Their brainwashing was not conducted at the Japanese village, since as new arrivals they could not be taken to a secret, restricted-access area. Those in charge of the training commuted every day from the village to Ishioka and Matsuki's accommodations to lecture them about the magnificence of the Great Leader Kim Il Sung and his *juche* ideology.

Ishioka and Matsuki were filled with distrust and dissatisfaction. They probably at first could not understand the truly unbelievable situation in which they found themselves. After all, they had not been violently abducted, which delayed their understanding of what had happened. They wanted to trust the women with whom they had spent so much time in Madrid, chatting and sharing meals. And, I have to add, Matsuki had fallen in love with Mori Yoriko.

The explosion came one day at the guest house where Ishioka and Matsuki were staying.

Mori Yoriko came to the guest house together with the other Yodogō wives.

The instant Matsuki saw her, he yelled, "You deceived me!"

He jumped at her in a fury. He grabbed her by her shirt front, and slapped her in the face. She fell to the ground. It all happened in an instant.

"You led me on and then you tricked me!..."

Hearing the ruckus, the Yodogō men came running.

"You blame her because you were tricked? It's your own fault for letting yourself be tricked!"

The men took Matsuki away from the wives and beat him. Blood ran from his mouth. This was when Matsuki found out that Mori was actually one of the Yodogō wives. After this incident, Matsuki was confined alone to a room in the guest house, and only the men continued his ideological instruction.

We know many details of how the students were taken from Madrid, thanks to the testimony of witnesses. No matter how many times we review the details, we have to say that the wives did indeed flirt with and then deceive the students.

The brainwashing and ideological training of Ishioka and Matsuki made slow progress. Apparently they were referred to as "the short one" and "the tall one." I understand that the tall one, that is, Matsuki, was the more rebellious of the two.

The matter came up frequently in the group's criticism meetings. How could they succeed in Ishioka and Matsuki's training? At one meeting, one of the wives said, "Maybe the problem is that it is just the two of them, two single men, on their own."

Hearing this, another wife spoke up, "Well, if it's going badly because it's just the two of them, let's bring in some women."

And, with this, it became their agenda to acquire and bring Japanese women to Pyongyang. It is no exaggeration to say that this was the start of their preparations to abduct Arimoto Keiko. The brakes had been released.

Three pictures had been glued onto Arimoto Keiko's travel insurance document, which Ishioka had included in his letter. One picture was of Ishioka, another was of Arimoto, and, until I saw it, I did not know that the third picture was actually that of an infant. When the letter and photos had first been made public, the copy of the third picture had come out all black, making it impossible to see the subject. Because Matsuki's was one of the three names given and there were three pictures, it was long assumed that the third picture was his. But, when I saw the actual picture myself, it showed an infant lying on a bed, head lifted, looking at the camera. I was astonished when I saw this picture, because I had been able to deduce through my conversations with the Yodogō members in Pyongyang that Ishioka and Arimoto had probably had a baby. After the revelation of the existence of the Yodogō wives and children, I had asked them several times how many children there

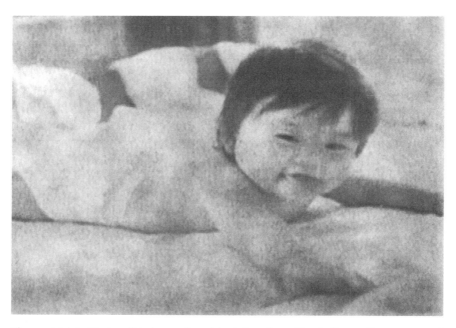

Figure 14.03. Photo of baby enclosed in letter from North Korea. From personal collection of Takazawa Kōji.

were now. Strangely, however, the answer differed slightly depending on who was answering. I found it odd that they didn't know how many children they had. However, the matter cleared up when I realized it depended on just which children they were including as part of their group. The same thing happened later when I learned about Okamoto Takeshi's children. His children were not included in the count until I had made their existence publicly known. It was no surprise to learn that Ishioka and Arimoto had had a child. His letter had hinted that they lived together. And having them marry and have children is typical of the ideology of Kim Il Sung. After all, children represented the next generation of revolutionaries—and they served as hostages as well.

One line of Ishioka's letter reads, "It's especially difficult to get clothes and educational books, and the three of us are having a hard time." Many North Korea watchers had taken this to mean that they were involved in teaching North Korean agents. The letter contains several strange passages like this. But it seems most straightforward to interpret the line to mean that Ishioka was complaining about the lack of educational materials and Japanese books for their child.

If we interpret the sentence in this way, another mystery becomes clear. If the third picture was of a baby, and not of Matsuki as expected, it meant they did not have a picture of him. The letter says "the three of us are helping each other out and living in Pyongyang." But, although Ishioka's and Arimoto's addresses and phone numbers are given in full in the letter, the only information for Matsuki is that he was from Kumamoto city; no address or phone number was given for him. Perhaps this means that Matsuki was not there when Ishioka wrote this letter as a "proof of existence." Had he been there when they decided to prepare this letter, surely his family's complete address and phone number would have been included in the letter.

Matsuki was no longer in the guest house with Ishioka and Arimoto when they decided to send the letter, so Ishioka could only write what little he knew about Matsuki. He had suddenly disappeared, and Ishioka, worried about him, included in the letter the "proof of existence" of this man whom he had befriended in Madrid and who had been brought to North Korea with him.

Matsuki's sudden disappearance probably brought home to Ishioka the precariousness of his own existence at the guest house. The danger always lurked that they, too, would someday suddenly be taken away and never allowed to return. They imagined their family and friends must still think they had disappeared forever in London and Madrid. No one could know that they had been spirited away to North Korea. Their feelings of loneliness were bottomless. Despair at the idea that their very existence might be forgotten must have been what motivated Ishioka to take the risk of writing his "letter of existence."

The sun had set, and it was already nearly dark when I finally left the Ishioka family's house. The mercury-vapor street lamps shone with a chilly light in the streets of Sapporo. I felt as cold inside as the wind that blew past me.

CHAPTER FIFTEEN

The Trap in London

When my flight landed at Heathrow Airport, I went straight to the address where Arimoto Keiko had lived while in London. According-ing to her letters, Arimoto had changed addresses twice between her arrival in London in the spring of 1982 and her disappearance the next year.

The first house she lived in was in a quiet neighborhood some dis-tance from the city's center, probably recommended by her language school. Her room was a remodeled attic on the third floor. The rather long commute to the school in Piccadilly must have been inconvenient, because after three months she found another family to stay with and moved into the downtown area. She lived in a room on the second floor of an elegant two-story townhouse in a residential block. This was the Poll residence.[1] Arimoto helped with the housework and babysat in addi-tion to attending classes. When the Polls moved in May of the next year, she went with them, making her second change of address. The third house, a fashionable English-style building with a garden full of flowers near the downtown area, was her residence until the end of June. Chris-topher and Caroline Poll still live there. If there were any hints of her imminent disappearance, the timing dictates that they would be in this house, and I had some questions for the Polls. After finding their house,

---

1. The *katakana* spelling of this name could be either Paul or Poll in English. Takazawa no longer remembers which it was. There are families with both names in London, and genealogical records suggest that the spellings are interchange-able, so we have used Poll.

I called from a nearby public telephone to set up an appointment. That day, however, no one was home.

After graduating from Kobe University of Foreign Languages, Arimoto Keiko left Japan on April 10, 1982, to spend a year in London studying English at the International House. She was referred to this school by the International Language Study Center in Osaka. In addition to English language classes, the school trained teachers and offered extra courses besides the regular English conversation curriculum. These extra courses were taught by trainee teachers without official certification; the tuition was lower, since the courses were specifically designed to provide teacher training. This lower tuition made these classes popular among foreign students from Japan and other Asian countries since they were less of a financial burden. The school was in a low-key building on Piccadilly Street facing Green Park. To my surprise, the school was next to the Japanese embassy, with only a small building separating them. It didn't seem to be a likely place for a kidnapping.

That evening, in my inexpensive lodgings near Hyde Park, I once again read the copies of Arimoto's letters from London that I had with me. I was looking for something, some clue in her letters that might have been overlooked earlier.

In the postcards she sent soon after her arrival, she briefly expressed her excitement about studying in England, something she had long dreamed of, and her impressions after setting foot in London:

> I arrived safely in London yesterday. I took a taxi and arrived at this house at around 10 o'clock. It's still cold, so the heaters are kept on. But the days are very long, finally getting dark only after 8 o'clock. The house has three stories, and my room is on the top floor. It is the only room on this floor and has its own sink. Today a girl from Switzerland came, and she is going to live here for two months. Many Japanese live in the area, and lots of shops carry Japanese groceries. Today was a holiday, so there was no school. It starts tomorrow. The Underground here is easy to understand, and I can get to it easily. I think things will go very well.
>
> ——London, 1982.4.13

> It's slowly getting warmer and warmer here. It's about ten days since classes started. There are many Japanese at the

school. The school is near Buckingham Palace and a large park called Green Park. I went to Bath last Saturday. I bought this postcard there. Bath is an old city with Roman hot spring baths. It's a beautiful place. Tomorrow I am going to Cambridge.

——London, 1982.4.23

It has been more than three months since I came here, and I have really gotten used to the life here. The school has twelve course levels, and I am in the seventh. I have been moving up one level every month.

——London, 1982.6.29

After four months had gone by:

There is a part of London called Soho, where you can eat food from all over the world. There are Chinese, Indian, and Italian restaurants, and lots of places where you can eat pretty cheaply.

The family is going to their cottage tomorrow, and they won't be back until Monday. All I have to do while they are gone is feed the two cats.

——London, 1982.8.24

At any rate, there didn't seem to be anything strange here. She was gradually getting used to her school and getting to know her way around London.

She went on a few short trips during breaks from school. As she gained confidence, she ventured farther abroad. She left London several times to make short trips to the continent.

Now I am in the town of Bergen, in Belgium. I left London yesterday, crossed the Straits of Dover, and arrived here after about five and a half hours. I'll only be here for about three days, then back to London. Antwerp is a small and very old city. I am here for the weekend and will return to London on Monday.

——Antwerp, 1982.9.11

This weekend, now, I have come to Paris. I took the night train and arrived in Paris this morning. The weather is wonderful—it isn't cold at all. I have already walked along the Champs Élysées.

——Paris, 1983.3.4

It took me a while to realize the significance of these letters in pondering her disappearance. She wrote to her friends and family with surprising frequency. With a careful reading, her letters allowed a nearly complete reconstruction of her life in London. By the time she returned from her short trip to Paris, she had been in London for nearly a year, and it was time to start thinking of her return to Japan. Her plan was to stay with the Polls until the end of June. On the sixth of that month, she wrote in a postcard to her family, "I've bought the ticket, so I can tell you the date I'll be back." She included her precise itinerary and flight number.

Then, something strange happened.

About a week later, she wrote a letter to a friend:

I will leave London at the end of this month. I feel a little sad, but I have so many things to do now. London has been so much fun! And I'll come back again someday. I already bought a ticket home, but, what do you know, suddenly I have found a job.

The job is in "market research" and involves doing research into the prices, demand, and supply of foreign products. If I take this job, I will be able to see all different parts of the world. I really want to give it a try! I don't know many details yet, but the person who introduced me to the job is in Hamburg, Germany, and, for now anyway, I'm planning on going there at the end of the month to find out more about it....

I feel pretty lucky! I never thought I would find a job so easily, and I am very happy now about being able to work overseas!

I'm pretty sure this will be my last letter to you from London. I will write again from Hamburg.

——London, 1983.6.13

There is no letter from Hamburg.

Sometime in the week between her writing the postcard to her parents on the sixth of June and sending this letter to her friend on the thirteenth, some fateful meeting took place: she met the person who told her of this "job." A marketing research position that involved traveling all over the world would have been irresistible to her, since she had hoped to find work abroad. She began to think she had to give it a shot. North Korea and the Yodogō group had laid their trap well.

Surprisingly, her next postcard is from Copenhagen, Denmark.

> I arrived in Copenhagen yesterday evening. The weather is similar to London's, if a bit cool for summer. There is a fairground called the "Tivoli" just across from the central train station, right in the center of the city. Now it's the tourist season, and the city is full of sightseers. Travelers can get around easily with English. I left the hostel early this morning to walk around and explore.
>
> I am meeting a friend here on July 15, so I will be here until then. I will write more postcards. Take care.
>
> ——Copenhagen, 1983.6.30

Why did this postcard come from Copenhagen and not Hamburg? Arimoto had left the Polls' house on the twenty-eighth of June and, according to this message, had arrived in Copenhagen on the evening of the twenty-ninth. She could not possibly have had time to go to Hamburg. Perhaps the meeting place was changed suddenly to Copenhagen. Probably the "friend" who introduced her to the job, mentioned in the earlier letter from London, was the same person she now waited for. Moreover, this person had either found the job for Arimoto or else approached her saying there was such a job available. In that case, a Japanese person could play such a role the most naturally, able to take into consideration her concerns and circumstances. Also most likely, their conversations were all in Japanese.

Market research is not a simple job. The constant traveling requires a considerable level of language ability, and one needs a great deal of knowledge about merchandise. Despite this, Arimoto was offered the job without regard for her qualifications. In addition, her contact was someone whom she could refer to as a "friend." We might conclude that it was a Japanese person, not so removed in age from Arimoto, and possessing a vague knowledge of business and marketing. That is, the contact may have been just a hired mediator or may have been offering the job under false pretenses. As such, we can create a fairly clear profile of this person.

We know Arimoto did not go to Hamburg. The plan to go there may have been changed for reasons known only to the contact. It seems unlikely that Arimoto would have suddenly canceled her plans to pursue the job she had been so excited about. There must be some reason why their meeting place was changed from the originally agreed upon Hamburg.

Other puzzles in the story of Arimoto Keiko's disappearance remain seemingly inexplicable unless we assume the job offer was a fake, offered with a hidden agenda. Then the picture begins to come clear. Looking at the whole picture, I could see traces of the Yodogō group's characteristic methods all over it, just as in many other similar cases. If we assume the Yodogō group's involvement, then the puzzle is solved easily. Before I lay it out here, though, let's return to what I found in London.

I finally succeeded in making an appointment with the Polls after several days. They had just come back that day from a trip abroad. I really only had a single question for them. The various reports of Arimoto Keiko's disappearance added up to the following course of events:

1. In early May of the year Arimoto disappeared, she made a short trip to Amsterdam. According to the Polls, "After this trip, she became more withdrawn. We have no doubt her disappearance is connected to whatever happened to her in Amsterdam."

2. In early June, she informed her family she would be returning to Japan on August 9, on a Singapore Airlines flight to Osaka. Her message included her intention of staying at the Polls' until the end of June, then traveling in Europe before returning home.

3. In mid-June, she suddenly told Mrs. Poll that she had found a job. She had also written the same thing in a letter to a friend in Japan. She told her friend that her contact for the job was in Hamburg; to the Polls, she said she would go to Copenhagen about the job. The Polls cautioned her against taking this job, saying it could be dangerous. They told me that, around this time, Arimoto was searching the classified ads looking for employment.

4. On leaving the Polls, she went to Copenhagen, not Hamburg.

5. On August 8, the Arimoto family in Japan received a telegram sent from Athens containing the message "FOUND WORK RETURN DELAYED." She may also have sent a letter from Athens (I have

not been able to confirm this). She was not among the passengers aboard the Singapore Airlines flight she had planned to take.

6. Arimoto suddenly visited the Polls in London in the beginning of September. She apparently spent one night there.

7. The letter from Copenhagen arrived at the Arimotos' home in Japan. She had written that her work was trade-related. This letter gives us reason to think she was abducted in Copenhagen in the fall of 1983. This was the last time her family heard from her.

8. Five years later, Ishioka's letter announced that she was in North Korea with the students who had disappeared from Madrid. Included in the letter were her travel insurance card and her family's home address.

This gives a rough outline of Arimoto's case as generally reported. The question I wished to ask the Polls concerned item 6: I wanted to know whether she had actually visited them in London in early September, after leaving at the end of June. If this was so, then the circumstances of her disappearance are very different. This was a crucial point in solving the puzzle.

The Polls started their story with their memories of Arimoto after her return from the trip to Amsterdam.

"Well, it was a long time ago. Indeed, it has been quite a while. She was a really nice girl. She was not suspicious about things, and she was not wary of people. We tried to teach her to be careful about the kinds of people she met, especially in a big city like London. But I don't think we did a very good job with it. She didn't talk to us very much after her trip to Amsterdam. She didn't seem to want to communicate with us. When she told us she was going to start working in Copenhagen, we tried to warn her, saying she'd be better off not doing that, because it could be dangerous. But she said she trusted the other person....

"She was a changed person after her return from Amsterdam. Before then, she was happy to spend time with us but not afterwards. She started going out a lot more around then....

"She told us she was leaving because she had found a job. She packed up and left at the end of June. Of course, we asked her where she was going. We asked her the usual questions, such as where we should forward her mail and what her address would be. But she only said she didn't know. We don't know if she really didn't know or if she just didn't want to tell us.

"Or, no, come to think of it, I think what she said was, she didn't know. She just didn't know.

"She probably really was looking for work. I remember her reading the want ads in the paper. I think she looked in the *Evening Standard*, but I can't say for sure. Then, after a while, she said she had found a promising job, and she looked very excited about it. When we asked her more about it, she said she didn't know much yet. But the pay would be very good, and, when she left, she would be going to Copenhagen. When we asked about the plane fare, she said it had been paid for.

"She didn't know anything about marketing or promotion. She had no business experience, nor had she done any studies of that sort. As for her English, she didn't have any problems communicating with us, but it was hardly good enough to work at a British firm. We are not criticizing her, not at all. She was a very nice child, and, when we say "child," we mean that she didn't have much experience. She was not adult enough to support herself with those jobs in the paper she was applying for."

I listened with interest to their stories about her changed personality after her return from Amsterdam, though I felt it had little to do with her disappearance, except perhaps indirectly. By now it was apparent that Arimoto's disappearance was an abduction in which North Korea was involved; had there been any developments in Amsterdam, it seems unlikely she would have been allowed to return to London. Although she seemed dispirited, she returned to the Polls' house. Probably her melancholy was unrelated to her later disappearance.

Finally, I asked the question to which I most wanted an answer. I thought it was best to be direct.

"Is it true that she visited you suddenly without notice after she had already moved out? It would have been in early September of that year."

They looked at each other.

"Do you remember her ever coming back?"

"No. You?"

"Perhaps she came to collect some luggage she had left behind and stayed overnight?"

"I don't remember anything like that. I don't know. I can't remember. Surely if she had, we'd have some memory of it. Is it some story someone has made up?"

"Did she leave anything behind?"

"I don't remember anything like that either."

"Well, if she'd gone off leaving something behind, we would have found it, right?"

"I can't think of anything."

"I don't remember her coming to pick anything up either. I don't have any memory of her returning here even once."

The Polls have no memory of Arimoto ever returning to their house or visiting them. This is an important fact. If it is true, we have to move the actual date of her disappearance up from the generally accepted time of late October or after. Although it has been generally accepted that she disappeared after sending that last letter, in fact she was not seen again after she left the Polls' house at the end of June. The postcard that she wrote two days later confirms that she actually went to Copenhagen, but it is not clear where she went from there. This is why the question of whether the Polls met her again is key.

The only adequate explanation is that her kidnappers baited their trap with a sweet job offer in marketing research, without explaining too precisely just what the job would entail, and lured her to Copenhagen, where she was finally abducted. If she was led to Copenhagen for this purpose, their plan would not have allowed for any waste of time. They could not give her time for second thoughts. The more time that went by, the greater the likelihood that their plan would fail. She might change her mind, or she might become suspicious about the lack of details when she started asking questions about the job. For those who were intent on abducting her, nothing could be more important than getting her on an airplane bound for North Korea without her suspecting anything. For this reason, it is most likely that her abduction took place very soon after July 15, the date in the message on the postcard she wrote soon after arriving in Copenhagen.

Her kidnapping was meticulously planned. Recall that the original arrangement had been to meet in Hamburg, but this was changed at the last minute before her departure to Copenhagen. This makes sense if the plan involved an abduction right from the beginning. Hamburg was chosen as a blind to cover up any traces; they could have used any city for the purpose. Frankfurt, Brussels—it wouldn't have mattered. One thing that is certain, though, is that Copenhagen would not have been mentioned until the last minute since it was an important operations base for the clandestine activities of the Yodogō group and North Korea. Her kidnappers were wary of exactly this, which is why she was given false information, corrected only at the last minute. And, in fact, she mentioned only Hamburg in her letter to her friend. Informing her of the actual meeting place right from the beginning might supply a clue to put the police on their trail, putting them in danger. They made only one miscalculation in their careful preparations: she was a better corre-spondent than they realized.

Strangely enough, Arimoto Keiko's "whereabouts" can be traced for a short while after her disappearance, thanks to the telegram announc-ing her delayed return to Japan and the letter sent from Copenhagen in the fall. Neither of these documents really tells us where she was when they were sent, however, since anyone can send a letter or a telegram.

At the top of the telegram, letters in all capitals read "GRAS." This is the country dispatch code for Greece. The message itself is written in roman letters: "SHIGOTO GA MITUKARU KIKOKU OKURERU KEIKO" [found work return delayed Keiko]. This international telegram arrived at the home of Arimoto's parents in Kobe the evening before she was due to return.

The telegram form has other marks and codes on it. On the line below the one giving the country of origin are the words "AEROLIMIN HELLINIKOY EAST 14/13 7/8 1845."

I traced the telegram based on the information in this line. "AERO-LIMIN" was an airport; "HELLINIKOY" was Greece. With the rest of the line, it meant this telegram had been sent from a post office in the Ath-ens airport at 6:45 p.m. on August 7. The east terminal of Athens airport served international flights, whereas the west terminal was for domestic flights and the national airline. Apparently, the telegram was sent from a temporary booth for the use of international transit passengers in the east terminal departure lounge of the airport, perhaps in the waiting period between check-in and boarding.

Once I had figured all this out from the information on the tele-gram, I had more questions: If she made a stop in Athens to do some sightseeing, why didn't she send this telegram from some tourist spot in the city? She would have been able to send a telegram about her delayed return from anywhere in the city, or from a hotel; she would even have had time to make a telephone call. From the time and date of delivery at her parents' house, it appears this telegram was sent hurriedly at the last minute. Moreover, if she sent it from the international departure lounge, she must have been on her way to her next destination. Why didn't she mention where she was going next in the telegram? My sus-picions grew with each new question. It is highly likely this telegram was a cover manufactured by Arimoto's kidnappers.

A possible reason for this scheme was to prevent her family from immediately notifying the police when she failed to appear among the passengers on her scheduled flight. Ishioka Tōru's disappearance in

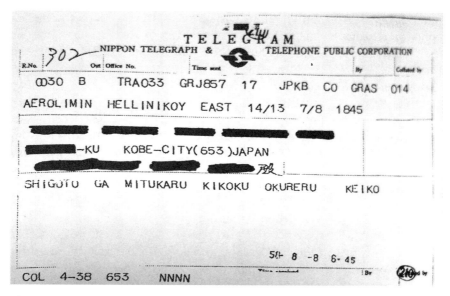

Figure 15.01. Telegram Arimoto Keiko sent from Athens airport delaying her return to Japan. From personal collection of Takazawa Kōji.

Figure 15.02. Office in Athens airport from which Arimoto's telegram was sent. Photo by Takazawa Kōji.

Madrid involved a similar ploy, with someone other than the victim appearing to have sent a message to the family to throw off pursuit. If this was her kidnappers' plan, then it should be consistent with the activities of the Yodogō group and North Korea at the time. What was the Yodogō group doing then?

In 1983, a socialist government had recently been established in Greece after the end of military rule in October of 1981. The Greek government started an active exchange with North Korea in this period and discussed establishing diplomatic relations. This period coincided with a time of increasingly active leftist terrorist organizations within the country. Members of the Yodogō group were frequently in Athens during this time while trying to set up another center for their operations there. So the Yodogō group was there at that very time.

For North Korea, 1983 was also a time of increased tensions that affected their operations in Europe and Asia. In February, the entire country went on full wartime alert in response to "Team Spirit," a joint military exercise conducted by the armies of the United States and South Korea. Kim Il Sung's visit to Eastern Europe and North Korea's export of weapons to Iran and Libya were matters of great importance. Establishing a base for their covert activities in Athens became an urgent task for the Yodogō group. Tensions between North and South Korea hit the boiling point with the attempted bombing assassination of the president of South Korea and other VIPs at the Aungsan Mausoleum in Burma [Myanmar], when North Korean terrorists attacked in the so-called Rangoon Incident.[2]

Then, there is the matter of the letter sent from Copenhagen in the middle of October (the text of the letter is in chapter 14, "Proof of Life").

With the clarity of hindsight and additional information, we can only conclude that this letter was simply another cover concocted by the Yodogō schemers. After rereading the letter several times, I noticed a subtle difference from Arimoto's earlier letters: it is filled with abstractions. There are no concrete descriptions of the city or of her activities. Though she is supposedly working in trade, the only types of merchandise she mentions are souvenirs, such as furs, pottery, and glass. And

---

2. On October 9, 1983, a bomb exploded during a ceremony for visiting diplomats from the Republic of Korea at the Aungsan Mausoleum in Rangoon, Burma. The attack was apparently intended to kill the South Korean president, Chun Do Hwan, but instead killed other South Korean diplomats. The incident is widely believed to have been the work of North Korean agents.

the description of the season seems off. "The cool of autumn has come to Europe; it's getting chilly." The weather in late October in Denmark is truly cold, the beginning of bitter winter. In addition, the line "Japan is just entering into a beautiful season now" is inappropriate with November so near; it is more usual to say something like "The weather will be getting cold in Japan, too," in anticipation of the colder weather. What is the reason for these subtle notes of discord?

In fact, the puzzle is easily solved: Arimoto wrote this letter in July, imagining what Copenhagen would be like in the fall. Under some pretense, the Yodogō members would have persuaded her to write this letter; it is not difficult to imagine their using the job as a kind of bait, using it to give some plausible explanation. She wrote the letter unaware that snow falls in Denmark in October. This also neatly explains why she gave no date or return address, not even the name or telephone number of the company she was supposedly working for. These omissions are especially strange given that she promptly informed her parents of her new address and phone number each time she moved while living in London. Mostly likely this letter was put in the mail in Copenhagen by one of the Yodogō operatives or a North Korean agent.

There is one more important piece of evidence hidden in this letter. If we set Arimoto's abduction in mid-July, the letter shows that, when she wrote it, she still completely believed the offer of the position in marketing research and trade. It reveals that the Yodogō members never broached political matters with her but continued with the deceit of offering employment. Later, concerning the Japanese people they acquired in their schemes, they repeated many times, "We truly were searching for comrades in our political activities. However, we never brought anyone to North Korea in disregard of their own desires or by deceiving them." The letter from Arimoto in Copenhagen reveals this statement as a lie and is evidence of how they really acquired people. The letter, meant as a cover-up, is actually a monument to the true story.

After speaking with the Polls, I visited a library in London to check the help-wanted ads in the *Evening Standard* from the period immediately before Arimoto's disappearance. However, I could find nothing that matched the job she had been offered. There was only a single advertisement in marketing research, and it specifically sought a British national for a very high-powered position. She would not have met the qualifications.

On leaving the library, I was struck by an idea and made my way over to Oxford Street and Soho. I thought I might visit some of the Japanese restaurants and shops in the area. Where would she have heard about this job she said she had found? How did she find the job? These were my remaining questions. If I could find answers for them, I might be able to unravel the tangled netting with which the Yodogō group had laid its trap.

I went around to several stores asking how information about available jobs circulated. It seemed likely there was some kind of network for Japanese travelers and students seeking part-time jobs. Eventually my endeavors uncovered the existence of a message board at the Japan Center (the Japan Bookstore) and, to my surprise, of message boards at the various language schools. When I checked with the International House, I found they, too, had a message board for students. Moreover, a manager told me that many Japanese find part-time jobs through friends.

It is highly likely that the "job" that Arimoto Keiko found was through a connection she had made somewhere within this network. Clearly, she did not find it in the newspaper want ads. In 1983, this network of Japanese people in London hid the Yodogō agents' quietly but craftily laid trap. It was a trap they could set only because they themselves were Japanese.

When I went to have a look at the message board at the Japan Center, I found the board full of messages from people looking for roommates and help-wanted ads for part-time workers. A crowd of students came by, took some notes, then left quickly. Suddenly, I could see her there in the crowd, notebook in hand, eagerly scanning the offerings on the board. Illusion and reality crossed paths for a moment, there in front of the message board in the basement of the Japan Center. I returned to the ground floor of the building, trying to brush the vision away. It was nothing more than a glimpse of a moment that had occurred fifteen years earlier.

Arimoto took souvenir photos at Westminster Cathedral and the Tower of London with her sister and others who came from Japan to see her. With a little extra time before leaving the city, I visited these same spots. I quickly found where the snapshots had been taken.

I had someone take a picture of me standing in the exact same spot where she had stood. Standing there, I experienced an uneasy feeling of being caught in a web spun by North Korea, a trap I could not escape. I felt a sensation close to fear. It was the fear of being deprived of my freedom against my will.

Figure 15.03. Arimoto Keiko sightseeing in London with her sister. From personal collection of Takazawa Kōji.

The Tower throws its shadow out over the River Thames as it flows by. As I stood on Tower Bridge watching the water on its way to the North Sea, I was assailed with uneasiness at the thought of Copenhagen, far away across the sea. I knew I would have to go there; the city in the North began to occupy my thoughts.

CHAPTER SIXTEEN

Tivoli Summer

Tivoli Park lies just to the east of Copenhagen's Central Station, occupying a vast space between the station and City Hall Square. For the people of this city of the North, the annual opening of Tivoli marks the beginning of the long-awaited summer. For a few months from May to September, it delivers the dreams of summer to throngs of visitors, but, with the end of the season, all falls back into winter hibernation.

The short season is treasured, and people pass many pleasurable hours at Tivoli. The number of visitors to the park is supposedly equal to the population of Denmark. Crowds of children during the day and, later, pairs and groups of adults who remain until late into the night ensure there is never a quiet moment. With concerts by world-famous artists, jazz festivals, pantomime shows, a carnival, a row of well-known restaurants, boating, a carousel, festive lighting decorating the palace and pavilions, it is not hard to understand what draws people in. More than anything, Tivoli evokes its namesake, a city in southern Europe, borrowing along with the name a sense of summer ease and vitality and bringing a feeling of openness to people's hearts.

Arimoto Keiko visited Tivoli soon after her arrival in Copenhagen in July of 1983. I can imagine she entertained bright dreams of her own that summer. If this opportunity worked out for her, it would be a turning point in her life. She felt proud of her decision to go and study in England. The waltzing melodies and the glittering fountains of water seemed to be celebrating the new possibilities opening up before her. "I feel pretty lucky!" she had written. "I am very happy now about being able to work overseas!" These must have been the thoughts running through her head as she wandered about the city.

Like nearly all visitors to the city, she began her stay in Copenhagen with a visit to the tourist information center in front of the train station, where she found an inexpensive place to stay. Arimoto had come to meet her possible employers, but the scheduled date of the meeting was still two weeks away. She could not afford to stay in a regular hotel, so she had to find a cheap pension or youth hostel suitable for a long stay. She finally settled into one of the many such places scattered around the city.

Having found a place to stay, she started exploring the city the next morning. There was plenty to see: the City Hall clock tower, Christiansborg Palace, the art museum on Strøget, the park with the statue of the Little Mermaid. Just outside the city, Frederiksborg Castle with its flock of swans; Kronberg Castle, the setting for Shakespeare's Hamlet; and Dragør, famed for its cobblestone streets all were worth visiting. She had plenty of time. Moreover, she felt like she had found herself inside a Hans Christian Andersen fairy tale. She never tired of the sightseeing and took her time wherever she went. But Copenhagen is not a very big city, and after a week she had fewer places to visit. Naturally, she returned to spend more time at Tivoli. During July, when she was there, Tivoli reached its seasonal climax with the opening of the Summer Festival.

Two weeks after her arrival in Copenhagen, Arimoto woke up early, got ready, and headed out to her appointment, her heart no doubt filled with excitement. Very likely their meeting place was somewhere along Strøget, or in front of the Little Mermaid, or near City Hall Square.

There is a certain pattern in the type of places the Yodogō members and their North Korean colleagues selected as their contact points. They preferred famous locations well known to anyone, where they could linger without arousing suspicion; moreover, there was always some unique, precise spot within the site that could not be mistaken. They deliberately avoided choosing places with many repetitive, similar features, such as train station exits or the entrance gates to Tivoli, where it would be too easy to mistake the exact location. The meeting places had to be easy to identify without mistake, even for a first-time visitor. Copenhagen's City Hall Square, with its famous clock tower, is a popular tourist area located in the center of the downtown. Asked for directions, anyone would know the place. But the square itself is quite large, and it would be easy to miss your rendezvous without a more specific spot, such as by the fountain or in front of the statue. The North Korean agents' most frequently used contact places were "in front of the fountain" in various famous parks. Anyone could find their way to the Little Mermaid statue. Another similarity shared by the locations is good visibility in all directions. This was important for the agents, since it allowed them to observe the whole area to secure their own safety before making any moves.

From the available clues, I can imagine how Arimoto's meeting went.

Once she arrived in the designated spot, she stood and waited. The Yodogō member observed her from a distance for a while. It was important to be cautious, to be certain no one had followed her, that she was in fact alone as instructed and not behaving oddly.

Arimoto checked her watch, and at that moment the Yodogō member approached her quietly. Her face showed sudden relief and brightened. She gave a greeting to this person, whom she had obviously met before. She could not hide her excitement.

That day, however, it was not only the Yodogō member who had been observing her carefully from a distance. At the same time, from a nearby vantage point, another person was watching them closely. They did not notice, but other eyes were following their movements.

Once contact with Arimoto had been successfully established, the Yodogō operative invited her to a nearby café to continue their conversation. After the women had seated themselves, a man approached like a shadow and joined them. The distant watcher keeping all of them in view may well have clicked his tongue at the sight of this man. "That's KYC. So he's active again."

Arimoto remained seated as she looked up at the newcomer. He was tall. Her companion remained seated as well, exchanging a few words of greeting with him. Arimoto realized they knew each other. He seemed to be in his late forties. Her companion introduced the man, saying he worked for a trading company.

"I'm Utsunomiya. I do business in trade here. I travel all over the world, so I don't have much time to settle down anywhere."

Arimoto was aware that her own nervousness must be showing. Suddenly, here was the man whom she was supposed to meet today. He chatted easily on various topics and joked as if trying to put her at ease.

As the conversation continued, Arimoto appeared to warm toward him. She listened and nodded at his stories about the trading business, the working conditions, conducting marketing research, interesting episodes in different countries. Caught up as she was in her high hopes, everything he said struck her as interesting and exciting.

"It's possible you won't be able to return to Japan often once you start working and become busy. Your family might worry about you then," he said.

She eagerly denied this, thinking that, if she didn't handle this moment well, she might lose the chance for this job. She told the man calling himself Utsunomiya that she had already sent her family a letter telling them about this job and that it might delay her return to Japan. In fact, the letter had probably already arrived, so there was no need to think they would be worried, she explained. Hearing this, the listening Yodogō member frowned.

Utsunomiya took in Arimoto's words and said, "That's excellent. That was thoughtful of you. It's important not to worry your family. I am glad the person I will be working with is so perceptive.

"I think you should prepare several letters like that in advance. You never know when or where you'll be traveling with this job. It's often necessary to go to one of the communist countries. Should you decide to send a letter from such a place, your family would be upset, no matter what the reason. Since there is no need to worry your family this way, you should write a few reassuring letters in advance and leave them with these people here. They can mail the letters from here. Since you will be working for me, please follow my instructions from now on.

"It's a little sudden, but I am flying to Moscow tomorrow, and I planned to have you come with me. Let's make the flight and hotel arrangements for that today. As for the work that needs to be done, you can pick that up on the job."

All she could do was nod. She finally found something appropriate to say and murmured, "I hope you'll guide me in my efforts."

She was, in effect, overwhelmed by him. Her fate was decided at that moment. The other observer continued to watch their actions as they left the café and headed toward Tivoli. As they walked, they seemed so friendly that their watcher thought they must be close associates. After noting the hotel they went to, he returned to his office. He had to hurry to develop the pictures he had taken.

The next day, Utsunomiya drove to the airport after collecting Arimoto from her hostel. The men watching them followed discreetly. Upon arriving at the airport, the two of them checked in for the flight to Moscow. Kastrup is modern and functional, with a row of check-in counters visible on entering the building. Passengers immediately go through the check-in procedures, then spend their time leisurely waiting for their flights. Arimoto and Utsunomiya passed through the lobby with its duty-free shops, entered the waiting area for their departure gate, and sat down. Their observers took several pictures at this point, using a small, hidden camera, and took note of every tiny detail until they disappeared through the boarding gate.

Driving away from the airport, the surveillance team's conversation may well have gone something like, "That young woman is new."

"There weren't any matches for her picture. But the other one, Uomoto Tamiko, entered the country through Kastrup on July 10. She didn't come via Moscow, either, surprisingly enough. She came directly from Tokyo."

"And what happened to that guy going by the name of Yamata Jera? Somehow that name strikes me as a fake."

In the mid-1990s, when North Korea's involvement in Arimoto Keiko's disappearance had become clear, a policeman from the External Affairs section of the Hyogo Prefectural Police received instructions from the National Police Agency to visit Keiko's family in Kobe with a photograph. In the photo, a man with hair elegantly graying at the temples sat on a bench next to a young woman. The picture seemed to have been taken in a waiting room somewhere. The woman had her legs

Figure 16.01. Arimoto Keiko with her abductor, Kim Yuchol, waiting to leave for Moscow. From personal collection of Takazawa Kōji.

crossed and sat slightly inclined, leaning toward the man next to her. The picture seemed to show her complete trust in him.

"Do you recognize the woman in this picture?" The officer from the External Affairs division watched Arimoto's father carefully as he asked. Apparently her father was surprised enough to nearly drop the photograph when he looked at it closely.

"That's my daughter! My daughter, Keiko!"

"You are quite sure that is your daughter?" The officer asked again, for confirmation.

"I am quite sure. Who could mistake a picture of his own daughter? When and where was this photo taken? Who is that man sitting next to her?"

The officer did not answer his questions. "I can't give you more details because the case is under investigation, except that we think the man in the photo is a known North Korean operative."

Until that time, Arimoto Keiko's family had been persistent in their efforts to push the Ministry of Foreign Affairs, the Japanese government, and several members of the Diet to begin a search for her and to make official requests for her return to Japan from North Korea. They had despaired over their inability to find their daughter despite clear evidence of her whereabouts.

The photograph the officer from External Affairs showed Arimoto's father was one of the pictures taken in July 1983, when a Yodogō agent and a North Korean operative were followed in Copenhagen on the same day Arimoto disappeared. The date on the photograph is July 16, the day after she had her appointment for an interview about a "job." It was taken in the departure lobby of Copenhagen's Kastrup Airport.

The man's identity was known from the start; Arimoto had never been identified because she had no prior connections with North Korea or the Yodogō group. The man was Kim Yuchol, from North Korea's intelligence agency, the North Korean Workers' Party Liaison Department Base (LDB). He was one of the Yodogō group's principal handlers for their clandestine activities.

Kim Yuchol was famous among the Western intelligence services. He spoke perfectly fluent Japanese and looked Japanese. He used the Japanese name Utsunomiya Osamu, stood about 5'7" with a slender build, had a gentlemanly appearance and sociable manner, and wore glasses. He was born in Pyongyang on April 17, 1938.

Kim worked in the North Korean embassy in Copenhagen from November 1978, transferring in 1980 to work at the embassy in Belgrade

Figure 16.02. Kim Yuchol. From personal collection of Takazawa Kōji.

in the former Yugoslavia and at the consulate in Zagreb. He was married, with a wife and children living in Pyongyang. He was known among the European intelligence agencies by his initials, "KYC," and was considered a primary actor in the North Koreans' European liaison section.

The day after Western intelligence agents had observed him in the Copenhagen café with a Yodogō member, Kim handed Arimoto a counterfeit passport prepared in advance, and they flew to Moscow. The name in her passport was Hown Suk Kim; he used a North Korean diplomatic passport. There was a direct flight by the North Korean national airline from Moscow to Pyongyang; he probably already had the airline reservations to continue to North Korea.

One afternoon several days into my stay in Copenhagen, I took a walk along Strøget in the city's center. From City Hall Square all the way to Kongens Nytorv, near the landing for sightseeing boats, Strøget is a pedestrian-only street, lined on both sides with stylish boutiques and restaurants.

I strolled along. When I reached the docks, I returned to my starting point by the same route. I was walking along the streets of Copenhagen trying to fathom the minds of the Yodogō kidnappers, bent on their mission of acquiring Japanese people. Copenhagen was the scene of the last of the student abductions whose traces I had followed in Madrid and London. There was no place more appropriate to ponder over the Yodogō group's mission to acquire and abduct Japanese citizens.

The sunshine in Northern Europe is rather pallid even in summer; it was already past the height of summer now. I could sense how the people here longed for summer and luxuriated in the light while it lasted. "Strøget" means "walk" or "stroll" in Danish. I concentrated as I walked and finally marshaled my imagination to become a kidnapper myself.

The people walking toward me looked Japanese. Perhaps they were college students traveling during the summer break. From their appearances, I guessed they were students from some women's college. They were intent on the window display of one of the swank little shops. I stopped to try and talk with them, but no words would come out of my mouth. As I eavesdropped on their conversation about styles and fashion, I knew this would not work; their talk was beyond me. I walked on. I began to think that my target should be alone. When I looked up, a woman walked past me at a brisk pace. Was she Japanese? Probably not. Maybe from Hong Kong or China. For a while I went along like this, absorbed in sorting out by sight which of those I passed were Japanese. I had to speak to someone who was. Would you like to come to North Korea with me?—ridiculous! I would never be able to get someone to come with me that way. But this was my mission, my duty. Of course, I could start with an invitation to tea. I could mention a trip to North Korea later. That could wait. But how could I initiate a conversation without revealing my ulterior motive to my target? Because, of course, my ideology did not allow me to reveal any hint of the principles I believed in, any clue to my real mission. That was real loyalty to Kim Il Sung. I must not distress the "Beloved Leader Comrade." Would you like to join me for some tea? How about having a meal together? That's it. I could get to know more about my target over a leisurely dinner. I had to conduct my preliminary background investigation perfectly. I needed to know about family, work history, place of origin—all necessary to see that there wouldn't be any inconveniences.

How many hours had I been going along thinking like this now? I had to meet at least one person and bring the conversation around to an invitation to dinner. Wouldn't you like to go to North Korea? There is work that would let you travel all over the world. You can play at being a spy, too. The living is secure, and you will live a luxurious life. The country will pay your salary; you will feast at every meal. How about it; why don't you join us? I sounded to myself like a shill standing outside a train station supermarket, shouting out advertisements for a big sale. No. That was not the right tone. North Korea is Shangri-La, an earthly paradise, the only such place in the world. There, the Leader and the People are working hand in hand, trusting each other and sharing hardships to build a rich society. You are young; won't you lend us a hand to create a fabulous future? No, no, this wouldn't work. Now I sounded like someone recruiting for a new religion. Though, had the Yodogō members used such an approach, they would not have been kidnappers. No matter how rotten their words, their targets would at least have had a chance to agree to the proposal. But they did not do so; their victims were given no options but deception.

And the reference to North Korea as Shangri-La—I have forgotten exactly when, but I once met Tamiya in a country other than North Korea. We were talking over coffee in the lobby of a Shangri-La Hotel.

Tamiya asked me, "What does "Shangri-La" mean?"

"Oh, it's something like "Arcadia" or "Paradise on Earth," I answered casually. When he heard this, a frown crossed Tamiya's face.

At any rate, now I needed to quickly find someone I could take to North Korea. That was the problem, finding them. The means for taking them there presented no difficulties. Once I had safely delivered them, the rest would work out on its own. They would be converted to the ideology of Kim Il Sung, to his philosophy of *juche*. Faced with this ideology, no one could remain unchanged. Even those adhering to defective ideologies could be "awakened" to become better people, given an encounter with the Great Leader's ideology. At that point, they would be grateful to me for bringing them there. That is certain, so it did not really matter who I brought. And my methods wouldn't matter either, since clearly they would thank me for it later. Where had I heard such language before? Of course: Aum Shinrikyō, the Japanese group that killed twelve people in the sarin gas attacks on the Tokyo subway system in 1995.[1] Aum Shinrikyō had a way of thinking similar to the North Koreans. But that was unimportant here. Now the issue was how to approach someone. I couldn't take anyone if I didn't meet anyone. The problem was how?

---

1. Aum Shinrikyō was an apocalyptic religious cult founded by Asahara Shoko that was active in Japan in the late 1980s and early 1990s. In addition to promoting its religious beliefs, those at the center of the group practiced various forms of forcible indoctrination and conducted mind-control, medical, and chemical experiments. In 1995 the group carried out a coordinated attack in which sarin gas was released in several Tokyo subway stations, resulting in twelve deaths and thousands of injuries. Key members including Asahara were subsequently arrested and tried, but some remain at large on wanted lists, including one named Hayashi, who had ties to North Korea.

I was engaging in a strange activity in a strange country: trying to approach a woman while pretending to be a kidnapper. Just thinking about doing this was exhausting me. Cold sweat ran down the back of my neck.

The sunlight was fading from Strøget.

Were the Yodogō members charged with a mission of picking up girls? As long as they engaged in kidnapping, such a label was unavoidable. But it seemed they couldn't even handle such a mission successfully. If their mission really was to pick up girls, they should first have kidnapped someone from Shibuya who was a real expert at it.[2] Then it wouldn't have taken them so long to complete their mission. I continued to wander around in my own world pretending to be a kidnapper, remembering a funny story I had heard in Pyongyang.

When the Yodogō members first flew to Europe on their mission of acquiring Japanese, some went to Madrid, but others went to Paris, Amsterdam, and Rome. Konishi Takahiro went to Rome and began his search for likely targets while working as a dishwasher in a restaurant. Every day he wandered around the Piazza di Spagna, the Trevi Fountain, the Colosseum, Saint Peter's Basilica. He was picking out Japanese tourists and exchange students as targets.

Once, on the famous stairs of the Piazza di Spagna, he saw for the first time a beautiful woman. He quickly spit out the gum he had been chewing and, making up his mind, straightened up. He hastily donned his sunglasses to hide the face made famous in many police bulletins. Telling himself this was his duty, he approached the woman shyly.

"Would you like to talk?"

"…?" A cold glance.

In other words, there was a world of difference between Konishi Takahiro and the newspaper reporter played by Gregory Peck. The Yodogō Hepburn in Konishi's *Roman Holiday* dream disappeared like a bursting soap bubble.

This story had come up because we were talking about why Konishi was so fat. Ever since that day, besides washing dishes in the restaurant, Konishi had begun devouring mountains of leftovers. The power he had possessed as a student at the Faculty of Medicine of the University of Tokyo did not work on beautiful Japanese girls in Rome. His own self-criticism was that "Rome wasn't built in a day." The others

2. Shibuya is a busy youth-oriented shopping and entertainment area in Tokyo where men frequently pick up young women.

frowned on him in disapproval. In the end, there were no Yodogō-related disappearances in Rome.

But not everyone was as inept as Konishi. Some among them carried out their missions faithfully, perfectly. It was an expression of loyalty to the "Great Leader" to do so, and many of them truly believed it would strengthen their own organization as well.

I was suddenly struck with the thought that the Yodogō group tried to achieve with their kidnappings the same goal of "communization in a single strike" that lay behind the United Red Army purge incident: anyone could be transformed, and the more radical the measures, the more effectively people would be remade at a single stroke. They were convinced that they were in the right, that their actions were just, and that anything was permitted for the sake of justice and revolution. In the light of this belief, ordinary people's lives had no value; a worthless life, no matter that it belonged to another, was unimportant. By bringing people to North Korea, they might achieve "*juche* in a single strike." This superb method of Kim Il Sung's ideology was maliciously labeled "brainwashing" by the imperialists.

With these beliefs, the Yodogō group members became true kidnappers. They were dictators and judges over the lives of other people. They considered themselves as chosen for this duty. Their extremely subjective views made them believe they were acting on behalf of good and justice. "We are the center of everything," they believed. "We are the masters of our own fates and of the fate of the world." Such was their *juche* ideology.

I gave up pretending to be a kidnapper and wandered in the bright summer night streets of Copenhagen with these thoughts coursing through my head.

Night had come to Tivoli.

Summer nights in Copenhagen are lit by a midnight sun. As the sky grows pale with dusk, Tivoli enters the hours most popular with adult visitors. The dazzling lights begin to shimmer, couples gather. Candles light the restaurants, changing them into venues for adults to socialize. Lovers scream from the jet coaster; the music of the merry-go-round lends an air of nostalgia.

Perhaps Arimoto Keiko rode the jet coaster and the carousel at Tivoli that day. Were the Yodogō members with her? Did Kim Yuchol join her for a ride on the "Magic Carpet" or enjoy an outing on the little boats? A strange closeness seems evident between them in the picture taken the next day in the passenger waiting area of Kastrup Airport.

This closeness could not have been the result of their meeting in the café about the "job," but still they have some sort of mysterious connection. They appear to have become close friends in a single day. Was it the magical power of the Tivoli summer?

She was caught in a dream that summer in Tivoli. Whether the dream lasted only a night or for the whole summer, the arrogance of the Yodogō group soon converted it into a nightmare.

She was not, however, the only one going about in a dream. The Yodogō students themselves must once have been filled with dreams, even Tamiya, even Konishi, Akagi, Abe, Tanaka....Even I was in a dream. I continued in my dreams of that period for a long time. At some point, though, we must all come to terms with the outcomes of our dreams. Those onetime heroes were now nothing more than common criminals nestling close to power. Those who had declared in their parting message, "We are tomorrow's Joe," should have followed their dream no matter how tragically it finally ended. They should not have destroyed the aspirations of others while using those same hopes as traps. The Tivoli night reminded me of how bitter the dregs of such dreams taste.

Soon the season of the midnight sun would be finished in Copenhagen. The pale blue of the night sky was growing darker. The screams had quieted down; the horses on the carousel were still. Summer in Tivoli was coming to an end.

CHAPTER SEVENTEEN

Smuggling Syndicate

Photos showing the Yodogō hijackers going about their activities overseas have been taken in many places besides Copenhagen. The photos include the men, their wives, and the North Korean handlers who accompanied them.

The scenes in the photos vary: standing in an airport waiting area, walking through an airport lobby pushing a luggage cart, deep in conversation in what appears to be a café, on a city street, riding in an official embassy car, shopping. Most of the pictures were taken in Europe, especially in Scandinavia. Though most of the photos in this large collection depict decidedly ordinary scenes, some of them are more interesting, such as a photo of one of the hijackers and his wife kissing passionately in a public park, or others where for some reason the couple combinations do not accord with the officially announced marriage pairings.

Few of these photographs have been made public so far. They and the reports that accompanied them languished for years in the files of the intelligence agencies of various countries. Some of these pictures, though by no means all, came to light in 1988, just before the start of the Seoul Olympics, partly because intelligence agencies around the world began cooperating and sharing information to prevent acts of terrorism more effectively.

Initially, most of these photos were nearly incomprehensible when they arrived at the public security authority, mainly because it was assumed that the Yodogō hijackers were still confined within the territory of North Korea. The public security officials hurriedly analyzed the photos and papers they had received. The Japanese National Research

Institute of Police Science also had a look. It was finally concluded that the people in the photos were the Yodogō members. Strangely, however, all these documents were merely marked "Top Secret/Indefinitely" and kept in locked files at the International Terrorism Prevention Section of the public security authority. These later came to be known as the "Pandora files."

The only time the contents of the file were put to public use was in August of 1988, when a passport recall order was issued for five of the women we now know as the Yodogō wives, based on the information gleaned from photographs showing the women meeting with North Korean operatives in Europe. They were charged on the basis of Article 19, Section 1.2, of the Japanese passport law, which dealt with "persons threatening the national interest and public safety of Japan."

On August 6, 1988, then foreign minister Uno Sōsuke issued a formal statement in a government newsletter, listing the names of Kaneko Emiko, Fukui Takako, Mori Yoriko, Mizutani Kyōko, and Uomoto Tamiko, and describing them as "persons suspected on the basis of sufficient evidence to be engaged in activities damaging to the national interest and public safety of Japan, such as meeting directly with known North Korean operatives in overseas locations."

The women's meetings with North Korean agents remained a puzzling question. At the time, it was not known that they were the Yodogō wives. The passport recall order issued by the Japanese government vividly illustrates the limitations of its understanding at the time.

However, several years later, some of these photos were submitted for the first time by the state to the court as evidence in cases concerning the passport recall order and the Yodogō members' violations of the passport law. These photos, obscured for so long in top secret files, suddenly came into the sunlight. The photos were undoubtedly just as astonishing to the Yodogō hijackers.

Tamiya was mystified by the existence of these photographs and the detail in which their paths had been tracked overseas.

"Why would they do that?"

He asked me this question several times. All I could say was that I didn't know what I didn't know, and I didn't understand what I didn't understand.

For me as well, this mystery was outside the usual range of possible interpretations. However, quite by chance, a brief encounter in Copenhagen gave me insight into a solution.

I had already been given a hint during my interview with the Polls in London. When Arimoto told the Polls she would be going to Copenhagen for her new job, they had immediately tried to warn her it could be dangerous. "That place is infamous for its drugs and smuggling. A job that pays so well has got to be dangerous," they told her.

What made them respond that way? Why should Copenhagen, a city famous for mermaids and Hans Christian Andersen's fairy tales, elicit such an immediate, negative reaction? This question remained in my mind. There had to be some reason for such a spontaneous reaction at just the mention of Copenhagen. The answer had beckoned to me from the distant northern city beyond the flowing waters of the Thames when I left London.

Searching for a clue to the mystery, I visited the office of the local newspapers the day after I arrived in Copenhagen. However, it turned out my visit was fruitless because my question was too broad. "North Korea?" I was told. "They have a bad reputation. Articles about North Korea? We have tons of them. In fact, there are so many that we can't help you unless you can be more specific!"

My concerns remained even after I had left the newspaper office, so, whenever I got the chance, I tried asking local people about their impressions of North Korea. The results of my survey were not positive. The hatred and fear evoked in people by the name of that country rose like a barrier between us and prevented me from getting any further when I asked. One person frowned in silence, turning away just at the mention of North Korea. Another spat out only, "North Koreans are all drug dealers and smugglers! Just go to the area south of the Central Station, and maybe you will find something there!"

Drug dealers and smugglers!

Now the Polls' casual remarks were shown to be somehow tied to the idea of "North Korea." My question just kept getting bigger.

I returned to the newspaper archives once again to pore over old articles. Visiting such a place requires a certain degree of determination, since it means struggling alone with piles of accumulated time and dust. However, it was there, in the yellowing copies of collected articles, that I found a ream of unexpected facts and the truth of the situation.

Tamiya may have been puzzled about why those photographs existed, but in fact the reason was simple. And pitiful.

To clearly understand the matter, I had to look back some twenty years to the period just before the Yodogō wives had left Japan. The wives were still living their ordinary lives in Japan, and the Red Army Faction students were still absorbed in their daily study of *juche* philosophy in their Japanese village just outside of Pyongyang. We now embark on a journey through time. Our destination: Scandinavia in the mid-1970s.

Copenhagen, January 1976

An unusual situation had been developing in the city of Copenhagen since the year 1975. A large volume of black-market cigarettes were circulating in the city. The city police were having difficulty controlling the flow.

"It is pretty strange. We tried checking all the sources, but there was no unusual activity there. The manufacturers say they don't understand what is going on either. There is no movement of such goods through the airport or ports. Everything is coming in through the normal routes. It is almost like magic. We try to arrest the dealers, but they don't lead us anywhere...."

The black-market cigarettes were being sold at almost half the regular price throughout the city. The mystery was that the goods were authentic despite the huge discount, and there was a wide selection of brands and types of cigarettes. Though they were on the black market, there were no signs of either counterfeiting or tampering. Normally this would be an indication that the goods were stolen, but no such thefts had been reported. Investigators had requested wholesalers and warehouses to beef up their inventory control and inspection, but no problems had been reported.

The city police were understandably confused. The cigarettes had not been stolen; airports and ports had been closely investigated, but in any case it would be difficult to smuggle in such bulky items unnoticed. The police had considered one possibility but rejected it because it was too ridiculous: that is, the cigarettes were being bought at full price but sold at half price. With all other possibilities eliminated, what else remained? But what for? What was the point of entering the black market and losing money? Could the goal possibly be to disrupt the economy? But, in that case, it was only cigarettes, surely too minor a product for such a project? It was impossible to make out what the dealers were thinking. If only for that reason, the case seemed ominous.

The city police organized a special team for the case, with fifteen detectives investigating. They tightened control with twenty-four hour surveillance. But, despite all their efforts, "authentic" illegal cigarettes continued to circulate.

The matter began to clear up thanks to the quick wits of one investigator. The testimony of a dealer arrested in another case provided the information that Asians from one of the embassies seemed to be involved.

"Diplomatic privileges? No, this cannot be true!?"

Copenhagen had an international duty-free shop for diplomats, and, though he doubted the possibility of his idea being correct, the investigator visited the shop. He found out that employees from one embassy had ordered incredible amounts of a variety of cigarettes there.

The investigation reached a turning point with this discovery, which revealed how to "buy at the full price and sell at half-price," a possibility the investigators had dismissed. In fact, the discovery revealed a loop-hole. Because diplomats could buy cigarettes for personal use at one-eighth the market price at their duty-free shop, it was possible to make a profit by selling them on the black market at half the regular price.

The Copenhagen city police proceeded cautiously with their inves-tigation. With the suspected involvement of foreign embassy personnel, a little clumsiness on their part could lead to an international diplomatic incident. They began an undercover investigation.

Soon after, in January, a North Korean embassy employee was seen meeting with a Syrian black-market cigarette dealer. By the time arrests were made, the North Korean embassy personnel had sold some 250,000 packs of cigarettes to black-market dealers and accepted orders for 125,000 more. Moreover, four people from the embassy, including the ambassador and a secretary, were found to be involved. Apparently, the entire embassy participated in the criminal activities.

This was not the end of the matter. Other crimes came to light, one after the other. Besides cigarettes, they were suspected of mass pur-chases and resales of whiskey, wristwatches, jewelry, and electronics, as well as other goods. Their illegal dealing amounted to nearly a million U.S. dollars in duty-free items.

In addition, later that year an officer continuing the investigation developed an unpleasant suspicion: the North Korean embassy person-nel were also smuggling and dealing marijuana and heroin. They had used sealed diplomatic mail bags to move about 150 kg (330 lb) of heroin.

The case expanded abruptly.

By this time, the Danish police had dug deep in their investiga-tion. They had discovered a tight network of cooperation in neighboring countries. The Danish police urgently requested the help and coopera-tion of the national police forces of Sweden, Norway, Finland, and Ice-land, as well as of other European nations. As a result, illegal cigarettes, whiskey, and heroin that had been smuggled into Norway and Sweden came to light. Some 300,000 cartons of cigarettes and 4,000 bottles of whiskey had been brought into Norway. A large quantity of heroin was confiscated. At this point, the Danish police made public some photos of the drug-dealing North Korean embassy employees. Thus the criminal activities of North Korean embassy personnel in several countries were brought to public attention.

These revelations, stemming from an investigation started by the Copenhagen city police into the excessive numbers of black-market cigarettes in their city, developed into a scandal that shook not only Scandinavia but the whole of Europe.

The governments of the countries involved made strong complaints to the North Korean government and decided to deport all involved embassy personnel. On October 15, 1976, the Danish government ordered the deportation of North Korean Ambassador Kim Hon Chol, Third Secretary Kim Sun Gil, and two other embassy employees; they departed Denmark on the twentieth. On October 18, Norway ordered the expulsion of Acting Ambassador Pak Ki Pil as well as three other embassy staff; they left on the twenty-second. On the twentieth, Finland ordered Acting Ambassador Chan De Hi to leave, along with three of his staff. The four of them at first said they would resist the order but then left on the twenty-fifth. Before the Swedish government could give the order, North Korea recalled five personnel from Sweden, including the ambassador to Sweden and Iceland. They returned to Pyongyang on October 22.

The mass media of every country in Europe gave wide coverage to these events. The Danish newspaper *Politiken* reported that "the North Koreans pay their diplomatic expenses by engaging in criminal activities." *Ekstrabladet* wrote that "all of the embassy personnel were a gang of smugglers." West Germany's *Die Welt* reported on "the smugglers' captain, Kim Il Sung," while France's *Chrétien de Paris* called him "the behind-the-scenes manager of duty-free shops."

Soon after this, North Korean diplomats in Denmark were involved in a hit-and-run accident when their embassy car driver ran a red light. Three diplomats, newly arrived on the nineteenth of the previous month to replace their deported colleagues, were in the car on November 1 when it hit a print shop worker riding his motorcycle to work; they fled the scene. The victim, Toben Paulsen, told reporters from *Ekstrabladet* that the diplomats got out of the car as if to help him but then pushed him back to the ground with a shove to his chest and drove off, leaving him alone. The citizens of Copenhagen were stunned by the unlawful acts of these North Korean diplomats. Danish feelings of antipathy toward North Korea continued to deepen.

The criminal activities of North Korean embassy personnel and operatives in Scandinavia did not stop there. Shielded from the consequences of their actions by their diplomatic immunity, they staged an attempted kidnapping in Copenhagen in 1980. They were discovered and foiled while attempting to abduct a tourist and a professor from South Korea who was attending the International Women's Conference. The attempt motivated the South Korean embassy in London to issue an unusual warning to South Koreans traveling in Scandinavia to be very cautious. In August, the *London Times* went so far as to quote the South Korean embassy, publishing articles warning about North Korean operations throughout Europe.

In fact, the stage of their operations was not limited to Europe but spread over the globe. Similar smuggling operations were revealed in Central and South America, in Malaysia, and, in 1980, in Australia and Nepal. With these discoveries, North Korea was cornered internationally; its image as a terrifying country dealing in drugs and smuggling became firmly embedded in European minds.

Ever since these revelations, European police authorities and intelligence agencies have kept all North Korean embassy staff and operatives under very strict surveillance. Such was the situation in Europe when the Yodogō hijackers were sent there on their missions as "*juche* warriors." They were to be substitutes for the North Korean agents, who were hindered from engaging in their usual activities by the strict surveillance of local authorities.

So the Yodogō group became responsible for these economic activities in addition to their mission of "acquiring" Japanese citizens. The economic activities were a unique kind of mission, for which they had to carry North Korean diplomatic passports.

For the record, the economic activities that discreetly take advantage of diplomatic privileges and duty-free shops for diplomats continue to this day, though the methods may have changed somewhat.

It is no surprise that the local authorities identified the Yodogō members as operatives from the very beginning of their activities overseas since, in order to pursue their tasks, they had to be in contact with North Korean embassies and agents. First of all, they used the embassies in various countries as their residences and as the bases for their operations. They met with embassy personnel on a daily basis. There is no question that everything they did was seen and noted by the local governments, police authorities, and intelligence agencies. The host countries were "letting them swim," as it is called, but unfortunately this term was not a part of their or their North Korean colleagues' vocabularies.

So I can now clearly answer Tamiya's question "Why?" It is no mystery why so many photos were taken of them engaged in their assignments; it was simply routine. In a later court case concerning the Yodogō passport law violations, a public security official testified about the circumstances surrounding these photographs: "Kim Yuchol, known as KYC, and other North Korean operatives were targets for intelligence surveillance. Anyone who came into contact with them was afterwards subject to surveillance as well."

Apparently the Yodogō members were the only ones not aware of this.

The record of their routes in Copenhagen is not limited to the kidnapping of Arimoto Keiko. The details of their daily lives and activities were also recorded as a matter of routine.

Behind Copenhagen's Central Station, in the southern part of the downtown area, there is a concentration of hotels. Starting near the station, the Astoria Hotel, the Grand, the Weber, and the Hotel du Nord, all relatively inexpensive business hotels, are lined up one after the other. The names of the Yodogō members and their wives, including Kaneko Emiko, Mori Yoriko, Uomoto Tamiko, and Fukui Takako, appear repeatedly in the hotel registers. Other entries include a forged Japanese passport number with the name Yamata Jera, supposedly used by a Yodogō member (the public safety authorities incorrectly suspected Abe Kimihiro); another forged passport with an illegible name of Ogawa or Ogawe, given name unclear (possibly Onoue? Ogawe Staio? Ogame?); and Kim Yuchol. Kim checked into the hotels as Utsunomiya Osamu, using a Japanese passport (number ME8352863).

The district just beyond the hotel is crowded with porn shops, gay bars, tattoo parlors, and bath houses. Locals fear the area as a drug zone. I wonder if it is only by coincidence that the traces left by the Yodogō group show they frequented this area. They used these hotels over a very long period of time.

The register of the Hotel Ibsen, though at some distance from this district, shows that Mizutani Kyōko, Tanaka Yoshimi's wife, stayed there for an extended period while she was renewing her passport. Mori Yoriko also renewed her passport at the Japanese embassy in Copenhagen. Countless reports of their surveillance tell of their daily activities and identify the hotels where they stayed and the cafés and restaurants they frequented. These data show how important Copenhagen was for them as a center of operations.

In fact, for the North Korean operatives, the city of Copenhagen was their window to the West.

After I finally finished the first round of my battle with the piles of dust in the newspaper's archives, I turned my footsteps to the porn district behind the railway station. Stopping in front of a shop plastered with photos of child pornography, bestiality, homosexuals, male nudes, and labia piercing, I was occupied by images of the Yodogō men and their wives, active in Copenhagen. This shop was just a step away from the Hotel du Nord. I wondered if they had ever been lost in thought in front of a porn shop like this. What did they think of this northern city so far away from Pyongyang? I kept hearing, again and again, Tamiya's voice asking me, "Why?" But the final answer was just too pathetic. Perhaps it was for the best that they did not know the whole truth. This naïveté suits those Red Army Faction students who so dramatically pursued their ideals. Even had they known the truth of the situation and sensed the real danger they were in, they would have been powerless to change anything. They were nothing more than the hands and feet of what is described in Kim Il Sung's ideology as "the living body of the State." They were forbidden to think for themselves or make judgments. That was someone else's job. Their task was to obey the will of the "Great Leader"; unquestioning obedience was the only way to express their loyalty to Kim Il Sung and the North Korean Workers' Party, to whom they owed so much. Questioning could lead only to accusations of rebellion and treason.

"It was best you did not know this," I said silently to Tamiya, who had continued asking why until his death. Only those who do not entertain doubts, who do not think, can survive in North Korea.

Not thinking, not questioning, loyalty—these phrases provide the keys that allow us to understand the lives and activities of the Yodogō group over a quarter of a century.

CHAPTER EIGHTEEN

Two-Faced Janus

In 1980, when the Yodogō group started its myriad activities in Europe, Tamiya wrote his first letter to Japan since their defection to North Korea. He titled it "Ten Years since Leaving the Homeland: A Message from Pyongyang."

In it, he criticized the theories and past struggles of the Red Army Faction and declared his own unconditional conversion to *juche* philosophy. Curiously, however, the letter was not a theoretical treatise or political propaganda; rather, it took the form of a personal essay in which he stated his feelings for Japan. What struck readers most were his explicit expressions of longing for home and his feelings for Japan and the Japanese people (*minzoku*) as symbolized in his use of the word "homeland" (*sokoku*). Historically, neither is a familiar term in the rhetoric of the left-wing movement in Japan. Readers' responses divided sharply into two camps. Leftists criticized his choice of words, saying they had no place in any communist movement upholding the principle of internationalism; the New Right, to whom the concepts of "the Japanese people" and "the Japanese race" appealed, gave him a large measure of support. Whatever the response they elicited, the contents of this essay were a surprise.

Tamiya's essay, published in the summer issue of the magazine *Shisha*, started as follows:

> Ten years since we left the homeland. "Ten years an epoch make," they say, and a span of ten years is no trivial thing....However, time does not make us forget everything. Our feelings for par-

ents, siblings, friends too far away to meet only deepen as time passes. Not only for the people to whom we feel bonds of love, but our longing for home and homeland also grows strong.

Looking back on these ten years, there has not been a single day when we did not think of our homeland.

The homeland! We were not in the habit of using this word when we still lived in Japan. Not until that day ten years ago when we were crossing the sea to Korea did we start thinking of Japan as the homeland, perhaps because we were aware that we would not be able to set foot on Japanese soil for a long while. Though we had left to seek a new path, our hearts burned with emotion as we watched the blue ocean of the homeland recede behind us, wondering when we could return; memories of twenty years growing up in the bosom of the homeland raced around in our minds....

Since coming to Choson, our first action in the morning has been to listen to the radio for news of Japan; the most important activity of the week or month is to pore over new Japanese publications the day they arrive. We have been greedy in our desire to understand everything about our homeland, past, present, and future.

No matter where they go, Japanese remain Japanese. No kind of water can transform the blood of the nation. In the course of ten years, we have changed greatly, physically and ideologically; however, nothing can change the fact that Japanese blood flows in our bodies. (Tamiya 1980, 116–117)

He went on to summarize the Japanese student movement of the past:

Our movement did not gain the sympathy of the Japanese people, nor were we successful in turning it into a popular mass movement....In short, we could not see the people's unlimited power, nor did we truly believe in the creative power of the working masses. This fact clearly shows how mistaken we were in our worldview at the time and consequently how erroneous we were in our ideological theory. (pp. 119–120)

He concludes his summary by saying, as a former cadre of the Red Army Faction, "We are responsible for an enormous crime against the Japanese people" (Tamiya 1980, 121).

His words, though apparently a critique of the ideas of the Red Army Faction, are nothing more than an unquestioning espousal of *juche* ideology and Kim Il Sung's philosophy. Certainly the Red Army made many mistakes in its struggles, but this analysis does not show the slightest hint of a critical evaluation of North Korea's *juche* ideology or an awareness of objective reality; he is merely using the *juche* point of view to dismiss the Red Army. This has become clear to me now, after retracing the lives and ideological transformations of the Yodogō men during their first ten years in North Korea. Of course, it was their tragedy that they had no alternative. We will have to return to this matter later.

Tamiya wrote briefly about the ten years they had spent in North Korea:

> We have been studying *juche* philosophy for a long time, engaging in debate and ideological struggle, critically examining our past and the present status of the organization to which we once belonged. Finally, we were able to find historical truth and the underlying principles of the social movement; we acquired a deeper, enlightened view of those days, clearly perceiving the mistakes we made as we wandered, groping in the darkness. We think nothing can be more precious, or more satisfying, than this. (Tamiya 1980, 120)

Had it really been this simple, there would have been no mystery. There would have been no need for me to do all this writing. Unfortunately, the matter was more complex and multilayered than Tamiya made out. Let me repeat once again: in North Korea, the true story is always hidden behind the public fiction.

Elsewhere, Tamiya later wrote, "We think of the homeland only once we find ourselves abroad. At the very least, it is true that life in a foreign country brings it home to us even more deeply that we are, in fact, Japanese." Also, in the same piece, "Living here among the Korean people, I am ever more strongly aware of being Japanese" (Tamiya et al. 1987, 36). These were honest statements. He said the same things to me on several occasions in our conversations in Pyongyang. However, there was a subtle strangeness to "Ten Years since Leaving the Homeland."

Naturally, extended stays in foreign countries make one homesick for Japan. Differences in lifestyle bring about a rediscovery of Japan. In this sense, Tamiya's references to Japan, the Japanese people, and the homeland are not difficult to understand. After all, it was Tamiya who recited a Japanese poem on board the *Yodogō*, holding a Japanese sword in one hand. While still in Japan, he once had the nickname *kumichō* (chief.) He loved the cherry blossoms and believed in the spirit of chivalry. I knew this side of him, so it was not too surprising to hear words like "homeland" suddenly coming from his mouth. But there really was something askew, some subtle difference, about that essay written in the tenth year.

Where did the strangeness come from? Perhaps the scope of his writing task made him nervous; perhaps his emotions got the better of him. Strangest of all were my own worries that the group might not have considered all the reactions such an essay might provoke in Japan. Even though ten years had passed, this was the first communication from the Yodogō hijackers since they disappeared so dramatically. Many readers felt no sympathy for their longing for the homeland, given the magnitude of their act of hijacking an airplane to North Korea. Several of those who had been passengers aboard the *Yodogō* said outright that they didn't want to hear such talk of longing for the homeland from men who had made so much noise about going to North Korea in the first place. It was a mystery to me how they planned to deal with such entirely natural reactions.

I believe I now have a satisfying answer to this question. I may not be able to explain it perfectly, but I think the choice of words like "homeland" and "longing for home" in this essay was deliberate, a strategic decision. The reason is apparent. The Yodogō group knew as well as the Workers' Party did that such expressions would be most effective in eliciting sympathy for their bid to return to Japan.

It is hardly necessary to repeat that 1980, the year in which this letter was published in Japan, was the year the Yodogō group's overseas operations swung into high gear. They were completely engaged in the mission of increasing their numbers by acquiring Japanese citizens in various cities, including Madrid; they were actively planning to create several bases for their operations abroad. If we keep these facts in mind, it becomes clear that Tamiya's letter is more than the essay expressing his longing for home that it purports to be.

To restate the obvious, the Yodogō men did not have the option of expressing their own thoughts or opinions, then or now. Regardless of the issue, they had to follow the guidance of the Workers' Party, and they needed approval from their Party handlers before taking any action. There is no question that they could only have presented this essay after the Party had inspected its contents closely and given approval for publication. Had they expressed their longing for the homeland, Japan, solely on their own initiative, they would immediately have been subject to intensive ideological interrogation and reevaluation. However, the Party and their handlers approved the letter. The letter was submitted to a Japanese magazine and published. The Workers' Party regarded the exercise as a strategic maneuver, using the Yodogō group to advance their efforts to subvert Japan.

The publication of the letter was merely the first move in a propaganda campaign conducted mainly in a political propaganda journal aimed at Japan, *Nihon o Kangaeru* (Think about Japan), published out of Pyongyang from 1981 to 1990.

The training the Yodogō Red Army Faction received at their Japanese village on special operation techniques and the repeated operations to "acquire" Japanese citizens conducted in Europe and elsewhere were both tied to North Korea's anti-Japanese operations. According to the group's more abstract explanations, their duty was to apply the philosophy of *juche* and Kim Il Sung to "the reality of Japan and develop the ideology and theory necessary to found a movement there" (Tamiya et al. 1990, 200); but it is clear that, to them, the abstractions of theory and ideology were meaningless unless they took action as well. From this perspective, the most urgent task in achieving their operational goals was to return to Japan. Unless they could return to Japan to pursue their mission, all their efforts were meaningless. They had to find a way to get back into Japan, no matter what.

One of the characteristics of the Kim Il Sung ideology presented by the Yodogō group was its use of the principle of usefulness, that is, a disregard for truth and a willingness to say anything that would serve their political ends. As such, the patriotic expressions of homeland and their longing for it were convenient tools for an effective emotional appeal to the Japanese people by describing their longing and feeling for the homeland in terms anyone could understand. They were laying the foundations for their return to Japan using any means available. The process was irrelevant because the only thing that mattered was their final success. If they failed, it was the fault of the method or means they had used; if they succeeded, it was thanks to the blessing of the Great Leader. Instead of laying out their political stance and intentions, they used phrases like "feelings for the homeland." This was sophisticated use of the techniques of the art of guidance.

The Yodogō group often used buzzwords such as "humanity," "human rights," "independence," "patriotism," and "ethnicity" in highly political guises. They phrased their appeal not only through these words, but also by referring to the events of the Zenkyōtō movement,[1] their memories of their own *zenkyōtō* experience, and the protest movement against the war in Vietnam.

It was true that their own backgrounds included participation in the mass movements of the time and their membership in the Red Army Faction; they were products of that period. However, ten years in North Korea had changed them profoundly.

They had already traveled a long distance since those days. They were disciples of an ideology with a completely different outlook. *Juche* and the philosophy of Kim Il Sung were not extensions of the ideas they had once followed, but were completely separate from them. The Japanese New Left took as its starting point a departure from Party bureaucracy and Stalinism; the North Korean Workers' Party, espousing the ideology of Kim Il Sung, gave explicit homage to Stalin ("Long Live Stalin!") both in its ideology and its official Party line.

Since shared experiences could gain the sympathy and compassion of their readers, they had to use them to the fullest extent possible. Any gain, however small, was proof of their skills as artists of "guidance."

Their real intentions were in stark contrast to the pretty sentiments of their disguised words.

When Tamiya's "Ten Years since Leaving the Homeland" appeared in Japan with help from the writer Oda Makoto, I read it with a feeling of unease. In retrospect, I should have realized that the Yodogō group, striving to be excellent adherents to the ideology of Kim Il Sung, would not have talked about the homeland in such a way without having hidden intentions. But my sympathy for them led me to underestimate them. The phrase "longing for the homeland" gave an impression of weakness on their part; however, the Yodogō members were crafty political dealers who knew this well and counted on it. Their use of words such as "feeling" and "longing" for the "homeland" was nothing more than carefully chosen strategic phrasing.

The Yodogō hijackers were like Janus: they always showed two faces. One looked to their supporters in Japan, the other to the Workers' Party and the Great Leader. A sharp contrast distinguished the faces

---

1. The Zenkyōtō movement was a broad series of protests on Japanese college campuses from 1968 to 1970 that involved student strikes and building occupations that were initially managed by an all-campus struggle committee, or *zengaku kyōtō*, with mass meetings at which all students could participate, but they frequently devolved into control by competing New Left sects. See Steinhoff 2012, 2013.

of the former Red Army Faction soldiers and those of the current *juche* warriors, adhering to the ideology of Kim Il Sung.

To their supporters and sympathizers in Japan, they never spoke of their lives in the village but always implied that they were exiles with few resources. They may have used the art of guidance at times, but they made no explicit political statements regarding *juche* or the ideology of Kim Il Song. Although in their political reevaluation period they must have concluded that their actions during the Zenkyōtō movement and the protests against the war in Vietnam had been misguided, still they shared nostalgic memories of those days with visitors from Japan. They did not denounce those days of struggle. They said nothing of their daily morning ritual of bowing and singing songs of praise to the portraits of Kim Il Sung and Kim Jong Il. Their words concerned their longing for the homeland, but their intentions lay elsewhere. They concealed the truth not only because it could have interfered with their other activities, but also because, within *juche* doctrine, playing off of two faces in this way was considered politically effective. It furthered their clandestine activities to do so. In front of their Japanese supporters, they displayed one version of their devotion to Kim Il Sung; they hid the true extent of their faith. They engaged in a softer, fake ideology that their Japanese friends would find easier to accept.

At the time when they started talking about the homeland and their longing for it, they also wrote a poem dedicated to their Leader, Kim Il Sung. This congratulatory poem was sent to him on April 15, 1982, in celebration of his seventieth birthday. The men, reborn as loyal followers of Kim Il Sung, produced this carefully polished work after a series of group sessions in one of the village conference rooms.

I reproduce the poem in full here, for the record. Because the original was so long, I have transcribed some of the middle sections in paragraph form. The original had each verse on a separate line.

Congratulations to our esteemed Chairman Kim Il Sung on his seventieth birthday

April 15, 1982
Auspicious day of April, fragrant with the lovely spring
Look—and see waves of bouquets covering Mangyondae
Listen—and hear voices singing praise from five continents
The true and loyal hearts of Choson look up to you as the benefactor of their liberation

The voices of the world laud you as the sun of Man
The seventieth birthday of our esteemed, our beloved Kim Il Sung
You swore at the age of twelve on the banks of the Amur
Never to quit until the homeland was free
Devoted ever since to the People and the Revolution
We bow our heads to your half-century and learn the truth
Along with the myriads who share the day's joy
We humbly extend our song of praise

You/Seek the dignity of Man in his autonomy/Place him at the center of the world/Awaken humanity with *juche* ideals/Make men the masters of revolution/Make them the agents of history/Domination, enslavement, all forms of constraint/Break them all without leaving a mark/Out of the storm of revolution/You founded the era of self-reliance.

You/Suffered with no equal in the struggle against Japan/Even at the price of death by starvation/Refused to take the property of the People/Put the good of the People above all/Made a pact of iron-clad principles/For the love of your People/Only your People/You led the fight against Japan to victory.

You/Defy America, skilled in invasion and war/Believe that those who fight for justice must triumph/Trust the power of the People to the end/With unshakable belief and an iron will/Led the newly freed People of Choson/Began the prologue of the destruction of imperialist America/No negotiation, no mercy for imperialism or domination/You took the lead in the resistance against the imperialists.

You/Standing on a field path wet with morning dew/Beside a machine in a factory/Stay close to the People/Always insist that the best is that which the People say is good/Advance the revolution based on what the People request/Lead on the path of autonomy, independence, and self-defense/For which the world longs/As a model for the world to learn from/You established the People's government, the People's paradise.

You/To the people in the world committed to revolution/Say that revolution can be neither imported nor exported/Teach them to take an independent stance in their fights / Rely on no one / Imitate no one / Lead them to the path where they create their own destiny / You spark new revolutionary vigor, autonomous power.

You / Lift to your shoulders the children who come running to greet you / Say that revolutionaries love and fight for the future / For the glory and happiness of the masses / For the love of the People light a path previously untrodden / For the peoples of the world / Show a blueprint for the future utopia / You are the beacon for the new human history of self-reliance.

O, Chairman Kim Il Sung!
It is you
The leader for whom all the people have been waiting
The teacher of struggle and production for revolutionaries to
      follow
It is you
Shining in this era when human destiny trembles on an edge
The sun of hope for tomorrow's new day
A hero to lead Choson, a hero for the world

During all the years of your long life
Every instant has been dedicated solely to the revolution
In a brief moment out of all the streaming years of history
You accomplished the work of a thousand generations
Your name
Will be engraved forever in the hearts of the people of Choson
And worn as a badge of gold brocade by the people of the world

You treasure the dignity and the value of people more than anything else / You dedicate your life to the love and service of the People / Thanks to you / You / Our life benefactor / Our respected teacher

We flew in on you illegally / You gave us a warm and safe haven / You helped us reach enlightenment over our mistakes

Your favor, your friendship / You value our desire to contribute to our homeland / You guaranteed us the right to study and learn to our hearts' content / What great consideration!

Thanks to you / Thanks only to you / We found and overcame our
mistakes to seek the true path of humankind / Now we can dedicate ourselves to creating the future of our homeland

To you, for whom a single moment is worth thousands in
gold / These twelve years / We have brought you nothing but
worry / Your embracing compassion / Like the passage of time,
like the changing rivers and mountains / We can never in our lives
forget your kindness

We left our homeland to live and learn in Choson
Our hearts overflow with respect at your wise guidance
Fill with gratitude for your unlimited virtue and compassion
Together with the People of Choson and the People of the world
For the Revolution and the Unification of Choson
For the present and future world heading toward the dawn of
    self-reliance
Please take great care of your precious person
We humbly pray for your everlasting longevity

                                                               April 15, 1982

Although there is a substantial difference between this poem that
the group composed together and the faces they (and their wives) presented for their supporters and the propaganda campaign in Japan, there
is no real conflict between them. One Janus, two faces. For operatives
like the Yodogō group, their supporters were targets, nothing more than
targets that had to be roused to serve their interests.

A document was adopted by the Central Committee of the North
Korean Workers' Party in 1974. Titled "Ten Great Principles for the
Establishment of the Party's Single Ideological System," it serves as one
of the foundations of the ideology of Kim Il Sung. The Party, of course,
refers to the Workers' Party, and the Single Ideological System refers to
the ideas of Kim Il Sung. This list is a sort of how-to list for would-be
followers of Kim Il Sung, with rules and behavioral guidelines. These
principles served as the primary creed of the Party. However, this document has never been publicly disseminated by North Korea or been subjected to public debate. It has been used only among devotees of *juche*
and the followers of Kim Il Sung, as a beautiful, secret document to be
memorized.

Why?

First we have to look at the contents of the document. The Ten Great Principles are

1. We must devote our lives to the struggle of *unifying the whole of society* with the revolutionary ideology of our Great Leader Kim Il Sung.
2. We must look up to and worship our Great Leader Kim Il Sung *with total loyalty.*
3. Great Leader Kim Il Sung's *authority must be absolute.*
4. We must believe in the revolutionary ideology of our Great Leader Kim Il Sung, and *his instructions must be our creed.*
5. We must follow the teaching of our Great Leader Kim Il Sung, keeping strictly to the *principle of unconditionality.*
6. We must strengthen the unity of our ideological commitment and the revolutionary solidarity of the whole Party, with our Great Leader Kim Il Sung as our center.
7. We must learn from our Great Leader Kim Il Sung and adopt as our own the practices of communism, the methods of revolutionary undertakings, and the correct attitude for doing the people's work.
8. We must treasure the *political life* granted to us by our Great Leader Kim Il Sung and repay his great political trust and consideration *with total loyalty.*
9. *Under the sole guidance* of our Great Leader Kim Il Sung, we must establish strong organizational discipline so that the whole Party, the whole military, and the whole nation can continue to engage in their activities forever without change.
10. The revolution begun by our Great Leader Kim Il Sung *must continue in each generation until the end* and must be completed. (emphases added by Takazawa)

In short, unifying all of society and the world under the ideology of *juche* is the goal, the primary party line of the followers of Kim Il Sung (according to the bylaws that accompany the Ten Great Principles). To achieve this, each generation (children and grandchildren and on and on) must continue pledging loyalty to Kim Il Sung and "fighting to the end for the victory of *juche the world over*." Loyalty means "living only for the Great Leader and happily devoting one's youth and life to him," making him the absolute leader to the point where "we do not know anyone else" and "handling with great care any portrait, plaster figure, bronze statue, badge, publication featuring his photo, or artwork featuring the Great Leader" (all in the bylaws). Furthermore, every written work and public speech must contain quotations of Kim Il Sung's words. Every person must spend two hours every day intensively studying the revolutionary ideology of Kim Il Sung.

It just continues on in this vein.

The concept of "unconditionality" is explained in the bylaws: it is "the fundamental requirement of loyalty to the Great Leader." So is the creed of Kim Il Sung: his teachings are to be "regarded as law, as a supreme order, with no explanations or excuses allowed." Of course, criticism of any of this was out of the question.

The Great Leader granted the people the priority of their political lives over their biological lives; in North Korea, the loss of one's political life was a more miserable and disgraceful event than losing one's physical life. And there was no guarantee that one's body would continue to live after the loss of political viability. Such a person would have nothing to live for. In North Korea, the concept of "human rights" as we usually conceive it does not exist. "We must think of our political lives as our primary life…" and be prepared to discard "our physical lives like dust and ashes for the sake of our political lives" (in the bylaws).

These "Ten Great Principles for the Establishment of a Single Ideological System" were the secret platform of the Workers' Party and the highest guidelines for the followers of Kim Il Sung. No one could argue against them. The same went for the Yodogō hijackers: by studying these Ten Great Principles and the accompanying bylaws every day, they internalized loyalty and unconditionality.

The Central Committee of the Workers' Party adopted these principles in 1974, and the ideological transformation of the hijackers paralleled the process by which these how-to rules were imposed and enforced on North Korean society. Their rebirth as *juche* warriors meant that their transformation into faithful and unconditional believers in these principles had been completed.

How can words such as "self-reliance" and "autonomy" coexist with terms like "unconditionality" and "total loyalty"? Here is my attempt at following their reasoning:

The theory of the "living body of the State"[2] (that is, a theory of

---

2. Although the North Korean expression includes a few more Chinese characters, this concept is strikingly similar to the term *kokutai,* or "national body," that in prewar and wartime Japan expressed the unconditional unity of the Japanese state and people under the emperor.

society and the body politic) within the ideology of Kim Il Sung teaches that the Great Leader alone is the brain and the People are the limbs, blood, and cells of the body. In this line of thinking, *juche* philosophy can be understood as just another term for the ideology of Kim Il Sung.

Although it is often misunderstood, the philosophy of self-reliance (*juche*) does not allow individuals their own agency. It refers to the agency, the initiative, of the collective group. Although the terms and characters themselves are the same "self-reliance" and "autonomy," the meanings of the words are diametrically opposed to their meanings in Japan and are used in a very different manner. They refer to the necessity of the will, the agency, of the collective. The vision in these words is to make "a single ideology (that of the Great Leader) into the will of the collective (the people)." Individual agency and ideology are only harmful to the leadership and solidarity of the group. Such is the essence of *juche* ideology.

With this being the case, the Yodogō members could talk about "self-reliance" and "agency" only once they had internalized and made completely their own the ideology of the Great Leader. It was a necessary condition. Through this process, the Leader's will became their own: this is what "unconditionality" meant. If their will was identical to that of the Great Leader, there was no need for any conditions; their acceptance was unconditional.

These are the meanings of "unconditionality" and "loyalty" in the ideology of Kim Il Sung. Their loyalty seems to be an expression of ecstasy in surrendering to the Leader. "O, our Father, Great General, may you live ten thousand years! Within the love of our Leader, we advance along the road of loyalty!"

None of this is socialism or anything like it. If anything, it most resembles the official cult of the Japanese emperor before the Second World War. If the North Koreans succeeded in their "unification," then, just as in prewar Japan and in modern-day North Korea, every household would have to display the precious portraits in every room. Instead of the emperor, of course, the portraits would be of Kim Il Sung and his son, Kim Jong Il.

This idea sends a wave of nausea through my stomach the way badly written futuristic novels do; I cannot stop shuddering in bewilderment at the fact that they turned, with all serious intention and with the support of North Korea behind them, to the task of transforming Japan into a nation of "self-reliance."

Mass games with tens of thousands of participants are frequently

Figure 18.01. Mass Games at Moranbong Stadium, with lettering produced by chil‐
dren's synchronized card display. Photo courtesy of The Mainichi Newspapers/AFLO.

held up as examples of the highest expression of *juche* ideology. Boys
and girls demonstrate their praise of and loyalty to the Great Leader in
perfectly choreographed performances that are truly extraordinary. At
some point there was a story that cannot be dismissed out of hand, of
a group of visitors to North Korea who attended one of these events at
Moranbong Stadium and at first mistakenly thought that the pictures of
natural scenes in bright colors created by the children's colored boards
were an electronic display. The background scenes and patterns change
continually, holding for a moment, then shift again. The boys and girls
are moved to tears while they perform these mass shows.

"Our Father, our Leader! Beloved Teacher Comrade! May you live
forever! May you live forever! May you live forever!"

The excitement of the performers infects the audience, and wild
enthusiasm floods the arena. "Isn't it amazing! It's beautiful! This is
juche! The embodiment of *juche* philosophy!" Even tour guides become
carried away in the excitement.

And, to be honest, even I could not help being astounded at their
incredible level of synchronization.

"Beautiful fascism!" The words left my mouth almost without my being aware of it.

Later, the Yodogō wives criticized me severely for this remark, but I believe that form of beauty had to be labeled as "fascism." They turned on me, rebuking me. "It is not fascism! Call it collectivism!" However, either way, I am not one to feel ecstasy in surrendering myself to a group.

At times like this, all of them were passionate when they spoke of *juche* philosophy and collectivism; however, they never voluntarily said anything of the "principle of unconditionality" or of "total loyalty." In this matter, they never showed their true selves to anyone. Of course, from their perspective as followers of Kim Il Sung, the Japanese people, their supporters among them, and I had yet to be "awakened" and prepared to hear the truth. However, their loyalty and eagerness to serve the Leader was clear in their willingness to engage in undercover operations along with the Workers' Party.

Only with absolute submission to the ideology of Kim Il Sung could they risk their lives for the sake of loyalty.

An incident in Europe in 1980 perfectly illustrates this. The Yodogō men and women had only just begun their careers as organized undercover operatives working overseas.

CHAPTER NINETEEN

Contact

Paris, June 1980.

The horse chestnuts lining the streets have passed the peak of their bloom. As the white flowers fall, the green deepens. Paris feels buoyant, cheerful as always when vacation season nears.

So why is the traffic so congested? The street is completely jammed. It's hot. He wishes it just weren't so hot. The temperature is unexpectedly high for June in Paris. He tries crossing from Montparnasse to Luxembourg, but all routes are blocked. He takes a detour at St. Germain des Prés, but even there the streets are crowded, apparently due to an accident.

Tanaka Yoshimi checks his watch in frustration. The set time for the contact is approaching rapidly.

Sunlight glows on a table. She takes a watch out of her bag again, looks at it. It is time. She rises from her seat in the café and begins walking to the meeting place. Even at a slow pace it is not more than five minutes away. She wears sunglasses, as if to avoid any passing eye contact. She arrives. She quietly looks around her.

Nothing.

Keeping her face blank, she strolls through the area. Someone is coming toward her. She continues on without pausing. She has passed through. She keeps walking; then, as if suddenly remembering something, she turns around quickly. She is soon back at the spot.

Still no sign of him.

Tanaka looks at his watch. It is time. He jumps out of the car and runs, runs, runs. He pays no attention to the people he knocks against. Without looking back he tosses over his shoulder Pardon, Excusez-moi!

He continues to shout, running as fast as he can. He leaps fences, runs across lawns. Running, running. Frustration burns. Running. No time to check his watch. Just keep running.

She discreetly looks at her watch again. The contact time has passed. She decides to move away from the meeting place, observe. She is lucky to find a shady spot under a tree and stands, wondering at the heat in June, in Paris. She regrets wearing such heavy socks. Suddenly the thought of him wandering around the village in his boxer shorts comes to mind. Tanaka prefers BVD. He must be sweating in this heat. Her thoughts continue. Tempted to check her watch again, she resists. She has to avoid any suspicious behavior. If anyone were watching, checking the time repeatedly would tell them she is waiting for someone. An enemy would then wait until the other arrives before taking any action. She looks around calmly. It is very quiet.

She feels a sudden surge of anxiety. Unable to restrain herself, she takes out her watch again. It is well past contact time.

Tanaka is still running.

Sweat streams off him; his shirt sticks to his back. He wants things to go as planned. His worst fear is that they will not make contact. He sends up a prayer, even though juche recognizes no god except the Great Leader. Running. Keep running. It is only a little farther. Nearly there. There, just ahead. He arrives. Finally, he has arrived.

Just before the meeting place, he stops briefly to wipe off the sweat with the back of his hand. He takes a deep breath—she is not there.

She has already left. He looks around. Not there. He suddenly feels weak; his knees shake. He takes another deep breath. Breathes....He has to control his breathing. He looks around once again, slowly, looking for a sign of her. He doesn't have the courage to look at his watch.

She is walking at a fast clip.

She must leave the vicinity as quickly as possible. Pursuers might soon find her here. Without any delay, she must get as far away as she can.

Something must have happened to him. She can't help imagining the worst. Her thoughts dwell on the possibilities, though she tries to stop them. He did not make the all-important contact meeting. She can think of no reason except that he must have fallen into the hands of the enemy. Evil and sadistic South Korean agents? American imperialists? The local police could hardly be involved. It has to be South Korean puppets. If he has been arrested, doubtless he is already being brutally interrogated in some underground chamber.

She walks on, terrified that a pursuer might grab her shoulder from behind at any moment. Looking around, she feels as if everyone is staring at her intently.

Tanaka will certainly commit suicide rather than endure torture. She thinks he could not endure the shame of living after being arrested. Such a thing would be unthinkable for a warrior of the Great Leader.

He must be swallowing poison even at this moment! Those South Korean monsters are probably panicking right now. Well, good. Think they can capture us that easily, do they? We are the glorious juche warriors, selected by the Great Leader himself!

She walks on, her thoughts focused only on putting as much distance behind her as possible. Unconsciously, her feet turn toward her room. If Tanaka has fallen into the hands of the enemy, they would soon discover the location of today's contact. Even if he does not talk, they might find and decipher the message. That would be the end of it.

Her pursuers may be closing in on her. They will not let her go free. It is only a matter of time before they find where she is staying. Maybe she is being followed, staked out. Please, hang on just a little longer, Comrade Tanaka, Tanaka of the iron will, just give her a little more time, until she has finished the matter. She could never let his death be in vain. Their Great Leader must be watching over them.

She feels her anxiety solidifying, sensing a real threat. The pressure increases. By this time, her face must be showing it. Sweat drips off her, but she is too preoccupied to wipe it off. She continues to walk at a frantic pace.

Tanaka is at a loss. He wonders what to do next. They failed to make the contact, all the fault of the brilliant sun. He has no way of communicating directly with her. His mission is a strict secret, as is hers. They have never made contact before in Paris, and they can do nothing without instructions. He decides he must first contact Pyongyang, ask them to schedule another contact meeting. He has been forbidden from making direct contact with Pyongyang for the security of his mission. The North Korean trade representative in Paris might be an option as go-between, but, since his activities are based in Paris, it would be very dangerous to ask unless there was a real emergency. Perhaps he could contact Pyongyang through the North Korean embassy in Copenhagen or Belgrade? He thinks it would be best for them to issue the orders organizing another meeting.

She finds herself outside her room.

She takes her key from her bag, inserts it into the keyhole and turns the knob. The door opens with an unpleasant squeak. Later, her memory of the day remains clear up to this point, but everything afterwards becomes disjointed and dim.

She goes around the room picking up her possessions. She does not have much in the way of clothing or personal items; she has to dispose of her activity reports and papers, notebook and address book. She burns them all after checking that the room does not have a fire alarm. Ashes overflow the ashtray, spilling out onto the tabletop. She makes sure nothing is still burning, sweeps it all into a trash can. She would flush it later, she decides. She must at all costs keep all her *documents out of the hands of the enemy. She looks around the room again. That is all of it. Is there anything left? Ah, in a pocket of the clothing she wore the day before and in her wallet. She stands. That is everything. Nothing remains that could cause a problem with the enemy. It is over. She thanks the Great Leader for granting her the time to clean up!*

After she finishes, she feels drained. The intensity of her emotions subsides. She sits down on the edge of the bed. Twilight is falling outside the window.

The sound of footsteps outside rouses her. She tenses. It might be her pursuers. The South Koreans might be outside her door this very minute. If Tanaka has been arrested, it might well be the enemy already. She listens silently. The footsteps belong only to one person and recede down the hall. She hears the distant sound of a door being unlocked. She presses a hand to her heart, realizes she is sweating.

Quietly cracking open the door, she sees nothing but the dimly lit corridor. No one is there, no sign of anyone. She slips out.

She has come to the rooftop terrace.

The Paris sky is red. Laundry left hanging flutters in the slight breeze. Concealing herself in the shade cast by a sheet, she leans over the edge to see people below on the ground. The air is hot, humid. Unenlightened slaves of capitalism! she cries out silently. The day will come when you knock your heads to the ground before the teachings of the Great Leader! Then the people of the world will be liberated from their slavery, and the entire earth will become a paradise, just like the Democratic Peoples' Republic of Korea, the country governed by the Great Leader. For the sake of that day, we fight in the battlefields of the enemy! But those puppets of imperialism, those South Korean creatures, have taken the precious life of Comrade Tanaka. They will pay for that someday. For that day, for the sake of that day....

Great Leader! Forgive me for falling into the hands of the enemy in the midst of this vital mission! In accordance with your teachings, I dedicate myself to loyalty here in the battlefield in enemy territory. Although my body may perish, my loyal heart will surely fly to Mansudae in the beautiful homeland of Mangyondae, to join in happy union along with the hearts of the People of Choson in the love and respect flowing from the compassionate heart of the Great Leader! May you be healthy and may you live forever!

And Dear Leader Comrade Kim Jong Il, thank you for the guidance you have given to us personally and to our efforts for the revolution in Japan. I offer up my heart, overflowing with gratitude....

And Comrade Tamiya! Somehow I must take responsibility for failing to fulfill my duties today and delaying Japan's juche revolution. How I wish you were here to offer me your warm and compassionate guidance!

She thinks of the village. Her memories of the days and years she has spent in North Korea since leaving Japan rise in her mind like phantasmagoric visions. The time she decided not to marry but to dedicate herself to the juche *revolution, the day her child was born in a room in Namsan Hospital, the day the children had their first birthday....*

The scenery of her mind shows her babies just learning to walk, climbing a rise in the village. She softly calls out the names of her daughters. Girls, stay loyal to the teaching of our Great Leader and follow the guidance of our teacher Tamiya. You will become fine juche *warriors, though we may not meet again....*

The neon lights of a café on a corner below her start to flicker with a rustling noise. She looks up with resolution in her face.

Sunset in Paris.

Lights appear on the hill of Montmartre in the distance. The bell tower of Sacré-Coeur begins to fade into the darkness.

...Memory ends here.

She awakens in water. Her body floats gently. It is dark here at the bottom. She is not sure where she is. She struggles under the water, cries out. Suddenly, a ray of light cuts through the dimness and continues to spread. The surface of the water is blindingly bright. Bubbles rise from somewhere, move up to the surface. She feels bubbles all around her body. Slowly, slowly, she feels her body rising with the bubbles. She is wakening from a long sleep.

White ceiling, white walls, white window; where is she? Why is she here? She understands nothing, remembers nothing. What happened to her? She closes her eyes, recalls the sight of the city in twilight, under a blood red sky. Straining to remember, she feels a splitting headache.

"Are you awake?"

She sees a man's face next to her.

"Very good. You survived. You have been asleep for a long time."

With that, he disappears through the white door. He seems to be a doctor.

Having received notification from the Paris police and the emergency hospital that she had regained consciousness, a member of the Japanese embassy staff visited the hospital several hours later. Since she was Japanese, the embassy became involved after her attempted suicide, and, once notified, the embassy had to deal with it.

The doctor reported her condition: "She has finally woken up. She survived because her injuries were not serious. She slept for a long time. We have treated her to the best of our abilities, and she should be ready to leave the hospital in a few days after regaining her strength. Once physically recovered, she should perhaps consult with a psychologist. She often cried out loudly while she was unconscious. She seemed delirious, calling out repeatedly the words 'Tanaka!' and 'Koryakorya.' The Paris police want to talk to her. Please ask her to cooperate with the investigation."

"Delirious? Tanaka? Koryakorya? What is this? Korya…"

The embassy official was surprised enough to feel a bubble of laughter rising inside, but given the situation, he forced it back.

"…Korea?"

The officer from the Paris police briefly explained. "She has a Japanese passport. Please check it later. According to her passport, the woman's name is Mizutani Kyōko. We believe she is Japanese.

"About the incident, she appears first to have thought of throwing herself from the rooftop terrace. Witnesses saw her standing there for a long while. Unable to do so, however, she returned to her room and cut her wrists. She had cuts on her wrists and at the base of her neck. She was found early, so we were able to save her life. According to the doctor, she seems psychologically unstable and even mentally deranged. This is common in foreign students living alone, far from home, especially at this time of year. She should probably get counseling. Or she should be sent back to her family. These cases usually improve quickly once they have returned home."

She had escaped death. The incident was treated as just another case of neurosis in a female exchange student. The embassy staff member recommended she return to Japan, and she agreed. The Japanese embassy in Paris notified her family. It was the first news they had heard of her in the three years since 1977, when she had left Japan.

The Paris police also treated the case lightly. But, had anyone been standing on the rooftop terrace on that hot and humid June evening in Paris, they might have heard her singing in a low voice.

> On the distant underground battlefield, I raise my eyes to our
>> Leader
> He leads us on that road to revolution, glory is in living, glory is
>> in death
> O, one heart, burning with loyalty
> To our Leader, to the Party, I dedicate this body
>
> I have only one wish, to report victory to our Great Leader
> Even if my body is destroyed….

This is a song the Yodogō wives composed to show their loyalty to Kim Il Sung. They apparently sang it often, intoxicated with their own heroism and elite status as chosen ones. This song was much on their lips when they began their clandestine missions. Giving up their lives as if they were nothing but dust would prove their loyalty as "brides of the Great Leader." It was also an iron rule for anyone engaged in a mission: the political life, granted to them by their Leader, always transcended the physical.

Probably Tanaka cannot be blamed for the incident, since in retrospect it may have been caused by the failure of a Party handler to contact him. Whatever the reason for its failure, the group's attitudes toward their missions were so intense that a failed contact would make one of them consider suicide. Soon after Mizutani's return to Japan, she received word that Tanaka was alive.

The matter did not attract the attention of the Japanese security authorities because her connection with the Yogodō group was still unknown at the time. However, it was noted in official records as a foreign incident, since the Japanese embassy had gotten directly involved.

After being taken into protective custody in Paris, she arrived at Narita on July 3, 1980; she spent about two and a half months resting quietly with her family and then disappeared from Japan once again. According to immigration records, she left Japan for Copenhagen on September 26. Detouring to Copenhagen was probably just a blind, and she was soon back in Pyongyang at the Village of the Revolution. She was afterward excluded from joining overseas missions and instead was put in charge of activities in Pyongyang, such as publishing newsletters and providing Japanese education to the children. She has never once returned to Japan since then.[1]

As this story shows, the group members were most cautious when they had to make contact during their overseas missions. They thought themselves extremely careful, never dreaming that, in fact, most of their movements were watched and recorded. In retrospect, their limited understanding of the situation and their mistakes in judgment appear to have been an indirect cause of a completely different matter, the tragedy of Okamoto Takeshi.

---

1. She did eventually return to Japan. See the editor's afterword.

CHAPTER TWENTY

Vienna Operation

Around that time, as one of their missions in the European arena, the Yodogō members working out of Vienna were heavily involved in the antinuclear protest movement. In contrast to their secretive economic missions and the projects to acquire Japanese citizens, their activities in mass political propaganda and agitation as antinuclear protesters were completely legal and conducted in the open.

Years later, Tamiya boasted that these propaganda and agitation activities were their most successful mission. "No one could do anything about it, see? The authorities in Japan may have known about it, but, even if they knew we were involved, they couldn't interfere. We had cultural figures, intellectuals, and other famous people involved. If they tried something on people like that, it would be a pretty serious thing."

Then he added, "You might write some history at some point, and, when you do, be sure to put that in about the Yodogō group, okay?"

"But there isn't any documentation on it, you know," I said.

"We put out some publications on it. You can ask K.[1] I think he has back issues of all our newsletters. You'll understand when you see them. You'll see what we were thinking then."

"Really?"

The idea of writing this book had not come to me yet when we had this exchange, so I had no reason to ask any further.

The K whom Tamiya mentioned was studying at a university in Vienna at the time, working in the antinuclear movement headquarters

---

1. Takazawa follows the convention of using only initials for people who have not been identified publicly as affiliated with the Yodogō group.

there just before the antinuclear protest movement really took off. He was a man of serious mind and high integrity, and Tamiya placed great trust in him.

Tamiya would sometimes tell me about their overseas activities. "That book *Twenty Years after Takeoff,* you know? It's good it got published, but it isn't really a complete description of everything we did. It doesn't say anything about our overseas missions. I think it is about time we went public with that. What do you think?"

"Ah, well, back then, you weren't talking publicly about your overseas activities. What about writing a sequel or something?"

"Yeah, I'll think about it."

After that, little by little, Tamiya told me about their international missions. He spoke of the protest movement, of events in Zagreb and Vienna, and of the time at a restaurant in Amsterdam when the Japanese couple at the next table recognized him. His stories were fragmentary and did not add up to a coherent whole, but this only added to my sense that they were true stories, not smooth, made-up fictions. Ever since Kim Il Sung had revealed the existence of their wives and families, it had become incumbent upon the Yodogō members to speak of their overseas activities. If they denied having worked abroad, how could they claim any truth to the wedding stories of their fateful encounters in Europe with their future wives?

"Do you mind if I write about this stuff?" I asked him once. His reply surprised me.

"No one will complain if you do the research and write about it. What you find in your investigations would come out in public eventually anyway."

After I began writing this book, I often became caught up in the memory of that conversation with Tamiya. His words kept gnawing at me, and to escape their influence I ended up taking a winter journey to Vienna and Zagreb, to UN-occupied Sarajevo and snowy Belgrade. During my travels, I often wondered what he really had meant about what I would find if I investigated. Was he implying that I would find out nothing even if I did do the research? Perhaps he didn't think I would actually travel from Western to Eastern Europe? Or was he trying to tell me something he couldn't say directly? At this point, no one can know what he really meant, because Tamiya then died suddenly. One thing is sure, however: had Tamiya not died so unexpectedly, I would never have set out on my European travels in pursuit of the Yodogō story.

Tamiya Takamaro died in the early hours of November 30, 1995.

The day before, on the twenty-ninth, Tamiya had met the former leader of the Red Army Faction, Shiomi Takaya, before his return to Japan. Tamiya had accompanied Shiomi to the Pyongyang train station to see him off. The two of them had stayed up late the night before talking politics, and we can imagine that Tamiya must have felt very tired. He had not, however, appeared to be on the point of death.

After Shiomi and his party departed on the Beijing-bound international train at 11:50 a.m. in the car designated for foreign passengers, Tamiya returned to the Project 21 building in east Pyongyang.[2]

"I'm tired," he said to the others who were in the office. He went home even before the early winter dark had fallen. This was the last time he was seen alive. His children were living in a dormitory near their school, and his wife, Mori Yoriko, had traveled outside of Pyongyang for the day on business. She had planned to come home that evening, but she didn't finish until late and ended up staying at the office overnight when she couldn't get a ride home. Tamiya arrived at his empty house in the late afternoon.

The next morning, he did not appear at breakfast. Thinking he was just tired, at first the others let him be.

As it got later, however, and he still did not appear, they became worried and went to his room. They found him lying on the floor as if he had fallen from the bed.

They immediately called a doctor, but his condition was obvious. The death certificate states Tamiya's estimated time of death as 4:30 a.m., November 30. The sixteen hours between his leaving the office in Pyongyang and the discovery of his body the next morning, already cold, are an utter blank.

Several months before his death, his sixteen-year-old daughter told him she had dreamed of his death.

Right up until he died, Tamiya was giving lectures to the Yodogō children to prepare them for their return to Japan. Most of the teachers at the Yodogō Japanese School were women such as Kaneko Emiko, Akagi Shirō's wife. The curriculum consisted largely of Japanese language, history, and customs. As the time for the children's return to Japan drew near, however, Tamiya himself, as school principal, began delivering the last lectures.

---

2. In the 1990s, the North Korean government built the Yodogō group a multistory building to house their international business activities and serve as their base in urban Pyongyang. It was called the Project 21 Building.

"I want at least for our children to return to Japan," he said right up to the end. "It became their destiny to be born as the Yodogō children. I want them to have the strength to throw off this destiny and live their own lives."

I believe he was under heavy stress. But I cannot let go of the feeling that his death was rather suspicious.

Winter in Vienna is always freezing, and, that year, the cities of Europe shivered under an intense cold spell. It was impossible to step outside even for a moment without adequate winter clothing. My hands were numb from the raw weather, and I kept them stuffed deep into my pockets whenever I went out. Even when I visited such heavily frequented places as Grabenstrasse or Haas-haus, the merciless cold made me miserable. The opera house lay under a heavy mantle of snow. I sat in a café off Kärtnerstrasse, thinking of the Vienna of the late 1970s and early 1980s. That was probably about the time when one of the hijackers, Okamoto Takeshi, had become active in the city; however, he had disappeared suddenly early on.

Japanese students in Vienna were the first to join the antinuclear protest that swept Europe in the late 1970s. The movement centered in Vienna spread out rapidly, reaching even Japan, where widespread interest was expressed by the "Writers' Antinuclear Proclamation." Slogans flew everywhere: "No Nuclear War"; "No Nukes, No War"; "Disarmament"; "No Atomic Power"; "Anti-America, Pro-Independence"; "Nuclear Firestorms"; "No Nuclear Weapons." People joined the protest motivated by fear of a nuclear war that would end in the extinction of humankind. The antinuclear protest movement appealed strongly to all people who felt the danger of such a nuclear confrontation during the tensions of the cold war between East and West; at the same time, though, the Eastern side had the hidden political agenda of working against the United States and President Reagan's nuclear policy of military expansion. Both East and West possessed nuclear arms, but, for some reason, the arsenals of the East were largely ignored by the movement, whereas the West was strongly criticized. Just about the only person to question this bias may have been Yoshimoto Takaaki.[3] One reason that nuclear weapons in the East did not get much attention is because the protest movement had its start in the Soviet Union and Eastern Europe. The

---

3. Yoshimoto Takaaki is a prominent Japanese intellectual whose ideas had great currency within the New Left in the 1960s and early 1970s.

Soviet Union was not alone in manipulating the protests to its own ends. North Korea played its own role in the Soviet strategy, with the Workers' Party giving the Yodogō members responsibility for some of the propaganda activities.

The Yodogō members spent a lot of time in Europe and joined protest groups in Vienna, Berlin, Paris, and the Eastern European countries. They wrote and published pamphlets and newspapers, attended meetings and demonstrations. They sometimes organized events, and a convenient stage for much of their activism was Vienna, long an important focus for many of North Korea's schemes. Vienna was an important base to the Yodogō operatives not only for their antinuclear propaganda work, but also for other ventures: Ishioka Tōru and Matsuki Kaoru, two of the Japanese students who disappeared from Madrid, appear to have visited Vienna during their travels with the Yodogō wives.

They began their antinuclear propaganda project by publishing a magazine called *O! Japan.* They formed a planning committee and held numerous discussions. The magazine at first was small, with a limited circulation. This was in 1978; as more issues were published, the magazine's contents and coverage became more comprehensive.

The original Yodogō editors later brought on Kuno Osamu and Ui Jun as consultants and editors, and *O! Japan,* first published out of Vienna, was soon established as the main Japanese mouthpiece of the antinuclear movement in both Japan and Europe. Eventually their offices were moved to Tokyo. K, mentioned earlier, was an important contributor in the early stages of the magazine, and Tamiya was important as a leading activist, but in fact it was Okamoto Takeshi who led the way in organizing the movement and keeping in contact with the leadership.

The antinuclear protest movement leapt from Europe to Japan, spreading as quickly as wildfire. In Hiroshima, Nagasaki, and other cities, it inflamed civil organizations and workers' unions. Tens of thousands of people joined in protest activities and mass assemblies in Tokyo's Meiji Park; large groups repeatedly performed "die-ins," lying on the ground and pretending to be dead. Though initially they represented possible victims of nuclear war, at some point the term "antiwar" replaced "antinuclear" and outstripped it in popularity. The protest movement introduced an invigorating new focus for Japan's sluggish civic movements of the late 1970s and early 1980s.

I remember being mildly surprised to discover that Tamiya was active behind the scenes of the antinuclear movement. Knowing the Yodogō group ran the protest movement's propaganda campaign under the supervision of North Korea and the Workers' Party gave me a new perspective on history.

What did the antinuclear movement mean to the Workers' Party and the Yodogō group? Besides being a direct protest against Ronald Reagan's military expansion strategy, the importance of the movement meant increased political clout for both the Workers' Party and the Yodogō members. It facilitated the dissemination of *juche* ideology under the smokescreen of the movement. This was a first step in the ultimate goal of the whole world and every society assimilating the ideology of Kim Il Sung and *juche.* Moreover, for the Yodogō group, there was a deeper, hidden benefit: the popularity of the movement made it easy to meet young Japanese intellectuals. These young people joining in protest against nuclear arms, with their elevated awareness of social problems, were unpolluted with ideological convictions from other sects and were perfect targets for the Yodogō group's mission of acquiring new Japanese adherents to their group.

In 1982, four years after the first issue of *O! Japan,* a group consisting of some of the editors and several central members of the Vienna-based antinuclear movement established a new political organization, the New Wave of Democracy. On March 21, in a restaurant in Vienna, some fifteen Japanese living in Paris, West Germany, Vienna, and other European cities gathered for the founding meeting of the new organization.

The following is from the group's initial announcement. There is no point giving the entire document; this is only a portion. Anyone who is familiar with the ideology of *juche* or who has read any of Kim Il Sung's books will immediately detect the traces of *juche* in it.

> From the Baltic Sea in the north to the Aegean in the south, Europe is now right in the midst of a new struggle. Hundreds of thousands of demonstrators and their tens of thousands of flags occupy the streets and public squares....They have stood up. For their own sakes, for their parents, for their children, for everyone they love, they have stood up. They stand to protect the homelands they love. They stand in a holy war as patriots against nuclear arms.
>
> They begin to understand. If they truly hope to achieve peace, they begin to understand that every nation, every people must respect others' rights of freedom as equal to their own and must aim for self-reliance. They have come to understand that they must cast away those of their national leaders who follow

the superpowers, that the citizens themselves must control their national polity, and they must actively pursue the goal of true democracy....

This is happening not only in Europe. The struggle against nuclear arms and for nuclear disarmament is gaining strength in Japan, and a renewed wave of antinuclear struggle, antiwar protest, and patriotism is spreading over the country.

We live in the era of "self-reliant liberation," when all countries and all peoples walk their own path of self-reliance, the democratic era when the masses become the masters of their own countries and direct their own politics; it is the "age of revolutionary struggle," when the people tear down the old and rebuild a new system....

While living overseas, we have been touched by the breath of the vibrant third world, and, seeing how the old yoke of stagnant European democratic ideology is being thrown off there in a new wave of democracy, we are excited to see the rise of a new political movement in our own country. As Japanese people, we enter the holy battle to create a new Japan, and so we proclaim the first European committee meeting of the New Wave of Democracy here today....

The New Wave of Democracy is an alliance of those with the noble mission of realizing true democracy in our country, a confederation, a campaign....

Friends, who respect democracy and self-reliance, who demand peace! Let us stand united to fight for the creation of the New Wave of Democracy. (*O! Japan*, April 1982)

I began to search for back numbers of *O! Japan*. I contacted K and visited libraries that appeared to collect limited-circulation periodicals and material on social movements, but I could not assemble all the issues. When I was having difficulty collecting them, K sent me a few editions.

The formation of the New Wave of Democracy was featured in the fourth anniversary issue (April 1982) of *O! Japan*. Many well-known people wrote messages to be read at the founding meeting, including such well-known Japanese intellectual and political figures as Iwai Akira, Doi Takako, Yoshikawa Yūichi, Ui Jun, Utsunomiya Tokuma, Noma Hiroshi, Kunō Osamu, and Maruki Iri, among others.

Apparently Tamiya Takamaro wrote the draft of the proclamation, and, when I read it with this fact in mind, I could detect it quite clearly in the phrasing and in his typical *juche* ideological language. Although it can be argued that the Yodogō group was merely riding a wave of popular feeling with this antinuclear movement in Europe, it was still one of the most successful of their projects there. Tamiya spoke of their antinuclear protest activities as an example of their successes, but this may well have been the only one, of all their projects in twenty years of activity, that they could pursue in the open. Later projects, such as their proposal of a "Respect the Constitution" movement and the "Humanitarian Association for the Return to Japan," showed similar traits of attempting to spark a public movement, but none of them developed into a mass movement.

Let's look at some other activities in which members of the Yodogō group were engaged during this period. First, there was their official participation in the International Congress of Journalists against Imperialism and for Goodwill and Peace in Pyongyang in July 1983; second, their attendance at the Second Pan-African Youth Festival in Libya the following month. When we retrace the course of their careers, these two events are important milestones in the lives of the Yodogō group members; I wish to consider the most salient points about their participation in them.

The International Congress of Journalists took place in Pyongyang from July 2 to July 6, 1983. There were 169 people representing 118 countries participating, most of them members of groups following *juche* ideology. Tamiya and Konishi Takahiro represented the magazine *Nihon o Kangaeru* (Think about Japan); on the second day of the congress, Tamiya made a speech titled "Anti-Imperialism is the Path to Peace." He concluded the speech by saying, "Thirteen years ago, we came to the Democratic People's Republic of North Korea in our struggle against Japan's militarism; today, armed with a new ideology and theory, we pursue justice through literary activities, and we will stand together with the ranks of our people in the struggle for an independent and democratic Japan. We hold high our pens and advance toward victory!"

The Pan-African Youth Festival, organized by the Libyan Student League and other organizations, was held in Tripoli from August 22 to 31 of 1983. This time, Konishi and Wakabayashi Moriaki attended representing *Nihon o Kangaeru.* No further mention would be necessary for a simple chronicle of their activities, but Konishi's report on this festival in Libya, "Think of Japan from Africa" (in *Nihon o kangaeru,* no. 9), contains some very interesting passages concerning their "passport problems." Let's just take a quick look at them.

Figure 20.01. Konishi Takahiro and Wakabayashi Moriaki in Libya. Photo from *Nihon o kangaeru*, Winter 1984, p. 7, in Takazawa Collection.

Figure 20.02. Konishi Takahiro and Wakabayashi Moriaki with conference participants in Libya. Photo from *Nihon o kangaeru*, Winter 1984, p. 7, in Takazawa Collection.

Because their visit to Libya was made openly, it was reported in Japan. However, since at the time their frequent overseas trips were still a secret, Konishi had to maintain the fiction that it was their "first journey by air in thirteen years [since the hijacking]." He was obliged to devote a few pages to explaining their "passport problems." Even though from our present vantage point his explanation reads like a joke, let us take a look:

> Well, when we decided to go to Africa, our first problem concerned passports. Of course, it is no surprise that we did not possess passports, since we had crossed the sea from Fukuoka without any documentation. We were determined to go as Japanese citizens; we had to. There is such a thing as a *"laissez-passer,"* a document that can be used instead of a passport. We applied to the relevant office of the North Korean government, and they agreed to issue one to us.
>
> The *laissez-passer* was not a certificate of citizenship in the DPRK. The first page of the document was printed with a message in Korean, French, and English: "This *laissez-passer* is for the purpose of international travel by foreigners only. Possession of this document does not affect the nationality of the carrier."
>
> In short, the "passport" was a travel certificate for foreigners, and you would not become a North Korean citizen by using it. (*Nihon o kangaeru*, no. 9, p. 55)

Perhaps Konishi felt it was necessary to mention the travel certificate (the *laissez-passer*) since their journey was public knowledge, but in fact there was no chance that anyone would be allowed to travel internationally using a travel certificate issued by the Democratic People's Republic of Korea. Immigration officials of any country would find such a document of dubious value and request to see a real passport. In fact, it later became known that they traveled under diplomatic or counterfeit passports and that this trip to Libya was not their first visit overseas. In his last interview (Tamiya and Takazawa 1996), Tamiya said clearly that they began going overseas in 1975, though these early "business trips" (as they called their activities outside North Korea) were always in the company of their Workers' Party handlers, who either worked with them or watched over them.

When Tanaka Yoshimi was arrested in Cambodia in 1996, the Yodogō members still in Pyongyang said in an interview with Japanese television that he had been using a *laissez-passer*. This was a fabulous joke since, by the time he was arrested, everyone knew he had presented himself as a North Korean diplomat named Kim Ilsu, traveling under a passport issued by the DPRK. Moreover, Konishi's report stated that the *laissez-passer* was merely a travel certificate for foreigners; it did not allow its bearer to work or engage in economic activities. In the same interview, the Yodogō group members stated publicly that Tanaka was conducting international trade in Cambodia. These contradictions irritated many who heard them.

This obvious lie is one more vital key in understanding the overall Yodogō problem today. In fact, if we didn't know how they create lies, it would be impossible to understand their explanations and reactions regarding the Okamoto Takeshi incident of a few years later.

When he spoke of the Yodogō group's involvement in the antinuclear protest movement, Tamiya asked me, "You know what was going on, don't you?" Unfortunately, however, I am unable to analyze closely the pamphlets they issued or the back issues of *O! Japan*. What I can see in the few copies I have been able to assemble is only the influence of *juche* on the contents, the mere shadow of the Yodogō group in the background. But these materials do reflect the Yodogō group's activities in Europe at the time. In the ads from cafes and restaurants and the like from all over Europe, in the letters to the editor from the magazine's readers, there are keys to understanding. But these clues only give me a glimpse of the activists' faces, a vague sight of the streets where they worked. Still, they were finally becoming engaged as activists within a wide network of contacts, even if they were as closely watched as fishing cormorants,[4] unable to escape their North Korean captors.

The era of increasing global outcry against nuclear weapons coincided with the beginning of the Yodogō group's overseas activities after a long period of confinement.

---

4. Cormorant fishing is a traditional fishing method in Japan and China. In Japan it is done at night by firelight, from small riverboats. The birds are attached by a leash to their fisherman handler and may also have a string around their necks that allows them to swallow small fish but traps larger ones. The cormorants dive underwater to catch the fish and then return to the boat, where the fisherman helps them disgorge the fish from their throats. Hence, the meaning here is that the Yodogō members were sent out to catch more converts but were closely tied to their North Korean handlers.

CHAPTER TWENTY-ONE

Shadows in the Background

Okamoto Takeshi was in Vienna.

1978, Summer, Vienna, Mariahilfer Strasse

Okamoto Takeshi could feel someone watching him from behind.

He turned a corner, walked along for a moment, turned back. He looked deliberately at the people passing by. The feeling disappeared.

Perhaps he had only imagined it, he thought, and returned to Mariahilfer Strasse near Vienna's West Station. Once back on the larger street, however, the feeling of being watched closely returned. He walked on, thinking that perhaps his nerves were reacting to the proximity of their temporary headquarters for the antinuclear protest project.

He slowed from his usual brisk pace.

One pedestrian passed him, then another. No one adjusted speed to match. He might be imagining things after all. He stared watchfully at the people on the opposite side of the street, at the backs of those ahead of him. He had learned in the village how to follow someone without being noticed, and using everything he had learned he examined the people around him. His tail was not necessarily alone; often, a team of three or four persons follow their target, changing their positions, now ahead, now behind, perhaps on the other side of the street, but always keeping their prey between them. With these thoughts in mind, Okamoto walked along, paying careful attention.

He had not noticed anything at the airport. He had taken the airport limousine bus from Schwechat Airport to the city air terminal. He first noticed the feeling

as he passed through the ticket gate in Mitte Station on his way down to the sub-
way to catch a train. Feeling an intense stare, he jumped on the train that had just
arrived at the platform. He changed trains after a few stations. He should have lost
his pursuer, but still he had the unpleasant feeling of being watched from behind.

He walked on. He kept walking for a long time.

Finally he thought the sensation had ceased. Not that he could be sure he
had been followed; it was just a feeling he had had.

Once again, Okamoto made his way toward the designated contact point.

1978, Winter, Vienna, Stephansplatz

When he emerged at ground level from the subway station at Stephansplatz,
Okamoto heard bells ringing out loudly from above. For a moment he was con-
fused, thinking he had taken the wrong exit, but it was only the bells of Stephans-
dom, and the street was lively and bright as day in the light from streetlamps and
shop windows. He had apparently come out in the middle of Kärntner Strasse. The
bells completely drowned out a street musician playing violin. Raising his eyes to
the bell tower of the cathedral, he saw the spire disappearing into the darkness
above. As always, he felt overwhelmed by its size and grandeur. He made his way
down the slope of Rotenturmstrasse toward the Donau Canal and noticed a man's
reflection in the window of a boutique as he passed. The man had been on the
subway with him.

He increased his pace. He stopped outside a restaurant and pretended to
read the menu, but it did not seem that the man was following him. Snow was
falling gently. Okamoto closed the front of his coat more tightly and continued on
his way toward the canal.

Several months had passed since Okamoto had begun his duties in
Vienna. He had been assigned to further encourage the antinuclear protest movement, which was picking up momentum in Europe. But this
momentum could still dissipate like fireworks, losing its brilliance in
an instant. To prevent this and to succeed in converting the quickening
antinuclear protest movement into a new wave of revolution, Okamoto
believed that he must extend his lateral network, establishing secret
connections with individual protest organizations in different European
countries. He also thought he should create a connection between this
surge of protest in Europe and the fledgling movement in Japan. Excitement rose in him at these ideas. He was reminded of his experiences in
the student movement of the late sixties and the Zenkyōtō movements

on university campuses.[1] His involvement in the antinuclear protests here in Vienna made him think often of those days.

Okamoto had been involved in the fighting at Yasuda Auditorium on the Tokyo University campus on January 18 and 19, 1969. The riot police had shot high-powered water cannons to disperse the protesters, soaking him and others. The weather had been freezing. Three others who would join the hijacking—Wakabayashi, Abe, and Akagi—had also been there.

Later, Okamoto had written about the battle at the auditorium in his essay for inclusion in the Yodogō group's collected memoirs, *Twenty Years after Takeoff*. Just before publication, however, his contribution was suddenly removed.

> I (Okamoto) was at the Yasuda Auditorium at Tokyo University. I fought in that battle. I thought, "It looks interesting. I'll give it a try." Apparently, however, this was an uncharacteristic move on my part; after I came here, I heard that my older brother had been astonished to hear I had gotten arrested for it.
>
> Before then, I had not been involved in any of the protest movement activities.... I had something of an inferiority complex about it, since my older brother was an activist, and I didn't think I could surpass him. That is why I never wanted to do the same things he did. When I was at Kyoto University, I was really into mountain climbing. I joined the mountaineering club, and we climbed most of the major mountains in Japan, starting with the Japanese Alps. The climbing gave me a sense of fulfillment and well-being, but it's true it wasn't quite enough. I was looking for something more worthwhile.
>
> That was the era of the Zenkyōtō movement on college campuses. Even at Kyoto University, the conflict was escalating. I had quite a wide circle of friends, including several activists. Knowing them made me interested in what was going on, though I had not joined in any particular activities.
>
> Toward the end of 1968, I heard the conflict at Tokyo University was heating up. People were saying there would be a big

---

1. See chapter 1, note 1, and chapter 18, note 1, for a general description of *zenkyōtō*. Okamoto was a Kyoto University student, but like many others he went up to Tokyo to participate in the two-day battle with the riot police in January 1969, which ended the six-month strike at Tokyo University. The campus remained closed for some time afterwards, and entrance exams were canceled, so there was no entering class in spring 1969. See Steinhoff 2013.

final battle early in the new year, and they were coming in from all over the country to join in. Some friends of mine asked me if I wanted to go as well.

I thought it sounded like fun. We might be fighting with Minsei[2] students or maybe clashing with the riot police. It was a fight for a real man to get involved in, and I thought, I'm a man, I'm going! I decided to go to Tokyo to join the battle.

Of course, my brother was surprised. In those days, my motto, very simply, was "If it's interesting and worthwhile, don't talk about it, do it!" In the end, this was my fundamental motivation for joining the Red Army Faction and then going along on the hijacking. Not that I wasn't thinking of social issues as well; I had read the works of Marx and Lenin, and I knew a little about the contradictions of capitalism and about revolution. But it was only knowledge, and at the time words meant nothing to me. Only action really had any meaning. That was my belief at the time.[3]

Later that same year, there was an intense and desperate fight at the clock tower of Okamoto's own Kyoto University. The streets around Higashi Ichi-jō glowed with the fire of exploding Molotov cocktails, but, as expected, the students lost the battle. This was when Okamoto started thinking he wanted a gun, that only armed struggle would tear down the wall of authority. He immediately joined the Red Army, then threw himself impulsively into the hijacking and, because of it, finally found himself in Vienna.

Early 1980s, Vienna, Autumn, Schönbrunn

Okamoto came to a halt.

He had noticed an apparently Asian man whom he thought he had seen before. When he turned around to look, the man was moving out of sight in a relaxed manner. Okamoto let out an abrupt laugh. He was too nervous, he thought. He must "be bold but cautious."

Okamoto resumed his stroll in the extensive gardens of Schönbrunn Palace, making his way toward the meeting place. Schönbrunn had belonged to Maria-

---

2. Minsei was the student organization of the Japan Communist Party, which was considerably to the right of the New Left student groups and often fought against them in campus conflicts. Minsei opposed the conflict at Tokyo University.

3. The content of this manuscript was removed from *Twenty Years after Take-off* (Tamiya et al. 1990), but the manuscript remained in Takazawa's possession.

Thérèse; Marie Antoinette had passed part of her girlhood there. Her luxurious rooms were still preserved in the palace. He had been amazed by their extravagance on a previous visit. A fountain played around a statue of Neptune at the center of the gardens, and the palace was visible through the curtain of water. He could see his contact approaching.

Once away from the contact and the meeting place, Okamoto told another Yodogō member about his feeling of being watched all the time, of sensing someone's gaze on his back.

"But it could just be my imagination...."

"Maybe you're just tired?"

"Well, maybe." Perhaps he really was a little tired. He had been working hard day after day and meeting with lots of different people. Even though he thought he had taken every precaution, that feeling of being watched had been growing stronger every day.

His colleague only repeated, "Please watch out. But be bold!" But he could really only look out for himself.

Along with Copenhagen, Vienna was an important center of operations for North Korea. Copenhagen was a hub for their comings and goings, their window to Western Europe, but Vienna lay at the geographical center of their European activities, and North Korea had several operatives stationed there. Austria may have been a neutral country, but, as far as North Korea was concerned, Vienna was nothing less than the heart of Europe.

For the Yodogō hijackers, Vienna was vital not only as the headquarters of the antinuclear protest movement, but also for its easy access to Zagreb (in the former Yugoslavia), where they had just established their own general headquarters for European activities. Everyone from the village came and went often, and their meetings with staff members of the North Korean embassy were frequent. It is no wonder their movements were under close observation; what is surprising is that Okamoto was the only one who noticed.

Early 1980s, East Berlin, Marx-Engels Square

The man was standing alone.

He lit a cigarette, then stood motionless. He did not seem to be waiting for anyone. What could he be doing there? Looking this way. Asian. Okamoto felt the man was watching him.

He turned toward the lone figure, who turned away in a deliberate man-ner but didn't seem to be leaving. Okamoto crossed the square in the direction of Friedrich Station on Unter den Linden. The linden trees lining the street threw it into shadow. The man continued to watch from a distance as Okamoto walked along the sidewalk.

Later, once again, Okamoto told a colleague that he had noticed he was being watched.

The projects Okamoto had overseen from Vienna were progressing well. The publication of the magazine was on track. An office had been established in Tokyo, and he would soon hand the entire operation over to the staff there. The protest movement had spread like fire through Japan, sparking an ever larger response in demonstrations by student and civic groups. Several of the wives had started slipping secretly back into Japan to carry out different tasks. The first level of Okamoto's mission was complete; it was time to move on to the next stage.

He went to Canada after finishing up in Vienna. His new task was to set off another wave of antinuclear protest among the large population of Japanese residing in Canada and to begin recruiting capable new activists. He did not think he would be in Canada for long, however, because soon he would embark on a bigger and even more important mission: his secret return to Japan.

The Yodogō group started planning their secret returns to Japan in the early 1980s. They considered many different routes for their reentry, including beach landings from boats or using counterfeit passports. Okamoto was the first assigned to make the attempt. He was given the task because of his earlier successes in Vienna. It would be an extension of his duties there because the antinuclear protest movement had become so big in Japan. Tamiya wanted to create a situation in which all the members of the Yodogō group could return to Japan, riding on the wave of antinuclear protest. He chose Okamoto to be the first to go.

A day in the early 1980s, Canada, Vancouver International Airport

It was nearly boarding time.

Okamoto was hurrying back to the village to prepare for his new mission. He felt his excitement rising. The reason was clear: the day for their return to Japan was finally approaching.

"This is going to be fun," he thought.

"Ten years since...." He was full of memories as he buckled the seat belt. As the prospect of his secret return became more real, he could not stop himself from indulging in thoughts he had long suppressed: memories of Japan; the faces of friends; his mountaineering days at Kyoto University; his hometown, Kumamoto. The pain he had caused his parents. He would not be able to see them while he was in Japan on mission, but at least he would be near them. Thinking of home reminded him of his younger brother, serving a life sentence at Ramleh Prison in Israel as the sole surviving gunman of the Tel Aviv airport attack in 1972. He found himself wondering if, in fact, they had indeed surpassed their older brother.

He turned his thoughts to the snow-tipped Canadian Rockies, visible through the tiny cabin window. Suddenly he was flooded with emotion and closed his eyes slowly. Strangely, with his eyes shut, he felt relief steal through him. He understood why. He had finally escaped the sensation of being watched from behind: in Canada, he had not felt it even once.

The plan for slipping Okamoto into Japan never quite came together. A secret landing from a smuggling boat presented too many pitfalls. Landing might be possible, but he would soon be stopped and apprehended. His ability to come and go freely was of primary concern, since it was vital to the success of their mission. He would need to return to the village in Pyongyang for various activities on a regular basis. A counterfeit passport would not serve his purposes, since he would be able to use it only once to enter Japan, after which it would be useless. He would be ineffective if he could not engage in his activities in Japan with all the rights of a legal citizen. The best solution was to obtain the real passport of a person who actually existed. This was not a simple matter of using a passport just once, as they often did overseas.

Everyone in the village bent their minds to this problem, but no one could come up with a workable solution. The Workers' Party's special Yodogō section offered to work with them on it, but around this period the members were starting to take on more responsibilities in other missions as well and could not devote much time to this project even though they considered it to be of great importance.

There was another reason they did not have much time to spare.

Much of the men's time was occupied with childcare. The wives, still not flagged by the authorities, were often sent to Japan and other countries for various kinds of business. Taking care of the children often fell to the men (although, given the resident nursery school teachers, nurses, and child-care facilities in the village, their burdens could not have been as heavy as they claimed in later years). Their numbers had more than doubled with the addition of the women and children, but still the Yodogō members' numbers were too few for the amount of work they had to do.

It was just around this time that the New Wave of Democracy was established in Vienna. In March of 1982, Okamoto flew to Vienna via Copenhagen to attend the inaugural meeting.

One day in March, 1982, Copenhagen, Strøget

He had not been in Copenhagen for a long time.

As he pushed open the door of his usual café, he had an unpleasant premonition.

He felt unease coil inside him. The atmosphere of the café was subtly different. Something was wrong; a warning went off in his head. He had returned to Europe, and already that uncomfortable feeling had found him again.

He sat down at a table instead of at the counter. A smiling blond waitress took his order. He drank coffee. Her eyes seemed to ask why he did not sit at the counter and have his usual beer, and Okamoto suddenly thought that he had used this café too much. It had often been the contact site to meet others from the village; he had even met Mr. Kim (Kim Yuchol) there. He had come to like the place because it was convenient, and its country-style décor reminded him of similar places in Shinjuku and the Kawaramachi district of Kyoto.

From where he sat, he could see the Strøget clearly through the café windows. When he had time, he liked to sit and watch the passers-by. The café was stylish, with bottles lined up on the shelves and posters on the walls. Coffee cup in hand, he looked around him. It was not a large place, and he could see everything clearly except some seats in the shadow of a wall in the back. All the other customers were probably locals. He heard or felt a note of discord, though he could not tell who made it; the feeling that something was wrong returned, even stronger than before. Okamoto finished his coffee and left the café immediately.

The following day, Copenhagen, Kastrup Airport

Once again he was being watched. What was this strange feeling that he could not suppress, the same feeling he had had the day before in the café? He raised his head, unable to escape the disagreeable sensation that someone was staring at him intently. Maybe he was just thinking too much. Who could be watching him, anyway? And from where?

Okamoto looked down once again at the magazine he held in his hands, trying to brush off the unpleasant feeling. But he could not absorb the meaning of the words he stared at. He was not alone; he glanced at his companion seated next to him. She seemed calm, serene. It must be him, thinking too much.

Okamoto may have decided he was just worrying too much, but if he had glanced up again from his magazine and looked directly ahead, he might have been able to hear the click of a camera's shutter.

A photo exists, taken that year, on that same date.

In the photo, Okamoto has turned his eyes back to the magazine in his hands. A woman in a vest sitting next to him also has her eyes turned down to something in front of her. The scene seems to show they have finished all necessary conversation and are merely passing the time. They do not appear relaxed.

The feeling that he was being watched dogged Okamoto persistently. And, indeed, there were times when he was being observed. That Okamoto sensed this correctly is proven by the pictures taken by intelligence agents. He was not the only one being watched. Not only the other hijackers but the wives were under observation as well. Okamoto tried several times to warn his associates to be careful, fearing a trap. They, however, dismissed his concerns, saying he was just too nervous. The Great Leader was knowledgeable about all things and would never make a mistake; it was impossible that anyone should be watching them....

This belief would put Okamoto into a difficult position with the rest of the group. His situation was about to take an unexpected turn.

Early 1980s, at the village in the Pyongyang suburbs

It was a Saturday near the end of the month.

The last weekly criticism meeting of each month was devoted to analyzing the activities of the whole month. That day, the Yodogō members were scrutinizing each other's ideologies in a session of mutual criticism.

One member of the group stood up. "I want to say a few things about revolutionary vigilance and our missions.

"Needless to say, our missions should be carried out with the utmost boldness. And, of course, we must operate with scrupulous care and revolutionary vigilance in all our efforts. However, the difference between caution and revolutionary vigilance, and pure cowardice is as great as heaven and earth.

"If we become caught up in cowardice or passivity, we won't be able to accomplish half of what we aim for.

"Cowardice raises the danger of opportunism and retrogression, which we abhor. We must take to heart the Great Leader's philosophy and carry out our mission of *juche* revolution with all care and boldness.

"However, I must point out that recently we have been seeing in our organization a tendency to confuse revolutionary vigilance and caution with personal cowardice and retrogression, spreading anxiety among our number. Boldness and recklessness are two completely different matters. Similarly, keeping revolutionary vigilance and falling into opportunistic wavering because of fear of some imagined watchers are polar opposites.

"We need to be cautious and also bold. I think the more faithful we are to the Great Leader, the more easily we will find the balance between caution and boldness.

"Unfortunately, one among our organization has lately been giving in to this tendency toward retrogression and cowardice. He has shown timidity many times when he claims that someone is following him during his overseas assignments or watching during his contact meetings. I have to say this behavior has thrown a shadow over the morale of our whole group...."

Okamoto listened in silence to this criticism from his comrade.

"While on assignment, this comrade has on occasion suggested to his fellows that they change dates or wait for another opportunity, because now it was too dangerous to go forward with the plan.

"The Dear Leader Comrade has taught us that 'we don't wait for chances, we make them,' but our comrade's actions show that he has not properly understood our Leader's thought and has retrogressed.

"Postponing any action because of danger will delay our revolutionary mission. If he knew of some danger, why did he not compensate for it beforehand? Or circumvent it? What if he only imagined the danger out of nervousness? If the matter was one rising from his imagination or from his own lack of commitment, then I must label this as a crime and traitorous to our revolutionary mission and to the Great Leader. We cannot deny that this reveals problems in his devotion to his duty to the people and his loyalty to our Leaders.

"This kind of thinking is a betrayal of the trust bestowed upon us by the Great Leader and the Dear Leader Comrade to carry out our glorious revolutionary mission. Even more, surely suggesting to a fellow comrade to wait until another time is nothing more than giving up on the mission.

"In addition, there have been several reports of this comrade engaging in 'liberal' activities while on his overseas missions....

"I think we need a strict analysis (*sōkatsu*) from this comrade."

Okamoto remained silent.

The afternoon sun threw long slanting shadows across the meeting room.

He remained silent, saying nothing in his own defense until directly asked to do so. But he had finally understood. He knew who had been watching him. He sat at the table, lost in thought.

In North Korea, some personal activities may be labeled as illicit by calling them "liberal." It was a favored trick for getting others into trouble. Until now, he had thought the watching eyes belonged to the enemy, most likely South Korean secret agents. But now he came to think that perhaps he had been mistaken. He looked back, reexamining the past. He remembered the Asian man who had stared at him in East Berlin and the other man in Schönbrunn. Perhaps that was why they had seemed familiar. He had heard somewhere that North Korea had an organization that kept a secret watch on other agents while they were on mission. Okamoto could not believe it. There was no room for such waste, and, if everyone did not work together with devotion to achieve the *juche* revolution, would that not in itself lead to retrogression, he wondered.

However, his imagination could not have been that far off the mark. When I reexamined the reports of the wives' secret missions into Japan and some of the traces of the Yodogō group's activities, I found strange bits of evidence everywhere that must have been due to observation by a third party.

Okamoto had departed for his first overseas duties earlier than the others. It is no surprise that the Party wanted to keep a close eye on him. Looking back now, however, it is clear that those men working for the Party did not realize that Okamoto and the other Yodogō members were also under close surveillance by Western intelligence agencies.

There was also a hidden reason for the criticism of the quality of Okamoto's devotion to the ideology of Kim Il Sung, of which he was unaware at the time. It was probably no coincidence that the issue had come up at the village criticism meeting.

From this time onward, differences between Okamoto's and the rest of the Yodogō members' interpretations of *juche* ideology gradually emerged. It is not surprising that the Party found this a matter of concern, though the concern was not the normal sort that comes when the solidarity of an organization begins to fall apart. For the Party, there could never be more than one interpretation of *juche* and Kim Il Sung's philosophy. There was no room for alternative approaches. There was no tolerance for even the slightest deviation, since even the smallest difference would go against the ideals of total loyalty and unconditionality. Unfortunately, Okamoto Takeshi had his own ideas and made his own judgments. To have one's own ideas within this fanatical collectivism was nothing less than antirevolutionary.

In political struggles, even the smallest matters from the past can be brought up again for more discussion. Such was the case for the criticism of Okamoto. The plans to send Okamoto on a secret mission to Japan were canceled.

CHAPTER TWENTY-TWO

Whereabouts Unknown

Of the nine men who hijacked the Yodogō, the whereabouts of two were unknown for a long time. They are Tanaka Yoshimi and Okamoto Takeshi.

Despite the Yodogō members' more frequent contact with support groups in Japan after 1990, there was no precise information about these two. They did not appear even when activists with whom they had worked in Japan visited Pyongyang.

The others always explained Tanaka's absence by saying he was "away on business, working," and Okamoto's by saying he had separated from the group and was happily married to a North Korean woman. During the period when I was traveling frequently to Pyongyang, many people in Japan asked me about these two. However, I could only answer by repeating what the Yodogō members had told me or by saying there was no information on them.

I had heard that Okamoto was living not far from the village and that sometimes one of the others would run into him on the street.

"I saw Okamoto this morning. He seemed all right. He seemed to want to meet his old friends from Japan, but it is apparently difficult because of something to do with his family," one of the wives said to me. They gave me another plausible explanation to the effect that family relationships were complicated in Korea, and Okamoto's family did not like him meeting his old friends or people related to his former activities. They asked me to please let him be. I really had no choice in the matter, and I tried to convince myself that everything was all right as long as he was happy. But no one who visited North Korea ever actually met Okamoto, and there was never any concrete news about him.

In contrast, several people actually did meet Tanaka in Pyongyang. They confirmed that he was seldom there, often being away seeing to business overseas. Though details about him were kept quiet, it was clear he was alive and well. He would not allow anyone to take pictures of him, not even when he met old friends or supporters; this is not surprising, since most of his activities overseas were secret. Looking back, what was really strange was how much information and rumor circulated concerning Okamoto, whom no one ever saw, whereas there was nothing to be heard about Tanaka, who was actually still with the Yodogō group.

Tanaka later resurfaced in a rather spectacular manner in March of 1996, with the sudden report of his arrest in Cambodia for involvement in the circulation of counterfeit U.S. bills. The CIA and the American Secret Service were involved behind the scenes, and news reports stated that Tanaka may have been laundering the counterfeit money.

In the early hours of March 24, a Mercedes-Benz had left the North Korean embassy near the Monument to the Independence of Cambodia in Phnom Penh. The car was an official embassy vehicle, a Mercedes 300E with the license plate number CD19004.

The Mercedes left the city on Monivong Boulevard and headed south, then turned east on Highway 1. No one in the car had yet realized it, but they were being followed by two Toyotas. Even now, the roads in Cambodia are not in good condition. Eventually, someone in the Mercedes noticed their tail, and the car accelerated suddenly. A car chase developed with the two old Toyotas in pursuit. However, one of the Toyotas turned back midway, and the other suffered a flat tire owing to the bad road. It looked as if the Mercedes would make its escape, when the appearance of the Mekong River saved the day for the pursuers, who just managed to make the same ferry. They abandoned their jalopy and commandeered an old taxi without passengers that was also on board.

The ferry crossed the Mekong and finally arrived at Bavet, Cambodia, on the border with the Vietnamese province of Svai Rieng. The area is busy with migrant workers and peddlers crossing into Vietnam by road. Once across the border, it is a short drive to Ho Chi Minh City (formerly Saigon).

The Mercedes was stopped by officials when it arrived at the border checkpoint. Besides the driver, the occupants included two embassy officials and another man. One of the embassy officials passed their North Korean diplomatic passports through the passenger seat window. The border official who took these documents noticed that the photograph in one of the passports looked exactly like that of a man reported as wanted by Interpol under suspicion of possession and use of counterfeit U.S. dollars. At that moment, the men who had chased the Mercedes from Phnom Penh finally arrived at the border crossing in the beat-up old taxi. The men were ordered out of the Mercedes, but they refused and barricaded themselves inside.

The Mercedes was forced to move into the border checkpoint compound. The North Korean embassy officials tried to use the prerogative of diplomatic privilege to persuade the border officials to let them return to Phnom Penh. They also tried to hand over a large bribe in U.S. dollars, but the border officials refused the money and also refused to let the Mercedes leave the premises. The man whom they appeared to want most spent the entire night in the car, not once coming out.

The next day, the North Korean embassy sent another car with personnel to resolve the problem; the Cambodian Ministry of the Interior sent out several dozen riot police.

The North Koreans angrily gunned their engine as if to drive right through the checkpoint barrier, and the gathered riot police immediately pointed all of their guns directly at the Mercedes. Tension crackled in the air. Finally, the North Koreans folded, cutting their engine.

The North Koreans must have realized that it was not business as usual on the part of the Cambodian police. Indeed, such heavy-handed actions by the Cambodian police against the embassy officials and the third man, even given the fact that his passport may have been false, must have been due to heavy pressure from the CIA and the U.S. Secret Service.

That evening, the Mercedes finally ended its resistance and returned to Phnom Penh in a cavalcade, sandwiched between police and government cars. The third passenger in the car, a Korean resident of Japan apparently named "Hayashi" who was on the Interpol list with an international warrant out for his arrest, was taken into custody. He insisted, however, that he was a North Korean diplomat named "Kim Ilsu." The North Korean embassy made a protest to the Cambodian Interior Ministry over his arrest. The embassy submitted a passport in response to the ministry's request, and the name in it was indeed "Kim Ilsu." It was suspicious, however, that the diplomatic passport had been issued that same day, and there were no passport control stamps in its blank pages. The man's original passport had been replaced with this new one.

The man calling himself "Kim Ilsu" was flown under the name of "Hayashi" to Bangkok the next day, because the Interpol warrant had

originated with the police department in Pattaya, Thailand. After preliminary inquiries in Bangkok, "Kim Ilsu"/"Hayashi" was to be sent to
the Pattaya police station on the twenty-seventh. It was at this point
that, suddenly, the man insisting he was the North Korean diplomat
"Kim Ilsu" spoke with a journalist from Fuji Television.

"I am Tanaka Yoshimi of the Yodogō group," he said, in Japanese.
It had been twenty-six years since the Yodogō hijacking.

The news that the Yodogō hijackers and North Korean embassy
staff were working together to circulate counterfeit bills was reported
the world over.

Immediately after this, Tanaka's wife, Mizutani Kyōko, and another
of the Yodogō hijackers, Wakabayashi Moriaki, gave a press conference
in Pyongyang to Japanese reporters and made the astounding gesture of

Figure 22.01. Tanaka Yoshimi is escorted to his trial appearance in Bangkok by Thai
authorities. Photo courtesy of The Mainichi Newspapers/AFLO.

kneeling down on the floor and bowing after apologizing to their supporters for "causing so much trouble" and "causing inconvenience to North Korea." The North Korean ambassador to Cambodia took responsibility for the entire incident and was recalled.

Tanaka Yoshimi was taken to a prison in Chonburi province and, at the time of this writing, is still on trial there. Since the trial is still in progress, I will not comment any further here,[1] except to note the extraordinary efforts made by the North Korean embassy to help a mere exile by going so far as to help him cross into Vietnam and issue him a passport. This proves that Tanaka was considered a VIP, and his mission was highly regarded by the North Korean side, even though many questions remain regarding the exact nature of his duties and just how he was involved in laundering the counterfeit bills. Within the North Korean system, the Yodogō members were accorded special status because they retained the direct confidence and support of Kim Il Sung. As long as they continued in their loyalty to authority, their positions were secure. In addition, because the special section of the Workers' Party under whose jurisdiction the Yodogō group fell was headed by none other than Kim Jong Il himself, it had unlimited authority in all of its actions. Even among North Korea's ambassadors, there cannot have been many who enjoyed the direct confidence of both Kim Il Sung and Kim Jong Il. Though worthless in other countries, this recognition by the North Korean leaders meant they held positions of the highest status.

There had been similar incidents in Europe of the North Korean embassy rushing to protect a Yodogō member. In those cases, a Yodogō member taken into custody by police would claim to be a North Korean diplomat, and, once notified, North Korean embassy officials would come immediately to confirm this and secure his release. The Japanese embassy responded to events too slowly to prevent it. In Cambodia, the efforts of the North Korean embassy had simply failed where elsewhere they had succeeded.

Another matter to consider is why the man claiming to be a North Korean diplomat named "Kim Ilsu" switched tactics so suddenly after his arrest and announced himself to be Tanaka of the Yodogō group. This decision illustrates Tanaka's quality as a warrior of *juche* and his unerring judgment as a follower of the philosophy of Kim Il Sung. The North Korean embassy would not be able to save him even if he kept to his

---

1. See the editor's afterword for what happened to Tanaka after his arrest and trial in Thailand.

story of being Kim Ilsu. He realized he had to act to save himself, since he would eventually be identified by his fingerprints anyway. There was also the risk that, if he continued to hide his nationality, he would be taken to the United States. If he revealed he was a Yodogō member and Japanese, he might be able to make contact with his supporters within Japan. He might even be able to enlist new sympathizers to his cause and find a way to further his movement through them. Furthermore, it might not be an impossibility to develop an effective propaganda campaign through a much-publicized trial.... Such may have been the thoughts behind Tanaka's calculated decision to reveal who he was. Some might surmise that he had tired of the mission and wished only to return to Japan. In fact, however, he chose to take advantage of his present adverse circumstances and try to expand the scope of his activities. Tanaka, at that moment, chose to switch the arena of his activities to Japan. He must have thought of how *juche* ideology teaches that everyone is the master of his own destiny, deciding his own fate.

From his prison cell in Chonburi, Tanaka wrote answers to some questions regarding Okamoto that had been put to him by a Japanese magazine. Around this time, Okamoto's long absence had caused people to start to suspect he had been purged.

"To be perfectly clear," he wrote, "Okamoto himself chose how he would live."

This simple statement sums up everything Tanaka thought about the issue of Okamoto's whereabouts. No matter what had happened to Okamoto, he meant, it was the result of Okamoto's own choices. It was on Okamoto's own head that the road he had chosen was unsuccessful. Behind this thinking, to be sure, lay that teaching from *juche* to the effect that every individual was "the master of his own destiny, deciding his own fate." In other words, "failure is one's own fault, and success is thanks to the Great Leader." The destiny Okamoto had to face was the destiny his own actions had shaped. This logic, based on the philosophy of Kim Il Sung, is very common in North Korea. There was nothing of the warm belief in each other that had filled the Yodogō hijackers when they posted their slogan "to live and die as one" on the wall of their residence so long ago. And, after his arrest, Tanaka himself had to follow this harsh path of reasoning.

Still, Okamoto Takeshi had disappeared, and no one knew where he was.

However, a single letter from Okamoto was delivered to Japan in the mid-1980s.

"I apologize for my long silence. . . . Good fortune has allowed me to live happily here, having married a North Korean woman. I do not think we will meet again, but I ask you to let me be."

So the letter went, more or less. In the letter, Okamoto wrote of his separation from the rest of his associates in the Yodogō group and of his desire to lay his bones to rest there. He was living happily with his wife and children, he wrote. His North Korean wife's name was Kim Sun Hi, and he went by the Korean name of O Son Nam.

Those to whom this letter was addressed were saddened but were willing to allow that, if Okamoto was happy, they could accept it. Everyone understood anyway that, even if Okamoto did someday return to Japan, he would only face a prison term.

By now it is clear, however, that, just like the students kidnapped from Europe, Okamoto was forced to write this letter full of untruths in a deliberate attempt to deceive his audience in Japan. And it was just around the time this letter was delivered that the last sure traces of Okamoto's whereabouts were lost.

Tamiya stated clearly that he did not know Okamoto had written such a letter. If this is true, we have to assume that a Workers' Party handler forced him to write it: Okamoto would have had no reason otherwise to write a letter so filled with lies. And we know from many examples that this sort of deception involving a letter is a favorite trick of North Korea and of the Yodogō operatives.

There were, however, unexpected consequences to Okamoto's letter. It became accepted that, as long as Okamoto had taken North Korean citizenship and was living happily, then he should be left alone if he so wished. The subject of Okamoto became a kind of taboo among his supporters in Japan and those who came to visit the Yodogō group in North Korea. They avoided the subject, and so Okamoto's life became a secret. The very secretiveness of the matter lent the deception an impression of truth. Here the tendency of the Left to be secretive anyway was used to conceal the existence of a secret. Anyone told discreetly that the matter was secret would keep silent about it, and no doubts whatsoever were allowed to interfere. In this way, the truth of Okamoto's life and situation were hidden.

Whether Okamoto was forced to write that letter by the Workers' Party or by the Yodogō group, it is at any rate clear that the Yodogō hijackers were actively involved in ensuring the success of this campaign of concealment.

During my first trip to Pyongyang in 1990, one of the Yodogō members approached me in the hall of the Koryo Hotel and whispered into my ear.

"Have you heard about Okamoto?"

"You mean about him being married to a North Korean woman?"

Another member brought up the same topic once when we were strolling around the fountain park of Mansudae. They didn't deny anything at all. And then there is the matter of that phrase, "Have you heard...?" Thinking back on it now, it seems to me they were fishing for information about how well known the rumors about Okamoto were in Japan.

A short while after my return to Japan, I received a very polite letter from them.

"Please keep in mind that we do not discuss Okamoto's situation in public, nor do we have any intention of doing so in the future," they had written.

Their ruse worked beautifully. Among Kim Il Sung's sayings, there is one that goes something like "A revolutionary must also be a psychologist." This psychological strategy was perfectly executed.

It is human nature that, on being told a secret, we often feel the urge to pass it on immediately. We whisper quietly, "This is a secret, but..." And Okamoto's story was not an awful one. Yes, it was a very good strategy, based on human psychology. It resulted in the story of Okamoto's naturalization as a North Korean citizen and his marriage to a North Korean woman being known far and wide. The only reason I did not wholly buy into it was because it was a "known secret," and everyone who heard it took it as truth.

Moreover, none other than the Japanese national security police played an important role in this deception. The North Koreans must have calculated from the first that the letter describing Okamoto's situation would fall into the hands of the police. Or we can speculate that they felt the letter was necessary as evidence of the truth of the rumors circulating about him.

Apparently, the security police obtained the letter quite soon, and they took it as evidence that the supposedly secret story was in fact true. Certainly the official who first saw the letter must have been happy enough to dance a victory jig after reading it. At the time, little or nothing was known about where the Yodogō group was or what they might be doing.

The final result was not only that Okamoto's true story was obscured. Years later, when the existence of the Yodogō wives and children became public and the police authorities were desperately trying to figure out the marriage pairings, for some reason they did not bother to try to clarify who Okamoto's wife was. In documents unofficially distributed to the media by the security police, she was referred to by the name of Kim Sun Hi.

Thus, the story of Okamoto having become naturalized as a Korean citizen became public knowledge, openly reinforced by the police. It was a perfectly executed strategy of concealment.

Finally, by introducing an imaginary Korean, Kim Sun Hi, this fiction of a story succeeded in erasing the existence of Okamoto's actual wife, a woman who had vanished, abducted from Japan. This was its true purpose.

CHAPTER TWENTY-THREE

The House of the Bayberry Tree

The hot August wind blew against my face as I stepped off the plane at Kōchi Airport in Shikoku. A haze of heat shimmered above the runway. How many times had I come here? I was continuing my search for a woman who had once lived in this city, though I didn't have much to go on. She had certainly lived here, perhaps only until the mid-1970s. Then it was likely she had left for a larger city.

I had little confidence that I would actually find the woman, given the vagueness of my information on her. Strong doubts filled me as I drove into the city from the airport. I had earlier attempted to follow her faint traces in places that seemed likely, but so far all had been in vain.

The house where she was born had had a Japanese bayberry tree growing in the yard. Bayberry is the Kōchi prefectural flower, and it grows wild in the meadows and mountains there. In spring, it blooms with yellow-brown flowers, and later it bears dark, reddish-purple fruit with a sweet-sour flavor. I had never seen a bayberry before and at the beginning of my search had made a special trip to Ryūga Cave to see them. But bayberry is a common tree in Kōchi prefecture: it was not much help as a clue.

Every time I thought I had found a trace of her, the woman's presence would fade again. I came to realize how many people in the world actually live under similar circumstances. I was searching for a woman who had disappeared in the mid-1970s and whose whereabouts were still unknown. However, the story after that was far from ordinary: for whatever reason, later she had ended up in North Korea. She was from Kōchi, born deep in the mountains. This she had told someone close to her in North Korea. There was no way to verify the truth of her words about the bayberry tree or the story of her home deep in the mountains; it was like trying to trap a cloud. I walked until I was exhausted, looking for a hint of her, until I began to doubt that she had ever really lived there or that she had even existed. There was no guarantee that her story hadn't been a fiction, after all.

However, even though I could not find evidence of her existence in Kōchi, it was certain that a certain Japanese woman had lived under the North Korean sky in the 1980s. That is, I knew already the whereabouts of the missing person.

She had existed. The question was, who was she?

I was searching among the list of people missing from Japan for a particular Japanese woman who had lived in North Korea. She had been the wife of Okamoto Takeshi.

There are times in our short human lives when we experience a moment in which we feel like we have been shaken by a great roar of thunder or hit with a blow strong enough to take the top of our heads off. That's how it felt to me.

Tamiya Takamaro and I had been strolling aimlessly in the streets of a dry and dusty foreign city. We walked along one side of a large park and entered a restaurant hidden in a corner within. The air was filled with an aroma of ethnic food. The sign advertising the restaurant had stood out on the main thoroughfare, but we had walked what seemed like a long distance to the place itself. It was just about lunch hour. We had plenty to talk about, and in fact we were more absorbed in our talk than in the meal we ate. Strangely, however, I can't remember anything about our conversation. That memory was completely eradicated by the shock of what Tamiya told me a few minutes after our meal. Even now, when I dig deep in an attempt to recall our conversation during the meal, the only thing that comes to mind is a vision of our menus lying on the table. I remember Tamiya suggesting we drink beer.

We left the restaurant and, turning our backs on the park, continued our wandering.

Tamiya said abruptly, "You don't actually believe us, do you?"

I could see amusement in his eyes.

"Right. I don't," I answered. I could feel my own face loosening in a smile. Our conversation up to this point still had a half-joking tone.

We had been talking about Okamoto Takeshi.

The street at our feet was arid, and the grass along its edges had withered. These details remain oddly clear in my memory.

"She was Japanese." Tamiya spoke suddenly, clearly.

I turned back to him without thinking. I had gotten a step ahead, and, when I turned toward him, he was standing there scowling. All traces of his earlier smile had quite gone.

"Do you mean his wife?" I asked.

"Yes."

At that time, the story of Okamoto's having separated from the rest of the Yodogō group and living happily married to a North Korean woman was still widely believed. The other Yodogō members were still diligently spreading the story, even the part about his having children with the woman.

"…Is that a fact? I thought as much. A Japanese woman…?"

I heard my voice cracking. The news was shocking. And I wondered why he had suddenly chosen this moment to reverse himself and tell me the truth.

I immediately believed the story he told me. It made sense, unlike the story of Okamoto alone marrying a North Korean woman when that country did not approve of international marriages.

I was silent. I guess I was searching frantically for something to say, but my mind was nothing but a white blank.

"How is he doing now?" I managed to ask in a low voice.

"He is somewhere where we can't reach him. We have no way of getting in touch with him."

I realized suddenly that we were standing in the middle of the street. People were looking at us with dubious faces. It seemed like a long while before we started walking again.

So the shocking truth was that Okamoto's wife was Japanese after all. In that case, she was someone no one had ever met or seen. And, for some reason, she alone had not come to light. I understood immediately that something must have happened.

I felt I might be able to open up a few more paths to understanding if I lined my clues up properly. I had the story Tamiya had told me and the fragmentary profile I had built later. The information about her parents' house and her hometown were based on the stories she herself had told in North Korea. I didn't know her exact name, but I had learned her family name was something like Fukutome.

I made an inventory of the fragments of information I had on her:

Her family name was probably Fukutome, given name possibly Kimija (someone had once referred to her as such).

She was from Kōchi prefecture, "deep in the mountains."

Her family may have been well known in the area. Her father may have been an elected government official.

She had once said her father had wanted a son, so she had been raised as if she were a boy.

She was twenty-four or twenty-five years old around 1977.

She had practiced *kendō* in either junior or senior high school and had once competed in the prefectural championships.

She had attended university in Tokyo.

She had worked for a while in Tokyo.

She disappeared around 1976.

Her manner was brisk and boyish.

A Japanese bayberry tree apparently grew in the garden of her childhood home. She had climbed it often as a child.

This was all I had in the way of clues. Perhaps it was hopeless to search for her based on such scant information. I even consulted with a professional people finder and was told the matter was impossible since I didn't even have her correct name. But I had no choice but to begin my search all the same.

Not having her exact name proved to be a real problem. Had I just been able to confirm her name and exact date of birth, I would have been able to make some progress, but I did not have even that much information.

The most promising clue seemed to be the one about her father being an elected official. I visited the Kōchi prefectural library, and, with the help of friends in Shikoku, I began my research. We started by checking the members of the national Diet but found no matches. Nor was there anyone in the prefectural assembly. We moved on to the lists of village-level assembly members, and found four by the name of Fukutome, but none of them were the man we sought. If not an assemblyman, perhaps he had been mayor or deputy mayor? We checked the list giving the top three officials of each village. Of course, the prefectural library did not have complete information for this level of government. We needed the entire period from the end of the war to the present. Finally we thought of looking at the pensioners' list but found no one after a thorough check.

By this time, I had started to feel more doubtful. My doubts sprang from the fact that I could not be 100 percent certain that I had the name right. As I wrestled with the vast lists, I gradually realized that similar names kept reappearing: Fukutome. Fukudome. Fukutomi. Fukumi…and so on. I had to check all the lists again for those names.

In addition, I looked in the prefectural telephone listings. And found a clue.

I found a township with a large concentration of the name Fuku-tome. I went there immediately, thinking it would be quickest to go and search directly. My main dilemma was figuring out how much I should explain my purpose. Just asking questions could pose a problem. This wasn't a place to go around spreading a story about searching for some-one who had been abducted to North Korea. It was such a small town that every rumor would immediately be known everywhere. If it became a matter of keeping up appearances before an outsider, I might never hear the stories that people would otherwise have told me. I had to act carefully.

Around that time, I also made an important discovery about the woman's name. "Kimija" was likely a Korean reading of the three Chi-nese characters that could be used to write the Japanese girl's name "Kimiko." If this was true, then the woman's name had very likely been Fukutome (or Fukudome or Fukutomi) Kimiko. I had moved one step forward.

And there was one other important clue in the list that had included the possibility that her father had been in the prefectural assembly: the fact that she had practiced *kendō* as a junior or senior high school student.

I began looking for junior and senior high schools in Kōchi that had *kendō* clubs. I heard encouraging news: we had found a woman from a neighboring township who had played *kendō* while she was in high school. Her whereabouts had been unknown since she had left her village. All the information matched precisely the clues I had; only the name was not quite right. Written in the *kana* syllabary, one charac-ter in the middle was off, but, if the name was read aloud, it sounded nearly the same. Furthermore, she had two of the same characters in her name: Miko. That would make it Mija in Korean. The person who gave us this information had been the teacher in charge of the *kendō* club at the high school. I traced the former student but was disappointed when she turned out to be the wrong person, alive and living in Tokyo.

The same thing happened several times. I would find a woman whose information matched my basic clues, but each time my checks showed that the person in question lived in Tokyo, Saitama, Yamagata, or Sendai.

Several months passed after I began my search, and I still could not identify the woman. I finally asked for help from two journalist friends. I told them about the work I had done but gave them the name Fukutome Kimiko as a sure thing so they would not fall into the same maze of confusion that I had found. "We'll give it a try," they said.

Two weeks later, I got a phone call late in the evening.

"Found her!" Their voices sounded cheerful over the telephone.

That was quick, I thought. Remembering suddenly, I asked, "Does the house have a bayberry tree in the garden?" The short silence on the other end indicated I had stumped them.

"Don't think so."

As it turned out, however, there had been one. When Kimiko was in the sixth grade, she moved with her family to a new house nearer to the foot of the mountain. The old bayberry tree still stands in the garden of the old house, near the mountain's peak. Later, one of the journalists who had found the place went with me when I climbed the mountain to take a look at the tree myself.

As I stood there looking up at the old bayberry tree, I commented that he had found it very quickly.

"Nah, I thought it would be impossible to find her using the regular methods, so I cheated a little...."

"You cheated? What on earth...?"

"Not the way you think. I just copied the page in the telephone book and started calling every household with that name. I asked them, 'Do you have a missing daughter around this age?'" He laughed.

She turned out to come from a place rather far away from where I had started looking for her. However, the bayberry tree that she had talked about in North Korea became the final proof that we had found her after all our searching. It seemed unlikely that she would make up a story about climbing that tree as a child. She had specifically mentioned that it was a bayberry, too. And we solved the riddle of her father having been an elected official as well: apparently he had once run for a seat on the village assembly when she had been an elementary school student.

For some reason, Fukutome had told stories only about her early childhood to those around her in North Korea, where she had been brought after her abduction.

Fukutome Kimiko spoke in Pyongyang of her birth "deep in the mountains." A visit to the house she was born in showed me she had not exaggerated. Her village lies at the edge of the Shikoku mountain range, and I understood what she had meant when I tried to go back in time to visualize the place where she had spent her childhood more than thirty years earlier. We climbed the steep mountain road leading up through the forest to the peak, and there, just before the road came to an end, surrounded by a grove of gingko nut trees, was the house she had lived in.

It must have taken an hour for such a young girl to walk to the elementary school at the foot of the mountain. When she was in the sixth grade, her family moved to their present house, lower down the mountain.

After graduating from the public high school, she began working for the main branch of a security firm in Tokyo. In high school, she had indeed practiced *kendō* and had gone to the prefectural competition. Several of her friends from high school had also worked for security companies or had become police officers. Kimiko's first security assignment was at the World Expo in Osaka in 1970. She wore a World Expo uniform and worked as a guard.

She was transferred from Osaka to Tokyo in September, when the Expo ended. At first she lived in the company dormitory, but she soon rented a small apartment in the Ebisu area of Shibuya ward. Her family and friends came to understand from her words around this time that she had started to realize she did not feel suited for security guard work. She finally decided on a change of profession. Working for a book distributor during the day, she attended evening classes at a junior college in Mejiro to obtain a nursery school teacher's license. On receiving her license at graduation, she interned at a nursery school. This was to be the start of the new life she had chosen for herself.

She nurtured one dream: she wished to visit Mongolia.

A notebook she left behind contains the genealogy of Genghis Khan, clippings from books about Mongolia, and various notes she had made, such as the following:

East from Xing'an Ling to Manchuria
West Altai Mountains; Central Asia
South Ying Mountain; the Great Wall of China
North Lake Baikal; Siberia
South-southwest Tianshan Mountains; the Tarim Basin
Southwest the Gobi Desert

I don't know what it was about Mongolia that attracted her. Perhaps her father had told her bedtime stories about China and its neighbors? She studied Mongolian on her own and practiced conversation when she could. The belongings she left behind included a language study book titled *Mongolian in Four Weeks.* She also left other books, including a collection of stories by Miyazawa Kenji.

Though we can't know if she was attracted by the wide open plains of Mongolia or by the heroic story of Genghis Khan, we do know she actually went to the Mongolian embassy with a friend to find out about getting a visa.

The friend recalled, "She said she wanted to walk alone on the Mongolian plain. She didn't like the idea of going there on a tour...." But they were told at the embassy that it was difficult and dangerous for women to travel alone in Mongolia.

She graduated from the junior college in March of 1976. Apparently her desire to travel overseas increased sharply, and she sought out some way to visit Mongolia. After working so hard to support herself while studying for her nursery school teacher's license, it was natural that she should wish to mark the end of that phase of her life by embarking on a trip before starting her new life. Such feelings are quite understandable. There was nothing to connect her with North Korea.

However, I am horrified to think that her traces show that the kidnappers successfully used her dream of traveling to Mongolia for their own ends. No ideological background that would connect her to North Korea appeared as I retraced her steps in Tokyo. But she appeared frequently in different places in her attempts to realize her ambition. Then she disappeared. An ordinary young woman suddenly vanished while dreaming of a journey to the Mongolian steppes.

She vanished in July of 1976, just before a planned trip back home to Kōchi during the summer holidays. She flew out of Haneda Airport in mid-July, after which she was not heard from again—except for a summer season greeting card that arrived at her parents' home in late August, when she was supposedly overseas.

It was a strange letter. It consisted of only one line, written in her handwriting: Sending you Summer Greetings.

There was no return address or contact number. The postmark was Japanese.

I don't have the energy to write any more about this familiar deceptive ploy.

Good friends saw her off from the train station in Hamamatsu when she left for Haneda Airport. Strangely, she wouldn't tell any of them where she was going. All she said was "I am going to a certain place, and there is someone I will try to meet. If we meet, then we will

Figure 23.01. Photo of Fuku-tome Kimiko. From personal collection of Takazawa Kōji.

travel together for a few months. But, don't worry, even if I am gone a while, I will be back before the end of the year. If I can't meet this person, I will return to Japan right away...."

One of her friends believed that she was moving closer, step by step, to realizing her big dream. But all she left behind her were these few words.

It is not difficult to imagine that the "someone" she went to meet was in fact a North Korean operative, especially when we compare this with the other cases we have seen.

After her disappearance, Fukutome's family collected her belongings from the little apartment in Ebisu where she had lived. They found a passport application form that had been torn into little pieces. Piecing them together, they saw that she had written "Mongolia" as her travel destination. Her mother worried that she had met with some kind of accident during her long-dreamed-of trip and asked her daughter's friends about her. The hope that her daughter would someday return whole from her trip sustained her for twenty years and continues to do so.

Later, however, I discovered that the destination on the passport application Fukutome actually submitted had mysteriously changed to Sweden. Here is where the mystery surrounding her fate takes over.

After this point, it is difficult to say where she went. The missing person report that her mother filed with the police lay untouched in a storage area. The police appear to have processed her as just another runaway. Considering the tens of thousands of such missing person reports the police receive every year, I can't really blame them for handling Fukutome's case as they did. But I also can't deny that this mistake so early in the case effectively obscured her disappearance from all of us.

Later investigations show that, just as in the cases of the students abducted from Europe, Fukutome Kimiko was also deceived and kidnapped. The timing of her disappearance, in July of 1976, coincides exactly with the period during which the special section of the North Korean Workers' Party launched Operation Marriage for the Yodogō men. The Yodogō group later changed tack and admitted that she became the wife of Okamoto Takeshi after she was brought to North Korea.

Fukutome Kimiko's abduction case became the first admitted to by North Korea and the Yodogō members in later exchanges, and it was the first to shed any light on the kidnappings and the victims' later lives in North Korea. However, compared to how the other marriage projects were handled, this one was conducted with outrageous force. Its result was to cast a subtle shadow over the fate of her husband, Okamoto Takeshi.

CHAPTER TWENTY-FOUR
Ideological Conflict

I t was probably late 1982 or early 1983 when Okamoto Takeshi's ideology and political line began to diverge sharply from that of Tamiya and the other Yodogō members. We know this because Okamoto continued his overseas activities until then, and photographs taken by Western intelligence agents place him in Europe as late as the spring of 1982.

Apparently the differences began over the interpretation of *juche* ideology. Okamoto was more aggressive and radical in his thinking, and politically he was even farther to the left than the others. It was the revolution in Japan that occupied him. He felt strongly that they should be working more actively toward infiltrating Japan rather than following their current indirect path. He was growing annoyed over having spent more than ten years in North Korea. He and Tamiya agreed in their intention of raising the revolution in Japan, but the years in North Korea had forced the Yodogō members to revise their Red Army Faction political line. Okamoto had converted along with all the others to the *juche* line, but his ideas for their next actions differed. Unlike the other Yodogō members, who believed that successful reunification and revolution in the Korean Peninsula must precede the revolution in Japan, Okamoto did not think these events had to be connected: the Japanese revolution should be sparked directly on Japanese soil, without reference to what was happening in the peninsula.

At the time, the Yodogō group's instructors in the North Korean Workers' Party held that the Korean reunification and revolution and the Japanese revolution were like two wheels on a cart. Once the peninsula had been reunified, the Japanese revolution would soon be achieved.

Under this logic, the Yodogō members had been included in covert operations against the South and allowed to go on overseas missions. Only after the peninsula had been reunited could they turn their attention to the revolution in Japan. And, of course, "revolution" meant Kim Il Sung's revolution. Thus, the primary assignment was the South Korean revolution, in order to set the stage for the later Kim Il Sung revolution in Japan. Their involvement in missions against South Korea occupied a large proportion of their time and energy.

The tasks they undertook after forming a new political party, the Independent Revolution Party, bore little relation to their original activities. Yet Tamiya and the other Yodogō members did not find the logic of the Workers' Party completely unpalatable. This was because, apart from the specific content of *juche* and Kim Il Sung's ideology, the concept resembled an extension of the Red Army Faction's theory about international bases for the revolution in a different form. Thus, they were able to view the future reunified Korea in the role of the international base that would trigger the Japanese revolution.

Tamiya persuaded himself and the others that this was international communism. Only Okamoto remained unconvinced. Certainly he was for the Korean revolution, but he could not understand why they must delay the Japanese revolution for it. Why should they put off their operations in Japan? Okamoto's experience with the antinuclear protest movement in Europe had profoundly influenced his thinking. He had begun to think of the practical strategies of covert operations and plans for action in Japan as his own mission. Perhaps Okamoto's later fate would have come out differently if he had not initially been assigned to conduct the first undercover task in Japan and then later had that assignment taken away from him and canceled altogether.

Tamiya and Okamoto would sometimes talk all night, but their discussions only widened the gap between their ideological and political positions. Apparently they even engaged in physical fights after particularly heated arguments. Their different interpretations of *juche* and their different plans for action soon became known to the others and unsettled the group.

Okamoto was adamant in his views, and he was not alone in them. "The Japanese revolution must occur according to the independent demands of the Japanese people," he insisted. "Isn't that what our Leader means when he says we must apply *juche* ideology to the Japanese revolution? We can't apply *juche* as we have learned it directly to Japan. Japan's revolution must differ from Korea's because of the difference in the two countries' international circumstances, standards of living, ways of thinking, and cultural traditions. We have to construct a *juche* ideology that fits the needs of the Japanese people if we want to apply *juche* ideology to Japan as it exists now."

From the time they had started to take their teachings on *juche* seriously, it had been the task of the Yodogō group to consider the theoretical ramifications of their new ideology. Their problem was to understand what form their *juche* ideology must take for it to be applicable to the reality of Japan.

They raised the issue often during their weekly Saturday criticism sessions and during their study hours. It had finally become a lackluster and lifeless discussion. No one had any concrete or creative theories on how to apply *juche* ideology to achieve the Japanese revolution. In addition, by this time no one in the group was frank in voicing opinions. There could only be one outcome to speaking honestly in this organization that so valued "unconditionality." Speaking out could be life-threatening.

"Comrade Tamiya has misinterpreted *juche* ideology." One day, during a criticism session, Okamoto singled out Tamiya directly. That utterance became a fateful turning point for Okamoto. By this time the original hijackers who had come to Pyongyang were no longer single but were living with their wives. Most of the women had originally come from *juche* study groups in Japan. The little community was organized in a three-tiered system with the North Korean Workers' Party at the top, the Yodogō men next, and the *juche* study group women at the bottom. In adherence to time-honored Confucian tradition,[1] the women were excluded from the men's meetings and were apparently often treated like rank outsiders, but, even so, the Yodogō men found themselves caught in the middle, like a slice of ham between two pieces of bread.

Before I can describe the furor that Okamoto's words raised in the group, I have to explain Tamiya's position within the group. Tamiya had been acknowledged as the group's leader ever since the hijacking. This is an important point. As anyone who has visited North Korea as part of a tour group will know, the group leader is for some reason granted a special status. Similarly, within the Yodogō group, we can see that Tamiya held a position of power. Furthermore, at about the time

---

1. The teachings of Confucius about proper human relationships are part of the shared cultural tradition of China, Korea, and Japan. These relationships are hierarchical: followers should be obedient to their leaders, and wives should be obedient to their husbands.

when their ideological remolding was nearing completion, Tamiya had received recognition as the group's leader from none other than Kim Il Sung himself. As far as the group was concerned, these facts meant Tamiya's authority was beyond question.

We can accept that Okamoto's open criticism of Tamiya sprang from the unreserved relationship that had developed out of their shared experiences as hijackers and their close living circumstances. But, for the people around them, the implications of Okamoto's criticism were not so simple.

The North Korean Workers' Party and the instructors sent by the Party immediately perceived Okamoto's criticism of Tamiya as a criticism of Kim Il Sung, who had anointed Tamiya as the group's leader. The women in the *juche* study group found his criticism to be an incomprehensible breach of manners toward the organizational leader, to whom they owed their unconditional allegiance and looked upon it as a revolt against *juche* ideology itself. For these women, schooled in the ideals of unconditionality and total loyalty, Okamoto's behavior showed the most extreme disrespect.

Within such an organization, Okamoto's criticism of Tamiya was completely out of bounds. Judgment was forthcoming in the weekly criticism meeting.

"Comrade Okamoto criticized *juche* itself when he said that Comrade Tamiya was mistaken in his interpretation of *juche*."

"His interpretations of *juche* during our literature and theory study sessions conflict with the best interests of the working class."

"He holds a distorted view of *juche* ideology."

Okamoto was criticized and denounced by everyone. He refused, however, to take back his words or to engage in self-criticism.

Tension began to take hold of the group.

Minority opinions are often drowned out when the majority prefers to adhere to a perceived safe option. But, if we take a closer look here, we can see that it was not a matter of a simple conflict between majority and minority opinions. At the bottom of the trouble lay the darkness of Kim Il Sung's ideology. A difference of opinion within the organization went against the principle of a single ideological system, which in this case meant whatever position Tamiya held. Everyone accepted Tamiya's decisions as final in all matters. It had been his decision to begin the mission of infiltrating Japan, and later it was his decision to call it off. Any expression of dissatisfaction with this state of affairs was taken as opposition. Every member of an organization must work together like gears in an engine. This was true for the North Korean Workers' Party as well as for the Yodogō group, so I must add here that none of Tamiya's decisions or policies were entirely his own: though leader of his group, Tamiya was in turn obliged to give the Party his own unconditional loyalty.

Okamoto was ordered to give a *sōkatsu*[2] and self-criticism.

Okamoto grew angry and depressed. He was probably filled with despair in the face of this intractable miscommunication and misunderstanding with his comrades.

One member later spoke of the madness that seemed to take over Okamoto in this period. He cut a photograph of Tamiya into tiny pieces. He tacked a picture of the whole group to a wall and used it as a target for knife-throwing practice. He was trying to find a way to release the fury that the lack of understanding had aroused in him. He could not escape his feelings of overwhelming despair and helplessness. He took to drinking and was often drunk even during the day.

Tanaka Yoshimi later wrote about the Okamoto affair in *Tsukuru* (February 1998). His words give us a picture of Okamoto Takeshi's psychological state at the time:

> The rhythm of our daily lives in Pyongyang repeated in a simple pattern day after day. We read Japanese newspapers and journals to study current events and gave presentations of our findings. We repeated many kinds of political debates; wrote essays and criticized each other's efforts, often rewriting numerous times; and, when even the slightest hint of frivolity or slackness appeared in the narrow confines of our lives, we were strict in our ideological criticism. Though we believed that someday we would return to Japan, it seemed a distant thing, like knowing without being able to see them that some islands called Japan lay out beyond the horizon; none of us could predict when the actual date of our return would be. We lived from day to day supported by our vision of the distant future, and the belief that we would return gave meaning to our lives. I can say from my experience that it was not an easy life.

> He had tired of it and had begun to think that he wished to have an ordinary life. He wanted to work, and meet different people, and sometimes climb mountains or travel. We knew from our

---

2. See chapter 6, note 3.

reading in the newspapers and journals that the political movements in Japan had died down. I think that in fact Okamoto began
to despair at how different things were from the time when he
had lived in Japan. It would not be incorrect to say that his desire
for an ordinary life sprang from these circumstances.

Even people living in the same environment will not always
experience the same desires or have the same ambitions. It is a
matter of course that any one person's life and destiny are determined by his ideas, his way of thinking, and his desires....

This is a very different story from one of people discovering
their differences after traveling abroad together and deciding to
go their separate ways. It seems obvious to me that his wish for
an ordinary life could never happen in this country to which he
fled as a political refugee and that is still at war with the United
States and Korea. (*Tsukuru*, vol. 28, no. 2, pp. 141–142)

Tanaka's account at least gives us a picture of Okamoto's psychological state around that time. It does not, however, give us any information as to why Okamoto began to wish to be alone and to live as an
ordinary person.

From the way Tanaka describes it, Okamoto wanted to "abandon
the revolution and have an ordinary life" because he had "tired of the
monotony of their daily lives as exiles," and so he left their organization.
But the daily lives of the Yodogō group members were never as Tanaka
describes, and Tanaka's own story is proof that he traveled to every corner of the world. I see Tanaka's explanation as another example of his
excellence as an operative loyal to the ideology of Kim Il Sung. The sole
point of his essay was to show there had never been any sort of policy
conflict within their group, a point vital to any collective ideology controlled by an ideal of absolute loyalty.

In the same essay, Tanaka wrote that they had lost all common
ground with Okamoto, and they found it impossible to talk to him or
engage him in discussion. Once their ideologies grew apart, they could
no longer even have friendly relations. It was not only Okamoto who
had lost interest in communicating with the others; those around him
returned the feeling. As seen in the description of the Ten Great Principles (see chapter 18, "Two-Faced Janus"), according to the ideology of
Kim Il Sung, anyone adhering to a different ideology cannot be regarded
as a friend or colleague, or even as fully human.

Tanaka criticized his own role in Okamoto's situation with only the following words: "We didn't have the capacity to persuade him, influ-ence him, or even tolerate him" (pp. 142–143). In other words, their only fault as *juche* soldiers in the confidence of the Great Leader was in their failure to bring about Okamoto's political reeducation.

Okamoto spent his time in deep gloom at the village.

One day he got into an argument with another member who rebuked him for his behavior. First they wrestled, and then they started hitting each other. Okamoto smashed a beer bottle he had in his hand and threatened his opponent with it. This prompted others who were watching to jump in, and they overcame him easily and held him to the ground.

Okamoto's face was covered in blood and tears. He was crying.

His companions tied him up with rope. Okamoto had lost the will to fight, and he was left lying there on the ground. They did not release him even when he begged to go to the toilet.

Okamoto's wife happened to be in the village at that time. She could not bear to watch, and she intervened, raising her voice in protest at their treatment of him.

At times like this, a champion coming to the victim's defense is likely to be accused of the same crimes by the attackers. So it was for Okamoto's wife. In modern North Korean society, where married cou-ples refer to themselves as "closest comrades," their political relation-ship takes precedence over their personal one. If a woman speaks out as a man's wife and not as his political comrade, she will lose her own political life (and we have already seen that, in North Korea, "political life" does not mean the same thing it does in Japan).

So of course they tied up Okamoto's wife as well.

They tied her up for another reason besides her defense of Okamoto: they accused her of being responsible for his behavior. Here another of the principles of the ideology of Kim Il Sung reared its head: all credit for any success belongs to Kim Il Sung, but all blame for failure is due to one's own carelessness. In the husband-wife relationship, this principle translates as all success being thanks to the husband's steadiness and any failure or unpleasantness being the fault of the wife and her flight-iness. This Confucian perspective penetrates deeply into the daily life of North Korean society. Okamoto's wife protested for a while, but no one listened to her.

"Madness overtook Okamoto," one of the members has said in recent years. But, rather, it was the others who were filled with madness.

"We'll have a problem if he runs away."

With these words, they retied the ropes holding him until he was almost completely encased.

"It is not good for children to live with such parents!" These were the words of one of the other wives. The children were taken away from their home. Okamoto's little daughters were only five and six years old at the time.

Okamoto was isolated from the rest of the group. He was taken away, still tied in ropes at the hands of the others. Separated from their children, Okamoto and his wife were left to the Party. They were still tied up when they were bundled into an instructor's car and taken away from the village.

In the Okamotos' abandoned quarters, the others found the picture of Tamiya cut into tiny pieces and graffiti denouncing the Yodogō members.

Tamiya, however, asked the Party for mercy, and, granting his wish, the Party decided to try to reeducate Okamoto and his wife. They were installed in another guest house, and Party instructors began the work of the Okamotos' self-examination (*sōkatsu*) and political reeducation.

Self-examination here means an ideological examination through a systematic and complete process of self-criticism. The ideology of Kim Il Sung allows only one specific method of self-examination. Any deviation from the accepted method results in an incomplete self-examination. In effect, the instructors will not accept that the process has been completed. Appropriate quotes have to be selected from the *Works* (as Kim Il Sung's writings and teachings were known) and accompanied by a confession to the leader, couched in terms of admiration, of how one has gone wrong, and of how one would act differently in the future. Finally, one finishes with an expression of gratitude toward the Great Leader.

Tamiya in fact visited the guest house where Okamoto and his wife were undergoing their reeducation several times to urge Okamoto to engage in the self-examination and to see the light.

"Let's begin again," Tamiya would say persuasively every time he visited.

They were once even brought back to the village to see their children, in the hope that it would help in some way with their ideological reevaluations and reeducation.

But Okamoto was no longer listening to anyone. He was stubborn.

"Why wouldn't he understand?" sighed one of the other members only about a year before this writing.

One of the background factors underlying the problem over Okamoto was the fact that the Independent Revolution Party that the Yodogō group had created in North Korea was a very different organization from the one that had claimed the members' support and commitment at the time of the *Yodogō* hijacking. This new organization was a totalitarian structure based on the ideology of Kim Il Sung. The rigid society and ideology that surrounded it acted as a safety valve to contain any problems within it. While they were living inside such an organization and society, people could never understand the true nature of the problem.

Okamoto's troubles began with the disagreement over policy and his different approach to handling their covert operations. Later these grew into a loyalty problem specific to the ideology of Kim Il Sung. I now think that Okamoto's supposed desire for an ordinary life and his loss of the will to fight were his way of expressing his opposing ideological stance. Certainly wishing for an ordinary life as an ordinary citizen is a perfectly valid ideological stance, as far as it goes.

But that isn't what actually happened. Okamoto did not wish to lead the ordinary life of an ordinary citizen in North Korea. His true desire was to return to his native Japan. Okamoto remained dedicated to the revolution in Japan until the end. And, unlike the other Yodogō members, his vision was not for a revolution that would transform Japan into another North Korea. If his true intention had been to lead an ordinary life, he would not have chosen the dangerous path he later chose—and which I will describe below—during his period of segregation. He would not have chosen the path of revolt against the North Korean state.

I see in Okamoto's story a reproduction of the events of the United Red Army incident of 1972. Despite the adage that says "the first time is a tragedy, the second a comedy," this story can only be viewed as tragic. The Okamoto events came just ten years after the United Red Army purge. Sadly, the deadly United Red Army purge did not provide a painful lesson for the Yodogō group. The tragic events that overcame their former comrades across the Sea of Japan were nothing more than a distant fact.

Exiled to the distant guest house and undergoing reeducation, Okamoto Takeshi never returned to his comrades' new organization.

CHAPTER TWENTY-FIVE

Escape to the Sea

H e could see the sea from the guest house. Okamoto Takeshi and his wife had been exiled from the village and were undergoing their ideological reeducation. Their daily life was monotonous. They spent day after day studying *juche* ideology and the *Works* of Kim Il Sung. This reeducation regimen did not consist of the polite lectures and gentle handling the Yodogō group members had received on their arrival in Pyongyang, nor did any professors from the Social Sciences Institute come to teach them. Their instructors simply handed them assignments and required them to do self-criticisms. The regimen was exceedingly strict. Instructors came every few days to examine their ideology. They were alone at the guest house, with only a housekeeper and their guards. Their time was unscheduled, but they had to spend their days and nights feverishly trying to finish the mountains of work they were given. Oka-moto and his wife were naturally not free to meet. They were prohibited from doing anything other than studying.

Unfortunately, I do not know the exact location of the guest house. None of the Yodogō members said anything about it except that it was a North Korean Workers' Party guest house close to the sea.

Given its proximity to the ocean, I can speculate that the guest house may have been near Pyongyang at Nan'po, where the Party main-tains a variety of facilities. Nan'po is an industrial port at the mouth of the Daedong River. Near to shore is Wau Island, with its white sandy beaches and amusement park. The silhouette of the offshore island resembles a cow lying on the ground, which is what the name of the island means. Visitors flock to the amusement park that occupies the whole island. The Sohe locks lie not far away, between the Daedong and the open sea near Nan'po.

Another possible location, since it has connections with the Yodogō group as well as an ocean view, is the guest house at Songdan on the east coast, near the city of Hamhung in Hamgyongnam province. Facing Riuwon Bay, Songdan has a boardwalk along the waterfront lined with flowering crabapple trees. There is a sanitarium for Party cadres and a separate cottage that the Yodogō members could use when they wished. The Yodogō hijackers had been brought here on their first outing during their initial ideological training, after which Abe Kimihiro had written so emotionally in his memoir, "We could see the ocean, our first sight of it since our arrival in North Korea" (quoted in chapter 6). The Yodogō members came frequently for relaxation, and several Japanese people underwent the process of ideological remolding here after being brought from Japan. The grounds have a private beach that is closed to the public and an endless view out over the East Sea toward Japan. Okamoto Takeshi stares at the ocean.

He has met and befriended some local fishermen while out on one of his walks. Although his life at the guest house is regimented, he does have some freedom to escape the watchful eyes of the guards. He may be undergoing reeducation, but he is after all one of the Yodogō members, and Kim Il Sung's onetime approbation still carries great weight. The day might well come when Okamoto will be reinstated at the village, and in that case he will once again be an important person with a direct connection to the central authority of the government. Naturally, he is treated with respect by the people around him, including the fishermen, who know nothing about the foreigners who leave the guest house to go for walks except that they are different. They cannot be treated disrespectfully.

One day Okamoto brings a bottle with him from the guest house, and the fishermen are delighted when he invites them to share it with him. Alcohol is a precious rarity in North Korea, and this bottle Okamoto has brought with him from the guest house is beyond the reach of ordinary citizens and fishermen.

They sing. They drink.

Okamoto continues to fill the fishermen's glasses until the singing and talking die out and he can hear them snoring. They have all fallen asleep. He looks around. He is alone.

In front of him, a fishing boat rises and falls invitingly on the swell of the waves.

There is no telling what went through Okamoto's mind. Very likely he felt great stress in that moment before making his big decision. We can't know whether his wife was with him, but, if she was indeed undergoing her own reeducation in the same guest house, then it is quite possible she was there too.

Okamoto jumps onto the boat from the wharf.

By the time he recovers his poise, the engine is running. He grabs the helm, and turns the boat around. He guns the engine to maximum throttle and the prow begins to make headway through the water. Once out of the shelter of the bay, the boat rocks on the waves of the open sea.

He wants to get as far away from the shore as possible. Having once been an ace swimmer on the Kumamoto high school swim team, he has no fear of the water. But, without either compass or sea charts, he has no choice but to head straight out to sea.

If only he can make it past the North Korean territorial limits: he might be all right if he can reach international waters. The North Korean fishing boat cannot have had much fuel aboard, so it is unlikely he will be able to reach a safe harbor. But, if he gets into international waters, he might be rescued even if he were forced for a while to drift in the current. He would be saved if he could be picked up by some foreign ship. He literally leaves his fate to the heavens.

The wide sea spreads out around him.

The salty sea breeze reminds him of the sea in his hometown. The fishing boat continues to cut through the waves.

Land falls farther and farther behind.

Okamoto is far out to sea.

Finally, the sea stretches to the horizon with no glimpse of the coast.

Ocean all around.

Waves. Wind.

Ocean.

He feels he has already come quite a long way out, when, at the edge of his field of vision he catches sight of a patrol boat coming on at high speed.

The patrol boat approaches rapidly, throwing up a white spray of water.

A fishing boat certainly isn't much for speed.

The other boat is closing in.

Irritation. He has the fishing boat at full throttle.

A loudspeaker blares.

"Chonji! Chonjihera!" ("Stop! You must stop!")

Okamoto continues speeding along without looking around.

Obviously, a fishing boat is no competition for a patrol speedboat. The gap closes.

Soldiers aboard the patrol boat hold their guns trained on him.

"Stop!" The voice on the loudspeaker roars again.

A gun fires.

It is a warning shot. The second will find its target. There probably won't be a third.

The fishing boat gives a shudder and rocks wildly. The patrol boat draws up alongside.

He can see soldiers jumping onto the rear of his vessel.

His venture has ended all too soon.

Okamoto's desperate but short-lived bid for freedom is over. He has failed to escape from North Korea by sea.

I do not know whether Okamoto planned his attempted escape or if he grabbed an unexpected opportunity to make a run for it. I have no way of confirming if this was even how he took the boat. This is all I know: Sometime in the mid-1980s, while sequestered at the guest house, Okamoto commandeered a fishing boat and attempted to flee from North Korea. He failed and was arrested. The North Korean state found his revolt and defection an insult to the prestige of Kim Il Sung and the North Korean Workers' Party.

The incident was kept a strict secret. Had the news leaked to the outside world that one of the youths involved in the flamboyant hijacking of a Japanese airplane to North Korea had now attempted to run away, it would have meant nothing less than a complete loss of face for their sponsor, the Great Leader.

The incident, still obscure, long remained completely shrouded in darkness.

An act like Okamoto's is probably considered treasonous in North Korea. There is, however, no record of any trial. Without any prompting from the outside, the rest of the Yodogō group branded Okamoto as an "anti-Party, antirevolutionary element."

This desperate and hopeless action of attempting to escape from North Korea in a stolen fishing boat was probably rooted in the despair Okamoto felt toward the other Yodogō members and the Party.

No one has seen Okamoto Takeshi since.

I have described how Tamiya said that Okamoto was in a place where they could not reach him. I immediately thought he meant a prison camp for political criminals. "Like this?" I asked, holding out my clenched fists as if manacled, but Tamiya only shook his head. Even if Okamoto was in fact in a prison camp, Tamiya might not have been capable of frankly admitting the fact. After all, faithful followers of *juche* are sure that no such places exist in North Korea. The statement that he was somewhere they couldn't reach him has some special meaning. The facts of the matter are still not entirely clear.

Sometime after Tamiya died, I requested an interview with a former Socialist Party Diet member. He had long served on the Japan Socialist Party's select committee for Korean problems. He had also been to North Korea on about seven occasions and had met with Kim Il Sung twice as well as several times with Workers' Party cadre Ho Dam and Kim Yongsun. I wished to ask him some questions directly.

My reason for this visit was that, when Okamoto came under criticism for his liberal ideas, one of the first things for which he was denounced was his meeting with a group of visiting Japan Socialist Party members that included this former Diet member.

Okamoto personally visited the Socialist Party delegation's lodgings and told them of his desire to return to Japan. Another important fact is that he had actually met with this Diet member before the hijacking. And the several people in this Japanese delegation to North Korea who met Okamoto were probably the last outsiders to meet him.

The former Diet member spoke with me in the living room of his home.

I must have met Okamoto in October of 1980, because that is when I was in North Korea for a Workers' Party convention. We were staying in a Party guest house instead of a hotel. One evening around 10:30, he came unexpectedly to the guest house. Thinking it would be a bad idea to meet with him alone, the group leader and I both met him. He seemed very remorseful, and he apologized to us, saying, "I did something unforgivable." He seemed to be talking about the hijacking. Then, I remember he gave us some North Korean ginseng, saying it was a local souvenir. I sent the ginseng to his father in Kumamoto. He mentioned that he wished to return to Japan. I thought he meant he wanted to return to Japan to continue his political activities. After that, I received a few letters and New Year's greeting cards from him. The last New Year's card I got came in January of 1982.

I didn't know anything about his marriage, and he didn't say anything about it. He had come alone; he didn't bring his wife with him. This was the first time I met any of the Yodogō members in Pyongyang.

The second time was in 1985. One of the members was having serious medical issues—who was it now? Oh, right, it was

Yoshida Kintarō. That time three or four of the Yodogō members came to visit. I can't remember exactly who did come, but Okamoto definitely didn't. When I asked how Okamoto was doing, one of them replied that he was "getting a lot of exercise" and laughed. They said Okamoto had gone off on a different political line. I didn't learn any more details than that.

There is plenty of important information in this testimony. First, Okamoto unexpectedly visited the delegation late at night in October 1980. This would have been shortly after the plan for Okamoto to go to Japan had been canceled and he had begun to speak out about his wish to return home. Second, Okamoto stopped writing New Year's greeting cards after 1982.

Finally, in 1985, Okamoto did not come to see his acquaintance, but a few of the other members did. We can infer from this that, by then, Okamoto had already been isolated and was undergoing reeducation. I am impressed by their deceptive answer of "He is getting a lot of exercise" to the inquiry about Okamoto, but, since it didn't really explain why he had not come, they probably felt they had to admit that he had chosen another path.

There is another interesting piece of testimony to introduce here. In the Yodogō group's memoirs (Tamiya et al. 1990), Konishi Takahiro gives the following account of a discussion the group had early in their stay, when they were still training for their early return to Japan:

Shall we swim? Not for fun, but how about serious swim training? Yes, training is a good idea. The only way to get back into Japan is from the sea. Would we leave the ship far out and swim the rest of the way in? Well, I guess. But I wonder if the North Koreans would just give us a ship? If they don't and we don't swim back, then we won't ever be able to finish the job we started with the hijacking! Our battle will be successful only once we return to Japan, right? But we can hardly swim across the Sea of Japan. Since that is impossible, then late some night we could swim out down the Daedong River and seajack a ship from Nan'po to go back to Japan. (Tamiya et al. 1990, 169)

This is a sketch of a conversation they had when they were engaged in their swim training in the Daedong with Okamoto as coach. Staring at the sea during breaks from his boring daily sessions of self-criticism, Okamoto must have often recalled this discussion. There is no evidence that he didn't suddenly decide to try it. In fact, they all joked about it often. Another point of interest to this journal entry is that, when Konishi wrote it, Okamoto had already made the attempt they spoke of, and of course Konishi knew this. So, in fact, in this story that he relates in a joking way, Konishi was writing the truth.

More than ten years passed before the true story of what had happened to Okamoto and his wife began to come to light. Around the same time that Tanaka Yoshimi was detained in Cambodia on charges of trafficking in counterfeit U.S. currency, the following news was reported from Beijing by the Japanese wire service Jiji (Current Events).

> Okamoto Takeshi tried to flee from North Korea and return to Japan with his wife and two children in the late 1980s. He was stopped and remains incarcerated in a North Korean labor camp.
>
> According to a reliable source from North Korea, while Okamoto was isolated and receiving reeducation after falling out politically with his colleagues, he escaped when he was out of view of his guards and apparently tried to leave North Korea by illegal means. This can be seen as an act of despair at the intransigent North Korean political system and his fellow hijackers who were so embedded in it. After being taken into custody by the North Korean security police agency, he has been incarcerated in a prison camp in North Korea since around 1990. His children have been taken in by other group members.
>
> ...The (Japanese) security police agency took note of the fact that Okamoto did not attend the funeral of Tamiya Takamaro in December of last year.[1]

This news was immediately followed by more details:

> ...Okamoto and his family made a bold bid for escape by seajacking a fishing boat and racing out to sea....Okamoto's relations with the rest of his group had deteriorated rapidly in the late 1980s owing to conflicts over their politics and strategy, and he, his wife, and their two children were subjected to reeducation at a separate government facility. Okamoto's increasing dissatisfaction with the North Korean system led him to decide to return to

---

1. The Japanese news report refers consistently to "Suspect Okamoto," which is how Japanese police sources refer to him because he was on the Interpol wanted list for his participation in the hijacking.

Japan with his family, resigned to the possibility of arrest. Apparently thinking there was a good chance of being picked up by a South Korean or Japanese ship if he was far enough out to sea, he set out in a boat. However, a North Korean patrol boat found him easily, and he was taken back.

The North Koreans were deeply shocked by this attempted escape and seajacking by one of the Yodogō exiles. There was great fear that the incident would become publicly known, and a strict gag order was placed on it. Not even the rest of the Yodogō members were informed of the incident. (Jiji, April 12, 1996)

This article appears to be largely correct except for the statement that Okamoto's children were involved and the date of his incarceration in a prison camp. The children had been separated from Okamoto and his wife by the other Yodogō members and were being raised in the village. More shocking than these small inaccuracies, however, is the sudden appearance of news about Okamoto, whose circumstances had for so long been unknown. More surprising still is that this story, kept completely secret for so long, had leaked at all. Together with the slowly increasing stream of refugees from North Korea, it showed that the state's iron control had slipped.

I wrote several articles for a variety of magazines detailing the facts of Okamoto's story. Soon after, a Japanese television crew (Tokai Television) went to Pyongyang to interview the Yodogō group, and, during the interview session, the reporter directly asked one of the members about Okamoto. The reply went something like, "His story has already been reported all over Japan. Do we need to go into it?"

Shibata Yasuhiro, the youngest of the Yodogō hijackers, who had just finished his jail term after being arrested in Japan, said in a press conference on August 24, 1996, "There were policy conflicts starting from the mid-1970s."

Finally, the veil of secrecy hiding Okamoto's story and the questions surrounding it was lifting. But another secret still remained hidden, at least until the existence of the Yodogō wives was revealed. Then the process of reinventing facts began again in a frantic attempt to save the situation.

The fact that Fukutome Kimiko, a missing woman abducted from Japan, was Okamoto's wife meant that the fabricated stories so carefully constructed by the Yodogō group and the North Korean government were all, quite simply, worthless.

CHAPTER TWENTY-SIX

Worthless Fabrications

"**I** see," the old woman said, and fell silent for a moment. I was visiting Fukutome Kimiko's tiny, eighty-year-old mother in the small mountain town in Kōchi prefecture where she lived. The only sounds were the buzzing of the cicadas and the electric fan. I had the feeling that, if I added another word, she would be overcome with emotion, and the conversation would be over.

"I wondered if it wasn't something like that, when she never turned up despite all my searching," she finally continued in a steady voice. I had just told her that her daughter, Kimiko, missing since the summer of 1976, when she had called from Tokyo to say she was going on a short trip, was in North Korea. Her mother had not stopped searching for her in the twenty years since Kimiko had vanished. She was quite alone now, her husband having died early and Kimiko's younger brother having been killed in a traffic accident. She had filed countless missing person reports, written letters to all the people listed in Kimiko's old address book, tried posting notices in the newspapers, and appealed to television programs that made announcements of missing persons. She never found anything. The news I brought her was the first she had had in twenty years. I told her that Kimiko had married Okamoto Takeshi, that they had two daughters in Pyongyang, and that she had once again disappeared from sight.

"What kind of man is Mr. Okamoto?" The mother's manner was very restrained. "I am very thankful to hear this news of my daughter finally after twenty years. I realize there are all kinds of difficulties involved, but I would be overjoyed if she could come back to Japan with her husband and children, and they could all live together, healthy and safe. I feel like I am in a dream."

When I called her the next day to thank her for seeing me, she told me she had been unable to sleep at all the night before.

A week later, on August 7, 1996, the morning edition of the *Asahi Shimbun* reported the news that Okamoto's wife was Fukutome Kimiko, a Japanese woman reported missing since 1976. Two days later, a more shocking headline appeared in every newspaper: DID THE OKAMOTOS DIE IN NORTH KOREA?!

One of the accompanying articles read:

> Missing former Red Army Faction member Okamoto Takeshi and his Japanese wife very likely died at their worksite in North Korea about eight years ago, in 1988, a source said on August 9. The remaining Yodogō members in North Korea apparently called the source with the message to "come and collect the remains of two people."…Okamoto's whereabouts have not been confirmed since he was last seen in 1982 by a delegation visiting North Korea from Japan. His wife, a native of Kōchi prefecture, has been missing since 1976. She may have entered North Korea around that time.
>
> According to our source, around 1988 the Okamotos entrusted their two daughters to the former Red Army Faction cadre Tamiya Takamaro before going to the worksite, where they died in an accident. There is said to be a grave.
>
> Sometime after the date of the couple's death, a letter stating that Okamoto had married a North Korean woman was delivered to his parents. From this it had been generally thought that he had no interest in returning to Japan. (*Tokyo Shimbun*, August 9, 1996, evening edition)

The Yodogō group seemed to have made this announcement through a supporter in Japan. Even so, the news was cruel and lacking in human feeling. Immediately after it was reported in Japan that Fukutome Kimiko was in North Korea married to Okamoto Takeshi, resulting in the realization that the story about Okamoto's marriage to a North Korean woman was false, it was announced that they were both dead. No explanation was given for the long deception about Okamoto's wife being a North Korean woman. And, in a reversal of their stance up to then, the Yodogō group asked their supporter in Japan to handle things

with Ms. Fukutome's family. They even sent from Pyongyang the Fukutome family's correct name and address.

I went to Kōchi yet again in mid-August, when this death story was
circulating. I spent several days in the little town there at the edge of the
Shikoku mountains. The southern wind was hot, and the sun burned my
skin. Every night the heat reached record temperatures.

I could not imagine how Fukutome's mother was affected by the
news of the deaths so soon after finally learning of the existence of her
daughter and grandchildren in North Korea. She told me again in a small
voice that she was unable to sleep after reading the newspaper article.
I can only think that she was unable to understand everything that had
happened.

The next day, after speaking to Fukutome's mother again, I visited
the little mountain hamlet where Kimiko had spent her early childhood.
From there I could see the mountains receding into the distance, the ter-
raced paddies cut into the slopes, and a river flowing through a distant
gap hidden in the mountain shadows. The rice was already starting to
bud in the flooded mountainside terraces. There was nothing to connect
this poor village community, rich only in fertile soil, with North Korea
and the destiny of one woman.

From the top of the mountain, the town and its cars and inhabitants looked small and distant. I sat on the ridge for a while, thinking.
At that time, the Yodogō group members were trumpeting the slogan
"Love the Country, love the People, love the Family," and there were
those within Japan who supported them. An organization called the
Independent Japan Association (with Shiomi Takaya as its spokesman)
adopted the slogan as well.[1] But what exactly does it mean to love the
Country, the People, and the Family? I had the strong impression that
the words denied their real meanings, because the actions and words
these people used were always so full of contradictions. In addition,
these words in their North Korean usage deviated greatly from their
meanings in Japanese. This slogan originally belonged to Kim Il Sung
and the North Korean Workers' Party. The words were really a collectivist slogan demanding that North Koreans continue to love the North
Korean state, love the North Korean People, and love the North Korean
ethnic family. It also meant that North Koreans should not hesitate to

---

1. "Independent" here is *jishu*, with the same confusing difference in
meaning as in the name of the Yodogō group's Independent Revolutionary Party
(see chapter 12).

make any sacrifice for their state. There was no way such words could be applied unchanged to present-day Japan. But the misunderstandings were never clarified, and the slogan was accepted as if it meant to love the (mother) country, the (Japanese) people, and the (Japanese) family. I had had enough of this kind of lying. Perhaps I had been affected by a mother's distress, but the thoughts continued to whirl in my head and I struggled to control the anger that kept welling up.

It had been six years since my Yodogō journey had begun, counting from that first trip to North Korea. I suddenly felt, there in the mountains of Kōchi, that I had come down a very long road. It was a feeling I had not had during my trip to Europe earlier in the year.

The death story broke in early August; near the end of the month, Fukutome's mother received an explanatory letter from the Yodogō group. Acting as their messenger was the former chairman of the Red Army Faction, Shiomi Takaya, now working with them again. The letter had been written by Konishi Takahiro, who became group leader after Tamiya's death.

> Kimiko married our colleague Okamoto Takeshi in the mid-1970s and began her life on North Korean soil.
>
> In the 1980s, much to our regret, Okamoto requested to leave our circle and be sent to work at a factory or on a farm. We continued to try and persuade him to remain true to our original intentions, but our discussions went nowhere.
>
> In 1984, Okamoto moved to another location, and Kimiko went with him. It was the kind of place often used to house foreigners. I think the North Koreans may have let them go off on their own to think things over, believing that, once they had done so, they would rejoin us. For our part, of course, we visited them often and continued talking with them. However, in the end, nothing came of our efforts.
>
> At the end of 1986, Okamoto and Kimiko broke with us for good. When they received assignments in a rural area, they entrusted [their children] to our care until their return and departed for their worksite.
>
> The next year, in the summer of 1988, our leader Tamiya Takamaro and I received a message from the North Koreans. It was a notification of Okamoto's and Kimiko's deaths in a mudslide.
>
> . . . Kimiko's body was laid in the same grave as Okamoto's.

Please let us know what the wishes of her family are concerning her remains.

It was a letter filled with transparent lies. If, as Tanaka Yoshimi wrote in his memoirs and the Yodogō group repeatedly averred, Okamoto had simply wanted to live an ordinary life on his own, he would hardly have left his children behind in the village. After all, doesn't living an ordinary life mean living together with one's family? But I have given many examples in this long book of their fictitious stories and deceitful actions. Surely it is no longer necessary to go into any more detail here.

One thing I do need to emphasize, however, is that, *even after the delivery of that letter, whether Okamoto and his wife are dead or alive is still unconfirmed, and there still remains a chance that they are alive.* Also, in order to understand the Yodogō group, it must be accepted that anything they say could be a lie, since they are prepared to lie without any hesitation. This needs some explanation, since I am not attempting mere character assassination here. The way cult groups think and use words is difficult to understand without looking very closely.

Every cult group has its own way of thinking and of using words. If we don't understand the ideas and the words, we won't understand their intentions. This is surely one of the reasons Japanese diplomatic exchanges with North Korea are always such strangely complicated affairs. The Japanese simply do not understand the other party's terminology or ideas and interpret them according to their own comprehension of the words and phrases. Though I have used the word "lies" several times here, the group members probably do not think of themselves as lying. They tell the story they consider to be the most politically correct, or they simply say what they must, and the truth of any given statement is of secondary concern. We can surmise that this is a natural attitude for a political group that exists in a country that puts its inhabitants' political lives above their biological lives. This kind of attitude reflects obvious cultural and ideological differences.

Konishi's letter can be understood from this point of view. Perhaps the group thought it would be accepted in Japan as it stood. Fukutome's family sent a letter to new group leader Konishi, asking for more details about the accident in which she had died. If "accident" were the correct term, surely there would be information about exactly when, where, and how it happened? He said it was a mudslide, and, if so, what were the circumstances in which it occurred? It is human nature to want to know such details. Beyond what was quoted above, Konishi's letter gave no concrete facts at all. Only that they had died "in a mudslide." The letter requesting more details that the family sent with the help of a lawyer never received any reply from the Yodogō group. Instead, Konishi wrote elsewhere, "Okamoto and Fukutome chose to leave our group. We do not have any responsibility for their actions" (January 15, 1997).

Where did this coldness come from? Is it a turn of phrase deeply colored by the idea within the ideology of Kim Il Sung that the fate of a person with different politics is unimportant? I felt that these words were finally revealing the truth of the exiles who, twenty-seven years before, had fled to North Korea aboard the *Yodogō* believing in the slogan "We live and die together!" The fabulous tale of the Yodogō had finally fallen to pieces.

To put it simply, by the end of my pilgrimage to discover the true story of the Yodogō, what I began to understand was that any note of grandeur, every last vestige of myth attached to the Yodogō legend, had completely dissipated by the time of the death of Yoshida Kintarō (reported "dead of illness" in 1985) and the events surrounding Okamoto's disappearance. Those heroes of the day, who had hijacked an airplane to bring on the revolution, had changed into something else entirely. I can only think that, of the nine of them, only Yoshida and Okamoto kept alive the spirit of the era and continued struggling until the end.

The remaining Yodogō members now take the political stance that all of them converted to the *juche* ideology at about the same time soon after their arrival in North Korea. They insist that every one of them exchanged the ideas of the Japanese student movement for those of *juche*, with no exceptions among them. They say they made personal advances by accepting the philosophy of the Great Leader. But this is not true: their words are merely parroting the political line that Kim Il Sung is great. In fact, there were numerous conflicts and doubts among the group members. And, whereas some of them pledged their allegiance, saying they had discovered the truth, others among them obeyed only reluctantly, and yet others never submitted. I think Okamoto's story can be understood as proving this point.

Even now, neither the Yodogō group nor any of its supporters within Japan has given reasons for their long deception regarding the question of Okamoto and his wife. Nor have they explained their little stories of having "seen Okamoto recently" or his "happy marriage with a North Korean woman." Eventually, it became clear that Okamoto's wife was not a North Korean but a Japanese woman abducted from Japan, but still

there has been no explanation of why the story of her death in an accident was not revealed to her family or the Yodogō group's supporters for
eight years.

Many of the stories the Yodogō group (now the Independent Revolution Party) continue to tell have already been revealed as completely
false. Their continued denial of their own marriages; the fabrication of
wedding stories and "revolutionary and fateful encounters" in Europe
once the existence of their wives and children became public; the story
of Okamoto's marriage with a North Korean woman and his supposed
desire to be naturalized as a North Korean citizen; the deceptions
regarding the abduction program in Europe; the appeal for the return of
their children to Japan on humanitarian grounds, while not being very
humane themselves—all of these stories have been clearly revealed as
nothing more than politically convenient fictions. However, even now
they continue to believe that the telling of these lies is their political
duty, that it is for the sake of the revolution, and that their actions are
right. I can only say that their revolution is nothing more than a fabrication of lies. Nearly thirty years have already passed since the hijacking
of the *Yodogō*. The continued lies of these men who changed their allegiance to a new ideology are both very empty and very sad.

Looking at things in this way, we can hardly continue to believe that
Okamoto wrote that surprising letter telling of his happy marriage with
a North Korean woman on his own initiative. He was somehow forced
to write the letter, and it wouldn't have been done by halves, either.
This brings to mind the stories of women who had been kidnapped to
North Korea from Lebanon. After the Lebanese government's protest had
secured their release, these women told of how they had been forced at
gunpoint to call their families to tell them they were safe. We can guess
that Okamoto would probably have been in a similar situation. Or that he
was forced to write in exchange for the safety of his wife and children.
The ploy of using a camouflaging letter was the same as in the abductions
of the students from Europe, but in Okamoto's case it did not work.

Incidentally, in 1998, certain information from the North Korean
Workers' Party regarding the Okamoto case began circulating unofficially. It was probably the first reaction on the part of the Party after his
story was taken up by the Japanese mass media: "The Workers' Party
did not participate at all in the events concerning the Yodogō group. The
management of their group is left up to their independent handling, and
the Party has thus far never interfered in their activities. The Okamoto
incident took place entirely within the Yodogō organization, and they

dealt with it directly. In fact, the Workers' Party, long committed to seeing to their best interests, found such behavior very inconvenient."

I will refrain from comment.

In fact, Fukutome Kimiko sent one letter to her parents after her disappearance, her mother told me. It arrived in August 1979, three years after her disappearance. It did not seem to be an alibi letter written for some third party.

"It came from a communist country. Kimiko's younger brother said the postmark was from East Berlin."

There was no address or sender marked on the envelope. The contents of the letter were strange. In addition to an ordinary greeting, it said she was now in a communist country, that she needed to remain abroad for just a little longer, and that she did not have any problems that they needed to worry about: "Now that I am overseas, I should like to stay for about one more year. I do not have any money problems, so no need to worry. I heard my cousin got married, but I can't send a gift. Send her my best wishes."

Her mother still wonders how Kimiko, overseas for so long, knew about her cousin's wedding. It had taken place just the previous April, only four months before the letter arrived. This letter gains greater significance in a different context.

One thing is clear: after her abduction to North Korea by persons unknown, Fukutome's family was kept under observation. In fact, all the Yodogō members regularly received reports about their families and their surrounding circumstances. This corroborates that there were watchers even in Japan.

Furthermore, Fukutome Kimiko left traces of a sudden visit to Tokyo in 1980. In March, she tried to visit a friend from her hometown in her old apartment building in Ebisu, in Shibuya ward. The friend, however, had already returned to her hometown. Fukutome asked a longtime resident of the building about her friend's whereabouts and left a short message: "I am staying at an inn in Ebisu, and tomorrow I am going to Yokohama."

She stayed for two nights with another friend in Yokohama's South ward. The friend stated: "I had no idea at the time that there was such a serious problem. I had only a vague notion at the time that she had been missing or abducted. I could only remember that she had gone traveling and not come back for some reason. She was herself, exactly the same as she had always been. I used to go and stay at places like youth hostels for a month or more without returning, too...."

"When she came? She just had a small Boston bag.[2] I had no sense that she had just come back from some faraway trip.

"She stayed with me for two days, but she spent her time in the apartment, just reading. When she did go out, she seemed to go to book-stores or the library. She seemed to be looking for a certain book, but I don't know what book it was.

"She left, saying she was going to see a friend in Osaka first and then to her parents' house in Kōchi."

This friend saw her off at Shin Yokohama station, where she boarded the bullet train. She never appeared at her parents' house in Kōchi.

Once again, all traces of her disappear.

Two things must be said about her visit to Japan.

First, why was a person who had been kidnapped to North Korea leaving traces in Japan? The timing of her appearance in Tokyo coincides with the period when Okamoto Takeshi was still a candidate for the plan to infiltrate Japan. If Okamoto was scheduled to return to Japan soon, it may well be that she had to return for a brief visit in order to make some initial preparations. In addition, her passport was nearing expiration. Probably she had to renew her passport for some other use. She would not, however, have been allowed to return to Japan alone. There would have been another person there to support her mission; it is very hard to imagine that she was sent alone. Or possibly the task was passed on to the underground support organizations within Japan. Anyway, whether by a colleague joining her in the mission or by members of the underground in Japan, all her movements would have been closely watched.

Second, visits like those she made to her old apartment building and to her friends were strictly forbidden while on mission. However, she went against the rules. In other words, she acted in a "liberal" manner, making her a target for a *sōkatsu* and self-criticism within their organization. Isn't it very likely that her observer rebuked her and ordered her back to North Korea immediately?

She was, in a sense, imprisoned even when she was in Japan. Besides the watcher at her side, there were her children, left behind as hostages in Pyongyang. She may really have been planning on visiting her mother in Kōchi, as she had told her friend in Yokohama. But we can

---

2. The Japanese original uses the term "Boston bag," which is a small oblong handbag with two handles that might be used to carry a change of clothing for a sports class or an overnight trip.

assume she was either warned against doing this or prevented from it by her companion or some other person who was watching her.

Who could her watcher have been? In her case, given that even her family was watched and reports went back to North Korea, we can understand that someone located very nearby was keeping an eye out on matters concerning her family. Whether this person was aware of playing the role of watcher, we have no way of knowing, since it is possible for a skilled informer to obtain information indirectly by drawing it out in ordinary conversation with someone near the family. If the task of watching Fukutome's movements in Japan was being shared by members of some underground organization, it is possible she was followed daily. There is also the possibility that someone had accompanied her from North Korea, since one of the other Yodogō wives is known to have been in Japan at that same time.

After being seen off at Shin Yokohama station, Fukutome Kimiko disappeared again. Her whereabouts can next be confirmed in the village, when she delivered Okamoto's second daughter there.

North Korea's purpose in allowing Fukutome's short return to Japan is something of a mystery. If she had made the trip in order to prepare for her husband Okamoto's secret return to Japan, it could be that Okamoto's return had been soon impending. If her actions while in Japan had for some reason displeased the North Korean government or the Yodogō group, then she might have cast a shadow on the plans for sending Okamoto there. I can only say here that, had the plan for Okamoto's return been carried out, the fate of these two people would most likely have been quite different.

The Yodogō plan for slipping back into Japan was eventually carried out a few years later by a different member.

CHAPTER TWENTY-SEVEN

Infiltration into Japan

In the spring of 1985, a man steps onto Japanese soil. He was born in Japan, but it no longer feels like home. Even his name is different. Fifteen years have passed since he left Japan, and it is clear the country has been transformed in that time. He shakes off his initial bewilderment and begins to walk the streets of a Japanese city for the first time after fifteen years of absence. He has neither the time nor the desire to lose himself in sentimental memories of the past. The streets are lively with bustling crowds that conceal the man as he walks along slowly. Finally, his figure fades into the shadows of the city and disappears.

After Okamoto Takeshi had been removed from his duties, the Yodogō hijackers continued to hunt for a way to further their plans of entering Japan. They considered many different options, almost certainly focusing on the possibilities of landing a boat on the Sea of Japan coast or of using forged passports. But each plan had disadvantages to outweigh its advantages. The biggest problems were the inability to come and go freely and the impossibility of acquiring the rights of citizenship, both of which were essential if they were to achieve their goals. They had attempted to obtain forged passports in Southeast Asia, the Philippines, and South America, but the results had been unsatisfactory. They needed the passport of a person who actually existed, and then one of them must become that person. Ideally, their target would have few if any relatives or dependents, since that would reduce the risk of detection. Their task was to find such a person and assume his identity. The Yodogō hijackers' scheme of infiltrating Japan was stuck on this point, and, as long as they could not resolve the problem, their plans could go nowhere.

Though the hijackers' own plans to reenter Japan were not progressing, their wives began making multiple return trips to Japan quite early on. Starting with Uomoto Tamiko's entry on January 20, 1980, and Mori Yoriko's and Kuroda Sakiko's on June 1, 1981, Uomoto, Mori, Kuroda, Kaneda Emiko, and Fukui Takako made several visits to Japan after 1982. These visits, as many as ten per person, ended only when the Ministry of Foreign Affairs issued a recall order on the women's passports. From the time of their initial departures from Japan until the recall in 1988, each woman had renewed her passport twice.

Several days have passed since the man's return to Japan.

He feels himself gradually becoming accustomed to his new environment, and now he thinks it is time to establish a settled residence. He has in his possession the signature stamp, certified family register, and national health insurance certificate of a person who actually existed. He tosses these casually into a briefcase and goes to a long-established real estate agency in the downtown area. The storefront displays apartment rental advertisements, simple room layouts liberally strewn with phrases such as "bargain," "plenty of sunlight," and "excellent access to public transportation." He opens the door and enters.

The Yodogō wives initially insisted that their purpose in visiting Japan was to "engage in economic activities." By this they meant to imply two things: first, that they were engaging in legitimate business in cooperation with the Yodogō men, and, second, that they took on part-time jobs in order to support their husbands and children, living modest lives as exiles in Pyongyang. Since they continued to maintain the story that the Yodogō group led restricted and quiet lives there, their testimony was sprinkled with such untruths.

Later, Tamiya Takamaro explained the wives' mission in Japan.

> What we expected of them was to do what we could not, that is, to enter Japan. In brief, we wanted to know the state of affairs in Japan. That is why we had to keep their existence a secret. Things are different now that the passports are no longer an issue, but back then that was not the case.... So we couldn't go public about them. That's why they could not make any contact with their families or meet any of their relatives while they were in Japan, though one of the women told me how she had walked around the neighborhood of her family home. (Tamiya and Takazawa 1996, 208)

In this interview, given late in Tamiya's life, the lies did not flow as they had initially; though the truth made something of an appearance, the story was far from complete. However, it would be a mistake to take Tamiya's line that they wanted to know the state of affairs in Japan to mean that the wives were working as spies. In fact, their duties were more complicated and secret than that. They were not merely spying.

The season is changing. It has not been long since his return to Japanese soil after his long absence, but already the spring wind is shifting into early summer. The man has placed a small, handwritten name card on the door of his apartment. It reads "A. Nakao." He has also visited a print shop near the subway exit to order business cards, selecting a basic pattern from the shop's design catalog. The cards give his company as "Columbus' Egg Trading Company." Once his address is fixed, the man has his picture taken, and he starts the process of applying for a passport. He does not hesitate in writing "Nakao" in the space for his family name.

The Yodogō group staged a performance to coincide with their mission of infiltration into Japan. They requested to be allowed to return to Japan, stressing their longing for home. Since they were making the effort, the performance had to be as flamboyant as possible, and it had to be effective. The target for their appeal was Prime Minister Nakasone Yasuhiro, the highest representative of the Japanese government. The Yodogō hijackers sent Nakasone a letter requesting a discussion of their return to Japan. On the part of the hijackers, it was a fine show of "the Revolutionaries of the North" addressing "the Premier of the East."

Greetings:

We are the Japanese citizens living as exiles in the Democratic People's Republic of Korea as a result of the so-called Yodogō incident.

It is said that even mountains and rivers change their shape after ten years, and it has been fifteen years since we departed our homeland. Not a few of our aged parents have passed away in that time. We hear that Japan has changed greatly.

In all these long years, we have never once lost our awareness of the fact that we are Japanese, and our desire to serve our homeland has only grown stronger. Our hope of returning to Japan to work for its continued prosperity and peace is now greater than ever.

In taking up our pens for the first time since our departure to foreign lands, we wish to express our true feelings and inquire about the government's stand on the issue of our return to Japan. There are those who think our case should be handled as nothing more than another criminal case. However, we cannot agree with this.

The movement in which we participated as young students in the 1960s was a demand for the democratization of our universities and a just struggle in opposition to the militarization of Japan by our government at the behest of the United States....

We have neither killed nor injured anyone. The airplane we borrowed was promptly returned. In contrast, in forcibly repressing the young patriots of Japan and in following the United States' lead in militarizing Japan, the Japanese government should recognize its mistakes and apologize to the Japanese people.

Recently we have received many letters from sympathetic Japanese who support and encourage our return. Many of them say our exile from Japan was inevitable against the background of events at the time, that our actions cannot be considered crimes, and that we should return home.

Although we are grateful for such words, we consider that the issue of our return can only be resolved once the government of Japan recognizes the mistakes of its policies in the past and corrects the situation that resulted. Our return is a political issue in which the Japanese government can show the world by its actions that it is ready to express its autonomy and lead the way on the road to peace.

However, during this time, not only has the government of Japan not righted its own wrongs, but it has ignored its responsibility to take any action on our behalf, leaving the management of our situation to the government of the Democratic People's Republic of Korea, a nation with which it has no diplomatic relations. Now that the possible normalization of relations between the two nations has been raised as a national issue, we believe that the demands of international good faith will not allow the Japanese government to continue denying its responsibilities concerning our treatment.

Mr. Prime Minister, you are the head of a government accountable to every single citizen. We believe that you must allow us, as Japanese citizens, to return to our homeland and that you must respond to the Japanese people's expectation and demand for peace and autonomy while simultaneously meeting your international responsibilities.

We demand the following from the Japanese government: first, to accept our return to Japan free of any criminal charges; and, second, to initiate measures to begin discussion of the issue of our return.

We trust we will soon receive a favorable response from you.

> July 17, 1985
> From all Japanese who must live in exile in
> the Democratic People's Republic of Korea

This is the text of the letter the Yodogō group sent to Prime Minister Nakasone. Their performance, however, developed in a direction they had not planned. The Japanese media, hearing of their request, trumpeted that "the Yodogō hijackers are asking with heads bowed to return to Japan" and covered the story using phrases such as "exile fatigue" and "homesickness." The government did not publicize the letter it had received and maintained a stance of "no comment." The Yodogō group hastened to protest against the media's coverage and to urge the government to acknowledge that they had indeed sent a letter. They sent Nakasone a second letter, but when it produced no results either, they had to resort to sending yet another letter, this time to Chief Cabinet Secretary Fujinami Takao.

...On July 17, we sent a letter to Prime Minister Nakasone concerning the matter of our return to Japan. However, though three months have passed since then, we have still not received a reply.

We have heard that the government is denying that it ever even received our letter; yet there is a completely false version of our letter making the rounds in the magazines and newspapers of the media that are supposed to report the truth....

These facts disappoint us greatly. In order to prevent a

similar situation in the future, we are taking the somewhat presumptuous step of sending, through you, a letter to Prime Minister Nakasone that is open to the public. We await his reply.

...We respectfully request that you forward the enclosed letter to Prime Minister Nakasone himself.

Sincerely,

(October 28, 1985)

Though their performance may have provoked a more complex situation than they had planned, still their ploy of sending a letter to Nakasone was effective: the wish of the Yodogō group to return to Japan and their request to the government to initiate negotiations for this were now known to the public.

Quite a long time has passed since his return to Japan. By chance, the man hears one day of a volunteer group that visits orphanages and homes for the elderly. After thinking the matter over for a while, he calls the group's leader, a plan in mind. The group leader warmly welcomes his request to join the volunteers and explains that they work with many elderly people and children with no near relations, and all the man needs to do is keep them company or play with them, or perhaps sometimes go out on a hike with them. The man says another job he holds may not allow him to join in every time, but he would like to participate and help as much as he can. The other work to which the man refers is academic and postgraduation counseling to high school students. He has already decided against starting up a cram school since it would require more time than he could give it, and anyway he does not think he is suited to teaching anyone how to study. For his purposes, he must have a legitimate venue for meeting and culti- vating youths outside of a cram school setting. It is imperative. And, in fact, the counseling work suits his requirements perfectly. Asking questions pertaining to the students' family situations and ideological tendencies is a matter of course, a natural part of his job as an advisor. He can ask the most personal questions without arousing suspicion. In short, he conducts his identity investigation openly and in public. He is rather impressed at his own cleverness in thinking of the guidance work and of volunteering with children without families at the orphanage.

Looking back, the motive for the performance of sending letters to Prime Minister Nakasone seems clear now. Their first plans to infiltrate Japan (by Okamoto Takeshi) coincided with their first confession of homesickness and the publication of their memoirs on the tenth anniversary of the hijacking; the second infiltration mission was under way when they sent their letters to the prime minister. These two public performances, sharing the theme of a return to Japan, hid reentry missions that were playing out behind the scenes.

Just as the frequent and short visits by the wives were explained as economic activities, the Yodogō men also needed a plausible and convincing explanation for their presence in Japan. Their true mission there had to remain concealed. The professions of wishing to return to Japan were a set up to provide an alibi and gain sympathy should they ever be discovered and arrested while on assignment in Japan. In other words, the men needed a story telling how their homesickness and irresistible desire to set foot once again in their homeland had pushed them into taking the risky step of returning secretly. How could they be blamed for their actions, when they were merely seeking to return to their rightful Japanese homeland by any means available? And, in fact, when one of them was arrested while on an undercover mission in Japan, this was exactly how they justified their actions.

More recently, Tanaka Yoshimi has mentioned the staging around the letters sent to the government in his account of the "Okamoto problem."

> Our situation and the circumstances surrounding Okamoto at the time led us in 1985 to send the letter to Prime Minister Nakasone demanding a discussion of the issue of our return. But it was completely ignored, and there was nothing we could do to turn Okamoto away from his decision to separate from us and live an ordinary life in the communist society.
>
> As a result, Okamoto entered North Korean society to begin his life as an ordinary laborer. He finally met with a terrible accident at his worksite that ended in the worst possible way. (*Tsukuru*, February 1998, p. 142)

The writer is implying nothing less than that everything, including Okamoto's fate, is the fault of the Japanese government and no responsibility of the Yodogō group. In Japan this kind of talk is clearly seen as a self-serving passing of blame onto others, but, apparently, in the ideology of Kim Il Sung, even in cases like this the Great Leader's principle that anything that goes wrong is the fault of others holds true.

The man is at the airport.

He needs to report to the organization that the mission in Japan finally seems to be on track. A secret order has come from the village for him to make contact outside of Japan. They must plan out the future course of the mission and discuss whether or not to continue the operations for acquiring their currently selected Japanese targets. The man's bag contains a list of names and data on the high school students he has counseled and the youths he has met through his volunteer activities.

The man takes a passport out of his pocket and presents it at the passport control window. It is a genuine passport issued by the Ministry of Foreign Affairs in the name of "Nakao Akira."

Were the feelings of homesickness and longing for their homeland expressed by Tamiya Takamaro and the rest of the Yodogō group merely a calculated tactic? This question bothered me, and I have returned to it many times. I think now that they were truthful when they talked about their longing for home. Their tactic consisted of tying truth and fiction together into a seamless blend. The strategy had to have been very carefully thought out or their words would never have been so close to their true feelings. They must have kept these feelings carefully hidden behind a screen of politics and theory. Above all, they were men who enjoyed games of bluffing and deceit. My point may be controversial, but in fact they used their deception in this case as an outlet to express their true feelings. Most astounding is how they ignored the difficulty of reconciling these tender feelings for their homeland with their intention of converting all of Japan, by force if necessary, to the *juche* way.

The man is sitting in a hotel, somewhere in Europe, hurriedly writing several postcards. He must soon return to Japan to continue his mission there, and he must finish this task before it is time to board his flight. He writes a few lines on the cards, then reaches into his bag for his notebook and begins mechanically filling in addresses. These are greetings from abroad to the youths who have been selected for acquisition. The man has been taught that such simple gestures are a basic technique for gaining the trust and confidence of a target. Once he finishes the last card, he grabs his bag, checks out of the hotel, and heads toward the airport. He drops the bundle of cards with their bland messages into a postbox on the way and then thinks nothing more of them.

A few days later, the man is once again walking the busy streets of Japan. A few more days after that, several high school students, including a boy and a girl in their junior year in Kanagawa prefecture, receive the postcards that were

*mailed in Europe. The sender has signed his name as "A. Nakao." They think it
strange to receive such a friendly postcard from someone they barely know.*

Over the years, the issue of the Yodogō group's return to Japan has taken
many turns. They sent another letter requesting a discussion of their
return when Kaifu Toshiki became prime minister after Nakasone. In
addition, as time went by, their initial demand for a "return with a full
pardon" moderated into a "negotiated return," and finally they asked
only for a return for "humanitarian reasons."

At times the Yodogō issue was like a thorn in the side of the political discussions between Japan and North Korea, but their true reasons
for returning to Japan were never clearly grasped. Many people thought
that, if they wished to return, they had only to accept their punishment or
fight the matter out in the courts. But they persisted in their demand for
a full pardon or a negotiation of terms. From the commonsense view in
Japan, their demands were simply preposterous. Their supporters spoke
of the statute of limitations and of how the Yodogō group's actions must
be seen against the background of events at the time, but their words
lacked conviction, since even they thought the hijackers' demands were
unreasonable. Even now the issue of their return remains unresolved.

I will step outside the chronological order of events here for a
moment to note that, although it has commonly been understood that
the Japanese government did nothing in response to their request for a
return, in fact, the group has been asked more than once through several
politicians to confirm their interest in returning and to settle the length
of imprisonment. In one instance I heard from the Pyongyang side, the
length of their sentences would have been considerably shorter than in
precedent cases. The Yodogō group, however, refused the deal. Although
it was suggested that they could come back and engage in a protracted
court battle, from their perspective their return to Japan would be
meaningless if they were arrested the moment they set foot on Japanese
soil. Perhaps their demands were preposterous, but, as far as the Yodogō
group was concerned, there was no point in returning if they would not
be free to pursue their mission.

Throughout the period of their grand performance of requesting
a negotiated return to Japan with the government, they continued to
search for ways to further their infiltration mission.

*The man's figure melts once again into the shadows. The city's darkness has hid-
den him well for the three years since his return after a fifteen-year absence.*

Before we trace the footsteps of this shadowy figure, there is another story that must be told.

At the time when the Yodogō group's letter to Prime Minister Nakasone and the issue of their return were hot topics in the media, another drama was playing out in Japan. From the shadows cast by this drama and the infiltration mission, the story of a woman caught in the vicissitudes of fate rises up out of the dark.

CHAPTER TWENTY-EIGHT

Betrayal

On the evening of January 22, 1988, a phone rang in the External Affairs section of the Kanagawa Prefectural Police Department. Regular working hours had long passed, and there were only a few people left in the building.

"At this hour?" the officer on duty wondered as he picked up the phone.

A male voice spoke. "Are the police working on that Korean Airlines incident that is all over the news right now?"

"Excuse me, but what exactly do you want to say?"

"I can't tell you my name, but, in fact, I know something that I think I should tell you."

It was a call from an anonymous informer. The police get many such calls, and the majority of them are pranks. This seemed like one of the prank calls, not to be taken seriously.

"May I ask who is calling, please?"

Abruptly the caller's voice came loud and harsh. "I told you already I can't give you my name!" he shouted. "I'm calling from Yokosuka!"

The officer turned to face the telephone. "So what is it, then?"

"There is a snack bar on Yonegahama Street in Yokosuka, called Yumemiha. The woman who runs it says her name is Satō, but she seems to have a lot of different names. She's about thirty. Foreigners come and go pretty regularly. The Korean Air thing has been on the news a lot lately, and I thought she might have something to do with it."

"What is her name, besides "Satō"?

"I don't know."

"Would you please give me your telephone number?"

"I told you, I can't tell you! Now it is up to the police to investigate. Oh, and she seems to be renting her apartment under a different name, so you should check that out, too." With that, the caller hung up.

It had to be a prank. The police officer took an unhurried look at the clock. It was past 9:00 p.m. He logged the call anyway and made a brief note of its contents. Once he had finished writing, he experienced a twinge of doubt. These kinds of calls were frequent, and usually they went to the Investigations Unit or the Public Security Division. This one, however, had come directly to External Affairs. He suddenly felt that perhaps there was something to it after all.

Satō Keiko was working at the bar that evening, as always.

The place had filled quite early. Perhaps it was Keiko's own youth and charm that made the place so popular and brought in so many customers so soon. Barely two months had passed since she had opened Yumemiha (literally, "dreaming-wave"). She had made up fliers and posted them around the town before opening day: "Look anywhere in Japan, and you won't find another café bar in this brand-new style. YUMEMIHA, a café bar square for men and women, opens on December 2."[1] Perhaps but not necessarily owing to the wording on the flier, most of the customers were young, many of them university students. Besides beer and liquor, the menu offered a wide array of popular appetizers and light meals. Given the youth of the clientele, the place had soon acquired a relaxed and carefree atmosphere. Occasionally a customer would come behind the counter and show Keiko how to make a favorite dish. Keiko herself was more like one of the noisy crowd, having a good time rather than playing the role of serious bar owner. With quite a lot of space for such a place, she had even managed to create a karaoke nook.

Keiko had just come out from behind the bar and was about to set up the karaoke microphone. A customer stood up to leave, and Keiko hurried to see him off at the stairs. Such moments were among the few times when she acted like a bar hostess.

When she returned, she turned immediately toward the karaoke machine, but one of her employees called out, "Mama—there's a phone call for you. Sounds like the same guy as before."

Out of the corner of her eye, Keiko caught a look of suspicion on the part-

---

1. The words "café, bar, square" were written in *katakana*, the syllabary used for foreign words, and were meant to evoke the image of a new, Western-style friendly gathering place for young men and women.

time girl's face. Keiko felt suddenly nervous. She had a bad feeling about who
the caller might be. She returned to the counter and took the telephone receiver,
outwardly calm. She heard only the hum of a disconnected line. He had already
hung up.

The External Affairs section of the prefectural police decided to begin a secret investigation. There was indeed a snack bar on Yokosuka's Yonegahama Street, just as the caller had said. It was a stylish place on the third floor of a multipurpose building facing one of the main streets. The customers were numerous and young, and, given its location, many of them were Self-Defense Force personnel. The business permit papers had yielded the name of "Yao Megumi" for Satō Keiko. The prefectural police sent an inquiry to the National Police Agency. A reply came at the beginning of February.

The response from the national police regarding Yao Megumi made excitement rise in the External Affairs section. The new information included facts such as how, during an overseas trip in February of 1982, she had a meeting in Copenhagen with Kim Yuchol, then vice-consul of the North Korean consulate in Zagreb, Yugoslavia; she had also been seen in the company of several Japanese women who were under suspicion, and records of her movements showed several visits to East Berlin and Eastern Europe.

Based on this information, the External Affairs section continued their quiet investigation. They suspected the woman of being a North Korean agent. Her neighbors were questioned, and she was followed and watched for quite a long period of time. A discreet query into her apartment lease revealed that the anonymous telephone informer had been correct: it was not her name on the lease contract.

The police made their move in mid-May, when they initiated a formal investigation. The arrest warrant cited her use of a false name on her apartment lease and charged her with falsifying official documents.[2]

Yao Megumi, a.k.a. Satō Keiko, was arrested by the Kanagawa pre-

---

2. Falsifying documents is a common charge that police use as a pretext to arrest someone and hold them for questioning. Any discrepancy in the name on a document, such as signing a hotel register with a false name for privacy reasons or failing to change the address on a driver's license after moving, can be the basis for arresting and holding someone for up to twenty-three days of interrogation. The arrest also allows the police to execute search warrants for any locations connected in any way to the suspect, which is often the primary motivation for the arrest.

fectural police early in the morning of May 25, 1988. Her apartment and the bar were immediately searched. The police expected to find evidence that she was a North Korean undercover agent. However, they found nothing of note. There was none of the equipment North Korean agents were assumed to use, such as random number tables, forged passports, and wireless radios.

The police continued to search her apartment and even visited the tiny, six-tatami-mat room she had lived in previously, going as far as removing the ceiling panels to look for hidden items. Even so, they could find nothing to support the information in the documents they had received from the National Police Agency. In the end, she received only a summary indictment of making a false statement on a government document for having used a false name on her residency registration and was fined 50,000 yen (about $390 at the then-current exchange rate).

At this point, the story takes an unexpected turn. Lacking sufficient evidence to indict her on the charge of "spying," the police released Yao after holding her for twenty-three days without pressing charges.[3] She emerged to find herself making media headlines as a "North Korean spy." Her story came to be known as the "Suspected North Korean Spy Snack-Bar Mama" affair, or the "Yumemiha Incident," after the name of her bar.

Ominous headlines sprawled across the newspapers:

"FORGED PASSPORT FOUND IN NAME OF NORTH KOREAN
UNDERCOVER AGENT"
"RANDOM NUMBER TABLE AND WIRELESS RADIO FOUND IN
APARTMENT"
"SUSPECT MET WITH KOREA AIRLINES INCIDENT'S KIM HYON
HEE"

Such were the headlines, with no relation to the actual facts of her story. She consulted with a lawyer after her release from police custody and immediately held a news conference.

---

3. In Japan, police can hold suspects for questioning for three days, after which they can go to court to get permission to hold the person for another ten days, which is renewable once for a total of twenty-three days. At the end of that time, they either have to indict the suspect for a specific crime or release the person. The usual strategy is to try to get the suspect to confess during this prolonged period of interrogation, which is carried out in a police jail. The suspect may claim the right to a lawyer, but lawyers are never allowed to observe the interrogations.

"I am not a North Korean spy," she declared.

Looking back now, it was a desperate move.

While the media were in a fever reporting on the "North Korean spy," several people, men and women, Japanese and Korean, were quietly but hurriedly leaving Japan from Narita, Kansai, and other airports. All of them left jobs without asking for permission, missed previously arranged meetings with friends, and left their apartments hurriedly in their rush to the nearest airports, though none of this would have been apparent to an observer. They had all received top secret orders to return immediately to North Korea.

Throughout her interview with the press, Yao Megumi hid in her heart a secret she could not reveal.

Afterwards, she filed lawsuits: against the national government and the Ministry of Foreign Affairs for revoking her passport on her arrest, against the police for investigating her on counts other than those for which she had been arrested,[4] and against several media organizations for libel and defamation of character. The courts later found that most of the newspapers, magazines, and broadcasting stations went too far in their reports concerning this incident. Except for two or three issues that are still under dispute, all have been settled by this writing.

The charges and claims made by the national government and the police, and Yao's countering denial of having any connection with North Korea were all similar in one way: they were all founded on falsehoods. The lawsuits were probably intended as a cover for her, an alibi. The story that needs to be told here is not that of either side in the court cases: none of the truth can found there.

Nine years after this incident, in May of 1997, birth certificates issued by the North Korean government were brought into Japan through the auspices of the "Yodogō Homecoming Humanitarian Association," a group supporting the Yodogō group in their quest to return home. These medical certificates showed that two female Japanese infants had been born in a North Korean hospital over a decade earlier; the documents were used to begin the process of obtaining Japanese nationality and family registration for the two girls.

---

4. Once a person has been arrested on a specific charge, it is against the law to interrogate that person about a different charge (*bekken taihō*, literally "different charge arrest"), although that is done frequently. This practice and the length of time a person can be held in custody before formal indictment facilitate and underscore the extreme importance placed on confession in the Japanese criminal justice system.

When the existence of the Yodogō wives had been revealed in 1992, it had provoked a variety of reactions in Japan. The women had made appearances before the media, and a call had been raised to allow their children to return to Japan for "humanitarian reasons." The North Korean government received a request to issue birth certificates for the Yodogō children, and the process of securing their Japanese citizenship had been started in Japan.

Including Okamoto Takeshi's two daughters, whose existence was kept secret for so long, there are a total of twenty Yodogō children. The parents of two of them did not, in fact, live in Pyongyang. These children had been separated from their parents and left behind in North Korea. The birth certificates named as their mother that very Satō Keiko who had owned the café bar Yumemiha on Yonegahama Street in Yokosuka: that is, Yao Megumi.

Yao has since apologized to the supporters of her lawsuit and other friends for not being able to speak the truth to them. Moreover, she has confessed that she had indeed lived in North Korea, that she had two children there, and that their father was one of the Yodogō group members.

How had she made the crossing to North Korea? Why did she have two children there? Why was she now in Japan, separated from her children? Why had she been silent on this matter for nearly ten years?

In my investigations of these background circumstances, I uncovered another twist in the complex Yodogō story, hidden in the darkness that is North Korea.

As I have written earlier, Kim Il Sung revealed the existence of the Yodogō wives on the eve of his eightieth birthday in April 1992. The interview he gave was reported in the political news section of the *Asahi Shimbun* early the same month.

The *Asahi Shimbun* reporter whose beat was the Tokyo Metropolitan Bureau of Police shook his head in puzzlement over this article.

"There are wives?"

His astonishment and doubt are not surprising, given what was generally thought of the circumstances of the Yodogō group at the time. Most people had the vague idea that they were living restricted lives as exiles in North Korea and that they had recently started confessing their homesickness, asking to be allowed to return to Japan without any charges being made against them. The idea of their having wives and children seemed to be outside the realm of possibility.

The reporter asked me, "Do you have any idea what is going on?"

I told him: "The guy who did the interview is one of your own colleagues. Why don't you ask him?" At the time, I had no other answer for him. I can still remember his words and the look of dissatisfaction that remained on his face as he walked away down a street in Shinjuku.

But Kim Il Sung's remarks were only the opening lines of the drama that was to follow, because his casual words allowed light to be shed on the story that until then had been hidden in darkness. Sometimes even the most skillful manipulator can slip up, and Kim Il Sung's breezy words threw his lieutenants into confusion. Their carefully constructed story began to show cracks and inconsistencies. Their elaborate structure began to crumble as each exposed lie revealed others. More than anything, this spelled the end of their operations in Japan.

The Yodogō group itself was quickest to organize a response to Kim Il Sung's words. Akagi Shirō met with a group of Japan Socialist Party members on a visit to North Korea and confirmed on being questioned that they were indeed married. He also had no choice but to admit, though reluctantly, that all of their wives were Japanese women. In North Korea, the Great Leader Kim Il Sung held absolute power. No one could disregard his words. If the Yodogō group continued hiding their marriages as before, they would be implying that Kim Il Sung had indulged in an outright lie, which was, of course, out of the question.

They had held an emergency meeting on the stunning turn of events. The group came to the conclusion that they had no choice but to admit the truth of their marriages to the public.

Although they felt no qualms about going public on their own behalf, still they had some doubts. At the time, they had a serious problem: those who had been arrested while in Japan.

Tamiya Takamaro thought long on the matter and finally came to a conclusion. They would not be able to avoid an uproar. However, he could not let the matter continue without taking some action. He sat down and began to compose a long letter.

In the interrogation room of the External Affairs section of the Kanagawa prefectural police on the day of her arrest, Yao Megumi answered questions in the following way.

"The charges you have made are correct. There are no mistakes. I did not wish to use my real name, so even with my friends I gave my name as Satō Keiko. I didn't think using a false name would bother anyone."

The interrogation report runs for only several lines and confirms the charge of falsifying documents. The investigation, however, continued.

The investigators next asked her about her overseas travels.

Since 1977, when she obtained her first passport at the age of twenty-one, she had traveled outside of Japan on seven occasions. The police were most interested in the first of these trips, when she was gone for seven years and during which her whereabouts were largely unknown.

She was not informed of how these questions related to the charges she had already admitted to. Under the current code of criminal procedure, a suspect may be held by police for a period of twenty days pending formal charges. Adding the three days allowed for police interrogations, a suspect can be held for up to twenty-three days without charges, during which time the police are free to make their inquiries as they see fit. They took full advantage of her arrest on other charges to conduct a thorough investigation into her suspected spying activities.

"I was traveling around Europe picking up part-time jobs in different places. I wanted to study, and I supported myself by babysitting, waitressing, washing dishes, that sort of thing," she said in answer to their questions.

Her answer did not satisfy the investigating officers. They persisted in questioning her; they grew impatient. The searches of her residence brought no additional evidence. They changed the focus of their investigation and looked into the source of her startup capital for the bar. They visited every place in Kanagawa prefecture where she had worked and even tracked down the records of every paycheck she had received. What they found was unexpected.

During the period they investigated, she worked so much she could have had almost no time to sleep. Factory assembly-line worker, stationery shop clerk, coffee shop waitress, vocational college office worker, word-processor instructor, pachinko parlor attendant, publishing company sales representative, all-night work as hostess in lounges and snack bars: she squeezed part-time work into even the smallest gaps of free time between other jobs. She had zero time to herself, and she did all she could to minimize travel time between jobs.

"She can't even have had time to take baths," one of the investigators apparently said in astonishment.

Certainly her lifestyle was in no way luxurious. She paid 20,000 yen a month (about $156 at the time and $200 in 2016) for a bare, shabby six-tatami-mat room with neither a bath nor a toilet. Even so, her savings could hardly have been enough to start her own business.

After several days, the police finally got a statement.

"During my travels, I received money on five occasions, totaling about 5 million yen, from an older man living in France," she said. The investigators felt that they had finally found the key. This was the opening that would reveal her connection with her co-conspirators.

"I became involved with him during my travels, but I didn't know his name or where he lived. I knew him as Mr. Liu, a Chinese man living in Europe.

"I met him on my first trip abroad in 1977. I was walking around Copenhagen when this Asian stranger spoke to me and invited me to join him for a meal. That was Mr. Liu. I told him my name was Satō Keiko. He asked me a few casual questions about my family and friends as well. I didn't tell him many details. He asked if I had ever been to Eastern Europe and said that, if I wanted to go, he would take me there.

"Mr. Liu called me when I was in France, about a month later. He said he wanted to meet me again. I agreed, and we arranged to meet in a café on Strøget in Copenhagen. I remember telling him there that someday I wanted to own my own restaurant and that I also wanted to found an orphanage.

"I met him several times after that. Once he showed me around Belgrade. I have also been to East Berlin and Moscow with him. I don't know how many times we had met when he said to me, 'You will need some money for your plans,' and gave me ten thousand U.S. dollars.

"Later he wanted to give me more money for my restaurant, but I was reluctant to just take it, so he said I could help him with his work. He said, 'It is easy work that anyone can do, and I know I can trust you.' So I decided to work for Mr. Liu."

After obtaining this statement, the External Affairs section showed her several photographs distributed by the national police to see if she could recognize any of the men in them. They lay spread across a desk. She took her time and looked carefully at each photo but found none of "Mr. Liu." The police officer, irritation clear in his face, pulled a photo out of a different file. He laid it on the desk.

The man in the photo was lean, wore black-rimmed glasses, and appeared to be in his late forties. She looked up.

"I think this is Mr. Liu."

Hearing this, the External Affairs section was flooded with excitement, for the man in the photo was Kim Yuchol, marked by Western intelligence agencies as an important North Korean agent. It had not previously occurred to the prefectural police investigating her case that Yao's "Mr. Liu" might be Kim Yuchol himself. Their suspicions regarding her deepened.

Gradually, more information supporting the material sent by the national police emerged in Yao's statements. However, much of their investigation was guesswork, and later events make it clear that they had probably reached some of their conclusions before they began actually investigating.

Yao filed her first lawsuit on April 17, 1989, against the Ministry of Foreign Affairs, protesting the revocation of her passport and asking for its return. She argued that article 19, section 1.2, of the Passport Law, which allows the confiscation of the passport of anyone considered a threat to "the national interest and public safety of Japan," did not apply in her case. The first hearing was held in Yokohama District Court on June 21. During this time, several civil organizations, labor unions, and human rights organizations lent their support and testified that she had been falsely accused. Later she spoke of her surprise at this show of support.

"I was deeply grateful. My heart warmed, and my courage grew a hundred times stronger. I had no support group at the time, nor did I belong to any civic group or labor union."

In retrospect, this was probably a profoundly moving experience. For Yao, alone and unsupported, even a slight show of support was a great encouragement. But, even so, no one around her knew the real reasons for her great emotion at this support. The secret she kept remained hidden.

The base of her support continued to grow. She began to file lawsuits against the media for their coverage of her case and their disregard for her human rights. A volunteer lawsuit support group was established to help support her case. They called themselves "Yumemiha" after Yao's café bar and organized a legal defense team. Over time, their numbers increased. They appeared to be making very good progress.

But a letter arrived to halt all forward movement. In the spring of 1992, a sudden catastrophe hit Yao Megumi.

Her hands shook as she opened the letter delivered to her through an intermediary. It was from Tamiya Takamaro in North Korea. Its contents threw her into deep despair.

I think you are aware from the media uproar that Premier Kim Il Sung has made public the existence of the Yodogō wives and children. Now I must ask you, Comrade Satō Keiko, to make no delay in announcing to the public that you, too, are one of us and in displaying the certificate of your marriage to our comrade Shibata Yasuhiro, currently in prison in Japan. From now on, you must struggle openly and praise the great work of our illustrious leader, Premier Kim Il Sung, and do your best in all matters. The two children who remain here continue to grow day by day, and they look forward with great longing to the day they will be reunited with their parents. Surely nothing would bring greater happiness than that the day the *juche* revolution is realized in Japan should also be the day of reunion between mother and children.

The people working in your support may be caught with momentary surprise, but I think they will certainly understand our true intentions. If it is necessary, we can explain matters further to them if they visit us here in North Korea.

Such were the contents of the letter. Shibata Yasuhiro was the youngest of the Yodogō hijackers. But it was difficult to obey the letter's orders when the lawsuits against the media organizations had only just begun.

In addition, it had been Tamiya himself as well as the Workers' Party instructors who had emphasized that she must under no circumstances allow her connection to the Yodogō group and North Korea to become known.

I had heard as much myself, directly from Tamiya in Pyongyang. Several years after Yao's arrest in Yokosuka, when the media were once again full of "spy reports," I asked them about their connection to Yao Megumi.

"No connection whatsoever" was the answer. They could say nothing else, since her work for them in Japan had to remain secret. My point is that at first they vehemently denied the connection that later they publicized so vigorously.

Yao Megumi was loyally following her original orders from the Yodogō group. In this she had no choice. After all, her children remained in North Korea.

She was bewildered and hesitated over the sudden order to go public. The other Yodogō members reacted critically to her hesitation. They regarded it as disloyalty to their group, and by extension it meant that she was lacking in loyalty to Kim Il Sung as well. It was the vicious judgment of a collective organization that regarded its members as mere cogs in a wheel.

Torn between her loyalty to the supporters of her lawsuit and her loyalty to the group in North Korea, she dithered helplessly for a while. Finally, no longer able to live with her conscience, she disclosed her relationship with the Yodogō group to her supporters working in the "Yumemiha" office.

Her supporters split into two distinct groups, those who continued to support and encourage her, and those who departed. The organization dissolved, and she was thrust into solitude even deeper than before. Only the hope of one day seeing her children again sustained her.

Ending the story here still makes it seem simpler than it really was. There remains yet another veil concealing the truth. To shed the light on this more deeply buried truth, we must once again call onto the stage the man who had so quietly slipped into Japan and who moved like a shadow in the darkness of a city's streets.

Campaign in Japan

A t about the time the Kanagawa prefectural police began their formal investigation of the bar Yumemiha in Yokosuka, the external affairs section of the Hyōgo prefectural police about 250 miles to the southwest were scratching their heads over a nearly incomprehensible telephone conversation recorded on a microcassette tape. There was a split in opinion in the department over the authenticity of the tape, and, based on what they could hear in the recording, it wasn't even clear why the conversation had been recorded.

The Hyōgo police had finished their secret investigation on "Nakao Akira" and arrested him on May 6, 1988, about two weeks before Yao Megumi's arrest in Kanagawa. The warrant for his arrest stated that he was under suspicion of passport violations. In fact, Nakao Akira was the name of a real person—a former Korean resident of Japan who had repatriated to North Korea more than ten years earlier. The man now holding the passport issued in Nakao's name had entered and departed Japan several times. The police suspected the passport was a forgery.

Early in the morning of May 6 (the date of such great significance to the Yodogō group!), after staking out his apartment in Shinjuku, Tokyo, officers from the external affairs division of the Hyōgo prefectural police arrested "Nakao Akira" and immediately transferred him to Kobe. They also searched his Tokyo apartment.

They found a national health insurance certificate, mail, telexes, and a certified copy of a family registration, all bearing the name of Nakao; they also found various documents, two word processors, floppy disks, and bank books. They found an address book containing the names and address of several high school students with whom the suspect had worked in his position as an academic advisor. Because they believed he was a North Korean agent, the police officers took their time in making a thorough search of his belongings.

They were still working when the telephone in the apartment rang. The answering machine was turned on and the cassette tape automatically began recording as the caller's voice came from the speakers.

"Hello? It's a little after 11:00 a.m., and I am in front of the ticket vending booth at the Tōkyū department store in Nihonbashi...."

The voice belonged to a man. After a short while, the phone rang again, and the same man left another message.

"Hello. Thank you for the information. Now I am at Mitsukoshi. I will wait for you on the roof."

The telephone continued to ring every few minutes. Each time, the caller's location changed: from Tōkyū to Mitsukoshi, from the ground floor to the roof, next to the elevators, then to the smoking area. Clearly, "Nakao" was missing an appointment with the caller, who was leaving messages for him after he did not appear.

All the officers searching the apartment listened to the voice in the messages. Several hurried to the described locations, but all were filled with crowds of people, making it impossible to identify the caller. The calls stopped coming after a while.

However, these telephone messages served later to focus the attention of the officers of the external affairs section on the recording machine cassette tapes, which might otherwise have gone unremarked. The telephone answering machine had two microcassette tapes, one with the greeting and one for recording the call. The first tape had only the usual sort of greeting message on it, but the second cassette had a strange conversation recorded on it. The inventory list of items confiscated from the apartment of the "unidentified person (male, using the name of Nakao Akira)" included the entry "cassette tapes, 2."

The fingerprint analysis done after "Nakao's" removal to Kobe identified him as Shibata Yasuhiro, one of the Yodogō hijackers.

A shock of surprise went through the public safety police at the news of Shibata's arrest inside Japan. The mass media also gave the event sensational coverage. The police and the media were equally caught by surprise because they had continued to believe—without any basis in fact—that the hijackers were living restricted, limited lives in North Korea.

On his identification as Shibata Yasuhiro, "Nakao" was arrested

Figure 29.01. Shibata Yasuhiro arrested in Kobe. Photo from *Asahi Shimbun*.

for a second time, by the Tokyo Metropolitan Police, for his role in the Yodogō hijacking. To foil any possible attempts to snatch him out of police custody, the police took the unusual precaution of transferring Shibata to the metropolitan police headquarters in Tokyo by helicopter.[1] The police came to regard this arrest of one of the Yodogō hijackers as perfectly executed.

Even after Shibata's transfer to Tokyo police custody, the Hyōgo prefectural public safety police and the external affairs section continued their analysis of the materials confiscated from the apartment as part of the intensive investigation of Shibata's activities. The one item they had trouble deciphering right up to the end of the investigation was the microcassette tape recording from the telephone answering machine.

The officers of the external affairs section listened to the tape again and again but could only shake their heads. It contained a conversation between a man and a woman, apparently in code.

---

1. The word for snatching someone from police custody, *dakkan*, was familiar to both police and student radicals. When the leader of a radical group was arrested, his followers often fantasized about staging a kidnapping to release him. The Yodogō hijackers had wavered over whether to carry out the hijacking or instead to try to spring Shiomi from jail. Then in the 1970s, the Japanese Red Army carried out several international hostage-taking incidents to win the release of members who had been arrested. Although these incidents used a very different strategy, it became common practice for police to move high-profile prisoners by helicopter in an effort to prevent such attempts.

"What?"

"Wait a minute! Just a minute!"

"Oh, good evening! Welcome!"

Music was audible in the background.

"I can't make it today!"

"Sorry."

"I can't make it today."

One of the speakers seemed to be in a store somewhere. Music was still audible.

"So, um, the second of December, how—"

"Just a sec, what is tomorrow?"

"May—"

"Oh, sorry, sorry, sorry."

"3-1, right."

"Sorry, sorry."

"I should just add."

"Tomorrow is no good, but if today is March third, the fourth, fifth, sixth, seventh, impossible."

"Okay."

"Can't do it."

"Okay, hold on a minute."

Here the woman's voice faded away, as if she had set down the receiver and moved away from the telephone.

"Idiot—!" A sigh.

"Hello?"

Another sigh. "Everything has to be done over, thanks to you."

"What?"

"You aren't the only one who contacted 985! There are several others! I have to do it all over again. I'm getting annoyed. Thanks to you."

"Yes. Is 1202-5031 okay, then?"

"What?! Are you stupid?! That's not the number! It's 9851923."

The man's voice was angry.

"Add a zero! To the date when you opened your place!"

"01202?"

"No! Who is the most important person? And the second most important? What is it? You, you don't find me of much importance at all, do you? What is it with you? Do you really understand who I am, what I'm doing?! How important it is? Everything must be redone!"

"Yes."

"It isn't just you and me. Don't you know that I keep contact with several other people?"

"Yes...."

"Mari-chan, Mari-chan, wait a minute! Mari-chan was a very important person! Do you understand?!"

"Yes, but this is not a good time to be telling me this."

"Well, then, when would be a good time? I have no spare time at all. Do you know why the departure is on the tenth? I have work to do. Do you know how many times I have tried to call you? Do you think it was only thirty or forty times?"

The woman seemed to be at work and very busy. That she was aware of her surroundings and a little distracted also came through clearly. She said very little.

"No."

"You are messing things up! You— wh—, why, why?"

"Oh, sorry, could you hold on for a second?"

Once again the woman's voice receded, and the background noises could be heard faintly through the telephone receiver.

"Hello, welcome! I haven't seen you in a while!"

A male voice overlapped. "How cute!" Laughter.

In the background, the din of music and voices continued.

The tinkling sound of bottles; a buzz of activity; the happy voices of the guests, men and women.

And then—a long gap. Only the tape continued to advance. Suddenly, as if speaking to himself, the man's voice could be heard.

"Forget it. I'm tired. You idiot! Fool! I want to hang up!..."

From here to its end, there was nothing on the tape except the ordinary din of a restaurant or bar. The woman's voice did not return.

The officers of the external affairs section, after listening to the long tape several times from beginning to end, could only be sure that the man's voice belonged to Shibata. There was no clue as to the identity of the woman, and her location remained unknown. The background noise indicated a bar or restaurant of some sort, but nothing else was clear. A character analysis based on the voices on the tape deemed the man as short-tempered and introverted. Even so, the external affairs officers had trouble making sense of what they could hear on the tape. Assuming the man's voice was in fact that of Shibata, the police could not understand why he would deliberately have recorded this conversation. Given his multiple entries and departures from Japan using a highly sophisticated forged passport, his background as a wanted hijacker, and his suspected history of engaging in secret and illegitimate activities, this action was unfathomable. The matter seemed beyond comprehension.

However, the tape finally yielded some clues that pushed the investigation forward. After cross-checking the information contained in the various documents confiscated from "Nakao's" apartment, the police were able to connect the person referred to as "Mari-chan" on the tape with the telephone messaging service number of Seibu Mullion.[2] The telephone exchange for the messaging service was 985, also mentioned on the tape. The digits 5-0-3-1 matched the date of Shibata Yasuhiro's birthday (May 31). Gradually, the signs and codes used most frequently in the taped conversation were deciphered, and what had seemed incomprehensible as an ordinary conversation slowly filled with meaning.

The Hyōgo police were moving as quickly as they could. Identification of the woman would lead to her immediate arrest. They continued to work in secret, analyzing every detail of the confiscated address book, memos, telephone call records, and name cards. But the woman on the other end of the conversation could not yet be named.

While the police in Hyōgo were puzzling over these matters, the officers of the external affairs section in Kanagawa prefecture had detected in their secret investigation into the background of Satō Keiko—that is, Yao Megumi—not only a connection with North Korea, but also the shadow of the Yodogō group. They came to this conclusion after analyzing material provided to the Japanese National Police Agency by European intelligence agencies and secret police, and their conviction was redoubled at the discovery of Shibata's presence in Japan. It would only have been a matter of time before the Hyōgo police found the café bar in Yokosuka. All of these circumstances must have lain behind the Kanagawa police department's hurried arrest of Yao Megumi on the pretext charge of giving a false name on an official document.[3]

The Hyōgo police kept the microcassette tapes for a while as part of their investigative material, then belatedly turned them over to the Kobe

---

2. Seibu Mullion was a department store in the Yūrakucho (Nishi Ginza) area in downtown Tokyo. In Japanese, the name "Mullion" both sounds and is spelled phonetically the same as "Marion," for which "Mari-chan" would be a diminutive name. The Seibu department store chain ran a messaging service that used the telephone exchange of its headquarters in Ikebukuro. In the days before cell phones, such commercial messaging services were commonly used to facilitate the passing of messages among people who did not have an office staffed with a secretary at a fixed location.

3. See chapter 28, note 2.

District Public Prosecutor's Office as supplemental evidence, without having identified the woman recorded on the tape. Coincidentally, the handover occurred on the same day that the external affairs division of the Kanagawa prefectural police arrested Yao Megumi. On June 10, the Public Safety division of the Tokyo Metropolitan Police took possession of the microcassette tapes from the Kobe District Public Prosecutor's Office as evidence in the case against Shibata for robbery and inflicting injury in his role in the hijacking and other acts.[4]

This series of events shows us that the microcassettes were concealed from the beginning as top secret evidence by the investigating teams. Their existence did not become public until five years later, in 1993, as the result of completely unrelated court proceedings.

After Yao's and Shibata's arrests, and with the involvement of the National Police Agency in the investigation, the separate sets of evidence collected by the Hyōgo and Kanagawa prefectural police departments were finally exchanged and compared. Analysis of the materials collected from Shibata's apartment and the materials from Yokosuka revealed many points in common: records showing Seibu Mullion's telephone messaging number, address books containing many of the same names and telephone numbers, the number of a travel agency presumably used by both suspects, the name of a hotel in Paris. In addition, the date the man forced the woman to say on the tape corresponded to the date on which Yao opened her café bar, Yumemiha. At this stage, the Hyōgo police were finally able to identify the female voice on the microcassette tape as that of Yao Megumi.

Now the police investigations shifted focus to Yao's and Shibata's activities in Japan. In her statement to the Kanagawa police after her arrest, Yao spoke of the work she did for "Mr. Liu."

"Mr. Liu showed me what he had written in his notebook as he explained the work he wanted me to do in Japan. I was to buy certain daily supplies and books, and to take photographs.

"The list of things he wanted me to buy included several Japanese-made Polaroid cameras, dress shirts, sweaters, underwear, cigarette lighters, and watches. He also wanted books like Japanese dictionaries and Chinese-Japanese dictionaries, maps of Tokyo, Osaka,

---

4. At the time of the hijacking, there was no law against airplane hijacking in Japan because the crime had never before been committed. The arrest warrants against the hijackers charged them with theft of the airplane, kidnapping the passengers and holding them against their will, and other miscellaneous acts.

Niigata, Toyama, Kyoto, and Hyōgo, and copies of the *White Paper on National Defense* and the *White Paper on the Police*.[5] As for the photographs, his written list included five parks in Tokyo: Hibiya, Yoyogi, Inokashira, Ueno, and Shinjuku Gyoen.

"One of my tasks was to do research on hotels in Tokyo, places like the Ginza Dai-ichi Hotel, Shinbashi Dai-ichi, the Imperial, the New Ōtani, and Hotel Ōkura. He asked me to get brochures for all of them.

"I remember all of this pretty well because I took notes of what he had in his notebook. He watched me writing things down and cautioned me, saying, 'When you have finished the job, please tear up your notes into little pieces or burn them. And, when you are taking pictures, don't do anything to make yourself look suspicious. You can avoid that by pretending to be a camera enthusiast.'

"He said other things, like 'Always be alert in case you are being watched' and 'Don't buy a lot of books at once. Break it up into several smaller purchases.' Also, 'You must say absolutely nothing about this work to anyone,' and he made me promise to keep it a secret. He said that one of his clients would contact me to tell me the unit costs and number of items, and to call him with the information. 'Be careful to get the numbers right,' he said.

"I guess I called him with that kind of information about thirty times."

Yao also testified that it was "Mr. Liu" who told her how to use the telephone messaging service number for Seibu Mullion and gave her the number and the personal identification number to use it. But none of the activities she described in her deposition were illegal. Shopping and taking pictures of parks are not against the law and do not constitute a crime.

On Yao's release in mid-June, when the twenty-three-day limit of interrogation before pressing charges had run out, the Kanagawa police apparently told her, "We hope you won't cross Hakone Mountain or the Tama River, either." Apparently their words meant they were determined that this case and the person of Yao herself would not end up belonging to the Hyōgo or Tokyo Metropolitan police.[6]

---

5. These white papers are standard government reports issued every year. At the time they were available in large bookstores or government publication outlets.

6. Hakone Mountain is the western border of Kanagawa prefecture, and the Tama River separates Kanagawa from the Tokyo metropolitan area on the east. Takazawa sees the terms as also having more symbolic meanings as the boundaries between police jurisdictions.

Of course, Yao Megumi's deposition was entirely fiction. In fact, she had done none of the activities she described, but her words were released without changes in the National Police Agency reports (such as *External Affairs Bulletin,* no. 109) and in the *White Paper on the Police* (1988). Thus, the story became widespread of her being an innocent Japanese woman, approached while traveling abroad and seduced with sweet words and money by a North Korean agent into unknowingly engaging in spying activities in Japan.

She later testified in court, in the lawsuits she brought against the media and against the police for conducting illegal investigations, that the depositions were untrue. She claimed that the police investigators "led" her into saying what she did, though none of it was true. The lesson we might take from this is that even persuasive testimony that seems to fit our suspicions is still not necessarily the truth.

So what was the truth? I must make it clear here that her story, with all its questionable facts, was completely scripted by someone else. The details in her testimony on how she was to conduct her secret tasks would have come out of the education she received in the village. It is often the case that, when foreigners ask questions of North Koreans, the answers are completely scripted and stereotypical. Similarly, the Yodogō members assigned to missions in Japan had been prepped with answers to a set of hypothetical questions in case they were arrested. In her testimony, Yao was only following the orders she had been given.

But why did they give her this imaginary script in the first place? The fictions were necessary in order to hide the larger truth. But the testimony that had been prescribed for her was against her own interests. Considering the betraying phone call that set in motion the investigation ending in her arrest, and given the contents of the testimony with which she had been prepared, am I the only one who senses an evil plot stirring behind the facade?

There was a group of people who directly benefited from her arrest and her testimony, though it isn't clear to what extent this benefit was anticipated and planned for. In the chaotic situation after her arrest, when the media were screaming about the "spy incident" and the police were chasing after supportive evidence, many North Korean agents slipped out of Japan. Included among them were other Yodogō wives. Surely these wives and other agents gained the most from her arrest And, most important, *all of them received a secret order to return at once to North Korea, whereas she did not.*

Later, in Pyongyang, Tamiya spoke about this incident.

"No matter what she might have said in a police interrogation, she didn't know anything that would have caused us any damage. Still, we didn't think she would get arrested."

He meant that they did not think she would get arrested because she had not done anything illegal and that, even if she was arrested, she would soon be released. His words imply not only that was she not engaging in illegal activities, but also that she was not being informed of anything. Cool judgment will allow us to see that taking photographs of parks, doing research on hotels, and buying books and maps as she described in her testimony to the police may seem suspicious, but these would have been meaningless and childish activities for North Korea and the Yodogō group. It is hard to believe North Korea had any need for such information gathering, since all of the information Yao was supposedly charged to collect was easily available to the public. This makes it much easier to understand that her suspicious activities were meant as a camouflage to hide a different aim. It seems most likely that her role was that of scapegoat in case of an emergency. She was, after all, a mere cog in the organizational machine ruled by absolute unconditionality, never allowed to doubt, totally loyal. Such ideas will arise in organizations that give the highest priority to the political life and require the kind of vision and discipline that will allow a physical life to be discarded as mere rubbish at the demand of the political organization.

Moreover, Kim Yuchol ("Mr. Liu") was the North Korean Workers' Party cadre in charge of the Yodogō group and someone whom Yao would have seen every day after she was taken to North Korea. There was absolutely no need for him to meet her in Copenhagen, or hand her large quantities of money, or recruit her as an agent. In fact, the money she was supposed to have received from Mr. Liu to use as capital to open her café was later found to be a bank loan taken out in the name of a relative. In addition, the money that she had earned by working so many jobs that she barely had time to sleep was money she was required to hand over to support the Yodogō group members. In this way, the Yodogō group's words that "the women worked in Japan so we could eat" were perfectly true.

Earlier I noted that both the police story and Yao's story were fictitious; that is, both parties were constructing untrue stories out of this very convoluted situation. Why was she so loyal to the Yodogō group, and why did she bear the burden of their activities in Japan? In following her and the other Yodogō members' paths through Japan, I discovered another fact in the incidents surrounding Yao Megumi. This fact is the key to understanding the lies and the riddle surrounding her.

Yao Megumi had disappeared suddenly from Osaka in February 1977. In the two-year period 1976–1977, there were a series of disappearances from Japan in which North Korea was presumed to be involved. Several couples vanished from Kyushu and along the coast of the Sea of Japan. The departures of the women who later became the Yodogō wives occurred in this period as well. Yao Megumi's disappearance must also be seen as one of these disappearances. Yao had taken the entrance exams for an art college when she graduated from a Hyōgo prefecture high school in 1975. She passed the exams but decided against entering the college for economic reasons. Set on making a living for herself, she gained employment at a cosmetics company. She lived with her parents and did nothing but commute back and forth to work every day.

One day, while walking along a street in Kobe, a poster for a movie showing by the North Korean Movie Society caught her eye. She was reminded suddenly of a high school classmate, a Japanese-Korean with whom she had been good friends, and she found herself longing for those days. She noticed that there was no entrance fee. She had no other plans for the date given, and the location was nearby. She decided to go to the movie. At the time her acquaintances were limited to people she had met at work, and going to the movie was a small expression of her sense of adventure and interest in learning new things.

Her suspicions were not aroused at being asked to write down her name and address when she arrived at the movie theater. One movie was an introduction to North Korea, the other a drama. Neither was particularly interesting, and apparently she thought only that North Korea seemed to be a "pretty nice place," as she told a close friend at the time about her experience.

A few days later something odd happened.

A person claiming to be a member of a *juche* ideology study group visited her at home. She was taken to a coffee shop and invited to join the group. She did not really understand what she heard of North Korea's greatness or the excellence of its leader, Kim Il Sung. Much more exciting was the prospect of making some new friends.

In this way she began attending the *juche* study group meetings, and she met several people. However, she stopped going after a few months, feeling that the meetings were too closed and restrictive. It was only natural for someone her age to feel that way. She sought friends, not ideological indoctrination. In 1976, Yao Megumi was twenty years old. She thought her association with the *juche* study group would end when she left, but the group persisted in its efforts to recruit her.

In the new year, she was introduced to another Japanese-Korean at a private party with some of her Japanese-Korean friends and friends from the *juche* study group. By that time, she had quit her job with the cosmetics company and enrolled in a nursery school teacher training program in Takaishi city, in Osaka prefecture. She was living in her own tiny apartment near her school. This new Japanese-Korean friend was seen several times visiting her there. Just two months later, Yao disappeared suddenly without a trace. She left her apartment as if she meant to return and remained enrolled at the school.

Her anxious family called everyone they could think of and began a search for her, but her location remained unknown. A year after her disappearance, her family received a postcard from her: "I am working as a nursery school teacher and am doing fine. I am very busy so it is difficult to keep in touch."

It was postmarked in Japan. But, in fact, by this time she was already in North Korea. The postcard was yet another cover-up ruse by an unknown third person.

Her passport application was hurriedly submitted in Osaka immediately after the new year. This efficiency does not seem typical of her. In her testimony after her arrest, she described how she spent several years traveling and working in Europe, but in those days the requirements for overseas travel were a little different from what they are now. In order to apply for a passport, a bank statement showing adequate funds for such travel was required. It was still difficult for Japanese to travel overseas for several years at a time unless they were exchange students or had friends or relatives to sponsor them. For Yao Megumi, just turned twenty, working part time, and attending a vocational school, this could hardly have been an easy hurdle to overcome. These circumstances imply that there must have been someone in the background arranging for her travels.

On the morning of February 24, 1977, shortly after receiving her passport, Yao Megumi appeared in the international flight terminal at Osaka's Itami Airport. She boarded a flight to Hong Kong. A few days before, she had told a close friend she would soon be back. This was only supposed to be a short trip. Even she had no idea that it would be seven years before she came back to Japan.

According to records in the National Immigration Office, her travel destinations were Hong Kong and Macao, after which her location was unknown. Perhaps North Korean agents made contact with her and maneuvered her journey in Hong Kong or Macao. This scenario fits those of several other women who also became Yodogō wives.

The South Korean movie actress Choi Eun-hee was abducted from Hong Kong by North Korean agents. In addition, during the Korean Air incident, Kim Hyon Hee testified that in Guangzhou there was a North Korean Trading Office accessible overland from Macao. It is clear that the area was a base of operations for North Korea.

Within several days, Yao Megumi found herself in Pyongyang.

It is not difficult to imagine that she was isolated in a Party guest house immediately on arrival to begin undergoing her ideological brainwashing and education. Soon after, she would have been introduced to the Yodogō group. Although she may have made the initial journey to North Korea willingly, it is unlikely she had any choice in what happened to her once she was there. This is because the group maneuvering to bring her to North Korea had the goal of forcing her into a meeting with one of the Yodogō hijackers, making her marry and have children with him, then using them both to conduct secret operations.

The tactics used in forcing Yao Megumi and Fukutome Kimiko to marry were the most brutal among the cases of the Yodogō group's "Operation Marriage."

When the outlines of Fukutome Kimiko's disappearance became known, Yao Megumi's story also became clear to me. As the details of Yao's disappearance became clear, so too did those of Fukutome's disappearance and marriage. Until then, neither of the women had been linked with the Yodogō group. There was nothing to connect Fukutome Kimiko with Okamoto Takeshi or Yao Megumi with Shibata Yasuhiro.

Both Fukutome and Yao were sent to Japan for temporary stays during the 1980s. It is an interesting fact that they were both the wives of the Yodogō members assigned to secretly infiltrate Japan. This fact may be the key to understanding what the women were supposed to be doing in Japan.

I have already described how the Yodogō group was proceeding with its plans to enter Japan secretly. Simply put, it was the women's task to assist in any way they could. In the second phase of the plan, the issue of setting up and maintaining a long-term funding source came up. For this purpose, Yao Megumi's mission was to establish a business. However, this scheme of the Yodogō group was destroyed with her arrest, and the café bar Yumemiha closed within six months of opening.

The lies she told in her testimony were a prescribed story designed to conceal until the very end her connection with the Yodogō group. The plans to infiltrate Japan had to be kept secret at all costs. She had to be prepared even to sacrifice herself in order to disrupt any investigations being made. Of course, she had not written this script herself. She may not even have been informed of its real purpose and meaning.

The Kanagawa prefectural police, when they were forced to release Yao for lack of evidence of illegal activities, apparently regretted not having let her "swim around" for longer. Still, her early arrest by the external affairs division prevented her from committing any real crimes.

So just what were the missions of Shibata Yasuhiro and the wives during their frequent visits during the 1980s?

Shibata's arrest in 1988 just before the Seoul Olympics coupled with his name appearing on a list of suspects in investigations aimed at preventing terrorist attacks during the games led both the public security police and the media to suspect him of plotting to disrupt the Olympics. But, of course, this was not the case, since we know plans for secretly entering Japan began long before the Seoul Olympics did.

Tamiya spoke once about the group's secret missions in Japan.

"Some people talk about us like we were spies, but we were not trying to spy on Japan. We desperately needed to go to Japan. After all, Japan is where you can find the largest number of Japanese people." He said something very similar in his last interview with me, published as *Talking about the Homeland and the People* (Tamiya and Takazawa 1996). Apparently, one of the lessons they had learned from the acquisition schemes that began with Operation Madrid was that, rather than chasing after Japanese people traveling or studying abroad, it was far more efficient to capture them at home in Japan.

Before moving on, I should once again touch on the subject of Yao Megumi's fate and the telephone call to the police that betrayed her.

The biggest mystery about the telephone call is who made it. But, before trying to solve that puzzle, let me describe another strange telephone call, made the same year that Shibata Yasuhiro was released from prison, more than six years after Yao Megumi's arrest.

This odd call was made to Fukutome Kimiko's family home in Kōchi prefecture in November 1994. The male voice spoke with an Osaka accent.

"The truth is that Kimiko has lost her passport in another country and is having trouble returning to Japan. I could arrange for a fishing boat to take her back to Japan, but that would be expensive. If you want me to help her come back, I would need 40 million yen.

"I am in Japan buying weapons, and now I am in Osaka. I will call again tomorrow."

Feeling suspicious, Fukutome's family notified the local police of this telephone call. The police set up a recording device on the family's telephone and waited for the call, but it never came.

The common factor between the two telephone calls is that both callers were apparently familiar with the inside stories. Both the call that betrayed Yao Megumi and the one made to Fukutome's family were made well before the women's stories were known publicly. This probably means the calls were made either by someone within the same organization or by someone closely connected to the women. This is about all I can write at this time.

In May 1997, having obtained their birth certificates from North Korea, Yao Megumi initiated the application process to establish Japanese citizenship for her children. On July 7 of that year, Yao Megumi appeared in the Civil Affairs office of the Hyōgo prefecture Judicial Affairs Bureau. It was the afternoon of the Tanabata festival,[7] and the cries of the cicadas filled the summer air. She had come to the bureau to attend the hearing regarding the application for her children's citizenship and their entry into her family register. On exiting the building after the hearing was over, her eyes sparkled with tears. After ten years of silence, finally she could allow the truth to make its first appearance on these official documents.

She had had no choice about her silence. She had been forced to keep secret the existence of her children, left behind in North Korea as hostages. She has spoken of her simultaneous feelings of confusion and great emotion at the degree of support she received when the Yumemiha group formed to support her in her lawsuits. Perhaps her confusion and her emotion were a response to her first-ever encounter with compassion from other human beings. Really, her surprise at such support without an expectation of reward is not all that remarkable; she had had to adapt in order to survive in North Korea's ideological environment, as a member of a corrupt organization that sought only to use the compassion of others for its own ends.

After the hearing at the Bureau of Judicial Affairs, the Government of Japan granted Japanese nationality to Yao's two daughters that same

---

7. Tanabata is a midsummer festival in Japan based on the Chinese legend of the weaver girl and the cowherd, about two lovers who can only meet once a year on the seventh day of the seventh month. It is celebrated by writing wishes on strips of paper and tying them to bamboo branches, often with other decorations.

month. Once the government had granted Japanese nationality to her daughters, there were no official reasons for Yao's separation from her children. However, her children were not yet allowed to go to Japan because of the stance taken by the Yodogō group.[8]

The second stage and all later steps in the Yodogō group's plan to infiltrate Japan had come to a halt in May of 1988, when Shibata Yasuhiro, a.k.a. Nakao Akira, was arrested. From Pyongyang, where the situation was regarded with great seriousness, came the order via secret radio broadcasts recalling all its active undercover operatives from Japan.

---

8. For more about what happened subsequently to Yao Megumi and Shibata Yasuhiro, see Steinhoff 2004.

CHAPTER THIRTY

Retreat

That evening, the woman has an unexpected visitor.

It is one of her friends from work. She happened to be passing through the neighborhood, the friend says after her sudden knock at the door. The visit is inconvenient, but the woman feels unable to refuse her friend entry. They chat for a while, then she realizes it is nearly time for the last train. She looks at the clock in a manner calculated to remind her friend of this.

"And my boyfriend..." The friend just continues talking.

With another meaningful look at the clock, the woman rises and begins clearing the table as an indirect way of interrupting.

While the woman is occupied with the dishes, the friend notices for the first time in the corner of the room a plastic-wrapped stuffed doll peeking out of a paper bag filled with children's toys. Has some relative of the woman just had a baby? She finds the bag of toys strangely out of place in the woman's apartment.

She calls out to the woman, "Would you mind if I stayed over?"

"I'm sorry, not tonight. I have a headache, and I think I'm catching a cold...."

The friend looks rebuffed at this response, but she can hardly insist on staying, so she collects herself and her belongings and departs. As she is walking along in the darkness, she thinks that the woman was not her usual self that evening and that it was odd how she suddenly developed a headache.

The next day, the woman does not appear at work.

Remembering her excuse the night before, the friend thinks that maybe the woman really had felt a cold coming on.

The woman doesn't come to work the next day either.

She hasn't called anyone to let them know she would not be coming in to work. The friend decides to go by her apartment again to see how she is doing.

On the way, she buys a pack of strawberries at a supermarket near the station, thinking she might try a few herself.

There is no answer to her knock at the door. The lights are out. She feels a sudden anxiety.

The door is unlocked when she tries the handle. She quietly pulls open the door and sees that the place seems different. It echoes emptily, deserted. It still holds furniture such as the table and cupboards, but all of the woman's personal belongings and clothing have gone. The bag of toys and the cloth doll have also disappeared.

For some reason a world map is pinned on a wall near the curtains. She stares at the map, thinking that it is a strange place to put a map of the world.

The woman feels distracted for a while after finally seeing her visitor off so late at night. She was relieved her friend put up so little resistance at being asked to leave. She had nearly panicked for a moment when the friend had said she wanted to stay. She has to be alone, at least tonight. She could not have anyone staying with her now.

She looks at the clock. Only a little time left.

She takes a set of earphones out of her closet and carries a large transistor radio to the table.

Another look at the clock. Almost time.

She flips the switch on the radio, tuning it to receive short-wave broadcasts. At first she hears only static and whistling noises, but suddenly they disappear. As if the tuning needle has suddenly hit the right spot, she can now clearly hear what seems to be a melody from some foreign country. Code numbers are being read out one after the other. It is her own call code!

She begins to write hurriedly on a piece of paper she has at hand.

362, 43, 358, 65, 293, 17, 146, 23, 597, 81, 158, 75, 325, 58, 794, 67, 463, 13, 275, 66, 987, 54, 886, 73, 473, 24, 175, 81, 436, 42, 638, 59, 321, 75, 679, 89, 649, 53, 273, 19, 326, 65, 877, 92, 484, 32, 616, 73, 253, 43, 912...

When she has finished writing, she begins matching the numbers to letters she has written out on the paper. It takes her a long time.

The May sky has already grown light when she finally finishes deciphering the message. The expression on her face has tightened.

She stands up to open a window. A light mist flows into the room, and she suddenly feels as if something unknown is advancing toward her. It is like some menacing presence moving stealthily to surround her, just like the morning mist. She shivers. She takes a deep breath to dispel her sudden nervousness and begins collecting her belongings. The coded message sent from Pyongyang contains an order to return immediately because of imminent danger.

She takes out a large suitcase and begins filling it with necessities. She will have to leave the furnishings as they are. Her eyes fall on the paper bag in the corner of the room, and she carefully packs the doll and toys into her bag. Her little daughters in the village will surely enjoy their gifts from Japan. She looks at the world map on the wall and decides to leave it hanging. Someday, she thinks, the day will come when this map will be shaded entirely in the color of the Great Leader's *juche* philosophy....

This was the story of the departure from Japan that Uomoto Tamiko told me years later when I was interviewing all the Yodogō wives in Pyongyang.

She continued, "While we're on the subject, I had only recently arrived in Japan at that point."

"I suppose you weren't allowed to meet your family or friends while you were there?"

"No, that's right, I couldn't, ever. So, anyway, I went to Japan about three times, living at different addresses. I moved my resident registration, too. That's why, when my father went to the ward administrative offices after my older brother died, he discovered that my registration had been moved and realized that I must be in Japan. I heard that he visited the address listed on my registration, but it was after I had already moved away.

"I found out about my brother's death in 1988. We had a lot going on in relation to the Seoul Olympics, and we were pretty busy. I was in Japan when I heard that Shibata had been arrested.

"After that the situation became very dangerous for us. We were given orders to return, which is why we all left in such a hurry. I don't know why exactly, but I had a feeling at the time that I would never be able to return to Japan again."

"Was it like a premonition?"

"Umm, well, I don't know if it was a premonition or what it was. But I ended up calling my mother from Narita Airport for the first time since I had left."

Uomoto had no intention of meeting her family even once when she was in Japan. Apparently she did visit her old neighborhood, but the fact that she lived in North Korea had to be kept secret from her family and friends. This was the case for all the Yodogō wives.

Uomoto made her call to her mother in Osaka from Narita Airport just moments before she left Japan as ordered by Pyongyang.

"Hello?"

She heard her mother's voice grow tense on the other end of the line.

"Who are you? Who is this?"

For a moment Uomoto's feelings welled up within her, but then she was able to answer. "It's me, Tamiko."

"What are you doing? Your brother died, you know."

These, she said, were her mother's words. There was no time to go into any long explanations about her situation. She felt an overwhelming desire to see her mother again, but the innocent faces of the small children she had left behind in the village rose up in her mind. Without saying any more, she hung up the receiver. As she turned away from the telephone, she heard the boarding announcement for her flight.

This is the story as Uomoto told it to me in Pyongyang. And, as she had thought, this turned out to be her last visit to Japan. She and the other wives summoned back at that time never returned because, two months after their departure, the Japanese Ministry of Foreign Affairs issued the return order on their passports.

The chain of events following Shibata Yasuhiro's arrest brought an end to all of the Yodogō group's activities in Japan. Their withdrawal began. The urgent orders to return to North Korea barely allowed the women to escape arrest.

As I have written earlier, the order for the wives to relinquish their passports was issued in the government bulletin *Kanpō* on August 6, 1988. The return order was issued because the women had been found in violation of the passport laws and were considered to be "persons threatening the national interest and public safety of Japan." The order named five of them: Fukui Takako, Kaneko Emiko, Uomoto Tamiko, Mori Yoriko, and Mizutani Kyōko.

We know that one of the wives, Kaneko Emiko, actually returned to Japan soon after Shibata's arrest. A disembarkation card she filled out on May 16, 1988, shows that she returned to Osaka from Singapore, but strangely there is no matching embarkation card to show when she left. By that date, the order for the women to return to North Korea had already been issued. Articles about Shibata's arrest and removal by helicopter to the capital were still filling the newspapers. Just what business Kaneko had in Japan to make her run the risk of returning is unknown. At any rate, she was in Vienna on her way to the base in Zagreb when the passport return order was issued in the bulletin.

She read the order in the North Korean embassy in Vienna. Although she could not know the background and the extent of the Japanese police authorities' investigation of the women's activities, she did understand that some part of their operations had been uncovered. One of the counts on which the enemy's passport return order was based was that she had "met with known North Korean agents."

She reread the order several times. Finally, finding a small error in the announcement, she took up a pen and began writing a letter of protest to the Japanese Ministry of Foreign Affairs.

> I am writing to make an inquiry. I am writing because I am not
> sure whether I am the same Kaneko Emiko included in the list
> of five names in the passport return order issued just a few days
> ago. Based on the name, birth date, and passport information,
> I seem to be the person referred to in the list; however, the
> address given is Gunma prefecture, Usui county, written with
> different characters than my own address in another Usui
> county. Please clarify this point, as it is an important difference.
> I ask that you print the correction in the October 5 issue of
> *Kanpō,* where I will certainly be able to see it.
>
>   Furthermore, I cannot accept your reasons for ordering me
> to relinquish my passport. I will make a decision on the matter
> once the above point has been clarified.
>
> (August 28, 1988)

This letter was mailed to Japanese Foreign Minister Uno Sōsuke in late August. The return address on the envelope was the North Korean embassy in Vienna.

At about the same time, Uomoto Tamiko read the *Kanpō* in the North Korean embassy in Berlin. She also wrote a protest letter to Minister Uno. Uomoto's letter was more properly executed than Kaneko's, because she styled it as a formal request for review addressed to the Ministry of Foreign Affairs.

> Reasons and purpose in requesting a review: I have never
> "met with known North Korean agents," the third item in the
> list of reasons for which I am ordered to give up my passport.
> Moreover, I have never had any intention of being a "threat to
> the national interest and public safety of Japan" and have no

intention of becoming one in the future....Also, the concept of "agents" as given is in itself unclear, and I do not understand what kinds of people are called "agents." In any case, who has the authority to label someone as an "agent?" I have no idea. I suppose any Japanese person living overseas, no matter who they are, must be in constant contact with foreigners. On these grounds, is it fair to say that all those Japanese living overseas must be a "threat to the national interests and public safety of Japan" just because they are "in contact with foreigners"? I hereby state my refusal to relinquish my passport and demand an immediate retraction of the return order.

(August 28, 1988)

Both Kaneko and Uomoto made the mistake of writing these letters without knowing how far the intelligence and police authorities had come in uncovering their activities. In the next stage, they shifted their arguments, saying they had met with North Koreans only in order to see their families. "Anyone who wishes to visit another country must go to that country's embassy and meet people of that nationality. What is wrong with that?" They made similar assertions in their later talks in Pyongyang.

We haven't done anything wrong. There are absolutely no grounds for the return order that has been issued on our passports. Despite this, the order was made merely because we had to get help from North Koreans in order to travel to the Republic to see our husbands, since our two countries do not have diplomatic relations. This is just a case of saying we met with agents because someone has decided they must be agents just because we met them, even though they aren't agents. And that this might make us a threat to the national interests of Japan. This is the entire basis for the passport return order.

Given that kind of argument, say I exchanged a few words with a thief. Then, by this exact same logic, that would make me a thief too. There are simply no grounds for it. (Fukui Takako, in the discussion published as "Progress in Our Return to Japan and Our Longing for Home," *Marco Polo*, January 1994, p. 147)

Fukui was not the only one among them to say she had met with North Koreans only in order to take care of the paperwork necessary to travel back and forth to North Korea for the sole purpose of meeting her husband. All the Yodogō group members repeated this statement many times. Probably it was a cover story hastily concocted in a group meeting soon after the passport return order was issued.

Whenever I heard their explanations, I was always reminded of *The Ventriloquist,* a manga story by Tsuge Yoshiharu about a handsome ventriloquist and his grotesquely ugly puppet. The ventriloquist's good looks and great skill made him hugely popular among young women. Whenever he appeared on stage, he was greeted with cheers and bouquets of flowers tossed by his audience. Once the curtains fell and he had left the stage, however, the ventriloquist would walk backstage and set the doll down in his dressing room. But it wasn't the ugly one of the pair that was left alone and silent in a corner of the dressing room, because, in fact, it was the handsome one who was the doll. This was the ironic humor of a story filled with pathos about an ugly man of tiny build who could make people believe his puppet was a real human being.

The true story of the Yodogō wives has the same kind of twist to it. Their arguments were just like the story about the ventriloquist. They contended that it was wrong to judge the people they met as being agents, that it was just "a hostile and prejudiced policy of regarding every North Korean in a suspicious manner." Their words rang true in one way: they were not meeting with agents, since they themselves were the agents. And very likely they did receive substantial support from the embassies in their overseas activities and in their travels to and from North Korea. They used North Korean embassies all over the world as if they owned them. In a way, they did, since they enjoyed the direct patronage of Kim Il Sung. Such being the case, it would be incorrect to regard all embassy staff members as agents. Among the Yodogō group, it was most often the wives who took advantage of the authority and power that came along with their membership in the Workers' Party's special section headed by Kim Jong Il to use the embassy staffs for their own convenience. When will the audience realize the truth of the roles played by the ventriloquist and his doll? Or will no one realize the truth and the puppet continue to play the part of the handsome hero? At any rate, there seems to be a lesson in this story where the hero turns out be a mere doll.

To return to the events, Kaneko Emiko arrived at the North Korean embassy in Vienna on June 17, following her short visit to Japan immediately after Shibata's arrest. Later that morning, a Mercedes-Benz exited the embassy grounds. It was an official embassy car, license plate number 8856-A-16, and its driver was a man with punch-permed hair named Choe Giljun.[1] The Mercedes coursed through Graz and Leibnitz toward the border between Austria and Yugoslavia.

At that time in the former Yugoslavia, North Korean diplomatic establishments and operational bases were scattered throughout the country. There was a consulate in Zagreb, now the capital of Croatia. Zagreb was a frontline base for their operations in Europe, as I have mentioned several times before.

Choe, the driver of the Mercedes, worked for Kim Yuchol, the vice-consul at the Zagreb consulate and one of the Yodogō group's handlers. Seated in the back seat was a woman with the code name of Kim Hyeja.

At the border to Yugoslavia, Choe Giljun showed the border officials papers showing him to be an employee of the North Korean consulate in Zagreb and a diplomatic passport. The woman also displayed a diplomatic passport, with the name of Kim Hyeja.

After crossing the border, the Mercedes drove directly southward for a while, until it arrived at the city of Zagreb along the Sava River. It came to a stop at the corner of a gently sloping street in the city's residential area. The door opened, and Kim Hyeja emerged from the car. She was standing in front of an elegant European-style house located near the center of what had once been the city's center. It was the Yodogō group's base of operations in Europe.

The Yodogō members and their wives at that time all had both Japanese and Korean names for use within their organization as well as passports in separate Korean code names and numbers. They used the different names depending on the situation in which they found themselves. "Kim Hyeja" was the code name of Kaneko Emiko, based on three of the five characters in her Japanese name.

Kaneko's hurried movements had the aim of saving the situation after Shibata's arrest caused the collapse of the operation in Japan. The main purpose of their projects in Europe was to support and ensure the success of their Japan mission. Now it became their central task to take remedial measures against the fallout after Shibata's arrest and to reor-

---

1. This was a men's hairstyle with very tight, short curls set with permanent wave solution. It was popular in the 1970s to 1990s among *yakuza* gang members, motorcycle gangs, and other working-class men in Japan. It was apparently also popular among North Koreans who worked at embassies abroad.

Figure 30.01. The Yodogō group's base in Zagreb. Photos by Takazawa Kōji.

ganize their operations. The Japanese authorities were not alone in their surprise at having arrested Shibata. North Korea and the Yodogō group were deeply shaken as well.

The Yodogō group (as the Independent Revolutionary Party) initially planned their retreat from Japan as a temporary measure only. Such was their intention, but in reality this withdrawal was the end of their infiltration operations in Japan. Changes in the international political climate hindered their efforts to regroup, and their new plans for the infiltration of Japan never even got off the ground.

Not only were they forced to end their operations in Japan, but an avalanche of events also pushed them out of Europe and the Eastern Bloc nations. At the time of the passport recall order in August 1988, the level of turmoil in Eastern Europe was still only at a murmur, but within six months it grew into a mighty earthquake that shook the entire world in 1989. A storm of reforms in Eastern Europe allowed by the Soviet Union's policies of *glasnost* and *perestroika* soon tore down the Berlin Wall, set off the civil war in Yugoslavia, and saw the collapse of the Soviet Union itself.[2] For both the North Korean Workers' Party and the Yodogō group, the sudden fall of the socialist regimes in Eastern Europe meant the loss of their most important bases of operations. The overseas missions the Yodogō group had been pursuing for over ten years tapered off. Finally, they had no choice but to retreat to Pyongyang when it became impossible for them to maintain their bases amidst the political unrest and fighting that broke out in Yugoslavia during this period.

With the closing of their headquarters in Zagreb, the Yodogō group's active involvement in the European protest movement also came to an end. The North Korean consulate in Zagreb, which had supported them so actively in their projects, closed at the end of 1991.

At the beginning of the 1990s, the Yodogō group, or Independent Revolutionary Party, after once again making Pyongyang their headquarters, changed the approach of their operations aimed at Japan. They began to focus on propaganda and organizing group visits to North Korea from Japan. They really had no choice in the matter, since their withdrawal and the later passport recall order had effectively prevented them

---

2. *Glasnost* means "openness," and *perestroika* means "to listen." The former initiated a policy of being more open about the Soviet Union's actions and intentions, including signals that it would not intervene in certain affairs of neighboring states. The latter was a policy encouraging the leadership to listen to what the people wanted, which encouraged the expression of dissent.

from traveling to and from Japan themselves. Under the new approach, they took the initiative in organizing group visits to North Korea. They set up a travel agency to promote Japan–North Korea friendship and made plans to recruit members of the visiting groups to their cause. They wanted willing recruits who would be active supporters able to work for them in Japan.

Let me hasten to add here something that might not even need to be said: their recruiting techniques did not include political persuasion or discussions of ideology. They used the arts of guidance as required by the ideology of Kim Il Sung. Anyone who is a target of these arts may never realize he is being manipulated. Strangely, under such influence, such a person will often believe he is acting on his own will. Nevertheless, this powerful psychological tool has an Achilles' heel: praise could reveal the manipulation to the target, and the game would be lost. A target of this guidance will find himself well and truly stuck when his manipulators begin to seem sympathetic and understanding despite holding very different political views and when they begin to play on old connections to revive warm feelings of friendship and obligation in their target. At that point, the target may well have already voluntarily fallen under their influence and guidance. Certainly practitioners of the *juche* art of guidance do not waste any time praising or befriending the politically useless. But I digress.

In 1989, the Yodogō group put into practice its plan of inviting to Pyongyang activists and supporters from Japan who could help in their efforts to spread propaganda and support Shibata Yasuhiro after his arrest. In the summer of that year, I received my first invitation to visit from the Yodogō group.

CHAPTER THIRTY-ONE

Loss of the Homeland

Tamiya Takamaro was standing in the shadow of a pillar in the lobby of the Koryo Hotel, his head slightly tilted to the side. It was my first visit to Pyongyang, about six months after I had received the Yodogō group's invitation to visit North Korea. I did not know that this was the beginning of a new chapter in the story involving Tamiya, the rest of the Yodogō hijackers, and me. Nor did I know that they had all only recently returned to Pyongyang after finishing up long periods of operations in Europe and Asia. I thought they had spent the twenty years since the hijacking living confined lives in North Korea as political refugees unable to return to Japan. This was what most of the people who could remember the hijacking believed, with the only difference that I felt some sympathy toward the hijackers and wanted to better understand what their daily lives had been like.

This was why I was most interested in learning more about their living conditions and the issue of their return to Japan.

In 1990, at the time of my visit, they were making no progress at all in their efforts to go home.

Tamiya and I sat in a room near the top floor of the Koryo Hotel, talking about this problem until we could see the dawn breaking over Pyongyang. The city streets were hidden beneath the morning mist. A decade had passed since the publication of Tamiya's memoir "Ten Years since Leaving the Homeland." The path of their quest to return to Japan had twisted and turned, and the letters to Prime Minister Nakasone had made it a topic in the Japanese mass media. With all these events in the past, I assumed Tamiya was being frank with me.

Figure 31.01. Tamiya Takamaro in Pyongyang. Photo by Takazawa Kōji.

Certainly he was sincere in his expressions of homesickness.

"I am thinking of starting up a trading company. Maybe I'll call it Nostalgia Merchants." Suddenly he added, "I want to go back. I am serious. But the truth is I can't."

"You don't think you want to go back and fight it out in the courts?"

"Fight it out in court? For something that happened twenty years ago? I don't think we could expect a fair trial, for one thing, because the witnesses probably don't remember much."

I told him to stop repeating the word "homesick" so much. Looking back now, I realize I may have been a little unkind. Despite the political reasons for their use of expressions like "homeland" and "nostalgia," eventually it became clear that these words conveyed their true feelings.

Tamiya smiled suddenly. What he said next rather surprised me.

"Do you have a cassette tape? Want to record for a while?"

I took a small tape recorder out of a pocket and switched it on. An instant later his face had returned to its usual serious expression.

He obviously had something he wished to say if he wanted it to be recorded. And, even though he was aware of being recorded as he spoke of his desire to return to Japan, I think his true feelings of distress at having been completely immobilized come through clearly in his words.

"... as for returning to Japan, it is a fact that we all definitely want to. It's just that we are not prepared to throw away our principles for it. We do want to return home, but we want to do it in a principled manner ...

"I guess if you are Japanese, you like Japan and you can't really stay away from there. When we were fighting before, we used slogans like 'simultaneous world revolution,' but really, under all that, our starting point was that we wanted to make Japan a better place. We grew up in Japan. We could hardly be called human if we did not miss the place where we were raised or miss our old school friends.

"To put it another way, I don't think anyone would blame a man for being attracted to a woman or a mother for loving her children. In the same way, who can blame someone of a given race for loving others of the same race and nationality? I am not just inventing here, it just seems like an obvious given.

"I really do want to go back to Japan someday. But it isn't that easy for us. Just because a man is in love with some woman doesn't mean he automatically has the right to approach her! [Laugh.] In the same way, will we give up our principles in order to return to Japan just because we want to go home? No, that won't happen. It absolutely will not happen. We want to fight for our country because we love it. We have to fight for it with our principles intact, and, if we return to Japan, it must be in a principled way. That's all there is to it.

"Somebody [laugh] just said we should stop repeating the word 'homesick, homesick' all the time, or we'll become unpopular. Well, I can't deny I understand what you mean, but, to tell the truth, isn't that just how human beings are?

"Often when the question of our return comes up, people ask us to tell our true feelings, they want to know what we really think, but the fact is both things are true. It is true that we want to go back to Japan, but we don't want to make a bad compromise either.

"So people are always asking us how we really feel. Do I want to go back? Yes, I do. That's the truth. Do I want to go back right now, face a judge, and go to jail? No, I don't. That's the truth too. It's a bad situation. Nobody wants to go to jail. Do I want to fight for my country, for my society? Yes. That's the truth as well.

"To get back to the issue of our return to Japan, truly, we all want to go back. The more time that goes by, the more we want to return. We don't feel that we are forgetting Japan with time. Rather, we grow to feel more and more that Japan is where we truly belong. We want to return because we want to do our work in Japan, we want to continue our struggle. That's what I want you to understand."

He meant that they had been brought to a complete standstill. He may have been speaking about principles, but I could hear behind his words a constant mutter of "we're in trouble, we're in trouble." This was what he really meant when he said, "Both things are true."

What had brought them to such a standstill? What shackles prevented them from returning to Japan? It has finally become clear only now, after I have retraced the facts of their lives in the twenty-plus years since they went to North Korea.

I return once again to the interview Kim Il Sung gave to a team of reporters from the *Asahi Shimbun* in 1992, on the occasion of his eightieth birthday. In it, he let fall a comment on the issue of the Yodogō members' return to Japan: "Surely they are 'not guilty' after all this time has gone by? Please consider the matter" ("Interview Outline," *Asahi Shimbun*, April 2, 1992). Let us go back even further in time to the interview Kim Il Sung gave in 1972, just before the press conference where the Yodogō hijackers appeared before the Japanese media for the first time. Asked about the possibility of their return to Japan, he said: "There is no need for them to stay here very long, but we aren't going to help the Japanese police. If the police weren't going to arrest them, I would let them go back now." These two interviews show us Kim Il Sung repeating the same opinion at an interval of twenty years. In the second interview, he even used the unambiguous term "not guilty."

As I have mentioned so many times in this long book, Kim Il Sung's words carry a stronger binding power in North Korea than their mere meaning would seem to allow. The Great Leader's words are teachings that carry an absolutely compelling power, and they are law. No one can go against his words. Even the slightest objection can raise immediate questions about one's loyalty and end in one's being branded a traitor.

This state of affairs applies to the cadres of the Workers' Party as well. Although members of the Japanese government had made repeated requests for the extradition of the Yodogō group to Japan, against such a background the requests never even made it to the negotiation stage. In addition, the Workers' Party cadres hesitated to take action because only the special section in charge of handling the Yodogō group had any authority to act on the matter.

As long as Kim Il Sung persisted in his viewpoint on the matter, the Yodogō group would return to Japan only if they were granted a full pardon. Though they knew perfectly well that their demand was considered absurd and not taken seriously in Japan, the Yodogō members had no choice but to keep parroting the same words of "return with a full pardon" again and again. They showed their loyalty by doing so. Speaking one's own opinions out loud could only mean one doubted the

Leader. Even today, this issue of the Yodogō group's return to Japan is occasionally brought up as an obstacle in the relationship between North Korea and Japan, but since the death of Kim Il Sung there remains only one person in North Korea who can resolve the issue.

No one better understood the fetters holding them than the Yodogō hijackers themselves. Throughout the period of their appeals to the Japanese government for a return with a full pardon and later for a "negotiated return," they were simultaneously continuing their efforts to enter Japan secretly. Taking into account the blockade imposed by Kim Il Sung's words, their sense of obligation to the Workers' Party, their own sense of pride, and the likely response of the Japanese police, logically there was only one way they would be able to return without being arrested and thrown into jail the instant they stepped onto Japanese soil: they had to sneak in.

Just how did they envision their return with a full pardon ever happening? Konishi Takahiro wrote about it in 1993. "Our return to Japan will not be easy. There are many barriers. However, it is not an entirely impossible thing. *When our goal of returning coincides with the needs of the times and the demands of the Japanese people, then we will be able to return to Japan.* In other words, *the day of our return will come when our homeland calls for us*" (in *Nihon o kangaeru*, no. 9 [Winter 1994], p. 59; emphasis added by Takazawa).

They were apparently thinking that their homecoming would occur in circumstances similar to Lenin's return during the Russian revolution. Or perhaps they had in mind the made-up legend of Kim Il Sung's victorious return to his homeland. Wouldn't the "people" cheer in celebration at their triumphant homecoming, when the long-awaited Yodogō heroes finally returned after the revolution had transformed Japan? They had concocted an imaginary revolution story. They were quite serious. It was in order to bring on the "demands of the Japanese people" that they had to infiltrate into Japan. The whole thing went beyond the word "absurd."

A story of revolution is always the truth to those who dream of it and a silly fairy tale to those who do not. Because there have indeed been occasions over the long course of history when the dreams have come true, we can't dismiss all such fantasies. In this case, however, the Yodogō group's imaginary revolution lacked one essential element necessary to making it reality: they had not one single supporter in Japan for their plans of revolution.

Nevertheless, they continued to add details to the story of their imaginary revolution. A few of the members thought about the new names that Tamiya and the others should take in the event of their triumphant return. The names they had had at the time of the hijacking would not match their new status as revolutionary leaders. Heroes needed heroic names. In this they imitated the story of Kim Sung Ju, born in the rural outskirts of Mangyondae outside Pyongyang, who began calling himself "Kim Il Sung" when he became an active partisan in the Korean anti-Japanese resistance. He named himself after a legendary hero, General "Kim Il Sung."

The Yodogō group was not alone in its story making. The special section of the North Korean Workers' Party was also completely serious in its visions of how these men, who had arrived so dramatically with the hijacking, would become *juche* warriors and convert the whole of the Japanese nation to the ideology of Kim Il Sung.

When the special section undertook Operation Marriage to provide the Yodogō members with wives, it was decidedly casual in its methods of selecting and inviting (and abducting) the targeted women, with one exception: the choice of a wife for the group's leader, Tamiya Takamaro. In her case, the Workers' Party took great care. It spent great efforts in the search for a woman suitable to be Tamiya's wife. All sorts of detailed information was collected and examined closely. Unlike the others, this woman would be the "queen" of the Yodogō group. Several candidates unknowingly underwent interviews in Japan. The Party's choice finally fell on Mori Yoriko as meeting all its expectations. As I have mentioned before, she was the daughter of a North Korean man and his Japanese wife. Her father came from a good family, and in fact many of her father's relatives were members of the Workers' Party. From the point of view of the Workers' Party, it meant that Mori combined in her person distinguished North Korean blood as well as Japanese.

Her double heritage was a fact of great importance to the Workers' Party. Though nobody knew exactly when it would happen, the day would come when the *juche* revolution was achieved in Japan; it was imperative that the children of the Yodogō group's leader, who would play such a central role in the revolution, should have North Korean blood. In this way, the revolution in the land across the sea to the east would be directly tied to the *juche* revolution on the peninsula. The North Korean Workers' Party's strategy stretched a surprisingly long way into the future.

In the ideology of Kim Il Sung, the theory of "revolution in successive generations" dictates the idea that a leader's children must also be leaders. A child of a revolutionary family will grow up to be a revolutionary, and a leader's children will be leaders. Thus, Tamiya's children must also become leaders at some point. This matter of mixing bloodlines could not be ignored, because family and ethnic genealogy were vital elements in North Korean nationalist ideology. We do need to consider the birth component, peculiar to the North Korean class system, in Kim Il Sung's ideology of revolution across generations, but I will take it up a little later.

In his 1990 memoir (Tamiya et al. 1990), Tamiya wrote, "We began regarding Japan as our true homeland...the moment we flew out over the sea separating Japan and Korea." From that time, the homeland appeared to them only as a distant illusion. However, the moment when they truly abandoned their country did not come until they pledged their loyalty to the ideology of Kim Il Sung. They truly lost their homeland when they transformed themselves into the loyal puppet soldiers of Kim Il Sung.

For them, "making Japan a better place" meant no less than converting the whole of Japan to *juche* ideology and making it a country in which the entire nation worshipped Kim Il Sung and Kim Jong Il. Even when they successfully managed to enter Japan on one of their infiltration missions, they were nothing more than agents of Kim Il Sung. Japan itself would never be more than a mere operational target. This homeland, for which they expressed such longing, became a symbol of the paradox that loomed larger the harder they struggled to show themselves loyal to the Great Leader by acting as his agents. Surely nothing could be more isolating than this. The Yodogō group, torn between their longing for home and their sense of loyalty, lost their homeland. Forsaken by the Japanese activist movement, having lost forever the support of their sympathizers, they clearly would never experience their heroic return at the "demand of the people and the times." The Yodogō group had suffered a double loss of their homeland.

When was it now? Ah, yes, springtime. Trees were bursting in full bloom, and a fresh green covered the mountains and fields. The ice had melted from the Daedong River, and people were overjoyed at the end of the long North Korean winter.

Spring had come even to the peak of Mt. Moran. A gust of wind sent a cloud of flower petals fluttering into the air.

Tamiya came to a sudden halt and recited,

O, flowers will fall
The flowers are falling...

The flowers are falling. Petals are dancing in the wind.

For a long while he stood letting the wind frisk around him. A delicate pink petal lay on his shoulder.

He told me then for the first time that he had gone secretly to Ueno Park just before the hijacking to see the cherry blossoms there. Perhaps it was a kind of ritual in preparation for abandoning his country, necessary for him to be able to cross the sea and leave Japan. Though now I can't help seeing it this way, it would have held a different meaning for him at the time.

Tamiya always thought his absence would be temporary. As he had written in his departure statement, his intention was "absolutely to come back to Japan." He probably renewed his determination to return to the homeland while he drank in the sight of the cherry blossoms of Ueno Park in full bloom.

A few days after the planning meeting at the classical music café in front of Komagome station in Tokyo, Tamiya made various arrangements in preparation for their eventual return. He said to the others, "We have to figure out how we are going to get in touch with each other after we get back. I'll put an ad in the classified section of the *Asahi Shimbun*, an advertisement looking for 'Maro.' Then we meet at Ueno Park at noon the next day. Other people might come too, so we'll all have paper shopping bags from some big department store, say from Isetan or Mitsukoshi."

They agreed to meet at the statue of Saigō near one of the park entrances.

However, their planned reunion never happened in the twenty-five years since that spring. Nor did an ad for a person named "Maro" ever appear in the *Asahi Shimbun*.

They wrote many songs about their longing for home, the number of songs increasing as the years passed. With their return to Pyongyang, their overseas ventures at an end, their homesickness must have grown only stronger. They composed both lyrics and music; one of them, Abe Kimihiro, usually composed with a guitar. Here is one of the songs expressing their feelings for the homeland.

> Where did they come from? The wild geese fly
> Into the far eastern reaches of the sky
> When you return to the homeland
> Tell them we are well
> Time has passed; the rivers and mountains have changed
> But our memories of you have not

Into the cold wind the wild geese fly
Carrying their fallen comrade
Winter in the homeland must be cold
Help each other, do your best
No matter how high, no matter how many
We will cross the peaks together. (Tamiya et al. 1990, 210–211)

Another song expresses the children's feelings for Japan:

Across this ocean lies my motherland
My mother used to sing a lullaby
Nen nen korori yo o korori yo
My homeland I know only through songs
But I love the land where my mother was born

Across this sky lies my fatherland
My father used to speak of the mountains and rivers
Snow-topped Mt. Fuji, bright burning symbol
My homeland I know only through tales
But I love the land where my father was born

Beloved by my father, beloved by my mother,
They gave you their youth
When will I see you, o my homeland?
(*Marco Polo*, February 1994, p. 137)

The children sang these songs for me on several occasions during my visits to North Korea. Tears would come to my eyes at times as I heard some of the very youngest, obedient to their parents' requests, singing the songs in their unsteady voices. Abe Kimihiro sang marvelously well, accompanying himself on his guitar. But even now as I copy out these lyrics, I find myself gnashing my teeth in vexation over the question of why, if they still had such feelings, the Yodogō members couldn't be more considerate of other people? Why couldn't they be more sincere in their responses concerning the kidnap victims they dragged to North Korea, about their own comrades and comrades' children? And yet I can't conclude that their expressions of homesickness and their children's emotions were simply an exploitation of human feelings for political purposes. In order to show why, I must relate the following.

What did the term "homeland" mean to the Yodogō group and to

Tamiya in his last years? In the period after their quest to return home had run aground, as they began to tend more and more toward national-istic ideas, Tamiya and I had the same argument several times.

"Let's talk," Tamiya would say. It always began the same way.

I have discussed the ideology of Kim Il Sung, the thinking in *juche,* and the various assertions of the Yodogō group throughout this book, so I am not going to repeat what I have said elsewhere. I only want to elaborate on one matter.

I had recently returned from Phnom Penh, where I had been observing the 1993 general elections conducted under the auspices of the United Nations Transitional Authority in Cambodia (UNTAC), so the subject came up on one of my visits to Pyongyang. I had seen enough of the brutality and genocide of Pol Pot's nationalistic regime to be sickened by it,[1] so, when Tamiya began to expound upon his ideas of nationalism and ethnicity in impassioned speeches, I responded negatively. Looking back, I think now that I told him something crucial when I said that, in the end, the Yodogō group members were nothing more than the pup-pets of the North Korean Workers' Party. Among other things, I spoke of Cambodia's government under Heng Samrin and its relationship with Vietnam. I argued that, even if the Yodogō group succeeded in achieving the revolution in Japan with the backing of the North Korean Workers' Party, it would not be the free choice of the Japanese people as they claimed. Their Independent Revolutionary Party, following the ideology of Kim Il Sung, would be nothing more than the puppet of North Korea and, as a result, so would any government it created. Surely that contra-dicted any arguments the Yodogō members made about independence? Tamiya listened silently. I continued. The Red Army Faction's theory of international bases for the world revolution contained this same contra-diction. Achieving revolution at home from a base in a workers' nation could result only in the creation of a government that is a puppet of the workers' nation. This has become even clearer with the end of the era of

---

1. In 1975, the Cambodian Communist Party (Khmer Rouge) under the leadership of Pol Pot came to power and conducted a radical experiment to turn Cambodia into an agrarian society through murder of all educated persons and the forced movement of city dwellers to the countryside. A quarter of the popula-tion died and the situation remained unstable until a United Nations peacekeep-ing operation intervened, conducted elections in 1993, and revealed the extent of the genocide. Japan supported the UN effort, and Takazawa went to Cambodia as a journalist to observe the election and saw the effects firsthand. He later wrote a book in Japanese about his experiences there: *Kanbojia, ima* (Takazawa 1993).

international communism and the Cold War, just as the Yodogō group has had to begin speaking of *minzoku* (ethnic nationalism).

Tamiya listened to me without saying anything.

Finally, he said, "You're telling us to review all our theories, starting with the one on international bases. And that we should not speak so much about nationalism without reviewing what we mean? That's pretty tough."

Thus went our arguments every time we met again after that. But separately from these discussions, Tamiya and the rest of the group began to lean toward more nationalistic ideas, taking as their own Kim Il Sung's slogan of "Love the Country, love the People, love the Nation" and claiming that "blood is ethnicity." More and more, our ideas parted. After a while, Tamiya and I stopped talking about the subject. We both realized that continuing the argument could only result in our hurting each other.

I met Tamiya several times in the spring and early summer of 1995, the year he died in Pyongyang. Sometimes our meetings were in Pyongyang; at other times we met in a third country. At the time he was thinking of forming a political group called the Patriotic Alliance, an organization that would emphasize the importance of nationalistic ideas. It was obvious to me his ideas were based on the instructions of the North Korean Workers' Party. The plan was to advance their campaign by organizing Japanese nationalist groups. Almost without thinking, I found myself telling him he should stop, that he should not be doing such things. It was obvious political maneuvering. Surely pushing the ideology of Kim Il Sung upon the Japanese people, making them give up the ideals of socialism and free choice, was nothing more than selling out the homeland.

At this, for an instant, Tamiya's face became grim. "It's too late," he said, practically shouting.

Around that time, a Japanese magazine columnist ridiculed the Yodogō group's nationalistic leanings as "the opposite extreme from their earlier line of world revolution that puts to shame even the 'Anti-American Love the Country' line of the Revolutionary Left group and Japan's ethnonationalists.[2] The Yodogō group's claims are just par-

---

2. The Revolutionary Left group that joined with the Red Army Faction to form the United Red Army in 1971 had a strange slogan, "Anti-America, love the country," that sounded very right-wing and was easily mistaken for the views of Japanese right-wing ethnonationalist groups.

roting the North Korean Workers' Party line" (in *Uwasa no shinso* [The Truth behind the Rumors], July 1995, p. 19).

This was probably the very first article written by the Japanese media about the relationship between the Yodogō group and the North Korean Workers' Party. Though the writer also discussed Okamoto Takeshi's confinement under house arrest and reported on Tanaka Yoshimi's whereabouts overseas, Tamiya's strongest response was reserved for the mention of the Workers' Party.

"We're in trouble. This is going to be a problem."

From where I sat next to him, he seemed surprisingly flustered as he held the article in his hand.

The Yodogō group's nationalistic statements had prompted a gradual increase of criticism against them in Japan, accusing them of leaning to the right and reviving Nazism.

Tamiya would sometimes say in desperation, "I'm a Stalinist, long live Stalin! Stalin was a great man, after all, wasn't he? They say we are trying to bring back Nazism, but what is wrong with Nazism?!" The Workers' Party espousal of Stalinism has long been well known, but, for some reason, Adolf Hitler is also well regarded in North Korea (at least it is best not to criticize him). This is as strange as the fact that Hamlet was left out of the North Korean collection of the translated *Complete Works of Shakespeare* (even if the reason for this is clear enough).

There remains much to be written, but, to tell the truth, I do not feel like writing about Tamiya during this period. Just let me say that it was obvious he often found his position as leader of the Yodogō group to be agonizing. Tamiya's distress made it clear to me that the Red Army Faction's leadership had committed an unforgivable crime when they sent Tamiya and his men to hijack the *Yodogō*.

When I think of the situation in which Tamiya found himself, of having to speak of Japan's autonomy and nationality, all the while hiding a secret agenda to "paint all of Japan the color of Kim Il Sung's *juche* ideology," I feel overwhelmed by the cruelty of political necessities.

In the winter of 1990, as we sat in a room in the Koryo Hotel, Tamiya had told me that he truly wanted to go back to Japan. "Isn't that how human beings are?" Perhaps even now the ghost of Tamiya continues to ask this question with the same sad smile on his face.

During a lull in the story, a hero from the past announced his return to the scene but was never allowed to complete his role. When the *Yodogō* flew into darkness on April 3, 1970, there was another person on board besides the hijackers and the flight crew: the "substitute hostage," Yamamura Shinjirō, then vice-minister of transport.

Twenty-two years after the hijacking, on the evening of April 12, 1992, Yamamura, still a member of the Diet, went to bed early in preparation for a trip to North Korea starting the following day. He was the leader of a group of Liberal Democratic Party (LDP) members visiting to attend the celebrations in honor of Kim Il Sung's eightieth birthday.

Yamamura had returned home to Chiba from his rooms at the Diet members' lodgings in Tokyo to take care of some final arrangements for the trip to North Korea. The 10:00 a.m. flight was from Haneda Airport, a long way from Yamamura's home in Sahara City in Chiba prefecture. He had to be up very early.

About three days earlier, Diet member Yamamura had been interviewed by a reporter in his offices at the Diet Office Building. He told the reporter that, if possible, he would try to meet the leader of the *Yodogō* hijackers while he was in North Korea. If he succeeded, it would be the first time he had seen Tamiya since the hijacking.

A little past midnight, a sudden scream was heard from Yamamura's bedroom. His aged mother, sleeping in the next room, was startled awake. She found Yamamura, covered in blood, still lying on the futon spread out on the tatami-mat floor of his room. His second daughter, wearing a sweatsuit and holding a large kitchen knife, was standing next to him looking dazed. In the ensuing investigation, the police concluded that the daughter, known to be psychologically unstable, had committed the murder in a moment of insanity.

After some consideration, however, it is apparent that this event and the *Yodogō* hijacking are fundamentally linked together. This second daughter was the young girl waiting at the foot of the stairs when "Yamamura, the Man" disembarked from the *Yodogō* after its return to Haneda Airport from Pyongyang. Photographs show Yamamura, at the time thirty-six years old, hugging his daughter with his face filled with pride and happiness. The girl was much spoken of as the daughter of the hero of the *Yodogō* hijacking. The *Yodogō* and North Korea threw dark shadows over her life, for she suffered many bad experiences attributable to them. Given this, her fit of insanity the night before her father's return to North Korea and his meeting with the Yodogō hijackers may have been brought on by a flood of fear and unhappiness stored up inside her since early childhood. In her madness, she may have been trying to protect her father and bring him back to her. She, too, was an innocent passenger forced on board this damaging story of the *Yodogō*.

Tamiya himself had told me he was looking forward to Yamamura's visit to North Korea and for the same reason I was. He was hoping his talk with Yamamura would cause a breakthrough on the deadlocked issue of the Yodogō group's return to Japan. This was the period after Liberal Democratic Party kingmaker Kanemaru Shin's visit to North Korea, when negotiations between Japan and North Korea had reached a new high. In this atmosphere, surely everyone was interested in the outcome of a visit to North Korea by Yamamura Shinjirō, who had leaped to fame during the Yodogō incident.

Yamamura's sudden exit from the scene was a blow to the Yodogō group. They had hoped his visit would somehow set into motion renewed discussions with the Japanese government about how to settle the issue of their return to Japan.

Tamiya was discouraged by the cancellation of the meeting with Yamamura and his group. He took the trouble of sending a telegram expressing his condolences to Yamamura's family. Once again, the Yodogō group found the road of their return to Japan blocked, this time by the death of Yamamura Shinjirō.

Now, finally, I have to investigate a fact that I have been avoiding throughout this long story. By inspecting the truth of this fact, I may end up once again rewriting the history of the Yodogō and perhaps solve the mystery of their transformation into such fine *juche* warriors.

All of the characters are now out on stage, but the fact is that there are nine hijackers but only eight wives. Try as I might, I could not get the numbers to match.

CHAPTER THIRTY-TWO

Labyrinths of Time

I imagine the Yodogō continuing on its flight through total darkness. No aviation map charts a route through the turbulence and the occasional flash and boom of thunder outside the aircraft. Brief bursts of lightning illuminate the cabin's interior, revealing for an instant the ghostlike figures of the hijackers and their wives inside the Yodogō. Like characters in a silent movie, they appear fixed in momentary tableaux from the past, but their faces remain indistinct. I can make out no details except the number of people.

There were nine hijackers on board the Yodogō when it took off from Kimpo Airport and flew to North Korea in April of 1970.

Seven years into the future and another flash of lightning should reveal the presence of nine wives as well as the nine hijackers. However, although I can count nine men, for some reason one of them remains in the shadows, his face hidden from my sight.

Another glimpse of the interior of the aircraft in the mid-1980s might reveal that the figures of Okamoto Takeshi and Yoshida Kintarō have disappeared, and the number of wives has been reduced to seven. But the faces of the wives still cannot be seen clearly.

Ten years later, another flash of lightning illuminates the Yodogō group. Kim Il Sung's disclosure of the existence of the Yodogō wives and children must have felt like a direct hit. The aircraft shudders violently in the turbulence. After twenty-five years of wandering invisibly in the darkness, the Yodogō has now been exposed to searchlights for the first time.

Kim Il Sung's revelations also triggered suspicions concerning the story of Yoshida Kintarō's "fatal" illness.

In August 1985, a letter from Pyongyang describing Yoshida's poor condition arrived at his old family home in Kyoto's Gion district. The letter was not from Yoshida himself but had been written by Tamiya Takamaro. It invited Yoshida's family to Pyongyang for a last meeting because Yoshida had been hospitalized after a sudden illness, and his chances for recovery were slim. Tamiya's letter was the first news Yoshida's family had received of him since his departure for North Korea aboard the *Yodogō*. His mother began to prepare for a trip to North Korea. However, the necessary formalities were complicated and extremely time-consuming.

In mid-September, a second letter arrived from Tamiya. It notified Yoshida's family of his death.

At the end of August, a delegation of Japan Socialist Party representatives from Kumamoto prefecture had visited Pyongyang. When they met with the Yodogō group, delegation leader Baba Noboru, a member of the Lower House of the Diet, was told that one of the Yodogō members was in serious condition.

At about the same time, Inoue Izumi, another Socialist Party Diet member, received a letter informing him of Yoshida's condition. Inoue showed this letter to a doctor, who made the rather harsh diagnosis that recovery looked impossible. After he heard the news of Yoshida's death, Inoue sent a letter to the Yodogō group.

> You must be saddened by the loss of Yoshida, the comrade who chose the fate of embarking upon the struggle with you. Despite making every effort, we were unable to arrange for his mother to visit North Korea in time to see him before his death. Yoshida died the day after I showed your letter to a doctor, who told me it was impossible for Yoshida to recover and that he would probably pass away very soon.
>
> I think, even though it may take months or years to do so, you must try to show Yoshida's mother how excellently he lived up to what he believed. The hijacking itself may have been a mistake, but you must show through your actions that it was your only option for keeping your ideals alive. You must show that your beliefs require young people to make it their mission to protect the Japanese people and that this is your way of life as men who love your homeland and your people above all else. We support and encourage you to continue. (Diet member Inoue Izumi, Kōchi prefecture, in "Readers' Column," *Nihon o kangaeru*, no. 16, [December 1985], p. 73)

Yoshida Kintarō died in a hospital in Pyongyang at 5:12 a.m. on September 4, 1985, from acute liver failure. His body was cremated on the following day, and the Yodogō members held a funeral then. Yoshida was thirty-five years old.

A passage in the Yodogō group's collection of memoirs, *Twenty Years after Takeoff,* describes Yoshida's death. Though it is rather long, I present it here in its entirety. This is the only account of Yoshida's death published in Japan, and most people think the story it tells is true. The passage is unsigned.

> Several months have already passed since Yoshida left us, yet we still feel that he is standing just over there with that smile on his face. But he is gone. It is hard to accept he will never return, and the sense of emptiness he left behind remains strong.
>
> We called him by his given name, Kintarō. He was everyone's pet, partly because he was the second-youngest member of our group but also because his fair skin and small stature made him an appealing figure. He possessed a quick mind and good sense. He was quiet and gentle, but he would calmly accept any task he was given and carry it out competently. He had an idiosyncratic laugh and a way of waving his hands whenever anything funny occurred that charmed us all.
>
> He fell ill with an incurable disease at the end of February 1985. It was a strange disease that brought on acute liver failure. He survived one or two serious crises thanks to the expertise of the North Korean doctors, but it was clear he was weakening. In June, he suffered a debilitating heart attack. Watching him become even thinner and paler, we wept inside.
>
> Hadn't we promised ourselves for fifteen years to dedicate our lives to the service of our country and our people? Would he leave us without ever setting foot in his homeland again? We could hardly bear to think of the regret he must have been feeling. He must have divined our thoughts, because he said with a smile, "I am never going to give up. Don't you worry about me." His voice was weak but cheerful.
>
> As his condition worsened further in August, his death became only a matter of time. The doctors told us he was doing well, but we had lost hope for his recovery. We decided to make contact with Yoshida's mother. We did not wish to sadden her

with the news of his fatal illness, but we felt it was our duty to arrange for her to see him.

We all went to visit him in the hospital on September first. Yoshida looked at us tenderly, already lacking the strength to speak. As we tried to encourage him, he responded to our words with nods and a weak smile. Afterwards there was a short silence, then his lips moved and Yoshida spoke. "It doesn't look good." He had tears on his cheeks, and we couldn't stop our own tears from falling. We all stood sobbing, unable to speak.

We cried not only in mourning at the loss of a comrade who had been closer than a brother to us for fifteen years. We cried in regret for a comrade who would die without achieving his goals, and we cried in anger at the Japanese government that would let Kintarō die without being able to return to his homeland.

Soon after, at 5:12 a.m. on September 4, 1985, Yoshida passed away. Apparently he went quietly after suffering another heart attack.

When we arrived at the hospital, his body had already been removed to the basement morgue. We wished him a last good-bye and stood next to his body for a moment in silent prayer.

Strangely, we had no tears to shed. All we felt was a vague emotion that Kintarō was no longer with us.

Yoshida's body was cremated the next day. We held a small funeral for him at the same time.

Tamiya's voice delivering the memorial address echoed around the quiet room. The text of Tamiya's address went like this:

> Our late friend, Comrade Yoshida Kintarō:
>
> Today we wish you a final farewell, our hearts filled with a deep sorrow and a righteous anger.
>
> You have left us so soon, so suddenly. With twenty years spent in the homeland and then fifteen in a foreign land, your life of thirty-five years was short, but it was very precious.
>
> You were a social activist, a genuine human being who loved life and understood its brilliance. Even as a teenager you chose the straight path of dignity, holding firm against those who would ridicule and trample upon life. Right up to the end, you dedicated your frail body to

your ideals on behalf of Japan and your fellow countrymen, continuing to cultivate and train yourself without flinching from any difficulties you faced.

We cannot express the sadness we feel at not being able to save you from this deadly illness, you who so loved life and devoted yourself to making it better; nor can we deny the depth of sorrow we feel at having to see you off on the path of no return with all your wishes unfulfilled.

Along with deep sadness, our hearts tremble in righteous indignation.

Though the homeland that inspired the dreams in your heart is not far away, you, who so longed for your home and family and friends, have passed away without realizing your greatest desire of returning in your lifetime. We can only imagine the regret you feel at dying in a foreign country, banished from your homeland, your name still uncleared, your youthful devotion to justice looked upon as a crime.

We are fiercely angry at those who forced your grievous loss. We will never forget those last moments when you finally had to close your eyes.

Yoshida Kintarō, beloved friend and extraordinary comrade, we raise our glasses to promise, in the name of the friends and the Japanese people whom you loved so, that your death shall not be in vain.

We will continue to stand with our comrades in the holy struggle, fighting until the day of victory when the autonomous, peaceful, and democratic Japan of which you dreamed has been made real.

Rest in peace, friend.

September 5, 1985

(Tamiya et al. 1990, 246–249)

These passages suggest that Yoshida was an equal member of the group of nine Yodogō hijackers, deeply lamented by his comrades when he sickened and died on foreign soil.

There is another passage in *Twenty Years after Takeoff* that concerns Yoshida besides the one above. I introduce it here, the only passage that describes Yoshida's daily life in Pyongyang, written by Tamiya Takamaro.

> He was very bright, but we could see he was not very good at doing physical labor. After our arrival in North Korea, there were times when we used shovels and pickaxes to clear out space in the mountains for exercise grounds and other facilities. Since most of us had been students, to begin with we weren't much good at that kind of labor. Yoshida was the only one of us who had been a "worker," so he should have been the most skillful, but in fact, he was the clumsiest one of all.
>
> One day, somebody made fun of him. "Hey, Kin, you're supposed to be a worker and all, how come you're such an amateur?" To which he answered with a straight face, "No. I painted ships in a shipyard. This is my first experience with a shovel."
>
> He had a funny way of talking. His manner was a little affected, and he spoke through his nose. In appearance he looked more like a pampered boy or a "young lord" than a worker. It didn't seem like him, with his princely manner, to have started working as a physical laborer immediately after graduating from high school.
>
> We asked him questions sometimes. "Why didn't you go to university? Why did you go straight to work? Weren't you interested in the student movement?"
>
> "No, that's not it. It's just that the student movement was only a student movement. Just another part of the petite bourgeoisie. I wanted to be a part of the working class; I wanted to do real labor." (Tamiya et al. 1990, pp. 44–45)

Yoshida's name does appear in several other places in the memoirs. However, they are all brief mentions, usually less than a sentence in length, often in the context of some action in conjunction with a larger group. For example, he was quick at learning Korean, and he had made sure to bring a language textbook titled *Korean in Four Weeks* along with him; once he was supposed to play the violin in a concert but was terrible; and, just after their arrival in Pyongyang when they were riding in the Volgas on their way to the Workers' Party compound that was to be their new quarters, he was described as "the smallest and the weakest among the members."

Yoshida is mentioned about as frequently as the other members.

Figure 32.01. Early photo of Yoshida Kintarō in Pyongyang. From personal collection of Takazawa Kōji.

A careful reading, however, reveals that every mention shows him in "visible" scenes. Tamiya's memoir introduces Yoshida's own words, but they only concern Yoshida's motivation and thoughts on joining their movement. In other words, nowhere in the collection is there any mention of Yoshida's ideology or ideas. This is a strange lack considering that *Twenty Years after Takeoff* was published as a summary of the Yodogō group's ideology. There are numerous descriptions by the other members of the process of their review of their ideological beliefs, of the contents of their self- and mutual criticism sessions, and their comments on these matters. It is as if Yoshida was not even present when these events were taking place. Yoshida's own words do not appear in these passages.

When *Twenty Years* was published, Yoshida Kintarō and Okamoto Takeshi were not included in the list of contributors. I have described above how Okamoto's section was left out just before the manuscript went to print. I had asked that Yoshida's writing also be included in the final publication, but, after my return to Japan from that first visit to Pyongyang, I received a letter from Tamiya explaining why this was not possible.

> You asked that we include an essay by our late comrade Yoshida Kintarō in the collection. Five years have passed since Yoshida's death, but still we can never forget that he died with his dreams unfulfilled, and his last words remain alive deep in our hearts. Certainly we would have liked to include his essay in this collec-

tion, but the location of his activities and then his sudden illness prevented him from ever writing anything appropriate. We truly regret that we have nothing from Yoshida Kintarō to present to our readers.

Tamiya is telling us that Yoshida was not in a location where he could do any writing. What sort of place is it that can prevent a person from writing?

When Kim Il Sung so unexpectedly revealed to the world the existence of the Yodogō wives and children, there were six hijackers and their wives remaining inside the aircraft floating through time. By then, the group consisted of Tamiya Takamaro, Konishi Takahiro, Tanaka Yoshimi, Akagi Shirō, Abe Kimihiro, and Wakabayashi Moriaki and their wives, Mori Yoriko, Fukui Takako, Mizutani Kyōko, Kaneko Emiko, Uomoto Tamiko, and Kuroda Sakiko. In addition, they had been joined after the hijacking by Ogawa Jun (a pseudonym) and by Akagi Shirō's younger sister Michiko. There were a total of nineteen children at the time (at this writing, there are twenty).

As the Yodogō group's true story gradually began to unveil itself after Kim's revelations, still only six of the wives came to light. Even if we accept their word that Yoshida Kintarō was unmarried, there should have been at least eight wives. Two were missing.

These two missing wives were later identified. The first was Yao Megumi, who had been arrested in Japan in 1988 and later identified as the wife of Shibata Yasuhiro. Later it became clear that Okamoto Takeshi's wife had not been a North Korean woman as the Yodogō group had claimed but Fukutome Kimiko, the Japanese woman from Shikoku reported missing since 1977. Given these facts, *could it really be true that Yoshida had not been married?*

Operation Marriage, the project to find wives for all the Yodogō members, was conducted over a period of about one year from 1976 to 1977. Yoshida reportedly died of illness in 1985. Tamiya himself said about this project, "So we held a meeting and decided that, before the year was out, we would all have found wives for ourselves. . . . It became our revolutionary task to find these women, and, *within a year or a year and a half, we had all carried out our missions in good faith.* That was around 1977, and it was also the beginning of a new era for the Yodogō group" (Tamiya and Takazawa 1996, 207; emphasis added by Takazawa).

According to Tamiya, all the members found wives. That is, there should have been nine wives. In that case, there might still be an unknown

Japanese woman somewhere in North Korea. If Yoshida Kintarō did have a wife, where had she come from? Where had she vanished? Surely we should search for her as well? In fact, in the storm of publicity after Kim's revelation of the Yodogō families, friends and concerned supporters asked about "Yoshida's wife and children left behind in North Korea" in the belief that they must exist. However, the truth of their existence was left unclear. Even later, when the topic of obtaining birth certificates in order to establish Japanese citizenship for the Yodogō children arose, nothing was mentioned about the family of Yoshida Kintarō.

This obvious inconsistency concerning Yoshida's wife and children made me suspicious. I could not help asking one last question: did Yoshida Kintarō really die of an illness?

I began to review intensively everything the Yodogō members had written or said about Yoshida, focusing on the events around the time of his death. My investigations led me into an elaborate labyrinth of time, its convoluted paths hidden in the North Korean darkness. At its heart, I found an unexpected and astonishing story.

How far can we really trace Yoshida's footsteps in North Korea?

The earliest trace we have of him is at the late-night press conference with Japanese reporters held at the Pyongyang Hotel on May 1, 1972. Eight of the hijackers appeared before the press corps, with only Shibata Yasuhiro, still a minor, absent. At the reporters' request, they each signed their names; Yoshida was no exception, and his signature appears alongside those of Tamiya and Konishi. He is also clearly visible in pictures of the press conference. His next appearance was in 1973, when the Yodogō members agreed to a meeting with a Japanese television crew. In these later recordings, Yoshida seems to be smiling sadly for some reason.

The third occasion was on November 11, 1976. During a visit to North Korea, the writer Oda Makoto met eight of the Yodogō members in a reception room at a theater in Pyongyang. After his return to Japan, Oda held a press conference at the Chōsen Sōren headquarters building on the twentieth of the same month,[1] and afterwards he gave an interview to a reporter from the *Mainichi Shimbun.* According to the resulting article, Tamiya had been absent from the group meeting with Oda, and Konishi had appeared in his place as the leader. Other magazines (such as the *Playboy Weekly*) carried articles about Oda's meeting, but none

---

1. Chōsen Sōren is the official organization representing North Korean interests in Japan.

of the articles gave the names of those who had attended. They only say that Oda met with eight people. They do mention that at least one cadre from the North Korean Workers' Party was also present. Neither the newspapers nor the weekly magazines had any pictures of the meeting, explaining that pictures were a technical impossibility because the meeting place had been too dark. Without pictures, it is unclear whether Tamiya really was absent. Since then, there have been no occasions on which all the Yodogō members were present for meetings or interviews; nor have any more pictures of Yoshida ever appeared.

What about letters? Although Yoshida's family did receive messages from him during the early period, such as those delivered by visitors to North Korea at the time of the 1972 meeting, they have never received any letters from him. On the matter of letters, there is the following story.

In 1979, Konishi Takahiro's mother telephoned Yoshida's family in Kyoto. A letter had arrived from Konishi in Pyongyang, and she was calling to ask if Yoshida's family had received one as well. They had not. This is a significant fact, because the entire Yodogō group sent letters to Japan almost simultaneously that year, the men's letters proving they were in Pyongyang, the wives' letters feigning to be updates of their travels in Europe. Let us not forget that around this time Fukutome Kimiko's family in Kochi prefecture had also received a letter from her, postmarked in East Berlin.

Why did the entire Yodogō group send letters to their families at the same time that year?

A closer look at the circumstances of the Yodogō group around that time reveals several reasons for sending the letters. This was the period in which the Yodogō members began their overseas operations, and the men's letters from Pyongyang were intended to provide them with alibis to hide their presence in Europe. The letters were unexpectedly effective. Even when they were seen and recognized by Japanese people living or traveling in Europe, reports of these sightings were disregarded, since the letters to the hijackers' families proved them to be in Pyongyang. During the 1980s, several newspapers and weeklies received reports from travelers of sightings of the Yodogō hijackers or others whose faces appeared in wanted posters, and many of these reports were published as short articles. But no one believed the reports. Even the public safety authorities remained in some doubt about the Yodogō group's European operations. Those in North Korea were aware that the police continued to follow up with the hijackers' families and friends whenever they received a report of a sighting. However, on being shown a letter from Pyongyang, the visiting officers would consider that they had confirmed the hijackers' whereabouts in North Korea and would take no further steps. For some reason, they could not believe that both could be true, that the hijackers supposed to be in Pyongyang and the men sighted in Europe could be the same. They chose to believe only half of the story. I have already described how letters became a manipulative tool in persuading the Japanese public that Okamoto Takeshi wished to remain in North Korea as a naturalized citizen. This time, letters served to prove that the men remained in Pyongyang, in a skillfully executed plan that took advantage of the Japanese people's conviction that the North Korean government would never allow the Yodogō hijackers any freedom of movement.

The purpose behind the women's letters can be easily understood from the fact that all of them were sent from Europe, Mexico, or other locations of operations. In contrast to the men's letters, the women's letters were necessary to prove that they were not in North Korea and that they had nothing to do with North Korea. The letters were alibis showing they were really in Europe. Yet another reason for the women's letters lies in the fact that, at that time, all of the women had been reported to the police by their families as missing. In addition, the women's families were also actively searching for the women by asking for information about them among their former friends and acquaintances. These actions hindered the women's ability to maneuver. The letters were ploys to have the families cease their searches and to cancel the missing person reports. The whole plan was almost certainly devised by the Yodogō organization, under the instructions of their handlers in the North Korean Workers' Party. The group had information on the women's families' requests to the police to search for them as missing persons and on the families' own actions to find out more on their own, and they used this information to formulate their plan of action. As bizarre as it seems, the Workers' Party may have known more about the Yodogō members' families than the members themselves knew.

This solves the mystery surrounding the letter sent to Fukutome Kimiko's family in 1979. It was part of a carefully devised plan, and she was obviously ordered by the Yodogō group to write it. She had been informed of events in her family by the Yodogō group and by cadres in the Workers' Party. This was how she knew of her cousin's wedding, information she could not have gotten otherwise.

What is the significance of the fact that, of all the Yodogō members' families in Japan, only Yoshida Kintarō's family did not receive a letter in 1979? One explanation could be that Yoshida did not need an alibi placing him in Pyongyang. In other words, he had not been sent on any overseas operations, nor were there any plans to send him on such missions in the future.

Since then, Yoshida's family has sent several letters to him in Pyongyang. In 1980, a group visiting North Korea carried a letter addressed to him from his family. However, they have never received any reply.

During my search for information concerning that time period, I came across a strange newspaper article from the *Yomiuri Shimbun*, dated September 25, 1985, not long after the time of Yoshida's death. Its title read "Yodogō 8 may return in November—prepared for arrest after fifteen years." The article goes on to claim that the hijackers had become unbearably homesick after the death of their comrade and wished to return home even if they must be arrested. That this claim is unsupported is not important; what is important is that the article says it is reporting the contents of a conversation between a former labor organization official and members of the Yodogō group during a visit to Pyongyang in August that year. The Yodogō members had told the official that they would not have any regrets as long as they could ensure Yoshida's remains were sent to Japan. My interest lies in the date on which this conversation is supposed to have taken place. This person met with Konishi Takahiro and Wakabayashi Moriaki in August, when Yoshida was in the hospital. It seems strange for them to have spoken of Yoshida's remains if he was still alive when they met. Even so, the conversation itself is not really very important either because, odd as it was, there is no way of confirming it. What really draws my attention is the Yodogō group's reaction to the *Yomiuri* article. It seems to have really rattled them; the following month they voiced a public protest against it.

> The article claims to be based on a conversation we had with Mr. A, the former labor union official. However, we have no memory of saying what the article claims. For example, in the article, we are quoted as saying that "we couldn't return to Japan and leave our sick comrade behind" and that "we will have no regrets as long as we can ensure that Yoshida's ashes are sent to Japan." From a purely objective standpoint, it would be impossible for us to make both of these statements in the same conversation, since Yoshida was still alive at that point. Why would we have referred

to the "ashes" of a comrade still struggling with his illness (he
died later, in September)? (From the Yodogō group's protest
published in the *Yomiuri Shimbun,* October 28, 1985, reprinted in
Nihon o kangaeru, vol. 16, p. 13)

Apparently their scheme had not gone according to plan. The protest seems especially odd considering that they usually denounced the
Japanese press as part of the "new bourgeoisie" and simply ignored
inconvenient articles. The article in question had focused mainly on
the matter of their homesickness and possible return to Japan. Chances
were good that no one had even noticed whether the labor union delegation's visit to North Korea had been in August or September. And
yet, the Yodogō group still took the trouble to write their protest to the
newspaper and even sent copies directly to their supporters in Japan.
Why? Not in order to deny the possibility of their return to Japan but in
order to ensure that Yoshida's death was thought to have taken place in
September. It did not serve their purposes to have been heard talking
about Yoshida's ashes in August.

Behind the Yodogō group's overreaction to the article lay their larger
plan of infiltration into Japan. That is, their reaction was rooted in their
secret plans to slip into the country and not caused by the rumor that
they might return because they were suddenly overwhelmed by homesickness. Their secret operation of infiltration, the public performance
of sending letters of appeal to Prime Minister Nakasone, and the story of
Yoshida Kintarō's death, all of which took place at around the same time,
were closely linked parts of a single plan. Let us remember that, when
the *Yomiuri* article was published, Shibata Yasuhiro had already covertly
entered Japan. Who would suspect that one of the Yodogō hijackers was
already there in secret when they spoke so publicly about their desire to
return openly? In that period, the Yodogō group's main mode of operation was to outwit their opponents. Their confessions of homesickness
to the *Yomiuri* served perfectly to conceal their real schemes of secret
infiltration.

Another reason for the members to make clear that Yoshida's death
had occurred in September was the letter they had sent to Yoshida's
family in late August that said he was still alive. It would be extremely
inconvenient for their plans if they were thought to have spoken of
Yoshida's ashes in August, because that would mean they had sent the
letter about his critical condition after he had already died. The letter's
real purpose was to publicize the Japanese government's inhumane

policies that made travel to and from North Korea so difficult (at the time, every Japanese passport carried the words "excluding travel to the Democratic People's Republic of Korea") by showing how Yoshida's family was forced to jump through hoops in order to visit their dying son. Ideally for the Yodogō group's plan, it had to take Yoshida's family much time and effort to organize their journey to North Korea, and, even then, the story had to end in the most heartbreaking way. They thought this would make for propaganda best suited to their purposes. The only catch they feared more than the possibility that the government would speed up the process in the Yoshidas' case was the very real restriction against any such travel to North Korea in the first place. To ensure that the Yoshida family would receive the necessary permission, the Yodogō group carefully prepared the way by applying to various Diet members belonging to the Japan Socialist Party with appeals for "humanitarian treatment."

In October, after completing all the necessary and complicated formalities, Yoshida's family finally traveled to Pyongyang via Beijing. The day after their arrival, five Yodogō members visited them in their hotel and gave them a wooden box containing Yoshida's ashes. The family was also given a Swiss watch said to be presented to Yoshida by Kim Il Sung and a certificate of death. There was no letter.

Of course, had Yoshida's family been able to navigate the official formalities more quickly to arrive in North Korea sooner, there would simply have been an earlier date on the death certificate. The Yodogō group had a good reason not to allow Yoshida's family to see him: he was already long dead.

In the early winter of 1993, I had the opportunity to interview all of the Yodogō wives in a suburb of Pyongyang. Seven women agreed to the interview: all the wives except the two who were missing and Akagi Michiko, who had joined the group later. Kim Il Sung had revealed the existence of the Yodogō wives and children about a year and a half earlier.

I had no time to prepare for the interviews, which had been offered to me unexpectedly when I happened to be in Pyongyang. I had no choice but to start right in, and I had only two days to speak with everyone. I remember my exhaustion after seven straight individual interviews, each lasting from an hour and a half to two hours.

I categorized my questions by topic. I asked each of them the same questions (as described in chapter 10). What impressed them most on arrival in North Korea? What had been their saddest and most shocking experiences? What were the women's perspectives on the Yodogō men?

Several of the women mentioned Okamoto Takeshi. Some were critical of him, and others seemed more sympathetic, but it was clear that he existed for them. However, not one of the women even mentioned Yoshida Kintarō's name. His absence from their stories was so complete it almost gave me the feeling that the *Yodogō* had been hijacked by only eight men.

Yoshida's funeral was in September 1985. Even though the women were often away from Pyongyang during that period, working in Europe and Japan, they had all had children with their Yodogō husbands, and Yoshida should have been one of their closest comrades. Yoshida's death was still eight years in the distant future when the women arrived in North Korea in 1977. Yet, for some reason, Yoshida Kintarō had no place at all in the women's memories of those years. This was very strange. According to the Yodogō group's memoirs, Yoshida had struggled with his illness for half a year after falling ill in February of 1985. If so, then it is natural to think they would have visited him in the hospital, and indeed the written memoirs mention such visits. It could not have been a small matter to lose one of their group when there were only nine of them to begin with. And, if his illness was as sudden as they claim, then Yoshida must have lived in the village along with all the others during those eight years before his hospitalization. Yet a man who really had existed had no place in the memories of the Yodogō wives.

What should we make of this fact?

There are two possible interpretations: either the subject of Yoshida Kintarō was strictly taboo, or Yoshida Kintarō had not been there and the women knew nothing about him.

Tamiya spoke clearly about the Yodogō members' marriages: "The marriage operation went on from 1976 to 1977, and by the end of a year all of us had accomplished our mission." However, I heard several times that Yoshida had not had a wife and children. The only logical explanation for this contradiction is that Yoshida was not included when Tamiya spoke of "all" the members. Either Yoshida was already dead by the time of Operation Marriage, or he had already left the organization.

The wives had never visited an ailing Yoshida in the hospital, nor had there been any funeral for Yoshida in Pyongyang in 1985. As far as they were concerned, he had never existed.

I was horrified by this discovery. Chills coursed down my back and goosebumps appeared on my arms. The long excerpts I gave above were invented fictions. Everything, the story of Yoshida's struggle with illness, the funeral, Tamiya's eulogy—all were complete lies.

My discovery revealed other suspicious circumstances as well. I understood why there had never been any letters from Yoshida, why, despite his long hospital stay and despite his supposed awareness that the end was near, he wrote nothing, not even a dying testament. I understood why, when the Yodogō members spoke about Yoshida in interviews, they always described the same thing, his habit of waving his hands when he laughed. That was the limit of their memory of him. The timing fits perfectly to explain his lack of a wife and the fact that the other men's wives knew nothing of him.

However, I could no longer feel any surprise at the discovery of a fabrication, or conspiracy, or shocking fact by or about the Yodogō group. Their true nature had already been exposed during my research into the fates of Okamoto Takeshi and Fukutome Kimiko. By then, I only hoped I would not somehow be tricked into playing a part in one of their schemes.

The wives said nothing about Yoshida Kintarō. However, their silence on the subject conveyed a single eloquent truth.

Even now, there remain several clear taboos within the Yodogō group. The greatest of these concern Yoshida Kintarō, as I experienced personally on one occasion soon after the first of my several visits to Pyongyang.

I met Yoshida's older sister at a meeting in the spring of 1990. Fittingly, as the sister of a man described as a "young prince," she was graceful and beautiful. We met only briefly, but we spoke about my recent trip to North Korea and the Yodogō group. I told her a little about them, and then we talked about her late brother. She said, "If I could, I would like the chance to talk with the Yodogō people."

"I think you should. It would make Kintarō happy if he knew," I told her.

Conditions for traveling to Pyongyang had been changing gradually since 1985, when Yoshida had died, and it was now possible to contact the Yodogō group directly. It would not be impossible for members of the Yoshida family to visit North Korea if they wished to do so. I brought it up with the Yodogō members the next time I saw them. Their response was clear-cut.

"We will deal with any matter concerning Yoshida. Please do not get involved."

I found this answer deeply disturbing. I mentioned the Yoshida family's interest to several of the members, and all of them answered in the same abrupt manner. It was depressing. That was my first clue that a taboo existed. I had no way at the time of knowing the truth hidden behind their words, but I have to admit their words made me very interested in finding out what had really happened to Yoshida Kintarō. As I deepened my understanding of North Korea and the ideology of Kim Il Sung, I slowly uncovered the truth.

Yoshida Kintarō was not hospitalized in Pyongyang in 1985. He did not suffer from sudden and acute liver failure. He was only called upon posthumously to serve a political purpose, to play a role in the Yodogō group's ploy to secretly enter Japan while publicly campaigning for a return. So when, exactly, had he disappeared from the village? As I have already described, I can confirm that he was still alive only until 1973. We can see him then, standing alone, smiling sadly into one of the cameras of the Japanese television reporters. It is impossible to confirm whether Yoshida Kintarō really was included in the group that met with Oda Makoto in November 1976 since there are no photographs from the meeting. Eight hijackers appeared, and the newspaper articles say it was Tamiya who was absent, implying that Yoshida was really there—or that someone was pretending to be him. But the articles also say the location was too dark for pictures, and the face of the "Yoshida Kintarō" present on that day remains obscured in darkness.

If the "Yoshida" who appeared was the real Yoshida, then he pulls us even further into the labyrinth of time surrounding him, because that meeting took place when Operation Marriage was nearing its completion. Fukutome Kimiko disappeared around that time, and the other wives had begun crossing to North Korea. There is no guarantee that a wife had not already been selected for Yoshida Kintarō. If Yoshida was in fact present at the meeting with Oda, that would prove that he was still politically viable at that time. Since Tamiya said that all the members had found wives, that would mean Yoshida must have had a wife, too. This can only leave us to suspect that a wife had been selected for him but had disappeared before a marriage took place. Was Yoshida one of "all" the members mentioned by Tamiya? "All" of the Yodogō members appeared before Oda Makoto at this delicate juncture. Tamiya's "absence" meant only eight needed to appear, proving that all the original members were still alive and well.

I began to realize that a greater historical shadow loomed in the darkness behind this delicately complicated mystery and that, in order to understand the truth of what happened to Yoshida Kintarō, I must investigate it more closely. I have still not found the path out of this labyrinth, but what I did find in the shadows sheds more light on the Yodogō group. In fact, there was another Yoshida Kintarō.

CHAPTER THIRTY-THREE

Pact of Silence

*Fire. In the distance, a sailing ship is in flames. On shore, people are creeping for-
ward to stare at the vessel, looking as if they could hear the flames. A young man
holding a torch beckons and seems about to give a command to the gathering
crowd. Everyone is wearing clothing in the Korean style of long ago. Reeds grow
along the shore, and the smoke from the youth's torch seems about to reach the
bow of the burning ship.*

This was a painting I saw at the Museum of the Korean Revolution.
During my first trip to North Korea, I saw the giant bronze statue of Kim
Il Sung at Mansudae and then visited the museum that lay just behind.
The museum contains relics and displays of the anti-Japanese resistance
and celebrates the revolutionary achievements of Kim Il Sung. There are
many larger-than-life-size pictures and simple descriptions illustrating
the Great Leader's life. The picture of the youth holding a burning torch
was one of these. However, the handsome young man is not Kim Il Sung
but his great-grandfather, Kim Eung-u.

For some reason, this picture remains in my mind, though not
because it had been skillfully painted or because it was especially
appealing. It was really nothing more than yet another piece of socialist
propaganda. Perhaps I remember it for the subtle feeling of wrongness it
gave me the moment I saw it. The scene, from 130 years before, is quite
different from the other pictures depicting the war against the Japanese.

A museum commentator armed with a long pointer gave us a
lengthy explanation of this painting and the other exhibits, full of praise
for the Great Leader. Our guide translated.

The *Sherman,* an invading ship of imperialist America, was forcibly sailing up the Daedong River in disregard of our warnings. The word spread that the *Sherman* was killing villagers with indiscriminate fire from its cannons and guns, plundering the villages, and raping women and girls. Hearing this, Kim Eung-u, the great-grandfather of our Great Leader, Premier Kim Il Sung, gathered up the people and led the fight against the invaders. He had fishing nets collected from all the village houses and stretched them across a narrow section of the river between a small island and the Mangyong headland, then filled them with stones to block the course of the pirate ship. In addition, he benefited from the great revolutionary wisdom of the villagers and formulated a plan to attack the ship using fire tactics. Several small boats filled with burning firewood and oil were sent downstream to set the *Sherman* ablaze. As this story proves, our Great Leader's great-grandfather was an exceptional revolutionary who could lead the people in a fight, a resourceful man who loved his country and his home.

This story refers to events that occurred in August 1866. On August 15, the American schooner *Sherman* appeared at the mouth of the Daedong and, ignoring warnings from the Korean side, proceeded up the river toward the royal capital of Heijō. This act sparked an armed clash with the local people, and, on September 2, the *Sherman* burned and sank just downstream of Yongak island, near what is now central Pyongyang. All aboard burned or were killed as they tried to escape. These events marked the arrival of the Black Ships in Korea.[1]

The Museum of the Revolution at Mansudae displays other pictures besides the one depicting the *Sherman* incident. In addition to Kim Eung-u, other paintings show Kim Il Sung's grandfather, Kim Bohyeon, fighting against the Japanese; his father, Kim Hyeonjik, organizing the Korean People's Assembly (the anti-Japanese underground resistance group); his mother, Kang Banseok, the woman who raised the Great Leader; and, finally, surrounded by children, standing heroically at the peak of Mt. Paektu on his triumphant return to Korea, the nation's "Father," the revered General Kim Il Sung himself. The paintings were

---

1. As had happened in Japan in 1853, the United States sent ships to Korea to try to open the country to trade. These imposing Western ships were known in Japan as "Black Ships."

not just a biographical record of the life of Kim Il Sung but the record of several generations of an exalted revolutionary family steeped in a long revolutionary tradition.

These pictures would come to mind every now and then as I did my research on Yoshida Kintarō. As it turned out, the painting of the burning of the *Sherman* over a century earlier was an important clue in solving the mystery of his disappearance.

Yoshida Kintarō sat on a rock and looked out over Kobe's harbor from the heights of Suwayama. The rooftops of houses crowded together below him, and he could see the dignified bulk of the newly constructed prefectural office building. The port had been developing rapidly ever since his arrival from Okayama, with the noise of construction echoing from all directions even now. Kintarō enjoyed coming here and had climbed to this spot for the first time soon after he came to Kobe. It seemed so long ago now. Then, there had been no rooftops blocking his fine view of the harbor, and he had followed a wide road from the settlement near the water. In those days, a lovely view of the furrowed fields had stretched far into the distance, and modern ships had been anchored in the bay below. Occasionally he had been able to hear the sharp whistles of steamboats.

Kintarō found the view of the city refreshing, helping his daydreams to expand grandly. Japan was about to enter the era of its continental empire, fresh from its victories in the Sino-Japanese War of 1894–1895 and the Russo-Japanese War of 1904–1905. Kintarō had finally found success in this burgeoning port city. He had named his business the Yoshida Kintarō Company, and soon he planned to build his own house here on the heights. It might be an inconvenient distance from the busy city streets, but he felt it would be worth it to live with such a view over the city and harbor below.

For several years after their arrival in Pyongyang, the Yodogō hijackers devoted themselves to ideological study and self-review. Once they had abandoned their ideology of world transition, their only goal was to master the ideology of Kim Il Sung. They engaged in intensive group debates they deemed suited to a collectivist ideal and also studied alone at their own desks. The process of self-review was a repetitive cycle of self-criticism, followed by sessions of mutual criticism, then self-criticism again.

They kept their identity as members of the Red Army Faction for about a year, devoting much energy to developing and defending their Red Army theories and ideas, but they began to tire of this during the second year. After two full years, in 1972 they sent the letter in which they pledged their loyalty to Kim Il Sung. Thanks to the skillful handling of their instructors from the Workers' Party, they began to feel a little awkward. They did not want to join the ranks of the "people." Since they thought of themselves as a chosen elite, they naturally believed they would lead the revolution to liberate the people. They did not question the privileged status they held in North Korea or the affluence of their daily lives (which they could not have experienced had they remained in Japan). Even now, they believe their lifestyle befits their status as revolutionaries. Probably their enthusiasm for Kim Il Sung's ideology and philosophy of *juche* began in the summer of 1971, when they started reading his collected works. Some of them spoke of how they had "discovered the truth" of *juche.*

In order to assimilate themselves completely into the new ideology, they increased the intensity of their self-review process by deepening their mutual criticism. They pointed out each other's shortcomings and mistakes in repeated criticism sessions.

They soon stopped making criticisms regarding everyday matters. Certainly there was no end to the self-criticisms to be made about their day-to-day lives, but this did not seem sufficient. They felt that their criticisms should be aimed at far more fundamental matters and that the process needed to work at a deeper and broader level. They must try to reevaluate everything they had ever done in their lives up to that point. They invented a technique of self-criticism that took the past as a starting point that lent new energy to their self-reviews. They all examined their entire lives from the moment of their births, extracted the problematic points, and reanalyzed them from a *juche* perspective. Their comrades would listen and, in the next stage of mutual criticism, would point out other problems. In this way, their self-reviews continued in repeating cycles of analysis and criticism. Naturally, their family backgrounds and class origins also came under scrutiny.

Yoshida Kintarō's review would have included his family background and his reasons for trying to join the working class, his family's capitalist rather than working-class background, and their slide into financial ruin and hardship after World War II. Yoshida was not alone in these circumstances. Even if they were not from wealthy capitalist families, on questioning most of the Yodogō members admitted that their families were petit bourgeois, with bureaucrats, merchants, South Manchurian Railway Company employees, and regular office workers among their family members.

They were skillfully guided into this new type of self-review by their instructors. A characteristic of the North Korean class structure is the importance placed on the birth component, or one's family origins. This must have been behind the Workers' Party's motives for encouraging the group to take a new approach in their reviews.

The North Korean population divides into three general classes depending on family background. The first class includes the core ranks of all those loyal to the ideology of Kim Il Sung: the North Korean elite class, all the cadres of the North Korean Workers' Party, as well as all the people living in Pyongyang belong to this class. It also includes the workers, working farmers, poor farmers, intellectuals, bereaved families of patriotic soldiers, bereaved families of revolutionaries, bereaved families of those who died in the war, heroic soldiers, Workers' Party members, and worker-farmers, thirteen categories in all.

The second class includes unstable elements kept under surveillance and has twenty-seven subdivisions that include intellectuals, workers, wealthy farmers, and patriotic capitalists. Also in this group are families of defectors to South Korea, people stripped of Workers' Party membership, collaborators, people connected with spies, families of executed criminals, former political prisoners who were released after serving their terms, worshippers of superstition, financial criminals, returnees from Japan, middle-ranked farmers, small- and middle-ranked merchants, and people involved in service trades.

The third class is at the bottom and contains all the hostile elements kept under strict surveillance: former landowners, reactionary bureaucrats, pro-Japanese or pro-American sympathizers, members of the former Democratic Party, defectors to North Korea, Christians, Buddhists, capitalists, and counterrevolutionaries.

These subgroupings are not absolute, and sometimes the categories change for reasons of convenience. However, once one is branded as a capitalist or counterrevolutionary, there is no way one can return to one's former status. When the Yodogō group labeled Okamoto Takeshi as an "anti-Party, counterrevolutionary element," they meant he had gone counter to the Workers' Party, not their own Independent Revolutionary Party. The North Korean Workers' Party devised this very detailed structure based on family origins in order to more easily identify any undesirable elements that may have slipped into Party ranks. To cite another example from recent times, Pol Pot's political organization in Cambodia imposed a similar structure in which people were sorted into five classes in two main categories, "new people" and "old people." More than two million people were slaughtered on the premise of eliminating "internal enemies."

In North Korea, the class subdivisions are designed to expose "class enemies," "spies," and "anti-Party, counterrevolutionary elements," and anyone uncovered in this way suffers a predetermined fate. The process of self-review and criticism in which the Yodogō group engaged, highlighting and analyzing every detail of their lives and family backgrounds, was nothing more than an exercise designed to reveal any "anti-Party, counterrevolutionary elements" within their group.

Yoshida Kintarō was having a bad dream. In the dream, dark clouds hung over him, and something terrible was about to happen. When he was awakened by the noise of the wind, his body was shaking. He coughed and went downstairs to ask his wife for a drink of plain hot water. It was raining in Suwayama. His wife, heavily pregnant, was worried that the excessive rain might be bad for her health. That summer she gave birth to their sixth child. Kintarō was particularly charmed by this child, naming him Aiji, written with characters meaning "beloved child" or "loves what is right." Three months later, Count Itō Hirobumi was assassinated at the Harbin railway station in Manchuria by a Korean named An Jung Gun. Kintarō could not forget Count Itō's face, for he had seen the count many times when he had visited the hot spring baths at Suwayama. The following May, of 1910, the world seemed to have gone mad when twenty-six socialists were arrested for the attempted assassination of the Meiji Emperor in the Great Treason Incident. In August, Japan annexed Korea and established a colonial administration there. The year 1911 brought the promulgation of the Compulsory Purchase of Land in Korea Act and the fall of the Qing dynasty in China. The Meiji era was coming to an end.2

Suwayama was suffering under a fierce storm, with strong wind and heavy rain blowing down from the peaks of Mt. Maya and Mt. Rokko. It had been raining without a break since my arrival in Kobe. I had no choice but to spend another day going through official documents and papers, part of my search for information about that other Yoshida Kintarō.

First I investigated the business history of the Yoshida Kintarō

---

2. Japan counts historical periods by the era names of the reigning emperor in each period, so they vary in length. The Meiji era (1868–1912) is the period when feudal institutions were dismantled and Japan developed into a unified modern state that began to participate as an equal with Western nations. By these references in the imagined reflections of Yoshida Kintarō's grandfather at the end of the Meiji era, Takazawa points both to internal political instability and to Japan's growing position as a colonial power over other areas in Asia, including Korea.

Company during the late Meiji and Taishō periods.[3] I started by looking in Kobe company directories and registries from that period in the city public library and public archives. Yoshida Kintarō's name first appears in the fourteenth edition of the Japan *Who's Who* (1910). He is listed in the Kobe section as a securities dealer. I could find no earlier references, so his circumstances before this date remain obscure.

Yoshida's business, located at 1–17 Motomachi, was a forerunner of today's securities trading companies. It even had a telephone number, still rare in those days. Income taxes for the company the year before had totaled 34 yen. In the section for rice, stock, and securities sales brokers in the 1911 edition of *Kobe Commerce and Industry Records,* his business and income taxes for 1910 are given as 73 yen and 35 yen respectively.

Listed as either "Yoshikin Company" or "Yoshida Kintarō Company," the business, with its subsidiaries Yasuda and Nomura, continues to appear in the *Kobe City Commerce and Industry Directory,* the *Who's Who* listings, and the *Kobe Directory* until 1937. The 1926 *Kobe City Company Directory* names Yoshida as one of the directors of the Kobe Rice Exchange Corporation. His name on the board of directors is replaced by another's during the year of the so-called Showa Depression, but his financial condition must not have been too badly affected by the economic downturn because his name soon reappears on the list.

Yoshida launched his business ventures around 1904 or 1905, and he did very well in the buoyant economy following the Japanese victory in the Russo-Japanese War. The war may not have added directly to his success, but it was certainly a contributing factor. Business boomed in the years leading up to World War I. Kobe was full of so-called ship profiteers in those days, and naturally such a high-growth environment brought huge profits to a securities business like the Yoshikin Company.

Around the end of the Meiji period, Yoshida purchased a parcel of land in Suwayama with a fine view over the city below and built on it a magnificent Japanese-style house of cypress wood that became known as the Suwayama Palace. After the war, Hyōgo prefecture bought the building to serve as accommodations for prefectural assembly members, paying about three million yen in 1950. By then the house was no longer in the hands of the Yoshida family, as all the sales records show a seller with a different name. Yoshida apparently was a devout Christian and associated with Uchimura Kanzō and Abe Isoo. He was on friendly

_____

3. Taishō (1912–1926) is the era name for the period following Meiji.

terms with the social activist Kagawa Toyohiko and the Salvation Army's Yamamuro Gunpei, acting as their patron.[4]

Kintarō's sixth son, Aiji, was involved in the business as a son and heir, and he prospered. He often went from Kobe to amuse himself in the Gion district of Kyoto, traveling in a chauffeur-driven Rolls-Royce. It was there that he met and fell in love with Momomaru, a beautiful young *maiko*, a girl in training to become a geisha. World War II was rapidly intensifying around them, but this love affair in Gion blossomed. Aiji and Momomaru were married in Kobe near the end of the war.

However, the end of the war sank the Yoshida Kintarō Company. A searchlight factory purchased during the war years had been destroyed in an air raid, and the Occupation Forces requisitioned their large house in Ashiya, just outside of Kobe. Finally, Aiji and Momomaru moved to Kyoto, settling in the familiar working neighborhood of Gion and operating a tiny shop selling skewers of grilled meat. People often saw Aiji walking along, carrying shopping baskets. In February 1950, they had a son.

The new father, remembering more prosperous days, named the child Kintarō after his grandfather.

How did Yoshida Kintarō answer questions about his background during the self-review sessions in Pyongyang?

He probably felt the distant past was irrelevant to his present life. On graduating from high school, he had not gone to college, choosing instead to go to work in a shipyard. Probably he did not want to be a financial burden to his parents. He worked as a painter in the Osaka shipyard in Sakai, where his participation in union activities led him into the left-wing movement. He joined the Antiwar Youth Committee (Hansen Seinen Iinkai),[5] an antiwar organization under the All Japan Industrial Workers Union that was associated with the New Left student movement, at a time when the Zenkyōtō movement was at its peak.

Yoshida joined the *Yodogō* hijacking as a natural extension of his protest activities. He carried along with him a book called *Korean in Four*

---

4. All four of the individuals were leading liberal intellectual and social figures in the Meiji era, and all were Christians.

5. Antiwar youth committees were sponsored by the Socialist Party to bring young workers into the antiwar movement. Although some such as Yoshida's were actually affiliated with labor unions, New Left students often organized antiwar youth committees in neighborhoods where young workers at nonunionized small and medium-sized companies lived. Takazawa himself organized one in southwest Osaka.

Weeks. He was a conscientious person and felt that he should study the language even if they were planning to stay only for a short while.

His dutiful nature was visible in other ways, too, not only when he was engaged in political actions. He went with some friends to visit his parents before the hijacking, around the tenth of March. Yoshida enjoyed some of his mother's cooking, and, when he left, he bowed formally to his father, saying, "Thank you for everything you have done for me."

His mother followed after and called out to him, but Yoshida only looked back briefly as he hurried off. He had said his farewells.

The Yodogō group's self-evaluations continued.

Only one thing had really changed as a result of the review process. Now the Party instructors had a very good idea of each member's personal history and family background. Of course, additional background checks were conducted on them, since the Workers' Party could not simply trust the Yodogō hijackers, given the circumstances of their arrival. Was it really possible that they had flown to North Korea only in order to receive asylum? There is no doubt the Workers' Party ordered their agents in Japan to be thorough in their investigations.

There would have been a day when Yoshida was suddenly requested to review the circumstances of his birth and family lineage. This demand would have come from the Party instructors watching over the process. The Yodogō members knew little to nothing of each other's grandparents or other relatives; before coming to North Korea, they hadn't even known each other's real names.

Asked about his family, Yoshida likely found himself at a loss. Born and raised in a working-class environment during the impoverished postwar years, he would have found it difficult to answer the sudden questions about a grandfather born in the Meiji era. The family in which he had grown up was in no way either capitalist or bourgeois. Anyway, Yoshida could not answer the Party instructors' questions. Perhaps he never understood why he was ordered to pursue such a line of self-review.

From our point of view, it seems natural to conclude that he could not answer the questions put to him because he found it impossible to analyze something about which he knew nothing. Yoshida's North Korean instructors, however, who valued their genealogies more than their own lives, could never have accepted that he did not know anything about his own grandfather. The problem lay in the issue of how family background determines social status in North Korea: as the son

Figure 33.01. Burning of the *Sherman,* photo of painting in the Museum of the Korean Revolution, Pyongyang, Democratic People's Republic of Korea. Photo from published catalog of the Museum of the Korean Revolution in Takazawa Collection.

Figure 33.02. Yodogō group press conference in Pyongyang, May 1, 1972. From right front, Okamoto Takeshi, Konishi Takahiro, Tamiya Takamaro, (unidentified person), Yoshida Kintarō, and Abe Kimihiro. At the far end of the table, the person on the right is Kim Yuchol. Photo from Kyōdō News.

and grandson of a capitalist, Yoshida Kintarō must also have been raised and educated as a capitalist. Even if he now showed no traces of it, he must still carry somewhere within him the mindset of a capitalist. So there remained only one possibility: he had joined the hijackers with a secret agenda of his own. According to the reasoning by which people were sorted into social classes according to family background, there was no other logical reason for Yoshida to have joined the labor protest movement.

This was not the only reason he came under suspicion. Yoshida had not entered university but had chosen instead to work. All the other hijackers had gone to university; why not Yoshida? The Party instructors feared he must have some hidden motive for his actions and that he must have insinuated himself in among the hijackers as a spy. His comrades could not provide satisfactory explanations when questioned on the matter, since they knew nothing about him. The instructors', and by extension the Party's, doubts and suspicions only grew deeper. The dynamics of psychological tensions within tightly closed groups can spin out of control like this, as we have seen with the killings in the United Red Army incident of 1972.[6]

We can still ask why: why did Yoshida become such a target? There is really only one good reason why he became the scapegoat for the Party's suspicions: he was unable to accept the ideology of Kim Il Sung and *juche.*

Again, why? I don't know the answer except that possibly he could see directly through the lies lurking in the ideology they were being made to study. His ordinary common sense would have inclined him to work among the people of North Korea rather than spend his time in the isolated and luxurious village of the revolution. He was the only hijacker with actual experience as a worker, the only one who had chosen to work over going to university, and he tried to preserve his sense of realism even in North Korea. He had no real desire to learn how to operate undercover or to become a hero. He had no wish to be involved in any conspiracy or espionage. Yoshida Kintarō had chosen to spend his life sharing the joys and sorrows of common men. This was his foundation, and with it he had no need for empty theories or ideas as a basis for thinking about activism and revolution in Japan. This is what makes me think that, of the nine hijackers, only Yoshida kept the interests of Japan

---

6. Takazawa is referring here to my analysis of the United Red Army incident in Steinhoff 1991.

in mind; only he remained loyal to the workers and the people until the end (*hi-tenkō*).[7]

I have already described how anyone who differs from them in ideology ceases to exist for the Yodogō group. This principle applied to Yoshida as well, though his case was special. Even if they had wanted to stand by him and to persuade him to rejoin them as their comrade, there was a clear obstacle preventing them from doing so: the painting of the *Sherman*.

The story of Kim Il Sung's grandfather, Kim Eung-u, and the role he had played in the burning of the *Sherman* made its first appearance around 1968. Many of the facts of this period are obscure, but Kim Il Sung had finally taken total power within the North Korean Workers' Party after purging all of his opponents one after another. The *Sherman* painting appeared soon after and became a regular feature in books and magazines from around 1972. With this, the legends surrounding the exalted revolutionary family and its revolutionary tradition solidified into fact. The catchphrases "family background" and "revolution in successive generations" were much heard. These events overlap with the period in which Kim Il Sung began to transfer power directly to his son, Kim Jong Il. Kim Il Sung needed the story of the revolutionary tradition of his exalted family to ensure a stable succession.

If all this is true, then the situation was obvious: nobody could afford to defend Yoshida. The other hijackers could only remain silent in the face of logic that insisted Yoshida must be a capitalist if both his father and grandfather had been capitalists. Speaking out would have been the equivalent of challenging the North Korean Workers' Party on one of its fundamental positions: that the children of revolutionaries grew up to be revolutionaries and the son of the Leader was destined to be the next Leader.

---

7. The term Takazawa uses is *hi-tenkō*, which means a person who refuses to give up his beliefs under heavy pressure to capitulate. It derives from the concerted efforts of the Japanese government of the late 1920s and 1930s to stamp out the small Japanese communist movement and later religious groups that refused to accept the emperor-centered state ideology. In addition to arresting such people, the state pressured them to renounce their deviant beliefs, a process they called *tenkō*. Those few who resisted the pressure were later valorized after the war. In the late 1960s, Japanese New Left students who were arrested and subjected to interrogation often called refusal to cooperate with their interrogators *hi-tenkō*. See my doctoral dissertation, "*Tenko*: Ideology and Societal Integration in Prewar Japan" (Steinhoff 1969).

Yoshida Kintarō stood alone and friendless.

Only those present know exactly what happened next. One day, Yoshida would have disappeared from the village of the revolution. I do not know whether the other Yodogō members took part in Yoshida's disappearance. All I know is that none of them will talk about it, whatever it was. From that day, a powerful taboo emerged in the Yodogō organization.

The incident cast a deep shadow over the hijackers' minds and hearts. They felt an overwhelming sense of emptiness as if a great hole had opened before them: "[Our theories]...seem increasingly hollow....We...have no idea what we should be struggling for, and our entire reason for existence [seems about to] disappear" (Tamiya et al. 1990, 190).

The feelings of emptiness they felt during the process of ideological remolding (described in chapter 6) were probably related to the complex emotions they experienced at Yoshida's disappearance. They threw themselves into the glorification of Kim Il Sung and his *juche* ideology. One of them had to be sacrificed so the remaining eight could complete the process begun in the thought remolding. This manipulation, of allowing them to live in luxury and privilege even as one of them paid the ultimate price, reminds me of the proverbial carrot and stick.

Their unspoken agreement about the necessity of Yoshida's sacrifice set them on a path of no return to become *juche* warriors. Their shared secret completed their transition from Golden Eggs to warriors of the creed. To this day, they remain the Great Leader's loyal soldiers by keeping to their pact of silence.

During my summer visit to Copenhagen and Tivoli, I purchased a copy of Hans Christian Andersen's *Fairy Tales*. As I strolled aimlessly along Strøget, I was suddenly struck by the idea of rereading the tale of the ugly duckling.

A duck sat on her nest waiting for the last egg to hatch. Finally, she grew tired of waiting. She thought, "It is just lying there doing nothing. I should just leave it, because it's time to teach my other eight ducklings how to swim!" But the egg finally split open, and out came a large and very ugly duckling. "It looks like a turkey chick! We will soon find out when it tries to swim!"...The other ducks talked about the ugly duckling. "Look at him! He's so ugly! He doesn't belong here!" One duck flew at him and bit him on the neck. The ugly duckling was bullied wherever he went.

One day, he went to see a wild duck. The wild duck said, "You are very ugly! I don't see how you are ever going to get married!" The duckling hadn't given any thought to getting married.... The duckling came to a dilapidated farmhouse where he was allowed to stay for a while. "Here is a good find," said the owner. "Now we can have duck eggs." But the duckling did not lay any eggs. The house belonged to a cat and a hen. Whenever they had the chance, they said, "We are the world!" They thought they were each one half of the whole world, and, secretly, each thought itself the better half. When they were together, they believed everyone in the world was there. The duckling thought there might be other points of view, but the hen would not allow it. "If there is anything you don't understand, you should ask Him," she said. "There is no one greater in the world! He knows everything!" The duckling said, "I don't think you understand me." "So tell me who does understand you! What a thing to say to us, who have only shown you kindness! You should be grateful and give thanks to Him for our kindness to you! You have been given a warm place to roost in, and we have taught you many different things! You will soon have to learn to crow, raise your children, and learn how to make sparks fly! All your brothers are already doing all these things!" It would be too sad to tell you here of all the suffering and unhappiness the duckling went through that winter....

At the end of Andersen's story, the ugly duckling realizes he is a swan and flies off into the sky. But in my own long story, the other eight ducklings and the hen send the ugly duckling to his death before he can turn into a beautiful swan.

Yoshida disappeared from the village when the Yodogō group members undertook the task of reviewing their individual pasts from the moment of their births. His political life had come to an end. There is no need for me to repeat here what this means in North Korea, since I have already described it several times. However, biological life can continue even after political death. I don't know when Yoshida's body died, and probably the Yodogō hijackers don't either. However long he continued on alone in that country, he would have seen with his own eyes the true North Korea, the one none of us can know anything about.

There was no funeral for Yoshida in 1985. When it became necessary for their machinations, Tamiya composed a fake eulogy for him, even though there seem to be hints that he was not entirely happy about the situation. When I reread the funeral address, one part seems out of place. The phrase "your name still uncleared" does not seem to fit in with the rest of the passage. Of course, Tamiya could be referring to some sense of disgrace the Yodogō group felt at being unjustly labeled criminals for their political activities during the student movement of the 1960s, but would they really have considered their actions, including the hijacking of the *Yodogō,* as disgraceful? Judging from their memoirs, the Yodogō members regarded their status as criminals for their involvement in the student movement and war protests as a point of pride, not of disgrace.

> ...Today we wish you a final farewell, *our hearts filled with a deep sorrow and a righteous anger.*...Along with deep sadness, *our hearts tremble* in righteous indignation....We can only imagine the regret you feel at dying in a foreign country, banished from your homeland, *your name still uncleared, your youthful devotion to justice looked upon as a crime. We are fiercely angry at those who forced your grievous loss. We will never forget these last moments when you finally had to close your eyes.* (Tamiya et al. 1990, 248–249; emphasis added by Takazawa)

Perhaps it is obvious what Tamiya meant when he regretted that Yoshida's name was "still uncleared." If I have to add anything, it might be to say that the words "deadly illness" could have been a metaphor for Yoshida's nonconversion to the *juche* way of thought. I can't help thinking that Tamiya was trying to telegraph a message in his wording.

In the winter twenty years after the Yodogō hijacking, Tamiya sent a message to Shiomi Takaya, who had just been released from prison. I read this message to a party gathered in the Kyoto University Hall next to the Kamo River. "I waited for you for a long time at Renoir. You did not come even at the time we had agreed upon....In the end, we came here. You, my brother, had to spend twenty years in prison. Had you been able to come with us, would things have been better, I wonder..."

Tamiya compares the twenty years Shiomi spent in prison to the twenty years the rest of them spent in North Korea. Which twenty-year sentence, in the end, was easier?

When the Great Hanshin Earthquake struck at 5:46 a.m. on January 17, 1995, an aging Japanese-style house in the Suwayama district of Kobe, known to the local children as the "Haunted House," collapsed with a roar. The earth rumbled and burning flames raged in the streets of Kobe for three days and nights. Pandemonium reigned, and people wandered dazedly all over the city. There was no one who knew the story of the fallen house.

On November 30 in the same year, Tamiya Takamaro died alone under strange circumstances in the winter-beset village of the revolution just outside Pyongyang. A flag was flown at half-mast, and his body was soon cremated. The death certificate noted only "heart attack" as the cause of death. It certified the death of the man who knew the entire story of the *Yodogō.*

EPILOGUE

Something about the man catches the attention of the police officer on duty at Ueno Park that day. The man is standing perfectly still, all alone. He doesn't seem to be admiring the flowering cherry trees, nor does he seem to be waiting for someone; nor is he about to leave. His instincts aroused, the officer watches the man from afar, memorizing his features. A gift bag from one of the big department stores hangs from his wrist. The man just continues to stand there for a long while.

Finally their eyes meet. The man stares directly toward the officer, his eyes unmoving. Uncomfortable, the police officer is the first to break eye contact. However, as he moves closer, he realizes the man is merely staring blankly without seeing anything.

The officer experiences a moment of disgust with himself for dropping eye contact first. Cherry blossom season always seems to give him strange ideas. Muttering under his breath in annoyance, the officer sets out to make his rounds of the park.

The man continues to stand perfectly still. He sees nothing of his surroundings but remains lost in thought, staring inwardly at his memories. Suddenly, he hears a voice murmuring in his ear:

O, flowers will fall
The flowers are falling . . .

That was in spring, on the peak of Mt. Moran. It was the voice of a slender man who had died at the beginning of the previous winter in a foreign land. Of all things, why was it his voice that rose again from the depths of all the memories?

"North Korea is a revolutionary society."

Where had he heard him say that? Was it at the Prater amusement park in Vienna? In the gondola of the ferris wheel? The streets of Vienna had glowed with dusky light.

"A lot has happened, hasn't it?" These were his words when we met again after twenty years.

"I will go and organize you-know-who, and then I am coming back to Japan!"

I guess it's been more than thirty years now since I heard him say that.

Suddenly the loud laugh of another man rings out from the darkness. He is laughing without restraint. It is him. The portraits that hang in every room, in every building, along every street of that other country shake and rattle with laughter that continues to fill the darkness, rolling on without stopping; dark laughter, echoing.

I have finally completed the task I set myself, of telling the whole, unhappy story of the *Yodogō* hijacking. The only thing left to say is that this is specifically the story of the Yodogō exiles, based on a variety of sources that include books, periodicals, government documents, and especially my own notes and tape recordings. I had originally intended to provide footnotes and references, but the documentation was so complicated that I decided to simplify matters and leave it all out. I have left in only those references that are fundamental to the story.[1]

I set out on my pilgrimage to discover the true story of the Yodogō after the hijackers' leader, Tamiya Takamaro, died suddenly in Pyongyang in the winter of 1995. My travels took me through Beijing, Yanji (Yeon'gil), Changchun, Moscow, London, Copenhagen, Madrid, Paris, Vienna, Belgrade, Sarajevo, Split, Zagreb, Bucharest, Bangkok....Much of this book was written on the road. My journey and the writing of this book made me rethink the meaning of my own experience of the 1970s and to question anew my own ideological beliefs.

T. K.

July 1998

---

1. For this English translation, references have been restored for direct quotes whenever possible.

AUTHOR'S AFTERWORD
FOR THE ENGLISH TRANSLATION

Even now Mori Yoriko sometimes becomes caught up in thinking of the circumstances surrounding the death of her husband, Tamiya Takamaro. She was left desperately alone to raise their two daughters, but now the girls have reached an age where they do not need so much supervision from her. She has never tried to bury the emptiness left by the loss of her husband, and there are times when she can't stop herself from becoming lost in her memories.

When she returned home after finishing work in the office in eastern Pyongyang on the day her husband died, Mori had felt something strange in the mood of the companions who were usually so friendly toward her. The previous evening, for some reason, Konishi Takahiro had told her to spend the night at the office, and Ogawa Jun and the others were reluctant to let her see Tamiya, behaving as if her return to the village was an inconvenience to them. She is filled with regret when she wonders if she might have been able to save his life had she hurried home sooner. Whenever she reviews the events of that day, she cannot avoid the conclusion that Konishi and Ogawa knew something was going on or that they had been told by the Party that they and their families must stay away from the village. Even worse, she is convinced that the Yodogō members must have been involved in some act of violence and that the friends who usually made sure she had a ride back to the village, no matter how late the hour, on that one day were under orders not to let her go near. She can never forget this.

I, too, have heard a hint of what really happened, from a cadre of the North Korean Workers' Party. At the time, I had crossed the Tumen River on my way from Longjing to Hunchun. I was there to tour and collect information on the Tumen River Special Economic Zone. In addition to economic reporting for a variety of magazines, I was reporting on events around Tamiya's death. In chapter 20, I wrote only that I could not let go of the feeling that the circumstances of his death were suspicious, but here I include excerpts from an article I later wrote on this subject for *Shūkan Shincho* in 2003.

Was the Leader of the Yodogō Hijackers "Purged" by Kim Jong Il?

Tamiya Takamaro died in Pyongyang on November 30, 1995. I thought this was strange news the moment I heard it. When I had last met him in Pyongyang only three months earlier, Tamiya had been just as energetic as ever, and nothing indicated that he might be unwell.

The year after his death, I visited North Korea again to tour the area near the borders between North Korea, Russia, and China slated for the development of the Tumen River Special Economic Zone. Several cadres of the North Korean Workers' Party were serving as our guides for the tour. As we traveled through Hunchun from Longjing toward the Tumen River, I spoke with a cadre I had known for years. We started out on the subject of the special economic zone, but gradually the conversation turned to the Yodogō members. Suddenly, this cadre said something unexpected.

"Do you understand why Tamiya had to die?" He fell silent after this enigmatic question. But I believe I understood: he meant that Tamiya had been killed....

During the remainder of my tour of the special economic zone, I puzzled over the reasons for his murder. Another hint had come from a different highly placed cadre in the North Korean government. In other words, I had the information from a source very near Kim Jong Il himself.

"A few days before he died, Tamiya was called to see Secretary Kim. I am not sure of the location, but at first they spoke quietly. However, the conversation grew louder, became an argument, and finally their voices were audible to others outside. Their shouts could be heard in the hallway outside."

Could there have been such a confrontation between the dictator and the exile under his protection? It is difficult to believe the story, but, if true, it is enlightening.

I have asked the Yodogō members if they ever met Kim Jong

Il. They answered, "Whenever we had an audience with Chairman Kim Il Sung or when he advised us, Kim Jong Il was always tripping along behind."

They did not feel that Kim Jong Il was so very senior to them. In addition, Kim Jong Il had played the role of matchmaker in the decisions of who would marry which of the women brought from Japan during Operation Marriage.

As a result, they felt on familiar terms with Kim Jong Il.

However, Tamiya made a fatal mistake. Chairman Kim Il Sung had died the year before, and the reins of total power had passed to Kim Jong Il. He was no longer the man who had only followed behind in the shadow of the great Chairman but had become the most powerful man in North Korea. Perhaps Tamiya had forgotten this fact.

Tamiya, perfectly fluent in Korean, may have raised his voice in argument when he disagreed with Kim Jong Il.

Such behavior would have been unacceptable to the golden boy of the Workers' Party. One did not argue with the Leader but accepted his every word without question. Such is "democracy" in North Korea.

There is no way to know whether the argument was over the issue of the Yodogō members' return to Japan or about the kidnappings of Japanese citizens. At the end of last year, Kim was widely reported to have said, "I think we should find out who would win in a fight between American nuclear weapons and our own." North Korea has defied the Nuclear Nonproliferation Treaty (NPT) and started down the road of developing its own nuclear capabilities. If he heard the word "nuclear," Tamiya would always start to shout.[1]

I find that the circumstances of Tamiya's death only become stranger the more I investigate.

The cause of death was given as heart failure, but no heart problems had ever come to light in any of Tamiya's regular health checks. Also, it is difficult to understand the actions of the Yodogō members immediately before his death.

Perhaps the surviving Yodogō members know what really

---

1. Like many Japanese, Tamiya was deeply opposed to nuclear weapons, and he had promoted the Yodogō group's role in the antinuclear campaign in both Europe and Japan.

happened to Tamiya. Or perhaps they had only received strict orders from the Workers' Party that no one was to return home that night. There is little doubt they were in some way involved in the "purge."

"Do you understand why Tamiya had to die?" Seven years later, this enigmatic question still rings in my ears. (*Shūkan shinchō* 48 [January 30, 2003]: 44–45)

It was with a sigh of relief that I finally returned to Beijing from my visit to the Tumen River and Yanji. I was finally able to relax. I went to a Japanese-style karaoke club in a new entertainment district in Beijing and requested the song "A Hill in a Foreign Land." Before the song began, I said to the hostess in a low voice, "This is for Tamiya Takamaro, who died in Pyongyang."

> Today too darkens on a hill in a foreign land
> Friend, I am cold, I am cold

I have heard that this song was first sung in the prison camps of Siberia.

At the dark end of 1989, I traveled through Beijing to visit Pyongyang. I had no idea at the time that it was the start of a new story for me. After that first visit, I returned again and again to meet with the Yodogō hijackers. In 1995, in a Pyongyang filled with the rustle of late autumn leaves, group leader Tamiya Takamaro died suddenly. His death moved me to travel the world tracking their trails so that I might tell their full story. I can't deny I sought to write a requiem to Tamiya. But it did not take long for real history, surpassing any attempt at commemoration, to make itself clear. I became more deeply engrossed in the study of North Korea.

All through the writing of this book, I have been thinking about the relationship between fiction and nonfiction. I have come to the conclusion that nonfiction does not just hold a position in contrast to that of fiction, but it provides luxuriously fertile ground to build "tales" from the "truth." Everything in *Destiny* is based on reported facts; I have only used the techniques of fiction to add the details not found through such reporting.

Kodansha awarded the book the Twenty-First Annual Award for Nonfiction on behalf of Japan's publishing industry. When I received the prize, committee members such as Tachibana Takashi said many kind things, but I was especially gladdened by Henmi Jun's comment about it as "a work that takes on the issue of whether it is possible to write nonfiction." During a recent visit to Yarimizu, deep in the mountains of Hachiōji in Tokyo's southwestern suburbs, I was thinking about the fact that one of Henmi's early books had been about this area. I was struck by the realization that it was from this writer, who in her youth traveled the area in search of its Edo period history, that I had long ago learned the basic technique of personally visiting places before I wrote about them.

That was probably why her words made me so happy. It would not be exaggerating to say that her teachings had resulted in my chasing the trail of the Yodogō hijackers all over the world. Walking is the basis for writing nonfiction, and, whether you are making a living on your feet or only looking around, walking to exhaustion doesn't mean there is anything to gain for the effort other than the satisfaction of being tired. But we continue to walk in search of that moment of catharsis. Such is the fate of the nonfiction writer.

Long ago in ancient China, three men competed to decide who would drink a large cup of wine. They decided that the one who could paint the best picture of a snake would be the winner. Once they had agreed on this, the men began their paintings. One of them painted so quickly that he noticed only when he had finished that he had given his snake legs. He shouted out that the snakes in the other paintings had no legs! And he grabbed the wine and drank it down in one gulp. This is the origin of the expression "legs on a snake." This chapter is kind of like the legs on the snake. The book *Destiny* is quite complete as it stands. It doesn't need an appended epilogue. Really, the only needed additions are a few items I made note of in the days immediately after the book was first published. Please read them in that spirit, as additions as unnecessary as legs on a snake. In another version of that story, the man says, "Those aren't legs, they are claws!" I do not intend the following to be claws.

Note 1: In the last scene of the book, Yoshida Kintarō's old house in Kobe collapsed at a certain date and time that all Japanese recognize as the date and time of the Great Hanshin Earthquake. It was the second enormous earthquake to destroy a Japanese city, the first being the 1923 earthquake in Tokyo. I visited Kobe just afterwards, on a quest to visit the old house, but there was nothing left of it but the stone doorstep and the trees in the garden.

Note 2: I thought I should share the following lame and ridiculous counterarguments that the Yodogō group in North Korea communicated to me through their supporters. They seem to have made no serious effort at all: First, I wrote that Mori Yoriko's Spanish teacher had said, "She was a relatively good student of Spanish." I don't need to explain the lameness of their rebuttal that "Mori Yoriko does not speak Spanish all that well." Second, in response to my statement that they paid about 60,000 yen in rent for the apartment they leased in Madrid, they write, "Actually it was closer to 58,000 yen." Third, on the snapshot of Kuroda Sakiko and Mori Yoriko with Ishioka Tōru taken in the Barcelona Zoo, they claim, "We took lots of pictures in lots of different places with lots of different people. We just happened to take one with Ishioka Tōru." Who believes that? Especially since, a month later, a cover-up postcard from Vienna arrived at Ishioka's parents' house, written in his own hand and stating that he would "go to Spain next." "So doesn't that mean that this Ishioka person went on to Spain?" I am only passing on what they said themselves.

Fourth, in the epilogue, I wrote a scene of a man holding a paper shopping bag, standing below the cherry trees in Ueno Park, staring without seeing the scene in front of him. He was lost in his memories, there beneath the blooming trees. Of this, North Korea (i.e., the Yodogō group) had only this to say: "The man is certainly Takazawa himself." I don't think any junior high school language arts teacher would give them a grade of "satisfactory" for that. This figure is the "I" who makes his appearance again and again in the story, sometimes in closeup, sometimes seen only from afar. He stands under the cherries, holding a paper shopping bag, waiting for Tamiya as agreed. On a scene of such symbolic importance, all they seem to have to say is "it is just the writer absentmindedly staring at some flowers." The language arts teacher would give it a big red "X." Later in the same episode, in a scene in Vienna, I used a device from classical Japanese poetry in which a poem may "borrow scenery" that links it to another poem and gives the new poem added layers of meaning. In this part, Tamiya and "I" are riding together on the great Ferris wheel in Vienna's Prater fairgrounds, and he says, "North Korea is a revolutionary society." This scene links with irony to a famous episode in Orson Welles' movie *The Third Man*, in which the boss of a gang of drug dealers talks to a reporter as they ride on the same Ferris wheel, the streets of the city visible in the background. As the movie reveals, everything the drug boss says is a mass of lies.

When *Destiny* was first published, even the North Korean govern-ment responded, despite its track record of remaining silent in the face of all criticism. A booklet appeared, titled *Our View against Takazawa's "Destiny,"* written by a Yodogō member but obviously under the direc-tion of the Workers' Party. The book bears the logo Kari no Kai Booklet,[2] but most likely it was published directly by the Party. In it Wakabayashi wrote: "A stooge is destined to be useless. If something is useless, it will be discarded, so a stooge will do anything to impress his betters. He will pile up his crimes, starting perhaps only with ten but soon increasing them to a hundred, even to a thousand evil deeds. Such is *Destiny.* To someone of any degree of sensitivity or decency at all, it would feel like being stuck in an anthill from hell" (Wakabayashi and Abe 1999, 70–71).

These words were probably written with the intention to criti-cize me, but in fact they perfectly illustrate the Yodogō group's current circumstances. Behind them, I can hear a cry of "Alas!" Wakabayashi wrote, "A stooge is destined to be useless. If something is useless it will be discarded." Accordingly, North Korea, until recently so generous in its economic support and political protection, has now discarded the Yodogō group as a useless burden. Perhaps there was only one evil act to begin with, but now the group's misdeeds have multiplied to ten, to a hundred, even to a thousand, and now, again using their own words, they are about to be "discarded." They have kidnapped, purged their own comrades, and hidden behind a cover of antinuclear protest while working to advance North Korea's own nuclear capability: unimaginably evil acts, all the while showing a falsely sincere face to the world. Yet now they have reached the limit of their usefulness and are to be thrown aside by those for whom they worked.[3] It is a picture-perfect portrait of

---

2. "Kari no Kai" is the organizational name under which the Yodogō group wrote a monthly report in the *Kyūen* newspaper during this period, reporting on the current status of their efforts to return to Japan and other matters.

3. There was a short period in 2000 when North Korea wanted to get off the U.S. list of countries supporting terrorism in order to obtain much-needed aid and indicated a willingness to send the hijackers home. The Yodogō group sud-denly announced that they were willing to return to Japan even if it meant going to jail, in order to avoid endangering their hosts with the threat of an American attack on North Korea. None of it ever happened, and several of the hijackers and members of their families remain in the "village" to this day, but this is what Takazawa is alluding to.

the fate of mediocrity. We are reminded of the harsh reality of the dictatorship in which they live when, despite their unhappy circumstances, they must still continue in their expressions of warm praise and loyalty to Kim Jong Il. My heart aches when I think of sitting in a restaurant in Beijing with one of the group members who remains in North Korea, his shoulders shaking and voice tearful as we spoke of Japan. He had joined the hijacking plot immediately after being released from jail for participating in the battle at Tokyo University. Maybe that battle had been the impetus.

When *Destiny* was awarded the prize for nonfiction, many of my good friends and respected colleagues gathered for a party. Unfortunately, shortly before the party, my friend and mentor Shima Shigeo was struck down by a stroke. Confined to a hospital bed while he underwent testing, he was unable to attend the party. Instead he composed a message titled "Takazawa Kōji receives a prize for nonfiction." Here is what he wrote.

> I am one whole zodiac cycle of twelve years older than Takazawa, so of course our experiences as youths and our experiences of struggle are different. Since that time, our adult lives have been spent in completely different conditions, so I don't really know all that much about his life and work these days. I can't claim to be qualified to critique this brilliant, prize-winning work, but two or three things stick in my mind concerning our previous meetings and my reading of this book, and I wish to include them in my note of congratulations.
>
> One day near the end of 1995, Takazawa suddenly visited me at my home on a small island off northern Okinawa. Our conversation wandered somewhat, though I did not ask what he was working on at the time. Suddenly the subject arose of Tamiya Takamaro, whose death had only recently been in the news.
>
> I had long felt a strong dislike for the little Stalinist dictatorship, and I muttered, "I bet they've purged Tamiya, too."
>
> A moment of silence fell between us, abruptly broken by Takazawa. He said shortly, but with meaningful emphasis, "I have finally decided I have to confront North Korea and the Workers' Party."
>
> I knew that Takazawa had already visited North Korea sev-

eral times to meet directly with the original hijackers and their wives, but I was also aware of some of the clandestine activities North Korea sponsored in Japan. In the face of his determination, I said only, as casually as I could, "Please, be careful."

When *Destiny* was published, I realized that Takazawa must have embarked on his pilgrimage around the world very soon after our meeting. As I read through the pages recounting the years of his struggle to uncover the story, my vivid memory of our impromptu meeting on that southern island kept seeping through the lines. It seems to me that when the Yodogō conspirators felt eyes watching them from behind, they were in fact sensing Takazawa himself pursuing his investigations. At least for now, his exhausting obsession has been satisfied and its result given a well-deserved reward. For this and in relief that the entire matter has been revealed to the public, I offer from afar the most enthusiastic applause.

This work is of immediate relevance to us all. It is also a strong warning to a dictatorship that wishes to exert its distasteful influence on Japanese and international politics. Finally, it is a riveting story of international conspiracy surpassing any fictional account. Yet I cannot help but also read in this account of the Yodogō exiles' foolish and sad lives over twenty-seven years, steeped in such extensive research and documents, a refraction of the anguish of the author Takazawa Kōji's own life, which has been lived painfully alongside theirs. His short biographical sketch above the publication information on the very last page of the Japanese edition notes simply that he "was involved in the Zenkyōtō movement." I am not very familiar with the details of his involvement in those years, but I do not believe that part of Takazawa's life can be condensed into such a short phrase and simply dismissed. The era of the 1970 student movement has long ago been ripped apart and thrown to the winds, but Takazawa, who during that brief period undoubtedly devoted himself completely to the struggle alongside Tamiya, Shiomi, Konishi, and all the others, has spent his entire life ceaselessly pondering deep in his heart the meaning of his youthful experiences. This book represents one form in which his quest has finally come to fruition. It is also expressed in Takazawa Kōji's role as the editor of the seven-volume anthology titled *Bunto no Shisō*,[4] whose publication was finally completed just as this prize was being awarded.

This was no ordinary reporter, watching and chronicling from the outside as he tore away the veils of secrecy one by one to expose the activities of the nine men over the twenty-seven years since the hijacking. It could be said that *Destiny* began when Takazawa embarked on an inner journey of his past, ruminating on his own ideas and actions as he fought side by side with the men who became the Yodogō hijackers. These hijackers belonged to a political group known as the "Communist League Red Army Faction." Their ideas can be traced back to Bund, the original Communist League of 1960. If we count from when the planning for the anthology began, Takazawa spent a total of seventeen years editing the entire history of Bund, which was the birthplace of the Red Army Faction. While I was involved with the project, his determination filled me with amazement and at the same time gave me a strange feeling. Reading *Destiny* cleared up some of the mystery. This work began as a mourning pilgrimage for Tamiya Takamaro, but is it not also the outcome of a long journey of the heart that Takazawa finally achieved when he reached his fifties?

---

4. Shima Shigeo (1931–2000) was a student leader at Tokyo University and secretary-general of Bund from 1958 to 1961, who became a psychiatrist and was deeply involved in the New Left–inspired movement for community psychiatry. In 1958, under Shima Shigeo's leadership, much of the national student leadership of Zengakuren (All-Japan Student League) split from the Japan Communist Party and formed an independent New Left organization called the Communist League, nicknamed Bund. Bund controlled the Zengakuren mainstream that played a major role in the 1960 Anti–Security Treaty protests. During the 1980s, Takazawa worked with Shima and other early leaders of Bund to edit and publish a definitive multivolume reprint collection of the materials that Bund had produced in the late 1950s and early 1960s. Editing these volumes during the 1980s brought Takazawa into close contact with this earlier generation of student leaders who were the revered elders of the revived "second Bund" that Takazawa participated in during the late 1960s protests, which then gave birth to the Red Army Faction. Shima's comments point both to this direct legacy of overlapping student movement generations affiliated with Bund and to the depth of Takazawa's knowledge about the New Left student movement as a result of his immersion in these materials. Both the published seven-volume work and many of the materials that were not selected for inclusion were later donated by Takazawa Kōji to the Takazawa Collection at the University of Hawai'i.

Exactly twenty years after the Yodogō hijacking, Tamiya sent a message to Shiomi on his release from prison. "I waited for you for a long time. You did not come....In the end we came here. You, my brother, had to spend twenty years in prison. Had you been able to come with us, would things have been better, I wonder?"

I think perhaps, while reading these words, in his mind Takazawa felt his own image float and blend together with those of his former comrades.

—Shima Shigeo, Okinawa, Setoko Island

I clearly remember that day. I called on impulse from a street phone in Naha, then flew up the brand-new highway in a taxi, taking the Setoko Bridge from the Motobu Peninsula to the island that lay not far off shore. After a long conversation with Shima and an enjoyable walk along the nearby beach looking out at the sea, I returned to Naha that same day. Looking back, I know that was the day my pilgrimage began. Hasebe Hideo has written that the Bund was no longer involved in the conflict between communism and capitalism, and the poet and philosopher Yoshimoto Takaaki has said that the Bund under Shima Shigeo adhered to neither "the Soviet nor the Chinese model, but rather was an independent entity." When Shima accepted my statement that I must confront North Korea, it was his ideas of "world historical meaning" and his leadership ability that gave me the courage to begin the task. I stared out over Setoko's northern Okinawa sea for a long while, then went to a beachside marine shop and called a taxi to take me back across the Setoko Bridge. Okinawa island stretches from north to south, and the highway travels in the same direction. As we sped through the forest that covers that part of the island, a bird suddenly flew out and hit the windshield, making the driver cry out in surprise. I remember the moment clearly.

We crossed the city of Naha to the airport, and I flew to Osaka. It was the beginning of my pilgrimage, my research journey, my travels in mourning for Tamiya Takamaro. As the airplane approached the Yamato region, a bad omen announced itself when the fuselage began to shake and shudder. We were flying over the tombs of the ancient emperors, and the shaking was bad enough to be caused by the spirit of Emperor Nintoku himself. I stared out into the strong wind and rain, and felt a strange mood envelop me as I remembered stories about the "storm demons."[5] Perhaps this was a parting gift as I began my endeavor.

This essay may well be nothing more than feet on a snake, but at the very least it allowed me to introduce Shima Shigeo's message and to speak of the meaning of "walking the site," Henmi Jun's view on writing nonfiction. These were my main desires here.

---

5. The legendary Emperor Nintoku is thought to have reigned in the late fourth century and is also thought to be buried in the world's largest tomb, a keyhole-shaped earth mound in the Sakai area very near Osaka airport that is administered by the Imperial Household Agency and has never been excavated. The keyhole shape of these huge earthen mounds can be seen from the air, but at ground level it just appears to be a wooded park surrounding a mound. Japanese early mythology includes storm and thunder gods that were the offspring of the original gods credited with creating the Japanese islands. Storms could be viewed as evil omens brought on by the gods. These storm gods also appear in Japanese popular culture as characters in contemporary manga and video games.

EDITOR'S AFTERWORD:
THE YODOGŌ SAGA CONTINUES

The saga of the Yodogō group has continued in real time since *Destiny* was published in 1998. Both Kim Il Sung and his son Kim Jong Il have died, and the country now ruled by Kim Jong Il's son Kim Jong Un is still under the tight control of the North Korean Workers' Party. News of the Yodogō group crops up periodically in the Japanese mass media when those still in Pyongyang or their supporters in Japan make some public announcement. There was a great flurry of attention when Kim Jong Il admitted in 2002 that thirteen Japanese had been abducted to North Korea, and the three persons that Takazawa had traced to the Yodogō group's operations in Europe were on the list of abductees but reported to be deceased.

Legal proceedings in Japan have also kept them in the news periodically. The group members still in North Korea and their supporters in Japan continue to publish newsletters, pamphlets, and articles in various venues. In addition, several people associated with the group have published books about their own experiences. I will not attempt to cover all of this material in the present chapter. Instead, I will briefly follow up on the stories of those members who were already outside of North Korea at the conclusion of *Destiny* and summarize where the others are now, providing references to the books by members of the group and scholarly work in English. I include a small amount of additional information that Takazawa has given me over the past few years as I was preparing to write this chapter. With the publication of *Destiny*, he has generally managed to put what Shima Shigeo called his "obsession" behind him, yet he has continued to pursue a few loose ends. Some of these have led him to revise his earlier views.

Shibata Yasuhiro

The first of the Yodogō hijackers to return to Japan, Shibata Yasuhiro, was arrested in May 1988 under the name of Nakao Akira. When his identity was confirmed a few days later as Shibata Yasuhiro, he was arrested again on charges related to the hijacking. In 1970, there was no law against hijacking, since it had been the first such event in Japan, so the charges were for the "theft" of an airplane and the "detention" of the passengers, along with some charges relating to his earlier participation in the Red Army Faction's guerrilla training operation at Daibōsatsu in the fall of 1969. As a high school freshman, Shibata had run away to join the newly formed Red Army Faction in the summer of 1969 and had lived as a member of Tamiya's underground "army" until he left for the hijacking in March 1970. Since he was a minor at the time he left Japan, his picture and name had been kept out of the massive publicity surrounding the hijacking, and he was far less well known than the other participants. When his first trial ended in December 1990, Shibata received a five-year sentence, with two years off for time he had already served in unconvicted detention. This sentence was confirmed on appeal, and he served the three remaining years. Although Yao Megumi had never been entered in Shibata's family register as his wife, she divorced him while he was still in prison. After he was released, he went back to his family in Kobe and began working there. It had been clear from fairly early in his trial that he did not intend to return to North Korea, but he remained in contact with the Yodogō group. In Japanese news reports he is referred to as a "former member" of the Yodogō group. Shibata died in Kobe in June 2011 at the age of fifty-eight.

More recently, Takazawa has discovered a link between Shibata Yasuhiro and Arimoto Keiko, who was apparently his high school classmate in Kobe. Shibata had close personal relations with a teacher at the school who was connected to a *juche* study group in Kobe. It was through that connection that Yao Megumi was later able to meet Arimoto in London.

Yao Megumi

Destiny left Yao Megumi happy that she had obtained a family registration for her two daughters,[1] so that she could begin the process of bringing

---

1. Legal status as a Japanese citizen and national is based on a person's inclusion in a family registry (*koseki*), which is maintained by the government

them to Japan. Unfortunately, things were not as simple as she had hoped, because the Yodogō group had its own plan for returning the children to Japan. Yamanaka Yukio of the Relief Contact Center (Kyūen Renraku Sentā) had helped her begin the process, but he was working closely with the Yodogō group, and they wanted the children to return in a particular order. They also objected strongly to the fact that Yao had entered the children in her own family register. Following patriarchal North Korean ideas as well as Japanese tradition, they thought the children should be placed in the family register of their father, Shibata Yasuhiro. To do otherwise would stigmatize them as illegitimate children. In 1998, Yao filed a short-lived civil lawsuit in Tokyo District Court against the Yodogō group in Pyongyang and Konishi Takahiro as its leader, demanding the release of her children, which I have written about in some detail elsewhere based on *Destiny* and my own research (Steinhoff 2004).

Yao became quite close to Takazawa while he was working on *Destiny* and provided insights that helped him put the pieces of the story together. He helped her write a three-part magazine article about her unhappy marriage to Shibata that coincided with the lawsuit. She later published a book about her life in which she writes in some detail about both her experiences in North Korea and her involvement with Arimoto (Yao 2002). She now lives quietly in Japan.

Tanaka Yoshimi

When *Destiny* was published, Tanaka Yoshimi was on trial in Thailand for possession and distribution of counterfeit U.S. dollars. His supporters in Japan as well as Japanese news media were able to visit him periodically in Thailand. During the trial it was reported that the U.S. Secret Service, which was investigating counterfeit currency produced in North Korea, had attempted to get both Tanaka and another codefendant to become informants for the United States. After they refused, the U.S. agents involved in the case pulled back their evidence, hoping this would lead to Tanaka's extradition to Japan to face arrest for the 1970 hijacking. Other irregularities in the trial included testimony that officials in Japan had apparently forged fingerprint identification linking Tanaka to the evidence by photocopying fingerprints they had on file. The trial

---

office serving the area of the family's permanent residence. This continuing document holds the legal registry of births, deaths, adoptions, and marriages that move persons in and out of a particular family.

in Thailand continued until June 1999, at which time Tanaka was found not guilty. Japan immediately sought to have him extradited, but legal proceedings stalled this effort for another year.

Then, in May 2000, Tanaka told the court in Thailand that he was ready to return to Japan voluntarily. In late June he was flown to Japan and immediately arrested. Over the course of the next two months he was interrogated and indicted on several other charges relating to incidents he had participated in as a Red Army activist before the 1970 hijacking. By then it was common practice in Japan for political offenders to be held incommunicado during the period of interrogation. Instead of being sent to unconvicted detention after the first indictment, he was rearrested and held for twenty-three days of interrogation on each new count. During the trial, Tanaka published a book about his experiences (Tanaka 2001). His wife, Mizutani Kyōko, was allowed to return to Japan while his trial was still proceeding, and their three children later joined her. He received a twelve-year sentence in 2002. Although Tanaka was greatly relieved and happy to have his family with him in Japan, he developed liver cancer while in prison and was given a humanitarian early release. He died January 1, 2007.

Return of the Yodogō Wives and Children

The remaining Yodogō wives in North Korea were Japanese citizens who had left Japan on Japanese passports and traveled back and forth on them. The passports of five wives had been revoked in 1988 while they were outside the country because of their documented contact with North Korean agents.[2] After their status as the wives of the Yodogō hijackers was revealed in 1992, international arrest warrants for passport violations were issued for all of them. In order to return to Japan, they had to petition the Foreign Ministry for temporary travel documents. The Yodogō group's supporters announced in October 2000 that they were seeking permission for Tanaka Yoshimi's wife, Mizutani Kyōko, to return to Japan on humanitarian grounds to assist with his trial and were also seeking travel documents for Kaneko Emiko and some of the

---

2. Akagi Michiko had joined the group later and married Ogawa Jun (see below). She was apparently not involved in the training and activities the group carried out in Europe, except for legal activities in Vienna. As a result, she did not have her passport recalled in 1988.

older Yodogō children. Both women returned in fall of 2001 along with the first three children. Abe Kimihiro's wife, Uomoto Tamiko, and Konishi Takahiro's wife, Fukui Takako, also returned within the next few years. Japanese authorities arrested all of the women on their return, but four of the five were able to settle the passport charges quickly by paying a fine. Kaneko Emiko faced additional charges relating to the kidnapping of Arimoto Keiko. Yao Megumi had cooperated with the Japanese police, and she testified for the prosecution in Kaneko's trial,[3] which deeply angered the Yodogō group. In order to get the Yodogō children into Japan, it was necessary to have them registered in the family registry of a relative in Japan. As Takazawa indicated in *Destiny*, this also required additional legal proceedings because the children had not been registered in Japan when they were born. Only after they had been entered in a family register could arrangements be made for them to get a temporary document from the Foreign Ministry that would allow them entry into the country. Efforts to bring them to Japan were delayed for several years because the Yodogō group insisted that they be given Japanese passports that would permit them to go back and forth between Japan and North Korea, and the Foreign Ministry was not willing to do that.

After working tirelessly on behalf of the Yodogō group to get the children admitted to Japan, and with many false announcements of success, Yamanaka Yukio of the Relief Contact Center was finally able to bring the first three children to Japan in April 2001. Following the Yodogō group's plan, the first to arrive were the eldest daughters of Konishi Takahiro (Konishi Takako), Tanaka Yoshimi (Tanaka Tomi), and the late Tamiya Takamaro (Tamiya Asaka). In Takazawa's view, these three were the most heavily indoctrinated in the North Korean *juche* ideology and thus could be sent to Japan most reliably. The remaining children were transferred to Japan over the next several years. The two daughters of Shibata Yasuhiro and Yao Megumi were subsequently entered into Shibata's family register and came to Japan in 2002 and 2004. They are living in the Osaka area with other Yodogō returnees, who have blocked all contact between Yao and her children. The two daughters of Okamoto Takeshi and Fukutome Kimiko were also brought to Japan during the same time. Their parents are reported to have died in North Korea and all

---

3. According to Takazawa, Kaneko was released after a brief trial on payment of an astounding 30 million yen, which was paid by North Korean sources. To save face because she had been involved in the same incident, police also arrested Yao but then released her without charges.

of their grandparents in Japan are now deceased, but they have contact with some Fukutome relatives in Shikoku.

Nearly all of the Yodogō children are now adults. Those who are not with their own mothers have been living collectively under the watch-ful eye of the Yodogō wives. Most of the young women live in Osaka under the supervision of Kaneko Emiko, whereas most of the young men live in the Tokyo area. Takazawa has described Kaneko in *Destiny* as a high-ranking cadre who acted like she owned the North Korean embassy in Zagreb, and he now sees her as exercising firm control over the Yodogō children living with her.

Although they attended schools in North Korea and were also given a Japanese education by their parents at the Yodogō compound in North Korea, the Yodogō children do not have the formal educational credentials that would allow them to pursue higher education in Japan. They are reported to be working at the types of low-paid service jobs open to those with limited education in Japan. Despite the efforts of the Yodogō wives to keep them in check, the children are still exposed to contemporary Japanese society and to ordinary Japanese people. Accord-ing to Takazawa, the younger daughter of Okamoto Takeshi and Fuku-tome Kimiko was working at a McDonald's in the Osaka area when she fell in love with a young male coworker who was in a motorcycle gang (*bōsōzoku*). She ran away with him, and they subsequently married and had a child.

In *Destiny*, Takazawa reported that a Japanese man using the pseud-onym of Ogawa Jun had joined the Yodogō group voluntarily after work-ing in Vienna on antinuclear protest activities along with Akagi Shirō's sister Michiko. They later married and joined the group in Pyongyang. In April 2003, Akagi Michiko was given permission to return to Japan along with her children. Once in Japan, she was able to register her husband in her family register as Akagi Kuniya. He arrived in Japan in June 2007 and was immediately arrested on suspected passport violations as well as possible involvement in the abduction of the three Japanese that the Yodogō group had found in Europe and lured to North Korea. Takazawa has learned that his original Japanese name was Yonemura Kuniya, but he used the name Ogawa Jun when he was with the Yodogō group.[4] Takazawa suspects that he was a trusted North Korean cadre who was sent to Vienna to keep watch on the group's activities there and that

---

4. The details remain murky, but this suggests that he may have been a Korean resident of Japan who had repatriated to North Korea earlier.

his marriage and entry into the Akagi family register were carried out in order to facilitate his entry into Japan. He observed that, although all of the other Yodogō children attended local schools and also a Japanese school that the group organized in the Yodogō compound, Ogawa and Akagi's children attended an elite nursery school for the children of high-ranking North Korean Workers' Party cadres in Pyongyang. Ogawa was also present during most of the taping of the final interviews with Tamiya that were published as *Talking about the Homeland and the People* (Tamiya and Takazawa 1996).

Who Remains in North Korea or Is Unaccounted For

As of 2016, only four of the original hijackers are still known to be alive, and all four remain in North Korea: Konishi Takahiro, who now leads the group; Akagi Shirō; Abe Kimihiro; and Wakabayashi Moriaki. With them are two of the wives (Mori Yoriko, wife of the late Tamiya Takamaro, and Kuroda Sakiko, Wakabayashi's wife), along with the younger son of the Wakabayashi couple, who is still a minor. There were already international arrest warrants outstanding for the two wives for passport violations, but in June 2007 the Japanese authorities added new arrest warrants for their participation in the kidnapping of Ishioka Tōru and Matsuki Kaoru. Although she remains in North Korea, Tamiya's widow, Mori Yoriko, has published her own memoir of her life with Tamiya (Mori 2003). In it she describes Yao Megumi as young, beautiful, and happily married to Shibata, and describes how she cared for Yao's young daughter for a year while Yao was away on an assignment. She seems bewildered by Yao's later actions against the group and suggests that she must have been "turned" by the Japanese police. The term she uses is *tenkō*, meaning an ideological recanting under police pressure. The book was published through Yodogō support groups in Japan, and contact information for three of the groups is listed on the copyright page of the book. In a short epilogue, she adds that Kaneko Emiko had been arrested on her arrival in her "homeland," Japan, and nine months later was still being held incommunicado. She bitterly blames Takazawa and Yao Megumi for turning against the group and slandering her husband's memory after his death.

The Japanese Foreign Ministry obtained further details on Ishioka Tōru and Arimoto Keiko from the North Korean government in 2004. Ishioka stayed in hotels in Pyongyang in June and early July 1980, and then spent a year in training and taught Japanese outside of Pyongyang until October 1988. Arimoto Keiko stayed in a hotel in Pyongyang for less than a month in July and early August 1983 and then spent a year in training outside of Pyongyang. From September 1984 to October 1988, she taught Japanese outside of Pyongyang. Arimoto Keiko and Ishioka Tōru were married on December 27, 1985, and later had a daughter, the baby in the photo that Ishioka sent to his family. At the beginning of November 1988, they reportedly requested a quiet place to stay and went to another city. The next day all three were found dead in their room of carbon monoxide poisoning from a charcoal heater. The North Korean authorities provided no photos or other documentation of their deaths but did include the weather reports for November 3 and 4. The Japanese government demanded answers to several questions and documentary evidence, but no further information has been forthcoming.

The North Korean government also acknowledged in 2002 that Matsuki Kaoru had been abducted to North Korea but later died. They handed over his remains along with those of Yokota Megumi.[5] DNA testing performed at Teikyo University determined that the remains were not those of either Yokota Megumi or Matsui Kaoru, but this finding was later contested in an article in the scientific journal *Nature* in February 2005. This ambiguity plus other conflicting information reported by North Korea has led some of the families of the abductees and their supporters to believe that they may still be alive.

Takazawa also continues to pursue the riddle of Fukutome Kimiko, who had no connection to North Korean ideology and simply wanted to go to Mongolia. Although he still does not know who may have been keeping close tabs on her family after she left, he has found the link that led to her being sent to North Korea. At the time, Mongolia was a closed country, so travel there was only possible through a "friendship association" that had the right political connections. To arrange her trip to Mongolia, she went to a travel agent who happened to be connected to the North Korean organization in Japan, Chosen Sōren, and she fell

---

5. Yokota Megumi was abducted from Japan on her way home from school in 1977, when she was thirteen years old. Many years later, a North Korean operative on trial in South Korea reported that she had learned Japanese from Yokota Megumi. Yokota was included in the list of thirteen persons that North Korea acknowledged as abductees but was reported to have committed suicide, leaving behind a husband and a daughter. She became the public symbol of the abduction issue and has been the subject of television documentaries, a manga series, and a related animation.

into their trap. He also now thinks that Fukutome and even her husband Okamoto Takeshi might still be alive. He has found slight traces of her after the time they were reported to have died in different scenarios and no longer believes the story that Okamoto tried to escape North Korea by sea. He was also able to find out from one of her old friends the name of the book she had been desperately searching for on her one brief trip back to Japan. The book is *The Spherical Wilderness* (*Kyūkei no kōya*) by the famous Japanese detective writer Matsumoto Seichō. I had no trouble finding it in Tokyo because it had been republished in 2003, but it might have been harder to find in the late 1980s. It was made into a movie in 1975 and has had several other dramatizations since then. A new two-part television dramatization was announced in 2010. It is an enigmatic tale about a Japanese diplomat who is thought to have died in Europe at the end of the war after being involved in some secret negotiations but comes back to Japan years later with a different identity and observes his grown daughter from a distance.

As of 2014, the once secret Japanese Village of the Revolution has been opened to visitors. Many of the facilities are no longer used, and one of the buildings has been turned into a guest house for friendly foreign visitors.

TIMELINE

YEAR	DATE	EVENT
1969	1/18/1969	Riot police end Tokyo University conflict after six-month strike
	8/28/1969	Founding of Red Army Faction after expulsion of faction from Communist League (Bund)
	11/5/1969	Guerrilla training exercise and arrest of fifty-three participants at Daibosatsu
1970	3/31/1970	Nine Red Army Faction members hijack domestic Japanese plane *Yodogō* and demand to fly to North Korea
	4/1/1970	Japanese Minister of Transportation Hashimoto Tomisaburō and Vice-Minister of Transportation Yamamura Shinjirō arrive in Seoul to negotiate
	4/2/1970	Message from North Korean Red Cross guarantees humane treatment and return of aircraft to Japan
	4/2/1970	Vice-Minister of Transportation Yamamura Shinjirō offers to serve as substitute hostage
	4/3/1970	Hostages on the plane exchanged for Yamamura Shinjirō
	4/3/1970	Socialist Party Diet member Abe Sukeya arrives in Seoul to serve as negotiator for the hijackers
	4/3/1970	"Party" aboard the plane, and Tamiya Takamaro recites "Kawanakajima"
	4/3/1970	Plane with hijackers and Yamamura Shinjirō aboard flies to Pyongyang
	4/3/1970	Hijackers arrive in Pyongyang after four days grounded at Kimpo Airport in Seoul, South Korea

YEAR	DATE	EVENT
1971	6/1/1971	Ideological remolding begins in earnest as hijackers question Red Army Faction ideas and begin to accept *juche* ideology
	12/31/1971	Hijackers send first letter to Kim Il Sung
1972	2/19/1972 to 2/28/1972	Asama Sansō siege in Karuizawa; five United Red Army members hold off three thousand riot police for ten days
	3/8/1972 to 4/1972	Revelation of United Red Army purge of winter 1971–1972 through interrogations of arrested United Red Army members
	4/15/1972	Hijackers send second letter to Kim Il Sung
	4/27/1972	Kim Il Sung interview with Japanese journalists
	5/1/1972	Nine hijackers meet with Japanese journalists
	5/6/1972	Kim Il Sung meets hijackers at village
	5/30/1972	Lod (Tel Aviv) Airport attack in Israel by three Japanese
	6/3/1972	Shigenobu Fusako announces "Arab Red Army" carried out Lod (Tel Aviv) Airport attack for Popular Front for Liberation of Palestine
	7/1972	Tamiya Takamaro invites Shigenobu and others to come to North Korea at request of Workers' Party
	12/1972	DPRK adopts new *Juche* constitution; Kim Il Sung becomes President and Head of State
1974		Ten Great Principles adopted by Central Committee of North Korean Workers' Party
1975	11/1/1975	Fukui Takako arrives in Pyongyang to reunite with Konishi Takahiro
1976	6/13/1976	Kuroda Sakiko leaves Japan to go to North Korea
	7/1976	Fukutome Kimiko leaves Japan for Mongolia but instead ends up in North Korea
	10/1976	Scandinavian countries expel North Korean diplomats for smuggling and illegal sales of cigarettes and liquor
	10/7/1976	Uomoto Tamiko leaves Japan to go to North Korea via Mexico

YEAR	DATE	EVENT
1977	1/25/1977	Kaneko Emiko leaves Japan to go to North Korea
	2/24/1977	Yao Megumi leaves Japan to go to North Korea
	3/29/1977	Mizutani Kyōko leaves Japan to go to North Korea via Hong Kong
	3/30/1977	Mori Yoriko leaves Japan to go to North Korea via Hong Kong
1978		Okamoto Takeshi begins working in Vienna on anti-nuclear campaign
		O! Japan begins publishing in Vienna in 1978; later moves to Japan as part of Yodogō group's public antinuclear activities
1979		Fukutome Kimiko's family receives letter mailed from Eastern Europe
	12/1/1979 to spring 1980	Yodogō wives arrive in Madrid, Spain
1980	3/1980	Fukutome Kimiko meets old friends briefly in Japan
	4/15/1980	Photo of Kuroda Sakiko, Mori Yoriko, Ishioka Tōru at Barcelona Zoo taken by Ishioka's traveling companion
	5/1980	Ishioka Tōru and Matsuki Kaoru abducted from Madrid via Vienna to North Korea
	6/1980	Mizutani Kyōko hospitalized after suicide attempt in Paris
	7/1980	Essay by Tamiya Takamaro "Ten Years since Leaving the Homeland" published in summer issue of *Shisha* as first account by the group since arriving in North Korea
	7/13/1980	Mizutani Kyōko sent to Japan by Japanese authorities after suicide attempt
	9/26/1980	Mizutani Kyōko leaves Japan and returns to North Korea via Copenhagen
	10/1980	Socialist Party Diet member meets Okamoto Takeshi in Pyongyang
1981		Yodogō group begins publishing *Nihon o Kangaeru* for distribution in Japan; continues until 1990

YEAR	DATE	EVENT
1982	5/21/1982	New Wave of Democracy group founded in Vienna as part of Yodogō group's public activities centered on antinuclear movement
1983	2/1/1983	Uomoto Tamiko arrives in Japan from Zurich
	4/1/1983	Kaneko Emiko arrives in Japan
	7/2/1983	Kaneko Emiko leaves Japan
	7/2/1983 to 7/6/1983	Tamiya Takamaro and Konishi Takahiro attend International Congress of Journalists against Imperialism and for Goodwill and Peace in Pyongyang, representing *Nihon o Kangaeru*
	7/10/1983	Uomoto Tamiko leaves Japan for Copenhagen
	7/16/1983	Arimoto Keiko abducted from Copenhagen to North Korea
	8/10/1983	Kaneko Emiko arrives in Tokyo
	8/14/1983	Kaneko Emiko leaves Osaka for Hong Kong
	8/22/1983 to 8/31/1983	Konishi Takahiro and Wakabayashi Moriaki attend Pan-African Youth Festival in Libya, representing *Nihon o Kangaeru*
	8/29/1983	Mori Yoriko arrives in Tokyo
	8/30/1983	Mori Yoriko leaves Japan for Sydney
	11/5/1983	Mori Yoriko arrives in Japan
1984	1/21/1984	Mori Yoriko leaves Osaka for Seoul
	3/17/1984	Kaneko Emiko arrives in Japan from Singapore
	5/1984	Shibata Yasuhiro arrives in Japan using passport in name of Ishioka Tōru, acquires passport for Nakao Akira
	7/3/1984	Mori Yoriko arrives in Osaka from Singapore
	7/21/1984	Kaneko Emiko leaves Osaka for Zurich
	9/15/1984	Kaneko Emiko arrives in Tokyo from Cairo
	12/22/1984	Kaneko Emiko leaves Osaka for Singapore
	12/25/1984	Mori Yoriko leaves Osaka for Seoul
1985		Socialist Party delegation meets three or four hijackers but not Okamoto Takeshi
	1/16/1985	Kaneko Emiko arrives in Tokyo from Brussels

YEAR	DATE	EVENT
	2/14/1985	Mori Yoriko arrives in Osaka from Seoul
	4/25/1985	Fukui Takako arrives in Tokyo from Vienna
	5/11/1985	Fukui Takako leaves Fukuoka for Hong Kong
	5/15/1985	Kaneko Emiko leaves Tokyo for Brussels
	5/15/1985	Fukui Takako arrives in Fukuoka from Hong Kong
	6/4/1985	Kaneko Emiko arrives in Osaka from Singapore
	7/1/1985	Yodogō group sends first letter to Prime Minister Nakasone seeking return to Japan
	9/10/1985	Mori Yoriko leaves Osaka for Seoul
	10/24/1985	Mori Yoriko arrives in Osaka from Amsterdam
	10/28/1985	Yodogō group sends followup letter to Prime Minister Nakasone's chief cabinet secretary seeking return to Japan
	11/9/1985	Kaneko Emiko leaves Osaka for Singapore
	12/7/1985	Mori Yoriko leaves Osaka for unknown destination
	12/12/1985	Fukui Takako leaves Tokyo for Rome
1986	5/15/1986	Kaneko Emiko arrives in Osaka from London
	6/5/1986	Mori Yoriko arrives in Osaka from Seoul
	8/7/1986	Shibata Yasuhiro, a.k.a. Nakao Akira, leaves Tokyo for Hong Kong
	8/17/1986	Kaneko Emiko leaves Narita for Hong Kong
	12/20/1986	Mori Yoriko leaves Osaka for Seoul
	12/29/1986	Kaneko Emiko leaves Tokyo for London
1987	1/12/1987	Mori Yoriko arrives in Osaka from Seoul
	1/13/1987	Kaneko Emiko arrives in Tokyo from Hong Kong
	3/10/1987	Mori Yoriko leaves Osaka for Seoul
	4/30/1987	Kaneko Emiko leaves Tokyo for Hong Kong
	5/8/1987	Kaneko Emiko arrives in Tokyo from Hong Kong
	8/3/1987	Kaneko Emiko leaves Osaka for Seoul
	9/7/1987	Kaneko Emiko arrives in Tokyo from Seoul
	12/16/1987	Shibata Yasuhiro, a.k.a. Nakao Akira, leaves Tokyo for Brussels

YEAR	DATE	EVENT
1988		Japan increases security in preparation for Seoul Olympics, with emphasis on terrorism threat from North Korea
	1/29/1988	Shibata Yasuhiro, a.k.a. Nakao Akira, arrives in Tokyo from London
	2/2/1988	Kaneko Emiko leaves Osaka for Hong Kong
	2/9/1988	Uomoto Tamiko leaves Tokyo for Hong Kong
	2/10/1988	Kaneko Emiko arrives in Osaka from Hong Kong
	2/16/1988	Uomoto Tamiko arrives in Tokyo from Hong Kong
	2/22/1988	Kaneko Emiko leaves Osaka for Singapore
	3/13/1988	Shibata Yasuhiro, a.k.a. Nakao Akira, leaves Tokyo for London
	3/24/1988	Shibata Yasuhiro, a.k.a. Nakao Akira, arrives in Tokyo from Amsterdam
	3/30/1988	Uomoto Tamiko leaves Tokyo for Singapore
	5/6/1988	Nakao Akira arrested in Kobe; identified 5/11 as Yodogō hijacker Shibata Yasuhiro
	5/16/1988	Kaneko Emiko arrives in Osaka from Singapore
	5/25/1988	Satō Keiko arrested by Kanagawa police; later identified as Yao Megumi
	6/1988	Japanese media sensationalize Yao Megumi as North Korean spy
	6/18/1988	Yao Megumi released by Kanagawa police
	7/1988	Yao Megumi files lawsuits against Japanese mass media for portraying her as North Korean spy; support group forms to help her
	8/6/1988	Japanese government recalls passports of Kaneko Emiko, Fukui Takako, Mori Yoriko, Mizutani Kyōko, and Uomoto Tamiko because of meetings with known North Korean operatives
	9/1988	Letter from Ishioka Tōru reaches his family in Hokkaido, reporting he, Matsuki Kaoru, and Arimoto Keiko are in North Korea
1989	5/1989	Shibata Yasuhiro trial begins in Tokyo
1990	12/20/1990	Sentenced to five years in prison and appeals sentence

YEAR	DATE	EVENT
1992	4/1992	Kim Il Sung tells Japanese journalists that Yodogō hijackers have wives and children
	12/1992	Shibata Yasuhiro sentenced to five years in prison with two years' credit for time already served
1994	7/21/1994	Shibata Yasuhiro released from prison
	7/1994	Kim Il Sung dies; Kim Jong Il succeeds him as supreme leader
1995	11/30/1995	Tamiya Takamaro dies in Pyongyang
1996	5/24/1996	Tanaka Yoshimi arrested in Cambodia for involvement in passing counterfeit U.S. dollars; taken to Thailand to stand trial for money laundering
1997		1980 photo of Ishioka Tōru and two Yodogō wives at Barcelona Zoo revealed during Japanese police investigations
1998		Yao Megumi sues Yodogō group for release of her children
1999	6/1999	Tanaka Yoshimi found not guilty by Thai court
2000	5/25/2000	Tanaka Yoshimi tells Thai deportation hearing he wishes to return to Japan voluntarily as soon as possible
	6/28/2000	Tanaka Yoshimi arrested on arrival in Japan and charged with *Yodogō* hijacking
2001	5/2001	Mizutani Kyōko, Kaneko Emiko, and three oldest Yodogō children return to Japan
2002	2/2002	Tanaka Yoshimi receives twelve-year sentence
2003	4/2003	Akagi Michiko and her children return to Japan
2004	1/2004	Two younger daughters of Tanaka Yoshimi return to Japan
2006	12/15/2006	Tanaka Yoshimi released from prison on humanitarian grounds
2007	1/1/2007	Tanaka Yoshimi dies of cancer in Japan
	6/2007	Ogawa Jun (Akagi Kuniya) returns to Japan and is arrested
2011	6/24/2011	Shibata Yasuhiro dies in Kobe
	12/17/2011	Kim Jong Il dies; Kim Jong Un becomes supreme leader

BIBLIOGRAPHY

Gold, Hal. 2003. *Neutral War: A Novel of Soul-Chilling Barter, Bioterror, and High-Stakes International Poker.* Guilford, CT: Lyons Press.

Mori Yoriko. 2003. *Itsumademo Tamiya Takamaro totomo ni* [Together with Tamiya Takamaro Forever]. Tokyo: Rokusaisha.

Sashō Henshū Iinkai. 1975. *Sekigun dokyumento* [Sekigun Documents]. Tokyo: Shinsensha.

Shigenobu Fusako. 1972. "Beirūto Tsūshin: Sekigunha no dōshi shokun narabini Rengō Sekigun no dōshi shokun soshite yūjintachi e!" [Communication from Beirut: To My Comrades in the Red Army Faction, My Comrades in the United Red Army, and My Friends]. *Moppuru tsūshin,* Tokubetsugō [Moppuru News, special issue], April 20, 1972, pp. 83–87, reprinted in *Sashō* [Visa], no. 4 (June 1972).

———. 2009. *Nihon Sekigun shi shi: Paresuchina to tomo ni* [Personal History of the Japanese Red Army: With the Palestinians]. Tokyo: Kawade Shobō Shinsha.

Steinhoff, Patricia G. 1969. "*Tenko:* Ideology and Societal Integration in Prewar Japan." Doctoral dissertation, Department of Social Relations, Harvard University.

———. 1991. *Nihon Sekigunha: Sono shakaigakuteki monogatari* [Japan Red Army Faction: A Sociological Tale]. Tokyo: Kawade Shobō Shinsha. Republished as *Shi eno Ideologii: Nihon Sekigunha* [Deadly Ideology: The Japanese Red Army Factions]. Iwanami Modern Classics Series. Tokyo: Iwanami Publishing Company, 2003.

———. 1992. "Death by Defeatism and Other Fables: The Social Dynamics of the Rengō Sekigun Purge." In *Japanese Social Organization,* edited by T. S. Lebra, pp. 195–224. Honolulu: University of Hawai'i Press.

———. 2004. "Kidnapped Japanese in North Korea: The New Left Connection." *Journal of Japanese Studies* 30:123–142.

————. 2012. "Japan: Student Activism in an Emerging Democracy." In *Between Protest and Passivity: Understanding Student Activism in Asia*, edited by M. Weiss and E. Aspinall, pp. 77–105. Minneapolis: University of Minnesota Press.

————. 2013. "Memories of New Left Protest." *Contemporary Japan, Journal of the German Institute for Japanese Studies* 25:127–165.

Suh, Jae-Jung, 2013. "Making Sense of North Korea: *Juche* as an Institution." In *Origins of North Korea's Juche: Colonialism, War, and Development*, edited by Jae-Jung Suh, pp. 1–32. Lanham, MD.: Lexington Books.

Takazawa Kōji. 1993. *Kanbojia, ima* [Cambodia, Now]. Tokyo: Shinchōsha.

————. 1995. *Onnatachi no Pyongyang: Yodogō Gurupu no tsumatachi* [The Women's Pyongyang: Wives of the Yodogō Group]. Tokyo: San'ichi Shobō.

Tamiya Takamaro. 1980. "Sokoku o hanarete jūnen: Pyonyan kara no messe-ji" [Ten Years since Leaving the Homeland: A Message from Pyongyang]." *Shisha* [Messenger], summer 1980, pp. 116–125.

Tamiya Takamaro et al. 1987. "Wareware ni totte Nihon to wa" [What Japan Is to Us]. *Nihon o kangaeru* [Think about Japan], no. 23, pp. 35–45.

Tamiya Takamaro, Konishi Takahiro, Wakabayashi Moriaki, Akagi Shirō, Abe Kimihiro, Tanaka Yoshimi, and Shibata Yasuhiro. 1990. *Hisho nijūnen: "Yodogō" de Choson e* [Twenty Years after Takeoff: To North Korea on the *Yodogō*]. Tokyo: Shinchōsha.

Tamiya Takamaro and Takazawa Kōji. 1996. *Sokoku to minzoku o kataru* [Talking about the Homeland and the People]. Tokyo: Hihyōsha.

Tanaka Yoshimi. 2001. *Yodogō, Chōsen-Thai soshite Nihon e* [Yodogō, North Korea–Thailand and Then to Japan]. Tokyo: Gendai Shokan.

Wakabayashi Moriaki and Abe Kimihiro. 1999. *Takazawa [Shukumei] ni taisuru wareware no kenkai* [Our View against Takazawa's *Destiny*]. *Kari no Kai Booklet*, no. 002.

Yao Megumi. 2002. *Shazaishimasu* [I Apologize]. Tokyo: Bungei Shunjū.

INDEX

Page numbers in **boldface** refer to illustrations.

ABOUT THE AUTHOR

Kōji Takazawa is a former student activist who later went on to become a prolific author, editor, and independent investigative journalist. He is a leading authority on the Japanese New Left and has close ties to some of its surviving participants and institutions. During the late 1960s and early 1970s, Takazawa was a student member of the New Left organization known as Bund (nickname for the Communist League) and became part of the Red Army Faction that was expelled from Bund in the summer of 1969. He helped produce the Red Army Faction's publications and was close to the leader of the Red Army group that hijacked a plane to North Korea in 1970. Little was heard from the hijackers for nearly two decades, until communications opened up after one of the members was arrested in Japan in 1988. Over the next several years Takazawa traveled to North Korea several times to meet with the group and facilitated the publication of their writings in Japan. He later became suspicious about what they were telling him. After the leader's sudden death in 1995, he launched his own investigation into what they had been doing. *Destiny* is the result. Takazawa subsequently donated his research materials for *Destiny* to the Takazawa Collection at the University of Hawai'i.

ABOUT THE EDITOR / TRANSLATOR

The editor and one of the translators of the work, **Patricia Steinhoff**, is a Japan specialist sociologist who studies New Left social movements in Japan and has been a faculty member at the University of Hawai'i since 1968. She first met Kōji Takazawa in the early 1980s in the context of her research on the Red Army Faction. In 1993 he donated his vast collection of Japanese social movement materials to the University of Hawai'i. Since then Steinhoff has overseen the cataloguing of the collection and developed its bibliographic website with the help of Japanese graduate students at the university and funding from the University of Hawai'i Japan Endowment and the National Institute for the Humanities. When *Destiny* was published the students read it and decided to translate it into English as a group project, with Takazawa's permission. Along with extensive polishing of the translation in collaboration with a graduate student who is also a professional translator, Steinhoff has added an editor's introduction, detailed translator's notes, and a follow-up chapter to make the material accessible to an English reading audience.